Perspectives in Cognitive Neuroscience

Stephen M. Kosslyn, *General Editor*

Psychophysiology

The Mind-Body Perspective

Kenneth Hugdahl

Harvard University Press

Cambridge, Massachusetts
London, England
1995

Library of Congress Cataloging-in-Publication Data
Hugdahl, Kenneth.
    Psychophysiology: the mind-body perspective / Kenneth Hugdahl.
        p.   cm.—(Perspectives in cognitive neuroscience)
    Includes bibliographical references and index.
    ISBN 0-674-72207-8
    1. Psychophysiology.   2. Mind and body.   I. Title.   II. Series.
    [DNLM: 1. Psychophysiology.   WL 103 H891p 1995]
QP360.H84   1995
612.8—dc20
DNLM/DLC
for Library of Congress   95-21933
                                CIP

To Märit, Anna, and Emilia,
and our crazy dog Zimba

Contents

Preface

The idea to write an introductory textbook in psychophysiology came to me about ten years ago. I was just taking up a new position at the University of Bergen in Norway, leaving my laboratory and friends in Uppsala, Sweden, where I had studied and worked up to that day. Psychophysiology is a rather new discipline in the mind-body sciences, and maybe because of its multidisciplinary emphasis only a few textbooks, and a larger number of advanced research volumes, have appeared. The book I had in mind to write might have remained just an idea if Stephen Kosslyn, general editor for the Perspectives in Cognitive Neuroscience series, hadn't asked me at a meeting if there wasn't a need for a book on psychophysiology that would introduce undergraduates and graduate students to the new field. This book, I hope, will fill that need.

The merging of cognitive science with neuroscience into cognitive neuroscience has added an important new branch to the brain-sciences tree, and psychophysiology belongs on that branch. But the physiology of cognition is only one part of the field covered by psychophysiology. Another is the physiology of emotional experience. I would like to call this aspect of psychophysiology "affective neuroscience," and I predict that it will be the next new area of brain science. In this book I explore the newest findings from the physiology of cognition *and* the physiology of emotion, from the perspective of both cognitive psychology and peripheral physiology—what I have referred to as the "mind-body perspective."

This is an introductory textbook, which means that it is intended for those with no previous knowledge of psychophysiological theories, models, and methods. At the same time, it is an attempt to integrate psychophysiological knowledge from the emotional to the cognitive domain, and to incorporate in this knowledge current findings about both the brain and human behavior, also including clinical psychology. In the first of three parts, I provide an introduction and overview of the field of psychophysiology. In the second part I review basic anatomy and physiology of the brain and the nervous system. In the final and largest part I cover the methods used to record and analyze psychophysiological data from the brain and from the electrodermal, cardiovascular, and other muscle systems of the body. Besides explaining the basic research methods, in each chapter I discuss what we have learned from the research about how mind and body interact to produce behavior. In many cases basic findings in the laboratory may be applied to clinical settings, and wherever possible I point out how psychophysiology may help diagnose and treat mental illnesses and brain damage.

Writing a textbook like this requires assistance from many people. Some have helped me indirectly, by being my mentors and colleagues when I entered the field of psychophysiology some twenty years ago at the Department of Psychology in Uppsala, Sweden, and some have directly helped me with this book, by commenting on the manuscript and correcting my errors. Among the individuals in the first category I especially want to mention my mentor and friend, Arne Öhman, who revealed to me the mysteries of electrodermal changes in the face of danger or threat (I'm talking about palm sweating) and how this response could help explain what it means to have a phobic reaction. Thanks go, too, to Mats Fredrikson, who worked together with me at Uppsala, and all the other members of Öhman's group at that time, particularly Ulf Dimberg, Staffan Hygge, and P. Å. Björkstrand, and also Lars Bäckström, Gunnar Ågren, and Lars Erik Larsson. I am also grateful to my colleagues and students at the Department of Biological and Medical Psychology at the University of Bergen, Norway: Helge Nordby, Dag Hammerborg, Arild Vaksdal, Solveig Rønne, Janniche Alvaer, Bjørn Helge Johnsen, Arve Asbjørnsen, Magne Flaten, Jon

Laberg, Kjell Morten Stormark, Gerd Kvale, Sara Saban, Åsa Hammar, and Bjørg Kocbach. Finn Jellestad and Alf Inge Smievoll also read parts of the manuscript. Special thanks to Knut Wester in the Neurosurgery Department at the University hospital for letting me catch a glimpse of the clinical world outside of the psychophysiological laboratory. Finally, I am happy to thank those friends and colleagues who have taken the time to read parts of the following chapters before they went to print: Richard Davidson, Robert Edelberg, Richard Jennings, William Lovallo, Arvid Lundervold, Helge Nordby, Mikko Sams, Håkan Sundberg, Sven Svebak, and the series editor, Stephen Kosslyn, as well as the editorial staff at Harvard University Press. Special thanks to Janniche Alvaer for providing the drawings for the illustrations in the book and to librarian Brita Hekland, University of Bergen, for help with the references. The University of Bergen and the Faculty of Psychology provided financial support by granting me a sabbatical semester while I was finishing this book.

I also want to express my appreciation for the present and previous members of the MacArthur Foundation Mind-Body Network: Robert Rose, William Lovallo, Richard Davidson, Eve van Cauter, Anne Harrington, Allan Hobson, Stephen Kosslyn, David Spiegel, John Cacioppo, John Sheridan, Esther Sternberg, Arthur Kleinman, and Mardi Horowitz. The intellectual and creative atmosphere in the meetings of this group has not only shaped my thinking on mind-body issues but also added to my understanding of the intricate interplay between mind and body in health and disease. Although much research on psychosomatic disease focuses on the negative, "downstream" effects of the mind on disease development, I am glad to say that the MacArthur Mind-Body Network tries to focus on the mind's positive, "upstream" inoculation effect on the body.

I

An Overview of Psychophysiology

1

Introduction

Psychophysiology embodies in its name not only a subject of study—the mind-body interface—but also a specific approach to its study. A basic assumption in psychophysiology is that behavioral, cognitive, emotional, and social events all are mirrored in physiological processes. Psychophysiology is therefore concerned with how mental events, like feelings and thoughts, may have pronounced effects on bodily processes, including effects on health and disease. As a discipline, psychophysiology shares common features with other specialties in the larger field of biological psychology, such as physiological psychology, neurophysiology, neuropsychology, psychosomatics, and cognitive neuroscience. All these disciplines have an interest in the interaction between behavior, brain, and body physiology, but psychophysiology has its own conceptual framework and methodological toolbox with which to study the mind-body interface.

The recording of psychophysiological responses may be regarded as a "window" into the brain and mind. In psychophysiology the focus is on the human individual, either as a research subject or as a clinical patient. For the experimentalist, recordings of bodily events may reveal effects of mental states not observable in overt behavior or in verbal reports. For example, the presentation of an emotional visual stimulus, too briefly viewed for the subject to be able to recognize it, may nevertheless induce a profound physiological change in the subject. For the clinical researcher, or clinician, psychophysiological data

3

may be used in a variety of ways. Psychophysiological correlates of abnormal behavior may be used as diagnostic criteria or as criteria for evaluating treatment outcome. Sometimes monitoring of psychophysiological reactivity is an integrated part of treatment itself, such as the biofeedback techniques used to treat, for example, anxiety disorders.

In this chapter I will draw out a more detailed definition of psychophysiology and its methodology, giving emphasis to studies of emotional and cognitive processes. Next I discuss the relation of psychophysiology to other areas in psychology and medicine concerned with the mind-body interface, such as psychosomatic medicine, behavioral medicine, and clinical psychology and psychiatry. Although psychophysiology has been the subject of research of its own since the turn of the century, and is currently taught at most major universities and colleges, the field has not yet had a great impact on neuroscience and neuropsychology. One of my purposes in writing this book is to promote the integration of psychophysiology with other major trends in the neurosciences, particularly cognitive neuroscience and neuropsychology. I will return to this point at the end of this chapter, in the discussion of future challenges for psychophysiology.

Psychophysiological Studies of Emotional and Cognitive Processes

As argued by Jennings and Coles (1991), psychophysiology developed as a discipline of its own along with the development of techniques for recording physiological responses. An example is the introduction of the electroencephalogram (EEG) by the Austrian psychiatrist Hans Berger in the early 1930s. It is probably also a fact that the first psychophysiological investigations were studies of emotional and affective processes, such as arousal or stress (cf. Ax, 1953), although there is a possible exception: as early as 1929 Darrow described a study using recordings of electrodermal activity (Chapter 6) to mark responses to what he called "ideational stimuli" or, in today's terminology, "cognitive stimuli." Darrow's subjects were asked to imagine various stimulus contexts while he recorded autonomic physiological activity. This study may, thus, have been one of the very first demonstrations of cognitive psychophysiology, a field that has grown rapidly during the last decade and that overlaps in scope and content with the newly emerging field of cognitive neuroscience (see Kosslyn and Koenig, 1992, for an overview of cognitive neuroscience).

The traditional focus on arousal and emotional processes had its origin in an interest in the autonomic nervous system which controls the activity of the involuntary muscles, like the heart, and the glands) and the controversy between William James and Walter Cannon regarding the nature of an emotional response. Cannon's view can be summarized as a "parallelist" approach (Coles and Gale, 1978), which assumes that different physiological systems function in parallel and that they are by-products of the psychological processes involved in the experience of an emotion. The Jamesian approach can be called an "interactionist" approach. It emphasizes the interaction between different physiological systems and their causal significance in determining the subjective experience of an emotion. This view was later taken up by Lacey (e.g., 1967) in his critique of the classic arousal theory, which was based on a parallelist view.

The challenge for psychophysiology today is, however, to understand the interaction of cognitive and emotional processes—that is, how emotions modulate cognitive efficiency and vice versa. As an example, in a recent study in our laboratory it was shown that the shifting of attention from one spatial localization to another was markedly distorted after the cue to shift attention had been given an emotional salience through classical conditioning. This study was based on the spatial attentional shift paradigm developed by Posner (e.g., 1988). In several experiments, Posner and colleagues have shown that manual reaction time (RT) is slowed when the target is cued from the opposite spatial location. Posner (1986) has suggested that a series of elementary mental operations is involved in the change of attention from cue to target. When the target and cue occur in different spatial locations, shifting attention to the target involves an interruption of ongoing activity in order to disengage attention from the location of the cue and move and re-engage attention at the new location. When the eyes are fixated, a peripheral visual stimulus attracts attention to its spatial location and gives priority to information there. Thus, targets presented in the cued location are usually processed faster than are those in the uncued location.

The main purpose of our study (Stormark, Hugdahl, and Posner, 1995) was to investigate shifts of attention from the cue to the target when the cue had acquired emotional significance through a classical conditioning procedure. Several studies have suggested that subjects orient their attention toward stimuli that have emotional meaning for them, and that they have problems in disengaging from these stimuli. For example, Mathews and MacLeod (1985) found that patients with anxiety disorders had great difficulties in naming the color of words that expressed a threat in a version of the Stroop color-naming task (Stroop, 1935). In this task the subject is requested to name the color a word is printed in while ignoring the word's meaning itself. Reliable performance on this task thus depends on the ability of the subject to shift attention from the irrelevant "message" of the word, which serves as the cue, to the color, which is the response target (cf. Posner and Snyder, 1975). The difficulties in naming the color of threat-related words demonstrated by anxiety patients could mean that the emotional salience of the cue impeded their ability to make the attentional shift. The major hypothesis was thus that response time after a cue with emotional significance would be greater than the response time following a cue with no significance. The control group had the typical longer RTs on invalid trials whereas to our surprise the conditioning group, overall, had faster RTs, with no difference between valid and invalid trials. The aversive conditioning had thus established an emotional drive to the cue that triggered attentional interrupt on both valid and invalid trials.

Methodology and Definition
Independent and Dependent Variables

In the typical psychophysiological experiment, manipulations in the mental, or psychological, domain are used as *independent variables* and the physiological responses to those manipulations are used as *dependent variables*. An independent variable is what is experimentally manipulated in a study, while the dependent variable is what is recorded, or measured. A classic dependent variable is the amount of sweating in the palms of the hands under different conditions; sweating increases, for example, when a novel, unexpected event occurs in the environment. This is an *orienting response* (Sokolov, 1963; Öhman, 1979a; Siddle, 1991), a rapid adjustment of the level of hydration in the skin as a function of a shift of attention to a new event (see Chapter 8). The sweat glands in the palms are innervated by nerve fibers from the autonomic nervous system, which is activated during states of arousal and surprise.

A model of how the brain may change the level of sweating in the hands in response to a mental event was provided by Edelberg (1972; see also Boucsein, 1992). Edelberg (1972) suggested that palm sweating in situations of "surprise" or "uncertainty" is related to increased grip strength. The model argues that for prehistoric man, an optimal level of hydration in the hands in an unknown situation may have meant the difference between life and death, for the ability to hold a weapon or climb a tree when fleeing is dependent on friction and grip strength. Thus, the rapid increase in sweat-gland activity in psychologically significant situations is a nice example of how subtle changes in cognitive and emotional efficiency may have profound somatic effects. (Sweat-gland activity is referred to as *electrodermal activity*, which is discussed in Chapter 6.)

The Human Subject

Psychophysiological studies for the most part use human subjects, in contrast to physiological psychology (see below). This is in part due to the focus in psychophysiology on mind-body interrelations involving complex cognitive and emotional processes, which are related to language and higher-order information-processing. Complex processes of this sort are not easily studied in animals.

In different kinds of experiments, psychophysiological responses being studied may be independent of verbal reports, and measurements may have to be made in situations where verbal reports are unavailable. Psychophysiology allows for unobtrusive recordings of ongoing physiological activity, whether it is "time-locked" to a stimulus or proceeds in the absence of any stimulation.

Psychophysiology has traditionally also been concerned with correlations between the recorded, or observed, physiological processes and inferred psychological events. In this respect, psychophysiology studies physiological *correlates* of behavior, rather than the direct causal links between the psychological and physiological domains. However, recent theory in psychophysiology stresses the intimate links between mental and physiological events on a more general level. Modern psychophysiological research can accept both psychological and physiological recordings as the dependent measure.

A Working Definition

In 1964 Stern stated that "any research in which the dependent variable is a physiological measure and the independent variable a behavioral one should be considered psychophysiological research." Sternbach (1966) extended this definition by specifying the kind of recording usually done in psychophysiology: "Psychophysiology is the study of interrelations between the physiological and psychological aspects of behavior . . . It typically employs human subjects . . . whose physiological responses are . . . recorded on a polygraph . . . while stimuli are presented which are influencing their mental, emotional or motor behavior." Furedy (1983) added that psychophysiology concerned itself only with "unobtrusively measured physiological responses," thus excluding all intrusive measures, like single-cell recordings.

These definitions may, however, be too narrow, for they exclude recent advances in psychophysiology. A more modern definition would be: *Psychophysiology is the study of brain-behavior relationships in the framework of peripheral and central physiological responses.* This definition does not exclude studies that use physiological recordings as independent variables and record consequences in the behavioral domain as dependent variables. It would thus accept studies that screen individuals on physiological parameters—for example, differences in electrodermal activity—and measure depressive behavior in terms of scores on a questionnaire.

All the definitions of psychophysiology given above share a focus on methodology and recording technology, as opposed to the theory of the subject matter. This focus has followed psychophysiology throughout the years. It is still customary at the annual conventions of the Society for Psychophysiological Research (SPR) to talk about "the cardiovascular" versus the "electrophysiology" psychophysiologists, referring to those researchers who measure heart rate and cardiovascular function and those who record the electrical properties of the nervous system, like event-related potentials. One should not conclude, however, that psychophysiology is just a "recording technology." As pointed out by Haynes (1991), psychophysiology is both a conceptual system and a measurement methodology. Moreover, Stemmler and Fahrenberg (1989) made the argument that "psychophysiological assessment is not just the recording of a physiological measure and its analysis" (p. 72). Assessment can only be devised properly with reference to the research question, the particular theoretical constructs and their operationalization, the experimental design, and the statistical hypotheses. An important point I wish to make, therefore, is that psychophysiological assessment must always be placed within the context of conceptual and theoretical issues.

An example of the importance of theory may be recordings of heart rate, the frequency with which the heart beats, usually expressed as beats-per-minute (bpm). As also discussed by Stemmler and Fahrenberg (1989), a measure of heart rate may indicate a whole range of different theoretical concepts: a measure of sinus rhythm; an index of emotional state; an index of activation and attention; an index of brain laterality; an index of the organism's metabolic state; an index of hemodynamic regulation, and so on. Without a theoretical grounding, the psychophysiologist would be lost in the woods, seeing only trees but not the forest.

Autonomic versus Neuroendocrine Physiology

In addition to sharing a focus on methodology, the definitions of Stern (1964) and Sternbach (1966) both favor "dry" (or autonomic) physiology over "wet" (or neuroendocrine) physiology. Autonomic psychophysiology is usually studied by placing electrodes on the outer surface of the body (hands, chest, skull, or skin) to record the activity of organs innervated by the autonomic nervous system. Neuroendocrine psychophysiology is the measurement of hormone secretion from glands in the body as a consequence of psychological influences. Classic examples are the studies of stress and the secretion of cortisol from the adrenal glands (Frankenhaeuser, 1978; Ursin, Baade, Levin, 1978). In one study, Frankenhaeuser, Rauste von Wright, Collins, et al. (1978) measured cortisol and other stress hormones excreted by males and females during an important school examination. Hormone levels were higher during the examination than they were during a normal school day. This study utilized a physiological measure as the dependent variable (cortisol) and a psychological factor (examination stress) as the independent variable. By definition, then, there is no *a priori* reason why psychoneuroendocrinology should not be part of the psychophysiology family.

Physiological Psychology

As defined above, psychophysiology is the "opposite" of physiological psychology. Physiological psychology is concerned with manipulating physiological independent states (the independent variables) and measuring the effect on overt behavior (the dependent variables). A typical example of an experiment in physiological psychology is measuring how the electrical stimulation of a brain structure interferes with an animal's ability to find its way in a T-maze.

Although physiological psychology traditionally uses animals as experimental subjects, this is not always the case. One of the classic studies on the interaction between emotion and cognition could be reformulated as a human experiment in the tradition of physiological psychology. In this study, Schachter and Singer (1962) suggested that emotional experience results from an interaction between physiological arousal and cognitive interpretation of environmental cues.

The theory developed by Schachter and Singer postulates that autonomic arousal is necessary for emotions but that it does not determine the quality of the experience of the emotion, only its intensity. A necessary component for the experience of the emotion is a cognitive interpretation of situational cues, which is attributed to be causal in the emotion. If I experience increased arousal when I hear a strange noise behind me, and then turn around to find a threatening figure approaching, the emotion may be fear. If, however, I find that the approaching figure is my long-lost dog returning home, the emotion is probably happiness.

Schachter and Singer tested their theory by injecting epinephrine (a hormone that increases physiological arousal) into the bloodstream of human subjects while a control group received a placebo injection. Some of the subjects in each group were further given correct information about the effects of epinephrine, others were given incorrect information. Those subjects that knew the effects of epinephrine would have a good explanation for their arousal; those that had incorrect information would need to use other information from the environment in order to interpret their increased arousal.

All subjects were then put in a waiting room together with a confederate to the experimenter. The confederate tried to recruit the subjects for either euphoric (positive) or aggressive (negative) emotional activities. Those subjects who had incorrect information regarding the true reason for their arousal used the available cues in the environment to evaluate the situation. Thus, those exposed to euphoric scenes experienced euphoria, while those exposed to aggressive scenes experienced hostility and aggression.

The impact this study has had on theories of emotion, as well as criticism, during the last thirty years is not the important point here; instead, the focus is on the design of the study. Schachter and Singer used epinephrine to manipulate the physiological state of their subjects and measured the effect by asking the subjects how they felt after having been in the waiting room. In other words, the independent variable was a change in the physiology while the dependent measure, or variable, was a recording of subjective experiences—an effect on the psychological level. Although this study has had great influence on theories and models of emotion, it is important to realize that modern perspectives of emotions argue that there are specific physiological correlates of different emotional experiences. Not all emotions are accompanied by an increase in general arousal that has to be psychologically interpreted if the specific emotion is to be experienced (see Ekman and Davidson, 1994, for a discussion of theoretical approaches to the psychology of emotions).

Physiological Changes and Their Measurement
"Time Windows"

Physiological changes that can be temporally related to observable events, or stimuli, are typically of relatively short duration—that is, they rise and fall rather quickly. These are said to be *phasic* in character and are appropriately labeled responses. In contrast, *tonic* physiological changes are less closely related to observable events. Instead, they reflect the internal activity state of a particular effector or of the individual under study. Thus, tonic levels provide a background for the phasic changes.

Both tonic and phasic changes may be observed in most psychophysiological recordings. However, the time frame within which such changes occur differ depending upon which physiological system is studied. Because of these differences in temporal resolution, different physiological activities are more or less suitable for studying different psychological processes. Computers allow investigators to probe the brain's electrical activity for minute changes occurring in relation to significant psychological events. These event-related cortical potentials are seen in a time frame of milliseconds, which permits temporal coordination of the physiological change with sensory, attentional, and cognitive processes in the evaluation of a stimulus or in preparation for a response. Effectors innervated by the autonomic nervous system—the heart, blood vessels, or sweat glands—in general are slower: phasic changes may occur on a time scale of seconds, and tonic changes, in minutes.

Peripheral Versus Central Measures

Psychophysiological measures may be made of both the peripheral and the central nervous sytem. Within each category, recordings may be made non invasively (from the outside of the skin or the scalp) or invasively (from inside an artery, say, or inside the brain).

Peripheral measures include a range of responses both from effector organs activated by the autonomic nervous system (ANS) and from striated skeletal muscles. Central measures, like electroencephalograms (EEGs) and event-related potentials (ERPs), as well as more modern techniques like magnetoencephalography (MEG) or blood-flow measurements made by positron emission tomography (PET), are often linked to cognitive processing, such as attention and language processing, and more recently also to affective changes. Generally, most of the new imaging techniques have good spatial resolution (showing details in the brain), but their temporal resolution (how fast they can track a response) is poor (here the MEG technique is an exception.) See Chapter 13 for details about these new techniques.

Recordings from electrodes on the outside of the skin, on the other hand, usually have poor spatial resolution. Their temporal resolution, though, often far exceeds that of the imaging techniques. This is particularly true for ERPs, which tracks performance in milliseconds, and less so for electrodermal phenomena, which have a time window of seconds. Examples of different psychophysiological measures and their corresponding time windows are given in Figure 1.1.

Response Systems

A recording from a particular end organ, or receptor, in the periphery of the body or in the brain is a recording from a *response system*. This is a collective term for both the underlying anatomy and physiology of the end organ from which the recording is taken and the recording technology, including the electronics or mechanics of the recording

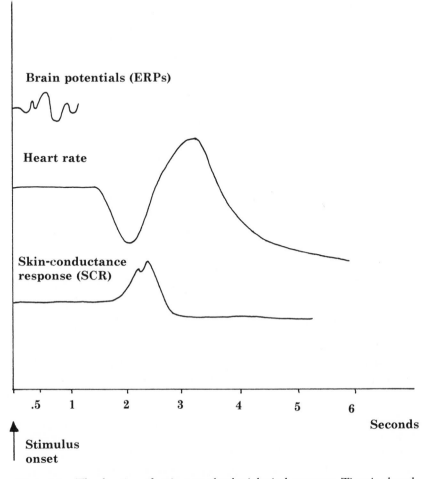

Figure 1.1. The duration of various psychophysiological measures. Time is plotted on the *x*-axis as seconds after presentation of a stimulus. In general, responses of the central nervous system (like event-related potentials, or ERPs) occur in milliseconds, while responses controlled by the autonomic nervous system (like the heart rate and skin-conductance responses) last for a few seconds. (Courtesy of Helge Nordby, University of Bergen, Norway.)

as well as the computer-digitizing of the recorded signal. For example, recordings from the electrodermal system measure a response system that includes the sympathetic branch of the autonomic nervous system, the sweat glands in the skin, specialized electrodes, various electronic couplers and amplifiers, and a computer with software specialized for this kind of data acquisition. Table 1.1 lists the response systems most commonly studied in psychophysiological research.

Before computers, a psychophysiological laboratory measured electrodermal activity (EDA) with a polygraph, on which the response signal was shown as a tracing on a paper chart. The polygraph has for the most part been replaced, however, by the modern personal computer (PC) equipped with an A/D-board and data acquisition and analysis software. Today, a typical psychophysiological recording passes through a series of stages, or phases, from the electrode on the skin

Table 1.1.   Examples of psychophysiological response systems.

Autonomic measures	
Electrodermal system	Skin-conductance response/level (SCR/SCL)
	Skin-potential response (SPR)
	Spontaneous fluctuations (SF)
Temperature system	Body temperature
Cardiovascular system	Heart rate
	Electrocardiogram (ECG)
	Heart rate power spectrum analysis (HRPSA)
	Vagal tone (V)
	Blood pressure (BP)
	Vasomotor response (VMR)
Gastrointestinal system	Electrogastrography (EGG)
Central measures	
Electrocortical system	Electroencephalography (EEG)
	Event-related potential (ERP)
	Brain electrical activity mapping (BEAM)
	Source dipole localization (BESA)
Magnetocortical system	Magnetoencephalography (MEG)
Brain blood flow, metabolism	Positron emission tomography (PET)
	Functional magnetic resonance imaging (fMRI)
	Regional cerebral blood flow (rCBF)

to the stored numbers in the computer. A physiological signal (such as the potentials from the heart when it beats) is picked up by electrodes on the skin. The signal is then fed to a series of amplifiers, magnifying the minimal signal (typically the signal is in the millivolt region, which is equal to 10^{-3} V). From the amplifier the signal is passed to an A/D-board in the computer, which converts the analog signal to its digital correspondent. The digitized signal is finally displayed on a computer screen, for later data storage and statistical analysis.

Figure 1.2 illustrates the setup of a modern PC-based psychophysiology laboratory, in which three PCs are connected together. The stimulus-PC is equipped with general-purpose software for easy programming of experimental parameters, like stimulus duration and interstimulus intervals. This software can also display scanned pictures as well as letters, words, and geometric shapes. It can also control the presentation of auditory stimuli, either from the PC itself or from an external sound source. Although the example in Figure 1.2 presents a PC-based laboratory, a similar logic would hold for a setup run by any type of computer.

The ANS-sampling PC has an A/D-board and special software for the acquisition and analysis of autonomic signals. For example, it may track R–R intervals from an electrocardiogram (ECG) or skin-conductance responses from the sweat glands in the fingers.

The CNS-sampling PC, finally, acquires and analyses EEG signals and performs signal-averaging calculations for ERP analysis whenever a stimulus is presented. The stimulus-PC sends a digital "trigger signal" to the ANS- and CNS-sampling PCs whenever a stimulus is presented by specialized software, thus coordinating the timing of the autonomic and central responses with the presentation of the stimulus for detailed analysis of phasic changes in these responses as a consequence of stimulus presentation. It is important to keep in mind that the example in Figure 1.2 can easily be modified depending on the resources available in each particular laboratory. With current technology it is probably as easy to have only one computer instead of two for the CNS and ANS sampling.

To illustrate the forms in which data may be recorded by these systems, I reproduce some examples of measurements in Figure 1.3: output from a polygraph recording from the electrodermal, cardiovascular, and oculomotor response systems. Note the compression of the ECG responses in this figure, which is due to the slow speed of

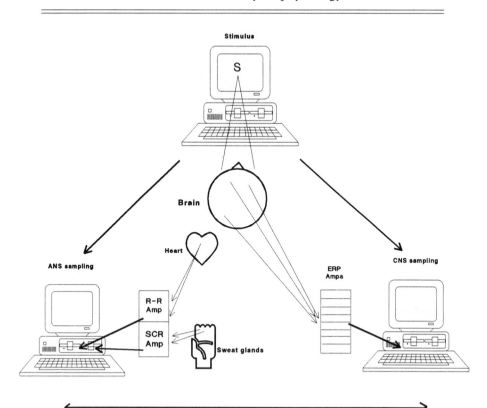

Figure 1.2. An experimental setup in a psychophysiological laboratory, with three interconnected personal computers (PCs). The top PC is equipped with software for presenting a stimulus, both auditory and visual. The software used in my laboratory in Bergen is MicroElectronicLaboratory (MEL), although other programs are available that serve similar functions. The PC to the left is equipped with a board for digitizing electric signals from amplifiers and couplers connected to electrodes placed on the subject for recording autonomic (ANS) activity. This PC is also equipped with software for data acquisition and analysis. The ANS activity that is being recorded here is the heart-rate (R-R amplifier) and skin-conductance (SCR coupler) response. The PC to the right is equipped with a board for digitizing signals from amplifiers connected to electrodes on the scalp for recording central nervous system (CNS) activity: specifically, event-related brain potentials (ERPs) from the brain. This PC also has software for data acquisition and signal analysis. Whenever a stimulus is presented by the "stimulus PC," a trigger signal is sent to the other PCs to mark the onset of a stimulus. The two signal-acquisition PCs are also connected so they can communicate with each other.

the polygraph paper as it winds past the recording pen. Stimulus presentations are marked as black horizontal lines, and the handwritten marks are the amplitude scores of the identified responses.

Central, Autonomic, and Sensorimotor Systems

Response systems may be classified with respect to the branch of the nervous system about which they provide information: autonomic, central, or sensorimotor. (These response systems are discussed in detail in Chapters 6–8, 11–14, and 15.)

Autonomic response systems are measured through recordings from the electrodermal system (sweat glands), cardiovascular system (heart activity, blood pressure, and peripheral vessels), and gastrointestinal system (stomach, intestines).

Central response systems are measured by the electroencephalogram (EEG) (electrical activity of the brain neurons), event-related potentials (ERPs) (discrete responses in the EEG), brain electrical activity mapping (BEAM), and the various brain imaging techniques (PET, fMRI, MEG). In addition, recordings from the oculomotor system (eye movements, eye blinks) are partly guided from the central nervous system, partly from the autonomic nervous system.

Sensorimotor response systems are measured through recordings of the skeletal muscle system (the electromyogram, or EMG), and respiration. The respiratory system is also innervated by the autonomic nervous system. Respiratory activity is measured by the end-tidal CO_2 (which records CO_2 concentration at the end of each breath) and the VO_2-max (the maximal volume capacity that the respiratory system can tolerate). As an applied example, Table 1.2 lists some typical changes in psychophysiological response systems during a phobic reaction. Note the general increase in physiological activity in most response systems, reflecting increased arousal and sympathetic activity.

Most of these response systems and measures will be discussed in detail in later chapters, and are listed here for the purpose of providing an overview of the field of psychophysiology. Respiratory and oculomotor recordings are in many psychophysiological experiments used as control measures, not to confound the parameters under recording. Gastric motility is seldom used in psychophysiological research, and recordings of muscle activity (EMG) are perhaps more frequent in health psychology and psychosomatic medicine than in traditional psy-

EDA_{LH}   EDA_{RH}   ECG   EOG

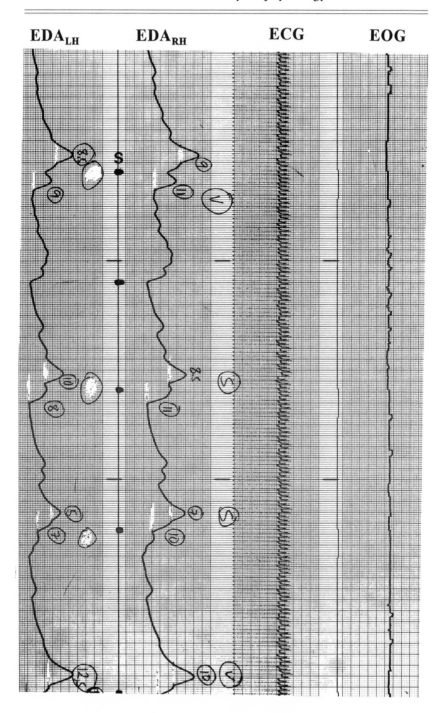

Table 1.2.   Psychophysiological response patterns typical of simple phobias.

Electrodermal system
Increased skin-conductance amplitude
Increased number of spontaneous fluctuations
Increased skin-conductance level
Large orienting response, retarded habituation

*Cardiovascular system**
Increased heart rate
Increased blood pressure
Vasoconstriction in peripheral blood vessels
Phasic acceleration of heart rate in response to stimulus

Skeletal muscle system
Increase/decrease in muscle tension

Electrocortical system
Reduced alpha activity in EEG recordings
Reduced contingent negative variation (CNV)
Increased P300 ERP amplitude

Brain blood flow
Increase in blood flow in occipital and frontal lobes, as shown by ^{15}O PET or rCBF

---

* An exception to this response pattern occurs when phobia involves the fear of blood or injury (see Chapter 2).

Figure 1.3.   A four-channel polygraph recording of approximately 1 minute duration. This is a record of the responses of an individual in an experiment on visual attention. The subject is being shown pictures of geometric objects in either the left or right visual half-field (the stimulus, indicated by dots on the straight line, labeled *S*, between the first two polygraph tracings). The two channels to the left are recordings of electrodermal activity (EDA; see Chapter 6) in the left and right hands (LH, RH): phasic skin-conductance responses are seen as "peaks" a few seconds after each stimulus. The handwritten marks on the EDA channels are "scores" of the amplitude of each response. The ECG (see Chapter 9) is a measure of changes in heart rate as a function of stimulus presentations. The large "spikes" in the recording are R-waves, representing each beating of the heart. The ECG is compressed since the speed of the polygraph paper is slower than in a clinical ECG recording. The channel to the far right is a recording of electrooculography (EOG), which measures eye movements (Chapter 14).

chophysiology, although there are notable exceptions (e.g., Dimberg, 1983; Graham, 1975; Svebak, 1986). Graham, in particular, has used the EMG to record subtle movements in the eyelid in response to startle stimuli, in studies of how the startle response may be modulated by cognitive and affective factors in the background of the presentation of a startle stimulus (see Chapter 15 for further details about startle responses).

Ambulatory Recordings

Ambulatory psychophysiological recordings are recordings taken from subjects not restricted to the laboratory setting or the clinic. They are achieved in two different ways, through telemetry and portable data storage (Turpin, 1990). Telemetry involves the transmission of physiological signals from transducers attached to the subject. The signals are transmitted, usually by a small FM radio transmitter worn by the subject, to a distant receiver for storage and later data analysis.

A major problem with classic telemetry is that signals transmitted over long distances may be distorted because of radio signal interference. As an alternative, the ambulatory subject may wear a recorder rather than a transmitter. Typically this is an instrumentation cassette recorder or a digital storage unit small enough to be worn by a subject during various activities. The data on the cassette or the digital device are later copied onto the main computer, every twenty-four hours or so. Ambulatory monitoring has proven valuable for recording changes in blood pressure over twenty-four-hour cycles, for example, and also in sleep research. It is, moreover, of great value for making continuous recordings of changes in autonomic activity in various anxiety disorders, like agoraphobia.

Psychophysiology and Disease

An example of a psychophysiological approach to disease is research on the so-called Type A behavior pattern and risk for coronary heart disease (Matthews, 1982). According to Jenkins (1971), Type A behavior is characterized by extreme competitiveness, striving for achievement, aggressiveness, a sense of urgency about time, and explosiveness of speech (see Chapter 10). Later research has focused more on the negative effects of hostility and repressed agressivity (Booth-Kewley and Friedman, 1987). Moreover, Miller, Turner, Tindale, et al. (1991) found a trend in recent research toward "null findings" regarding fatal heart infarcts and Type A behavior, leading some authors to question the utility for psychology of the Type A construct (Ray, 1991). In any event, the Type A paradigm would fit the definition of psychophysiology advocated in this book, that cognitive and emotional events can have causal roles in physiological changes in an organ in the body, changes which in this case may be fatal to the individual.

Psychosomatic Medicine

Psychophysiology shares a large body of theory and methods with *psychosomatic medicine*, which is also preoccupied with the influence of the mind on bodily function. A major difference, though, is that whereas psychosomatic medicine to a large extent has been concerned with how the mind has a negative influence on bodily function, stress and disease being the typical paradigm, psychophysiology takes a more generic approach that recognizes both positive and negative effects of the mind. David Graham's work (see, e.g., Graham, 1972) was pioneering the field of psychosomatic psychophysiology, particularly research on urticaria, or skin allergy. Among other things, Graham and associates developed a theory of psychosomatics in which attitudes determine the kinds of psychosomatic symptoms that develop (e.g., Grace and Graham, 1952; Graham and Wolf, 1950). The relevance for a psychophysiological perspective on disease of the studies by Graham and his colleagues is related to the issue of individual response specificity (see also Chapter 2). This term refers to the tendency individuals have to respond with the same response system to a variety of different stressors or mental challenges. It is clear from Graham's work that the attitude an individual has toward illness intervenes between the stressor and the specificity of the physical response.

Thus, in its focus on the mind-body interface, psychophysiology is concerned with both health and disease whereas psychosomatic medicine has traditionally been concerned with disease processes only. The story told by Norman Cousins in his book *Anatomy of an Illness*, about fighting his cancer by laughing and putting himself into a positive mood when thinking about his disease, is a good example of how the mind influences the body: the mind may have a destructive effect in some cases, but it may also prevent the outbreak of a disease or perhaps even "inoculate" the body.

This is perhaps a new field of research within psychophysiology and behavioral medicine, the study of those individuals who do *not* become ill when exposed to stress and other disease risks. It is an intriguing fact that some individuals resist becoming ill in situations where they should. An example of resistance to disease is provided in the study by Kvale, Hugdahl, Asbjørnsen, et al. (1991) on side effects of chemotherapy in cancer patients. (This study is further described in Chapter 4.)

Behavioral Medicine

The emerging discipline of *behavioral medicine* could be called an applied field of psychophysiology (Schwartz and Weiss, 1978). As the name implies, behavioral medicine approaches a problem in terms of objective behaviors, as opposed to the unobservable internal events studied in the classic psychosomatic model.

Behavioral medicine as a term was probably used for the first time by Birk (1973) in his edited volume on biofeedback. Apart from strong influences from classical psychophysiology, behavioral medicine owes a great deal to behavior therapy and stress research. Interest in behavioral medicine began partly as a reaction to the reification of mental events in the psychosomatic approach, which had created a classic dualism of mental and somatic processes (Engel, 1986). The people who contributed most to the development of behavioral medicine had backgrounds in behavior therapy, psychophysiology, or experimental psychology, fields in which greater emphasis was put on behavior than on mentalistic constructs when defining how psychology could contribute to medicine.

Individual Differences

The idea of screening individuals who are resistant to disease following exposure to stress is related to the issue of individual differences in psychophysiological reactivity. Davidson (e.g., 1984) has shown that individuals spontaneously differ with respect to preferred patterns of brain activation in a resting situation. In some individuals there is a higher level of activation in the left than in the right frontal cortex; in others there is greater activity in the right side. These stable individual differences have also been shown to correlate with affectivity and emotionality, with positive affect in individuals with a left frontal EEG activation pattern, and negative affect in individuals with a right frontal EEG activation pattern (Davidson and Tomarken, 1989).

Davidson's research has shown how individual differences in a psychophysiological parameter can predict stable mood patterns in individuals. Maybe individual differences in mood propensity (positive or negative) relate to the brain's control of the outflow over the autonomic, endocrine, and immune systems to target organs in the body. The common focus on the negative effect of the mind on the body may arise from the traditional view of health as the absence of disease. A perspective taken in this book is that health represents a positive category of its own; it should not be defined in terms of the exclusion of other categories.

Cognitive Psychophysiology

Although the study of emotion has been a key area of research in psychophysiology (Ax, 1953; Lang, 1968; Davidson, 1984), the application of psychophysiology to the study of cognitive processes in humans is today a major focus. Jennings and Coles (1991) argue that psychophysiology enriches cognitive theory by providing a bridge between traditional cognitive measures like reaction time and response accuracy with precise timing of brain events to the presentation of a stimulus.

Cognitive psychophysiology uses measures of both autonomic and central nervous activity. Typical experimental designs include measures of heart rate in situations of attentional demands (Jennings, 1986) and of ERPs to probe how the brain processes semantic information (Rugg, 1985; Kutas and Hillyard, 1980; see also Chapter 12). For example, it has been suggested that cardiac slowing is a correlate of attentional shift toward the source of an environmental event. Similarly, Näätänen (1990) has proposed a model of sensory memory based on recordings of ERPs to an infrequent stimulus interspersed among the more frequent stimulus, a phenomenon called *mismatch negativity* (MMN) (Chapter 12). Mismatch negativity is also a psychophysiological correlate of passive attention to a deviant event in a train of simultaneous events. It may reflect the activity of a brain processor specifically linked to the identification of physical stimulus features whenever there is a mismatch between what is presented and what is stored in short-term memory. Moreover, Kutas and Hillyard (1980) have identified a specific ERP component to incongruent semantic stimuli, occurring around 400 milliseconds (ms) after the presentation of the "surprising" stimulus. A typical incongruent sentence that would eliciting the N400 component is the following: "The man spread the butter on his socks." The N400 component is a negative brain potential occurring about 400 ms after the word *socks* is heard. If the sentence instead is ended with "the bread," the N400 component is absent from the ERP recording.

Clinical Psychophysiology

I have already defined psychophysiology as both a theoretical system and a recording methodology. I must now add that psychophysiology is also used for assessment, diagnosis, and treatment in clinical psychology. When discussing psychophysiology in clinical practice, however, one should make a distinction between the use of psychophysiological recordings for assessing the effectiveness of diagnosis and treatment and the use of psychophysiological methods directly in treatment. An example of the use of psychophysiology in treatment is biofeedback training, in which information about the change in a physiological parameter (such as heart rate) is given to the subject as part of the treatment process. See Gatchel and Price (1979) for a review of clinical applications of biofeedback in the treatment of fear and anxiety.

Turpin (1989), moreover, makes a distinction between psychological *processes* and physiological *correlates*, referring the former category to the "mind" and the latter category to the "body" when talking about the mind-body interface. Seen in this perspective, clinical psychophysiology is associated with psychosomatic medicine, as mentioned above. Whereas psychosomatic medicine largely has been preoccupied with identification of internal events, like personality traits, in the psychological domain (Alexander, 1950), clinical psychophysiology seeks to unravel the interactionist nature of *behavioral* processes and physiological correlates within a unified theoretical construct (e.g., Neuchterlein and Dawson, 1984; Cacioppo, Berntson, and Anderson, 1991). Cacioppo, Berntson, and Anderson (1991) also argued that the interaction of physiological and psychological levels of discourse should be phrased in terms of multi-interactional levels. Typical examples of a multi-leveled analysis are the classical conditioning models of the acquisition of phobic fear and anxiety responses (Öhman, 1979b), the information-processing approach to psychophysiological understanding of risk factors in schizophrenia (Venables, 1993), and the analysis of arousal patterns in psychopathy and antisocial behavior (Hare, 1978).

Emotional Imagery

Still another example of multi-leveled analysis is Lang's theory of emotional imagery. The underlying rationale for Lang's theory may be seen as an attempt to secure a foundation for the development of imagery therapies, like systematic desensitization. Only the relevance of the theory for the elucidation of the psychophysiology of simple phobias will be discussed here.

Lang et al. (1980) trained a group of snake phobics and a group of public-speaking phobics in imagery practice in a desensitization procedure. After training, subjects were presented with fear items relevant to their phobia. It was found that snake-phobic subjects showed larger increases in heart rate than did the social phobics, and especially at increasing intensities of experienced fear. The snake-phobic subjects also reported more vivid emotional images, indexed both by verbal reports and by psychophysiological responses.

By developing an imagery-training method that focuses the subjects' activity either on stimulus- or response-related propositions in the image-instruction scripts, the investigators showed that when response elements are reinforced in the instructions, both greater psychophysiological arousal and more intense verbal reports of the created image are obtained. An example of stimulus and response propositions is provided in Lang et al. (1980, p. 183) for a subject with fear of insects.

STIMULUS PROPOSITION: "You are alone in your car on an interstate highway and you notice an insect on the windshield. It is a large buzzing insect, a yellow jacket that has trapped itself inside your car. The bug has a yellow and black body, and moves back and forth against the windshield to get out."

RESPONSE PROPOSITION: "You are alone driving your car on the interstate highway and you hear the buzzing of an insect on your windshield. Your heart begins to pound as you notice that it is a yellow jacket trapped in your car. You perspire heavily and your eyes dart from the insect to the roadside while you try to watch the bug and look for a place to stop."

An important implication of Lang's theoretical work on emotional imagery is that the patients most improved after imagery therapy are those who are more physiologically reactive to fear-relevant scenes during therapy. Thus, focusing on response-related items in imagery scenes in therapy might improve prognosis for treatment through the mediating influence of increased psychophysiological activity and more vivid imaging of the fear scenes.

The Three-Systems Model

As noted by Turpin (1991), a central theme in psychophysiological assessment of psychological disorders, particularly anxiety disorders, is the *three-systems model* (Lang, 1968; Rachman and Hodgson, 1974; Hugdahl, 1981). The three-systems approach stems from Lang's classic 1968 paper in which he proposed that an emotional reaction was composed of *subjective experience, overt behavior*, and *physiological reactions.*

To take the example of a phobia, the subjective experience for an individual may be an intense fear of fainting or dying when confronted with the phobic situation. This may be accompanied by an escape or avoidance response, as the person tries to get away from the situation. Physiologically, a phobic reaction typically involves increased cardio-vascular activity. Lang (1968) suggested that different individuals may be differentially sensitive to the three components in an anxiety reaction, and that clinical assessment should involve measures of all three components.

Two individuals with a phobia for flying may show quite discrepant response profiles in a three-systems analysis. One individual may start ruminating and having negative thoughts several months in advance about not being able to fly to a favorite spot during the upcoming summer vacation. These negative thoughts and feelings may or may not be accompanied by increased physiological responses. When the time for the trip comes closer, the negative thoughts and feelings may have grown so intense that the person avoids the trip altogether and remains isolated at home.

Another phobic individual may not experience negative thoughts in advance, but at the moment when he or she is about to board the airplane may have an acute panic attack, triggered by a dramatic increase in physiological responses, notably the pounding of the heart. As a consequence, this individual also avoids going aboard the airplane. In both cases there is a phobic reaction, *avoidance* of a particular situation.

Both individuals thus display overt avoidance behavior, but their physiological and subjective responses are quite discrepant. A three-systems approach for assessment of anxiety disorders, including psychophysiological recordings of heart rate, blood pressure, muscle activity, and even neuroendocrine response, may thus be an important clue to the tailoring of individually based treatment. It seems obvious that the first of the two individuals described above should benefit more from a cognitively based treatment, involving the restructuring of negative thoughts and feelings (cf. Beck and Emery, 1985). The second individual, however, should probably be subjected to psychophysiological treatment involving *systematic desensitization* (Wolpe, 1982), or *relaxation training* to help him or her "quiet" the physiological system when exposed to the phobic situation.

Öst and Hugdahl (1981) have furthermore shown that phobic reactions acquired through a classical conditioning procedure (e.g., being bitten by a snake) are characterized by a greater emphasis on the physiological component, while reactions acquired through modeling and social experiences (admonitions from parents not to walk outside without shoes) load more on the cognitive, subjective component. It is important, though, to realize that subjective experiences of panic are not necessarily triggered by physiological concomitants, indicating a partial autonomy between the various components in an anxiety reaction (Margraf, Taylor, Ehlers, et al., 1987).

Intensity versus Quality of Responses

It is also important to realize that psychophysiology may give information not only about the *intensity* of a response but also about the *quality* of the response. This is particularly interesting in the study of anxiety reactions, in which diametrically different physiological response patterns may be obtained within the same response system to different fear-eliciting stimuli. A well-known example of this difference is that although heart rate typically increases during a phobic reaction, a significant decrease is observed if the phobia under study is related to blood and injury situations (Öst, Sterner, and Lindahl, 1984; Wardle and Jarvis, 1981). Thus, different physiological response patterns may be associated with different fear reactions. This is known as "stimulus-response specificity" and will be discussed in detail in Chapter 2.

Future Challenges to Psychophysiology

A major challenge to psychophysiology in the future will be to specify the functional architecture of interconnected structures and processes in the mind-brain-body network. This architecture has to be expressed in an algorithm explaining how the structures and processes may be transformed from one level of analysis to another, from a psychological to a physiological level. Such a strategy, thus, seeks to understand not only how the architecture of the mind interacts with structures and processes in the peripheral physiology and in the brain, but also how the mind-code is transformed into behavior.

A first proposition is that mind states have unique cortical representations, or "footprints," in the brain. This argument is valid even when a unique brain activation pattern has not yet been found. For example, if hypnosis is accepted as a state of the mind, then we should also accept that the hypnotic state is associated with a unique "footprint" in the brain, even if the cortical pattern for that state has not yet been identified.

The role of the brain in mediating the mind-body connection has traditionally not been in the focus in psychophysiology. The following statement from a chapter on the psychophysiology of classical conditioning (Öhman, 1983, p. 317) reflects some of the traditional psychophysiological views on the mind-body interface:

> Pavlovian conditioning is best viewed in procedural terms. Thus, its definition requires only the delineation of a set of empirical criteria for its observation. Such a definition, of course, remains completely uncommitted with regard to theoretical interpretation. In fact, it does not even imply that the procedure has its theoretical counterparts in a unique process.

In this respect it may be of interest to recapitulate some of Pavlov's (1927) original views of classical conditioning as a theoretical tool for explaining the functioning of the cortical hemispheres. For him, studies of conditioning provided insights into the functional properties of the nervous system, and particularly the cerebral hemispheres of the brain (Windholz, 1992). The behavioristic movement in the West during the period 1940–1980 is probably to blame for the standing Pavlovian conditioning incorrectly came to have as the "hallmark" of a behavioristic experiment.

A major challenge is, therefore, to understand how the brain modulates the mind-body link, in the sense that peripheral changes in the autonomic or endocrine systems are analyzed not only in terms of psychological processes but also in terms of the brain's control of the peripheral outflow.

An Interactive Model

A related argument for claiming that psychophysiology must join forces with other disciplines studying the mind-body problem, such as neuropsychology and cognitive neuroscience, is the emergence of the new brain imaging techniques (see Chapter 13). With techniques like positron emission tomography (PET) or functional magnetic resonance imaging (fMRI), complex cognitive and emotional processes can be functionally "mapped" in the intact human brain. Brain imaging will help unravel the mysteries of the mind's ability to exert such dramatic control of bodily processes as is sometimes exhibited by yoga experts, or to lead to the breakdown of physiological function under extreme stress. However, the brain imaging techniques will not replace the need to formulate exact scientific questions and to specify the independent variables and manipulations. Science proceeds not through development of new ways to measure the dependent variables but through the careful analysis and reformulation of the independent variables. There will always be a place for the psychophysiological approach—for setting up carefully designed experiments and recording the effect in a physiological subsystem.

Merging of Disciplines

The time is now probably ripe for a closer merging of the various disciplines and subdisciplines studying the mind-body interface. The emergent health problems related to mind-body interactions call for a closer collaboration between biological psychologists, independent of whether they call themselves psychophysiologists, neuropsychologists, or cognitive neuroscientists.

A good example of the "merging" perspective is a recent paper by Levine and Gueramy (1991), which applies psychophysiology in the field of clinical neuropsychology. A central argument in their paper is that psychophysiology has accumulated over the years a large body of evidence concerning physiological responses associated with the ability to orient, to attend, and to encode and recall learned material. Psychophysiology has, furthermore, developed careful experimental designs in order to probe and record these complex behaviors. Deficits in memory, attention, perception, and sensory integration are typical signs of dysfunction after focal or diffuse brain damage, and the use of psychophysiological measures when diagnosing brain damage may be a new branch for psychophysiology.

I would argue that neuropsychology has much to gain from the application of psychophysiological techniques and experimental designs. In the same vein, psychophysiology has much to gain from neuropsychology, with its focus on brain damage, especially its cortical effects. The study of mind-peripheral connections in brain-damaged patients will provide an excellent grounding for a closer understanding of how the brain regulates and controls the "flow of the mind" to the periphery.

Individual Differences

A third area that should engage future psychophysiologists is the area of *individual variability*. This includes variability in both spontaneous and stimulus-elicited physiological activity among individuals put under similar environmental conditions. As noted by Fahrenberg (1986, p. 65), "representative statistics concerning individual differences within the normal range are scarce. Apart from a few physiological measures like blood pressure and a few anthropometric measures describing gross body features, a *systematic* biology of *human variation* is virtually non-existent."

Research in psychophysiology has to a large degree been concerned with general laws of behavior and physiological response, and little room has been left for individual variations in responsivity in any given experimental situation. Although this has been the rule in the history of psychophysiology, there are several important exceptions. A classic example is Wenger's A-score, which is a weighted estimate of autonomic balance (see Chapter 2). Wenger's (1941) argument was that individuals differ in the degree to which they are dominated by sympathetic or parasympathetic influences of the autonomic nervous system. A low A-score indicates relative sympathetic dominance, while a high score reflects parasympathetic dominance. The A-score was a stable characteristic of an individual, which, however, could show phasic changes depending on the presence or absence of arousing stimuli.

Summary

This chapter has served as a broad introduction to the field of psychophysiology, specifically to its relation to emotional, cognitive, and clinical processes. Traditionally, psychophysiology has been linked to the study of emotional processes and the interaction of emotional and autonomic responses. This tradition goes back to early arguments about the nature of an emotional reaction as formulated by William James and Walter Cannon. However, modern perspectives on psychophysiology focus on how physiological responses may serve as a "window" to complex cognitive processes like attention, learning, and memory. In other words, the traditional view of psychophysiology as an index of general arousal and activation is an oversimplified view. Also discussed in this chapter is the relation between psychophysiology and health, particularly in the areas of psychosomatic and behavioral medicine.

Future challenges for psychophysiology lie in the integration of a psychophysiological perspective with neuropsychological and cognitive-neuroscience perspectives. The complexity of the human mind-body interface necessitates a closer integration of research areas devoted to the study of the relationships between mind, brain, and behavior. It is argued that psychophysiology can contribute to a better understanding of problems encountered in clinical psychology and psychiatry, too, such as the dysfunctions caused by brain damage and the processes that underlie psychopathology.

2

Concepts and Terms

In this chapter I introduce several theoretical constructs and terms frequently used in psychophysiology. These concepts usually cut across the various recording methodologies used. They also cut across central versus peripheral measures and approaches, although there are some exceptions. For example, the notions of sensory intake and rejection, as defined by Lacey (1967) and explained below, are traditionally linked to the cardiovascular response system and measures of heart rate. Other concepts, like autonomic balance, involves a whole range of different physiological measures. The concepts and distinctions introduced in this chapter have played important roles in defining psychophysiology as a discipline of its own.

Two important areas of psychophysiology, the orienting response and classical conditioning, are treated in a separate chapter (Chapter 8) because they have been so essential to the development of psychophysiology as a discipline within experimental psychology that they deserve to be treated more deeply and at greater length than the concepts discussed here.

Stimulus Specificity

A critical issue in almost every psychophysiological research agenda is the issue of specificity, the idea that there are distinct and specific physiological response patterns for each investigated psychological event (see Fahrenberg, 1986, for more on this issue). The topic to be considered here is *stimulus specificity*. Another aspect of the specificity issue is *response stereotypy*, the tendency for individuals to respond with the same physiological response system independent of the nature and quality of the stimulus (see below).

A classic experiment on stimulus specificity was performed by Ax (1953). In this study, an anger stimulus elicited a pattern of diastolic blood pressure increase and heart rate decrease, whereas a fear stimulus elicited increased frequency of spontaneous electrodermal responses. Moreover, the anger pattern was associated with the action of norepinephrine, while fear was associated with the action of epinephrine. The subjects were told the study was meant to detect physiological differences between those with hypertension and those without. In the fear situation the experimenter expressed surprise when the subject reported experiencing an electric shock to the finger. In the anger situation, the experimenter was described as an incompetent replacement for the regular experimenter.

Facial Responses

Another, more recent example of stimulus specificity is a study by Dimberg (1983; see also Dimberg, 1990), whose subjects reacted with subtle responses in the corrugator muscle, which controls the frowning motion of the eyebrows, when looking at pictures of angry facial expressions. When the same subjects looked at pictures of happy facial expressions, they reacted with increased activity in the zygomatic muscle, which controls the smile motion (see Figure 2.1).

Dimberg used EMG recordings from the corrugator and zygomatic muscles time-locked to the presentations of the pictures on a screen in front of the subjects. In this way he could identify specific changes in specific groups of muscles that were so subtle that the subjects themselves were not aware of them. However subtle these facial responses may seem, they may have been instrumental in survival of the species. Ekman (1972) has suggested that the basic facial emotional expressions are common to all individuals across cultures (fear, anger, surprise, happiness, disgust, to mention some). Anger, for example, is expressed by a frowning of the eyebrows, a staring gaze, and lifting the upper lip and showing the teeth. Fear, on the other hand, is expressed by a wide-open gaze and opening of the mouth. (See Figure 2.2.) Dim-

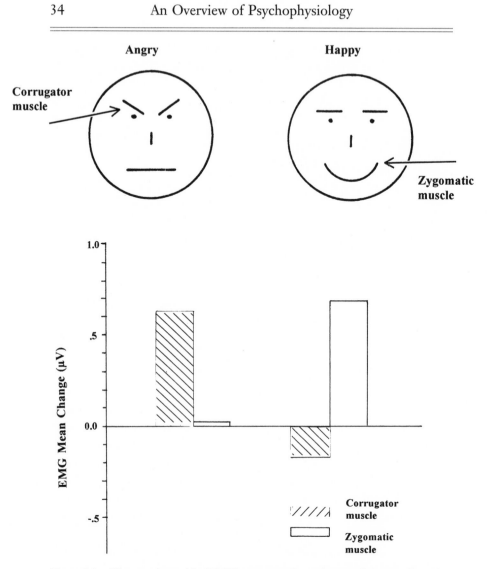

Figure 2.1.   Electromyographic (EMG) responses from the muscles controlling the eyebrow (corrugator) and mouth (zygomatic) when subjects were presented pictures of angry and happy facial expressions. EMG activity from the corrugator muscle increased when the subject saw pictures of angry faces, and EMG activity from the zygomatic muscle increased when the subject saw pictures of happy faces. (Data from Dimberg, 1983, redrawn with permission from the Society for Psychophysiological Research and the author.)

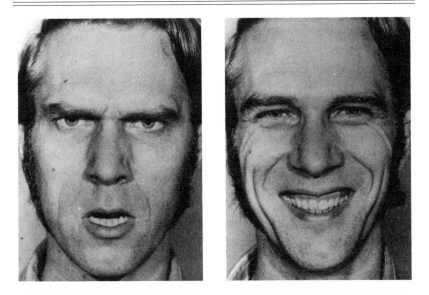

Figure 2.2. An angry *(left)* and a happy *(right)* emotional display. Note the frowning of the eyebrows and the lifting of the upper lip in the angry display, and the lifting of the cheeks in the happy display. (From Ekman and Friesen, 1976.)

berg's (1983) study indicates that at least some emotional responses can be differentiated physiologically (see also Ekman and Oster, 1979).

Since William James published his paper on emotions in 1884, different claims and theories have been put forward that discrete emotional experiences are associated with specific autonomic activity (e.g., Levenson, Ekman, and Friesen, 1990; see also Cacioppo, Klein, Berntson, and Hatfield, 1993). Cacioppo et al. (1993), who reviewed most studies published during the last decades, concluded that considerable variability exists between studies regarding ANS differentiation in emotions. They also concluded that "there is little evidence for replicable autonomic differences in pairwise comparisons of the emotions on the measures of bodily temperature, systolic blood pressure, facial temperature, respiration, skin conductance level and cardiac stroke volume" (p. 125). They also pointed out that the results of Ekman, Levenson, and Friesen (1983)—that skin conductance level increased more during sadness than during fear, anger, and disgust—have not been replicated, and also that this particular response pattern was observed only when the subjects *imagined* feeling sad or angry.

Phobic Responses

Another example of stimulus specificity is the different physiological response patterns seen during various phobic attacks. Öst, Sterner, and Lindahl (1984; see also Öst, 1989; Fredrikson, 1981) found that whereas snake phobics react with increased heart rate and blood pressure when exposed to a snake, or sometimes even to a picture of a snake, blood and injury phobics react with a dramatic *drop* in heart rate and blood pressure, and will sometimes even faint, upon exposure to the phobic stimulus. Graham, Kabler, and Lundsford (1961) concluded that the "fainting" response is caused by an initial sympathetic "fight-flight" response immediately followed by a massive parasympathetic response of the vagus nerve, which slows the heart and lowers blood pressure.

Thus, different phobias are associated with opposing physiological response patterns, which is another way of saying that phobic responses are stimulus-specific. As argued elsewhere (Chapter 7), the increase in heart rate and blood pressure in a phobic response may be an evolutionary remnant of an adaptive response to danger, as when our mammalian ancestors were attacked by a dinosaur reptile. Similarly, a dramatic drop in blood pressure may be an adaptive response to excessive bleeding, for it may help the individual to avoid bleeding to death. When the same responses occur in situations that pose no danger, however, the fear is called "irrational" or "phobic." In the examples provided by Öst (1989) and Fredrikson (1981), therefore, the same emotion elicits opposite cardiovascular response patterns depending on the nature of the feared stimulus. An alternative explanation may be that there are actually two different emotional qualities involved in a snake phobia and a blood or injury phobia, namely *fear* and *disgust*. The response of lowered cardiovascular functioning when a person is confronted with a bloody scene may indicate disgust, not fear. To summarize, the examples above may show a typical stimulus-specificity pattern; different physiological responses to different emotions (cf. Hugdahl, 1981).

Stimulus Specificity and Individual Differences

The issue of stimulus-specificity received much attention during the first decades after the Second World War. For example, Wenger, Engel and Clemens (1957) tried to develop a coherent taxonomy of specific stimulus-response patterns of physiological activity. Also, B. T. Engel (1960, 1972) made several attempts at a more coherent analysis of the specificity problem. In spite of all these efforts, there has been little progress in research on this issue over the last decades, with the exception of recent work by Ekman and colleagues on facial emotional expressions and Lacey's (1967) concept of "directional fractionation" (see below).

A different approach to stimulus specificity is taken by Davidson (e.g., 1992), whose work indicated that individual differences in positive and negative affective style correlate with EEG activation patterns over the right and left hemispheres of the brain, respectively. In a typical experiment (Davidson, Ekman, Saron, Senulis, and Friesen, 1990b), subjects were exposed to short film clips designed to induce approach-related positive emotion and withdrawal-related negative emotion. Happiness and amusement were the positive approach-related emotions, disgust was the negative, withdrawal-related emotion. The subjects were videotaped while watching the film clips, for a record of their facial responses, and EEG was recorded from various leads on the scalp.

An important aspect of studies on the dimensionality of emotion is that the investigators must try to ensure that the emotions studied do not differ in intensity, for a difference in intensity could explain the observed physiological or behavioral difference. Davidson and colleagues therefore had the stimuli carefully matched before the experiment, on the assumption that stimulus matching corresponds to physiological matching of the resultant emotions. In the experiment, subjects made facial signs of happiness (lip corners pulled up) in response to the positive stimuli, and signs of disgust (lowering the eyebrows, pulling the lip corners down) to the negative stimuli. By analyzing the EEG for the different frequency bands (such as alpha and beta; see Chapter 11), the investigators found that alpha power over the anterior left and right hemispheres of the brain correlated significantly with positive and negative facial expressions, respectively. The data are presented in Figure 2.3. Disgust was associated with less alpha power over the right anterior leads compared to happiness, which means more brain activation, while happiness was associated with less alpha power over the left anterior leads compared to disgust.

Response Stereotypy

Response stereotypy, or symptom specificity (Fahrenberg, 1986), is in a sense the "opposite" of stimulus specificity. Response stereotypy may

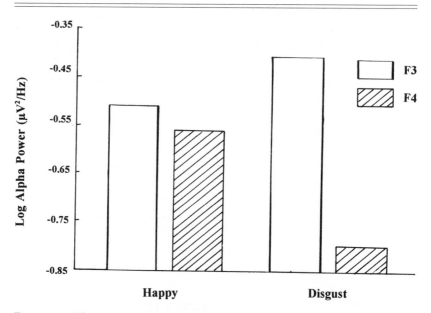

Figure 2.3. Electroencephalographic (EEG) recordings of alpha activity from the left (F3) and right (F4) leads of the scalp. Alpha activity was lower (= increased cortical activity) over the right frontal cortex when subjects showed signs of disgust than when they showed signs of happiness, and it was lower over the left hemisphere when subjects showed signs of happiness than when they showed signs of disgust. (Data from Davidson et al., 1990b, reprinted with permission from the American Psychological Association and the authors.)

be explained by reference to a classic psychophysiological study by Malmo and Shagass (1949). These authors studied psychiatric patients under stress. Patients complaining of head and neck pain showed increased EMG activity in these regions during experimentally induced pain, but patients complaining of cardiovascular symptoms experienced changes in cardiovascular responses during the same pain manipulation. Similar "sterotypic" responses to a stress manipulation were also observed by Engel and Bickford (1961), who recorded sterotypic changes in blood pressure in hypertensive patients.

Law of Initial Value

Although there are many laws in the natural sciences, psychophysiology has had only one "law," the law of initial value (LIV). This law (Wilder, 1967) says that the magnitude of phasic change in a response system is dependent on the tonic prestimulus base level. In other words, the "space" available for phasic changes in a response system is dependent on how close to the "ceiling" for that system the prestimulus level is. Thus, the "space" for a stimulus-elicited increase in heart rate is less if the tonic base level is 230 bpm than it is when the base level is 70 bpm.

In general terms, the higher the prestimulus level, the smaller is the potential response increase, and the larger is the potential response decrease under equal stimulus conditions. Geenen and van de Vijver (1993) argued that it is questionable whether the occurrence of LIV should be considered annoying or threatening to a study. They also questioned whether LIV is as widespread as sometimes indicated in the psychophysiology literature, and suggested that accurate statistical tests of the LIV may actually show that it describes a rather exceptional state of affairs. Their conclusion is that researchers should not "correct" scores for the LIV, since the "correction procedures" may be a much greater threat to the data than is the LIV itself.

Biofeedback

Biofeedback means "the feeding back of information to the individual about change in a physiological system." It implies that the subject is continuously, or discontinuously, informed about change in a particular physiological system under study. The information is believed to act as a reinforcer for further changes in either the same or the opposite direction. As a result of instrumental learning (see Kimmel, 1967, who pioneered this research), a physiological response may come under "instructional" or "volitional" control as a function of the feedback of information.

Lang, Sroufe, and Hastings (1967) were among the first to demonstrate the possibility of changing heart rate through biofeedback. They instructed subjects how to use information about their heart rate (a decrease in this case) in order to change their heart rate. At about the same time, Kamyia (1969) reported that subjects could learn to control the alpha rhythm of their EEG brain waves by providing feedback to the subject about the occurrence of alpha bursts (brief light stimulus when alpha was present). Kamyia's results have, however, been criticized on methodological grounds, and it has been difficult to replicate some of the findings.

The Question of Mediation

A major topic of controversy during the early years of biofeedback research was the question of mediation, that is, whether the effects obtained were the result of true learning in the autonomic nervous system or were mediated by muscle tension or respiration rates. For example, in a critical review Katkin and Murray (1968) concluded that what may have been happening in studies reportedly showing learning of autonomic responses was that subjects merely learned to modify their skeletal-muscle responses, over which they already had voluntary control. These modified muscle responses thus *mediated* the apparent change in the autonomic system under study.

Biofeedback Applications

Biofeedback has been applied to a large range of different supposedly psychosomatic diseases, like hypertension and muscle pain, with varying success. Mainly used in psychophysiology as an applied technique (see Gatchel and Price, 1979), the principle of biofeedback goes back to the idea that nonvolitional, autonomic behavior can be instrumentally conditioned in a stimulus-reinforcement paradigm.

Traditional learning theory at the time of the discovery of the biofeedback principle held that an autonomic, involuntary response could be conditioned only through the principles of classical, or Pavlovian, conditioning (see Kimble, 1961). Instrumental, operant learning could be applied only to voluntary behavior and responses (Skinner, 1953). However, in a series of experiments, Miller (1964) showed that autonomic behavior, like changes in blood pressure, could be operantly conditioned in rats.

Although replication of Miller's original experiments turned out to be difficult to obtain, the principle of operant or instrumental conditioning of cardiovascular responses soon became a popular research area in behavior therapy and behavioral medicine.

In a broader cultural context, various forms of "biofeedback" have been applied for centuries by yogis and monks in Eastern religions in order to gain mental control over their bodies. Dramatic examples exist of individuals being able to produce gross changes of their normal physiology by the sheer act of will. Examples in the literature range from the ability to hyperventilate over long periods of time to the ability almost to stop the heart and seemingly obliterate all signs of blood pressure.

Various "biofeedback institutes" and companies manufacturing "biofeedback equipment" grew up like mushrooms after a heavy rain in the 1970s and early 1980s. Despite the great promise these techniques held for psychologists, however, the clinical value of biofeedback has been limited, with a few exceptions (temperature feedback for treatment of migraine headache, to mention an example). Part of the problem seemed to be the magnitude of the obtained change (see Seer, 1979). Whereas a clinically relevant change in blood pressure, for example, would be in the region of 50–80 mm Hg, changes in the biofeedback laboratories seldom were larger than 5–10 mm Hg. Thus, although *statistically* significant, the changes seen in the biofeedback laboratory were often not *clinically* relevant.

Autonomic Balance and Individual Differences

Eppinger and Hess (1910) launched the concept of autonomic balance as a marker of individual variability, or *individual trait*. They argued that individuals could be characterized as either *sympathetically* or *parasympathetically* prone to respond to a stressor. Thus, Eppinger and Hess (1910) viewed autonomic balance as a kind of "personality" characteristic. Some individuals were more prone to balance the reciprocal activation of the two branches of the autonomic nervous system in favor of the sympathetic branch, others were more prone to balance the other way. Eppinger and Hess called these tendencies *vagotonia* and *sympathicotonia* to denote parasympathetic and sympathetic dominance, respectively. A few decades later, Wenger (1941) set out to test the concepts of vagotonia and sympathicotonia by testing a large group of children for twenty physiological variables, including blood pressure, muscle relaxation, heart rate, electrodermal responses, and respiration rate, to mention a few. On the basis of factor analyses and intercorrelations between the variables, Wenger reformulated Eppinger and Hess's concept of autonomic balance in this way:

> The differential chemical reactivity and the physiological antagonism of the adrenergic and cholinergic branches of the autonomic nervous system permit of a situation in which the action of one branch may predominate over that of the other. This predominance, or auto-

nomic imbalance, may be phasic or chronic, and may obtain for either the adrenergic or the cholinergic system.

Autonomic imbalance, when measured in an unselected population, will be distributed continuously about a central tendency which shall be defined as autonomic balance.   (p. 434)

As will be discussed in more detail in Chapter 5, Berntson and Cacioppo (e.g., Berntson, Cacioppo, Quigley, and Farbro, 1992) have introduced the concept of *autonomic balance* to underscore the important fact that the two branches of the autonomic nervous system do not always act in a reciprocal fashion. Sometimes there may be coactivation of both the sympathetic and parasympathetic branches, which describes the physiological activation pattern seen in a phobic patient afraid of blood. These phobic patients usually exhibit a brief sympathetic activation parallelled by a massive parasympathetic activation.

Vagal Tone

The concept of *vagal tone* (Porges and Byrne, 1992) and of individual differences in vagal tonus in relation to behavior is a more recent variant of autonomic balance. Vagal tone is a measure of heart rate variability in different stimulus contexts. Heart rate variability, in turn, is related both to respiratory patterns and to the influence of the vagus nerve on the heart. Porges has also demonstrated that vagal tone is positively correlated with emotional stability. See Chapter 9 for further details, including a critical appraisal of different measures of heart-rate variability.

Directional Fractionation

The concept of directional fractionation is linked to Lacey's (1958) observation that different physiological measures seldom covaried along a single dimension. As an example, an increase in skin conductance is often accompanied by a decrease in heart rate, despite the individual's exposure to an "arousing" situation or an unexpected stimulus. *Directional fractionation* refers to the observation that the direction of change in one physiological response system may be independent of, or even opposite to, the direction of change in another response system. In other words, the overall patterning of physiological responses to an external stressor is "fractionated" in various directions. Lacey used the concept to criticize the dominating view that "activation" meant that all physiological response systems must increase, or all must decrease, during a response. That this is not always the case is typically demonstrated in the "freezing" behavior of animals in danger, when heart rate is reduced even though the animal is cortically activated. (See the discussion below on "activation and arousal" for further details.)

Bottom-up and Top-down Processing

Another conceptual dichotomy often used in psychophysiology is the distinction between bottom-up and top-down modes of processing (Eysenck and Keane, 1990). Bottom-up processing, or data-driven processing, is the analysis of a flow of information from the level of sensory registration ("the bottom") upward to the higher, cognitive levels. In bottom-up processing, the sensory data are transformed and combined to produce concepts of perception, attention, and memory. Bottom-up processing may be compared with inductive reasoning.

Top-down processing, or concept-driven processing, focuses on an individual's concepts on shaping registration and "lower"-level processing. In top-down processing, existing concepts and memories modulate incoming sensory registrations, which combine into new concepts and models. Top-down processing may be compared with hypothetico-deductive reasoning.

Hemispheric Asymmetry, or Laterality

Hemispheric asymmetry denotes differences in the capacity for information processing between the right and left cerebral hemispheres. Hemispheric asymmetry, or laterality, is analyzed along several different dimensions, including functional (physiological) vs. structural (anatomical) laterality, stimulus-regulated vs. process-regulated laterality, cortical vs. subcortical (e.g., thalamic) laterality, and normal-functioning vs. neuropathological laterality. In general, the data favor the conclusion that the anterior left hemisphere is specialized for the processing of language and cognitive operations in sequence. The anterior area of the left hemisphere may also be specialized for positive emotional affect, although this is not settled. The posterior right hemisphere, on the other hand, is specialized for visuo-spatial processing and orienting in three-dimensional space. The right hemisphere is also specialized for face processing, particularly recognition of angry facial displays.

At a more fundamental level, the division of labor between the hemispheres may relate to the need of prehistoric man for effective symbolic communication between members of the same species and, at the same time, the need for good spatial orientation skills in hunting prey and fleeing from predators.

Activation and Arousal

The terms *activation* and *arousal* will be used interchangeably throughout this book, as both denote an increase in energy mobilization. In a narrower sense, however, activation refers to a process in the central nervous system, which increases activity from lower to higher levels of consciousness. Thus, activation is a construct denoting changes in the activity level of the brain, from coma to excitement. Activation is therefore traditionally measured with reference to the EEG pattern. Arousal, on the other hand, is related to motivation and mobilization of bodily resources, involving the peripheral nervous system, the endocrine system, and possibly also the immune system. Another, conceptually similar definition was provided by Pribram and McGuinness (1975), who suggested that arousal is related to short-acting, phasic changes, such as the elicitation of the orienting reaction, whereas activation is related to tonic maintenance of alertness over longer periods of time.

It is important to realize that the brain can control and regulate peripheral functions and target organs through four main "output systems"; the autonomic nervous system, the skeletal-muscle system, the endocrine system, and the immune system. Psychophysiology in a more restricted sense has traditionally been focused on the brain and the autonomic system rather than on the other systems.

Arousal is measured by monitoring the activity of the brain or changes in the autonomic nervous system and by correlating these with changes in behavior. As researchers soon discovered, however, these correlations were often minimal (although generally positive). The lack of substantial correlations between different indexes of arousal has created problems for arousal theory and, as noted above, led Lacey (1958) to propose that more than one type of arousal exists. Thus, we may see behavioral arousal as behavioral changes in a responding organism, autonomic arousal as physiological changes in bodily functions, or cortical arousal as electrical changes in brain waves.

Feedback from the periphery to the body was also important in Lacey's model of arousal. For example, he reported that distension of the carotid sinus (a nucleus in the carotid artery) causes EEG activity to change from alert, high-frequency activity to the low-frequency activity generally associated with sleep. This change indicates that feedback from various systems of the body can directly influence the arousal system and suggests that bodily systems may also play a role in determining the length of arousal episodes.

Although the concept of arousal still is frequently used in both research and clinical work, several problems with arousal theory remain. One major problem is the lack of a strong relationship between measures of behavioral, autonomic and cortical arousal. A second problem specific to Lacey's theory is that it assumes different patterns of bodily responses, yet clear differences remain to be shown.

Automatic versus Controlled Modes of Processing

Processing is said to be automatic if a stimulus is perceived and initially processed without conscious awareness or without attention. An automatic process is obligatory when a stimulus is present, and it will run to completion. Automatic processing also occurs without intention, and it does not demand attentional resources.

Processing is said to be controlled if a stimulus demands attention and the allocation of processing resources, usually from a limited-capacity central channel (Kahneman, 1973). Thus, controlled processing is intentional, aimed at specific goals. Typical everyday activities are to a large extent dependent on both automatic and controlled processes. Recent studies have shown that automatic processes develop early in childhood and stay relatively stable throughout life. Controlled processes, on the other hand, are subject to change across the age span.

Rogers (1993) reviewed evidence that automatic processes like visual scanning in a perceptual learning task show consistent differences between young and old individuals. In a visual scanning task the subject is presented with a single target item followed by a display of several items, the target plus distractor items. Younger subjects tend to solve the task in an automatic processing mode, without paying attention to the distractor items. Older subjects, on the other hand, are forced to shift attention, in a manner like controlled processing, between the target item and the distractors.

Some early (*exogenous*) components in event-related potentials (ERPs) recorded from the brain are said to reflect automatic processing, and later (*endogenous*) components are said to reflect controlled processing (Squires and Ollo, 1986; see also Chapter 12). Öhman (1979) has developed a model for the orienting response and its habituation based on the concepts of automatic and controlled processing. Automatic and controlled modes of processing are equivalent to unaware versus aware modes of processing (see Chapter 7).

A key element in the switch from automatic to controlled mode is the allocation of attentional resources to the stimulus. The distinction between automatic and controlled modes of processing is frequently used in cognitive psychophysiology, and particularly in ERP-research. See Öhman (1986) and Dawson, Filion, and Schell (1989), however, for analyses of electrodermal phenomena in terms of automatic and controlled processing.

Summary

Some of the major concepts and terms used in psychophysiology are defined and described in Chapter 2. The purpose of this chapter is to familiarize the student with psychophysiological definitions and concepts frequently used in later chapters in relation to different response systems and psychophysiological processes. Among the concepts discussed are stimulus specificity, response stereotypy, the law of initial value, biofeedback, autonomic balance, directional fractionation, modes of processing (bottom-up and top-down, automatic and controlled), hemispheric asymmetry, and activation and arousal. Emphasis has been put on introducing the reader to these concepts rather than on presenting an in-depth analysis of each one. Readers will find more detailed descriptions and analyses in specialized textbooks for the particular areas.

II

The Brain and Nervous System

3

The Nervous System

In the neurosciences, explanations may involve knowledge of the *anatomy* of the nervous system (the physical structures, such as the parts of the brain, the nerves, or the cells) and the *physiology*, or functioning, of these structures. The three chapters of this part introduce the basics of neuroanatomy and neurophysiology. (The interested student seeking a more in-depth treatment should consult, for example, Guyton, 1992, or Sobotta and Becher, 1990.) Given the focus of this book on psychophysiology, the overview presented here is intended as a foundation for exploring the intricate interface of mind, brain, and body. More specifically, it provides the anatomical and physiological background needed to study how the brain and mind regulate and control changes in the periphery of the body.

Chapter 3 begins with an overview of the central and peripheral nervous systems, with a focus on basic neurophysiology, and concludes with a description of the peripheral nervous system. Next, Chapter 4 presents the structures of the brain, as well as a brief introduction to hormonal regulation of stress responses and to psychological influences on immune system function. Brain regulation of stress and immune function is in many respects outside the purview of classic neuroanatomy and neurophysiology, but the topic is included here because of its importance to questions of interest in, for example, cardiovascular psychophysiology. Finally, the discussion of the autonomic nervous system, a branch of the peripheral nervous system, is given a chapter of its own (Chapter 5) because of the emphasis put on autonomic functions in traditional psychophysiology.

Anatomical terminology. Neuroanatomical descriptions require a set of specific terms and concepts to denote different positions and directions in relation to the brain or the body. These terms usually have Latin origin, although the language of neuroanatomy is mixed with Latin and Greek terminology. It is customary to name structures in the brain with reference to their position relative to some other structure. For example, the *hypothalamus* is so named because it is located under *(hypo-)* the *thalamus*, a structure deep in the brain which gets its name from the Greek for "inner chamber."

The "directions of the body" used to indicate relative positions of anatomical structures are illustrated in Figure 3.1. Moving toward the top of the head means moving toward the *superior* parts of the body. Moving toward the feet means moving toward the *inferior* parts of the body. Moving in the same direction as the nose means moving toward the *anterior* parts of the body, and moving toward the back means moving toward the *posterior* parts of the body. When one is referring to the whole body, rather than only the brain, the anterior direction is similar to *ventral* (toward the stomach), and posterior is similar to *dorsal* (toward the back of the body). In some instances, however, as in regard to the visual systems of the brain, *ventral* and *dorsal* are used to indicate the *bottom* and *top* of the brain, respectively.

Moving toward the middle of the body is the same as moving in the *medial* direction. Moving toward the side of the body is the same as moving in the *lateral* direction. Moving from the left side of the brain to the right hand is the same as moving to the *contralateral* side, that is, moving to the hand opposite *(contra-)* the place of origin. Consequently, moving toward the *ipsilateral* hand is the same as moving from one side of the brain to the hand on the same *(ipsi-)* side—as from left to left or right to right.

In addition to the directions, planes of orientation, or "slices" of the brain and body, are used to map anatomical structures. A vertical plane reaching from one ear to the other, across the top of the brain, defines the *coronal* plane. Also from ear to ear, or from side to side, but perpendicular to the coronal plane is the *horizontal* plane (called the *axial* plane in radiology). Finally, a vertical plane cutting reaching from the front to the back is known as the *sagittal* plane.

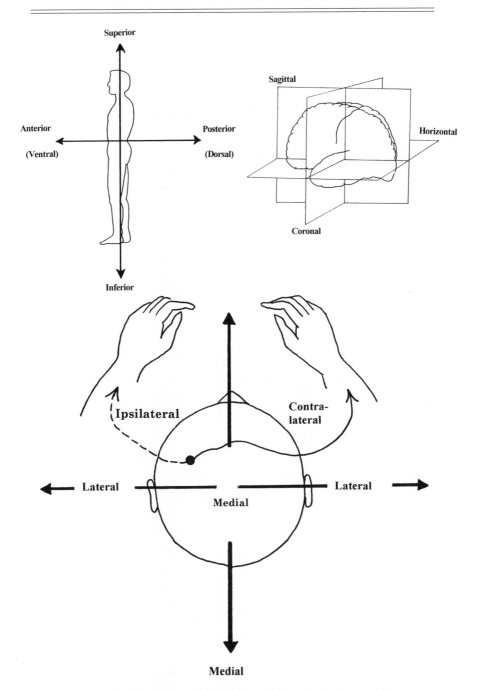

Figure 3.1. Terms for anatomical directions and planes in the human body.

The Structure and Function of the Nervous System

The nervous system consists of the *central nervous system* (CNS), which is the brain and the spinal cord, and the *peripheral nervous system*. The central nervous system is contained within the bony structures that embrace the brain and the spinal cord. Nerve fibers outside the skull and spine belong to the peripheral nervous system. (See Figure 3.2.) The peripheral nervous system can be further subdivided into the *sensorimotor* nervous system and the *autonomic* nervous system (ANS).

Like all organs in the body, the brain and the nervous system are constructed of cells. In the brain there are basically two types of cells, *glia* (literally, "glue") and *nerve cells (neurons)*. These two classes of cells have different functions. The neurons, which are the focus of interest here, are concerned with communication and information processing, while the glial cells are concerned with transportation of metabolites and protection of the neural cells and their environment.

The neuron consists of a cell body, called a *soma*, and several

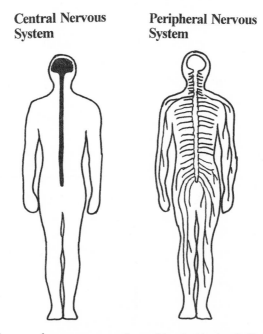

Central Nervous System   **Peripheral Nervous System**

Figure 3.2. The central nervous system (everything inside the skull and spine) and the peripheral nervous system (everything outside the skull and spine).

branching fibers, called *axons* and *dendrites*. Axons carry signals away from the cell body, and dendrites carry signals to the cell body. Each axon may have many branches, which themselves undergo further branching to make synapses with several thousands of other nerve cells. An axon may in some instances be several feet long (as in the spinal cord) or just a few millimeters (as in the brain).

The signals carried by neurons in the nervous system are electrochemical signals called *action potentials* and *synaptic potentials*. An action potential is a sudden change of electrical polarity on the inside and outside of a nerve fiber, which is triggered as a "response" when the nerve is stimulated. The action potential travels along an axon, sometimes jumping between the nodes separating the cells that form a protective fatty sheath, or *myelin*, around the nerve fiber. Eventually the action potential reaches the axon terminal, or knob, which is filled with small "bags," or *synaptic vesicles*, containing transmitter substance. This substance is released into the *synaptic cleft*, the space between the two cells at the contact point (see Figure 3.3), thereby affecting the connecting neuron by interacting with receptors on that cell's membrane.

Postsynaptic potentials. The effect of the transmitter substance on the postsynaptic cell may be either excitatory or inhibitory. If the receptor and the transmitter are excitatory, they may depolarize the receiving membrane, making the cell more likely to "fire"—that is, generate a new potential. An effect of this kind is called an *excitatory postsynaptic potential* (EPSP). If, on the other hand, the receptor and the transmitter are inhibitory, they may hyperpolarize the membrane, decreasing the likelihood that the cell will fire in the near future. This is called an *inhibitory postsynaptic potential* (IPSP).

The propagation of action potentials. Neurons are electrically charged, as a battery is, by the concentration of positive and negative ions on opposite sides of a barrier (for neurons, the cell membrane); as a result, there is a voltage difference between the inside and outside of the cell membrane. This difference, or electrical potential, can be measured with a pair of microelectrodes, one inserted into the cell, the other on the outside. The resting *membrane potential* of a nerve cell is about -70 millivolts (mV), with the negative charge on the inside. In the resting state, sodium ions (Na^+) are at a low concentration inside the nerve cell, where there is a higher concentration of positively charged potassium (K^+) and an even higher concentration of (negatively charged) anions, and chlorine (Cl^-) ions. The resting potential is kept

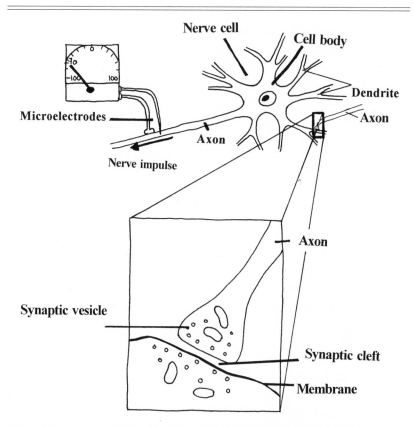

Figure 3.3. A typical nerve cell, with a nerve impulse traveling along the axon. The enlarged section shows the synaptic cleft and the membrane of the postsynaptic cell, dendrites, and structures that are important for the transmission of a synaptic potential.

at about -70 mV by passive transport (concentration and electronic gradients) and active transport (Na^+/K^+ pump) through ion channels in the cell membrane. When the nerve cell is excited, its electrical polarity changes to about $+60$ mV, a difference of about 130 mV. To oversimplify, the change in polarity is due, among other things, to a change in the permeability of the cell membrane, particularly for sodium (Na^+) and potassium (K^+) ions. Because of the increased permeability, Na^+ massively diffuses into the cell while fewer potassium ions (K^+) diffuse from the inside to the outside of the cell. The result is that the inside becomes positively charged relative to the outside. An action potential then travels, *propagates*, away from the cell body because the reversed charge spreads to adjacent areas of the axon. When ions travel across the cell membrane, either to the inside or the outside, they create a local current with an electrical polarity opposite that of the non-excited adjacent area. Since electrical charges of opposing polarity attract each other, the action potential will cause the "next" area of the axon to fire, reversing the polarity of the inside to the outside in that area of the nerve fiber.

Neurotransmitters

There are both excitatory and inhibitory synapses in the brain and nervous system. Inhibitory synapses make the neuron less responsive, while excitatory synapses make the neuron more responsive, resulting in a firing sequence when it is excited. Neurotransmitters are the chemical vehicles that "bridge" the synaptic cleft between an axon and a dendrite or between two axons. Thus the sequence of impulse propagation in the nervous system is electrical-chemical-electrical.

The major neurotransmitters in the brain and nervous system are norepinephrine (NE), acetylcholine (ACh), dopamine (DA), and serotonin (5-HT). In addition, there are some 30 neuropeptides and several amino acids that also have profound effects on certain functions in the brain. Of the amino acids, γ-aminobutyric acid (GABA) is an important transmitter in the brain. Other amino acids that have been found to act as neurotransmitters are glutamate, aspartate, and glycine. Concentrations of aspartate can today be monitored *in vivo* in specific areas of the brain by magnetic resonance imaging (MRI) spectroscopy, which is a variant of the use of magnetic resonance imaging (see Chapter 13 for further explanation of magnetic resonance imaging). Of the major neurotransmitters, NE and ACh are excitatory, while GABA has an inhibitory function. DA and 5-HT may be excitatory or inhibitory, depending on the receptor type. Glutamate is a major excitatory transmitter candidate, widely distributed in the brain. Of the putative peptide neurotransmitters, endorphins and substance-P are both involved in the regulation of pain and pain sensations.

Norepinephrine. Norepinephrine in the brain is synthesized mainly in the locus ceruleus, which is a nucleus (cluster of neural cells) situated near the pons in the brainstem. The locus ceruleus is part of the reticular formation, which is involved in arousal and activation. Svensson (1987) reviewed data showing that the locus ceruleus NE system responds to salient stressful stimuli within seconds, and that this system may play an integrative role for the initiation of biological and behavioral responses and, ultimately, for survival. From the locus ceruleus, NE is distributed over wide areas in the brain, including the cerebellum, brainstem, and the cortex.

Drugs that have an excitatory effect on the central nervous system, like cocaine and amphetamine, may act in two ways: either they prolong the effect of NE at the receptor site, or they substitute for NE at the synaptic cleft, "tricking" the brain to behave as though it were extremely aroused and leading to an effect similar to the typical "rush" felt by amphetamine addicts.

Norepinephrine in the brain should be distinguished from that secreted from the medulla of the adrenal glands. Adrenal norepinephrine is an example of a transmitter acting as a hormone in the autonomic nervous system. Norepinephrine, epinephrine, and dopamine are collectively called *catecholamines*. Effects caused by catecholamines are collectively called *adrenergic* effects.

Dopamine. Dopamine is a pharmacological precursor to NE, and dopaminergic neurons contain an enzyme not seen in NE neurons. The two most important dopaminergic pathways are the nigrostriatal and the mesolimbic systems. The nigrostriatal system originates in the substantia nigra in the basal ganglia, with neurons spreading to the frontal cortex, whereas the mesolimbic system originates in the tegmentum and spreads to limbic areas of the brain. Dopamine has major influences on motor function, and a shortage of this neurotransmitter is involved in Parkinson's disease. Excess of dopamine, on the other hand, has been linked to schizophrenia. A common side effect of dopaminergic drug treatments of schizophrenia is the development of motor disturbances resembling the motor dysfunctions seen in Parkinson's disease. Dopamine is also involved in the regulation of emotion through the mesolimbic system.

Acetylcholine. Acetylcholine neurons are mainly located in the basal forebrain bundle and brain stem. They are also frequent in the autonomic nervous system. Cholinergic neurons may be classified as *nicotinic* or *muscarinic:* the nicotinic function of ACh is to serve as the neurotransmitter at the neuromuscular junction for the control of muscle tonus; the muscarinic function of ACh is to serve as the neurotransmitter in the parasympathetic synapses in the autonomic nervous system. ACh is also important for memory and intellectual functioning. Impairment of the regulation of ACh is critically involved in the severe dementia that characterizes Alzheimer's disease.

Serotonin. Serotonin and serotonergic neurons are localized to regions in the pons, and particularly to a collection of nuclei called the *raphe nuclei.* Serotonin is believed to play an important role in sleep, although modern sleep theories (e.g., Hobson and McCarley, 1977; Hobson, 1990) also place emphasis on the adrenergic and cholinergic systems. Hobson (1990) has shown that there is a shutdown of the adrenergic system and norepinephrine activity in parts of the pons during REM sleep, which is the phase of sleep when we dream, characterized by rapid eye movements (REM) (see Chapter 11).

GABA. GABA, finally, is a major inhibitory amino acid transmitter in the brain. It exists in great quantities all over the brain. GABA is particularly linked to dopamine and dopaminergic action, inhibiting action in both the nigrostriatal and mesolimbic dopaminergic pathways.

Sensory and Motor Systems

The rest of this chapter describes the functional anatomy of the peripheral and central somatomotor, somatosensory, visual, and auditory systems. In addition to these systems, the specific sensory systems includes the olfactory (smell) and gustatory (taste) sensory systems. Phylogenetically one of the oldest sensory systems, the olfactory system differs from the others in that it projects ipsilaterally to the brain; in other words, olfactory information from the left nostril reaches the olfactory centers in the forebrain on the left side. Other sensory systems, as well as the motor systems, cross over the midline of the body and brain and thus project contralaterally.

The Somatomotor System

The somatomotor nervous system consists of nerve fibers controlling both volitional motor functions, like moving a finger or bending a knee. Nerve fibers coming from the brain to the periphery are called *efferent* or motor fibers, and nerve fibers coming from receptors in the skin, muscles, or joints are called *afferent* or sensory fibers. A more detailed description of somatic sensations is given in the following section on the somatosensory system.

The somatomotor system is subdivided into several subsystems, each with its own specific anatomy and physiology. The major motor system is the *pyramidal* system, which is made up of motor neurons and tracts and which runs from the motor cortex, via the medullary pyramidal cell bundles, to the *neuronal endplates* in the striate (skeletal) muscle fibers (see Chapter 15 for further details).

The pyramidal system has its name from the large pyramid-shaped bundles of cells in the medulla oblongata. The pyramidal tract originating in the *left* motor cortex crosses over to the *right* side at the level of the medullary pyramids and descends along the spinal cord. The tract eventually exits the spinal cord and extends to the periphery of the body. The crossover from left cortext to the right side of the body (or from right to left) is called *pyramidal decussation* and explains why damage to the left motor areas of the cortex will cause a hemiparalysis on the right side of the body.

A single peripheral efferent motor fiber innervates several different muscle fibers. The peripheral nerve fiber and its innervated muscle fibers is called a *motor unit*, which is the basic unit of action in the striate muscle motor system (see Chapter 15).

A second major motor system is the *cerebellar* or *extrapyramidal system*. The name *extrapyramidal* is somewhat misleading, since the pyramidal and extrapyramidal systems are integrated in a complex loop of neuronal activity in the cortex, the *basal ganglia*, and the cerebellum. Key structures in this system are the *cerebellum*, located at the back of the skull, posterior to the cerebrum (see Figure 4.9), and the basal ganglia. The cerebellum integrates fine-tuned movements and receives feedback input from the muscles through the *spinocerebellar pathway*.

Activity in the motor cortex is gated to the cerebellum through the *corticocerebellar pathway*, which is routed through the pons. The cerebellum is also critically involved in the maintenance of gait and balance through signals from the vestibular cochlea in the inner ear, the cortex, and the corticocerebellar and spinocerebellar pathways. The cerebellum is also involved in simple associative learning (Thompson, 1988; Daum, Schugens, Ackermann, et al., 1993), and may be critical for memory of motor responses.

The Somatosensory System

In the present context, the somatosensory system comprises the receptors, nerve cell tracts, and brain centers that provide information to the brain from the skin. The skin is covered with different *receptors* (sensors) that are differentially sensitive to stimuli: *Meissner corpuscles* are sensitive to touch, *Pacini corpuscles* to pressure, *Ruffini cylinders* to heat and warmth, and *Krause end-bulbs* to cold.

Pain is a complex sensation emerging from a combination of stimuli, like pressure, heat, and cold. Pain is sensed through *A-* and *C-fibers* from the skin to the brain, with "gating posts" at the spinal cord and thalamic levels. Melzack and Wall (1965) proposed a "gate-theory" for pain based on inhibitory control of activity in the C-fibers at the level of the spinal cord.

Except for facial sensations, sensory signals from the skin travel up the spinal cord to the sensory cortex in the parietal lobe. There are two major sensory systems in the spinal cord, *the lemniscal system* and the *spinothalamic system*. The spinothalamic system contains both crossed and uncrossed fibers, thus having both contralateral and ipsilateral input to the brain.

The Visual System

Visual information from the retina in the eye is transmitted through the optic nerve fibers in the optical tract to the lateral geniculate body in the brain stem. From there, information travels in a large tract, the optic radiations, to the primary visual areas in the occipital cortex. This is the *geniculostriate* visual system. There is also a secondary system, the *tectofugal* system, which involves the superior colliculus, the pulvinar thalamus, and projections to various cortical sites, including the parietal lobes.

Information presented to either the left or right visual half-field (see Figure 3.4) is initially projected to the contralateral occipital areas. The optical projections are arranged so that nerve fibers from each of the nasal portions of the retinal inflow projects to the contralateral hemisphere. The optical nerve fibers cross over at the *optical chiasma*. The temporal portion of each hemiretinae projects ipsilaterally to the visual cortex. This means that if the eyes are fixating on an object in the middle of the visual field, visual information presented in the left half-field will be projected to the right visual cortex, and vice versa. This is the anatomical principle behind the *visual half-field technique* frequently used in studies of hemispheric specialization.

Most of the impulses from the retina are transmitted to the primary visual cortex in the occipital lobe, including the V1 area, which extends

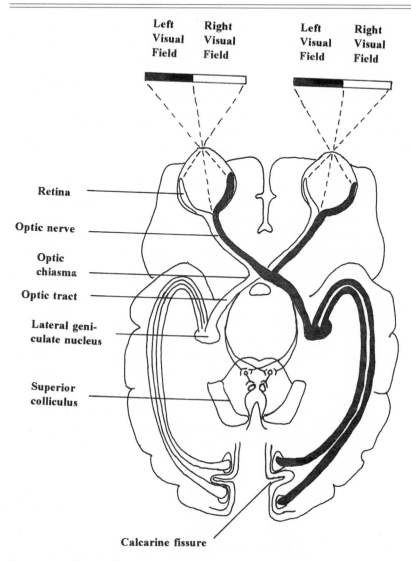

Left   Right   Left   Right
Visual   Visual   Visual   Visual
Field   Field   Field   Field

Retina

Optic nerve

Optic
chiasma

Optic tract

Lateral geni-
culate nucleus

Superior
colliculus

Calcarine fissure

Figure 3.4. The visual pathways from the retina to the calcarine fissure in the occipital (visual) cortex.

to the calcarine fissure between the two hemispheres at the far end of the occipital lobe. Research during the last decade has revealed that other areas close to the V1 area are selectively involved in the recognition of color, line direction (area V4), movement (area V5), and shapes (area V3). Regardless of whether color, shape, or direction is per-

ceived, however, areas V1 and V2 are always active in visual perception. Zeki (1978) has, on the basis on studies on monkeys, proposed
that visual information is first sorted in area V1 and thereafter trans-
ferred to the specialized areas in the visual cortex. Areas V1 and V2
thus act as kind of "control station" that directs visual information to
other areas for further processing. Although this idea may be intriguing as a model of visual functioning, areas V1 and V2 may not
be "smart" enough to sort information. An alternative view is that
visual information is simply "passed along" until it reaches an area
whose cells are "tuned" to respond to it (as area V3 is able to respond
to information about shape). The recognition of a visual object or pattern also engages areas in the temporal lobe. This is called the "what"

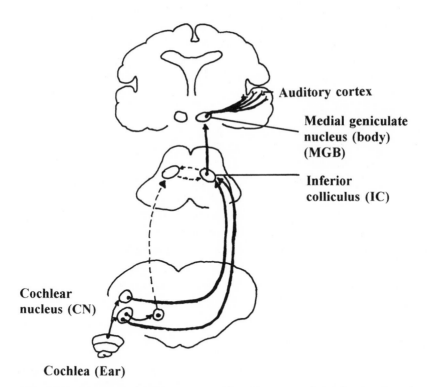

Figure 3.5. The auditory pathways in the brain. The auditory signal is transmitted
from the cochlear nucleus (CN) of the medulla, over the inferior colliculus (IC) at
the brainstem level and the medial geniculate body (MGB), to the auditory projections in the superior temporal lobe.

network and involves perception of shape, color, and speed of movement. Another neuronal network, the "where" network in the parietal cortex, is related to where in the visual field an object is located (see Gross and Mishkin, 1977).

A phenomenon that sometimes occurs after damage to the primary visual area (V1) in the striate cortex is the condition known as *blindsight* (Weiskrantz, 1986). Blindsighted patients can often discriminate between simple objects when asked to point at them, but they deny having seen the objects, thus demonstrating a dissociation between explicit and implicit (unconscious) perceptual acuity.

The Auditory System

Auditory information from the cochlea in the inner ear to the primary auditory cortex in the temporal lobe travels several tracts and pathways. It is carried by the auditory nerve to the cochlear nucleus and other peripheral nuclei and then goes to the inferior colliculus and the medial geniculate body, before reaching the auditory centers in the superior part of the temporal lobe. The major auditory projections are mapped in Figure 3.5.

As a rule, the contralateral nerve fibers from the cochlea in the ear to the primary auditory cortex in the superior temporal gyrus are preponderant over the ipsilateral fibers. This means that auditory information that is presented to the right ear has a stronger neural representation in the left temporal lobe, and vice versa. This is the principle behind *dichotic listening*, which happens when two messages are presented at the same time but directed to different ears. If the messages contain verbal information, there is usually better recognition from the right ear (the right ear advantage, REA), which is explained by reference to the stronger neural representation between the right ear and the left, language-specialized temporal lobe.

Summary

This chapter presents a brief sketch of how nerve cells communicate through action potentials and synaptic transmission. The major neurotransmitters were listed and described, along with some of the putative transmitters. Finally, the major motor and sensory nervous systems, including both central and peripheral pathways, were described.

4

The Brain

One of the brain's most distinctive features is the difference between grey matter and white matter. Cell bodies and unmyelinated neurons make up the grey matter in the brain and the myelinated axons make up the white matter. The white matter is so named because the glial cells covering the nerve fibers, or axons, form white, fatty sheets (the myelin). The grey matter gets its color from the cell bodies of the neurons and from the surrounding blood vessels.

The brain develops from a tubelike neural concavity, and the five ventricles of the brain—the two lateral ventricles, the third ventricle, the cerebral aqueduct, and the fourth ventricle—are the remaining parts of the hollow center of the neural tube. As the brain develops, the tubelike shape is markedly distorted. Table 4.1 lists some of the major structures in the brain and their developmental course. In a phylogenetic sense, the brain develops from a primitive "three-brain" division (forebrain, midbrain, and hindbrain) to a "five-brain" division (telencephalon, diencephalon, mesencephalon, metencephalon, and myelencephalon).

When the fully developed brain is viewed from the bottom, the first structure seen is the myelencephalon, which means the "spinal brain," consisting mainly of the medulla oblongata. Above the myelencephalon comes the metencephalon, or the "across brain," which consists of the cerebellum, the pons, and the fourth ventricle. The next division

Table 4.1. The divisions of the brain.

Early brainstem	Mammalian brain	Human brain	Functional divisions
Forebrain	Telencephalon (endbrain)	Cortex Basal ganglia Limbic system Olfactory bulb Lateral ventricles	Forebrain
	Diencephalon (between-brain)	Thalamus Hypothalamus Third ventricle	
Midbrain	Mesencephalon (midbrain)	Tectum Tegmentum Cerebral aqueduct	Brainstem
Hindbrain	Metencephalon (across-brain) Myelencephalon (spinal brain)	Cerebellum Fourth ventricle	

Source: Adapted from Kolb and Whishaw (1986).

is the mesencephalon, or the "midbrain," making up the tectum, the tegmentum, and the cerebral aqueduct. The two last divisions are the diencephalon, or the "between brain," which includes the thalamus, the hypothalamus, the pineal gland, and the third ventricle, and the telencephalon, or the "endbrain," consisting of the cortex, the basal ganglia, and the limbic system. The "brainstem" is the common name for all the structures from the cerebral acqueduct to the third ventricle.

A functional rather than structural division of the brain would include three major parts: the cerebrum (the large brain), mainly consisting of the cortex; the brainstem; and the cerebellum (the little brain). The cerebrum controls the higher mental functions, like language and abstract reasoning. The brainstem includes structures for vision and audition. The cerebellum is critically involved in motor control and movements.

The Cortex

Cortex, the convoluted outer layers of the brain, is the major part of the cerebrum. The cortex consists of about 10^{10} to 10^{12} neurons arranged in six different layers from the outer to the inner surface. The cortex is in itself only about 2–3 mm thick, but its total area far exceeds the rounded area of the skull because of the fissures and gyri, or ridges, in the cortical surface.

A fissure is a folding that cuts through the whole cortex, and the cortical cells in a fissure make direct connections to underlying structures. Examples of large fissures are the lateral fissure, also called the Sylvian fissure, which divides the frontal and temporal lobes, and the longitudinal fissure, which divides the two cortical hemispheres. A sulcus is also a folding, but one that does not make direct connection with underlying tissues of the brain. An example is the central sulcus, which divides the frontal and parietal lobes.

A gyrus is a ridge between sulci, and gyri are usually labeled according to their position in the inferior-superior axis of the brain. For example, the superior temporal gyrus is the superior gyrus of the three visible gyri in the temporal lobe.

Cerebral Hemispheres

The two hemispheres of the cortex, referred to as the right and left hemispheres, are the major sites for higher cognitive functions. The functional (and structural) differences between the two hemispheres of the brain are discussed in Chapters 6 and 12.

Functional differences are usually denoted by the term *laterality*, or *hemispheric asymmetry*, a reference to the fact that the two lateral half-spheres of the brain subserve different functions with respect to behavior. In simplified terms, the left hemisphere subserves functions related to language and the processing of verbal materials, as well as some aspects of positive emotions, and the right hemisphere subserves functions related to visuo-spatial functioning and to aspects of negative emotionality. An important point to mention when discussing laterality, often neglected in the literature, is that *subcortical structures* are also duplicated in a left and right version. As a rule, there are two identical versions of almost every structure and organ in the brain and the nervous system, one to the left and one to the right. Thus, there are two cortices, two thalami, two vagus nerves, and so on. One notable exception is the pineal gland, of which there is only one, oriented along the midline in the lower portion of the brain. The seventeenth-century French philosopher Descartes believed that the pineal gland was the seat of the "mind," perhaps because of this unique anatomical characteristic.

The two cerebral hemispheres are connected through the corpus callosum, a horseshoe-shaped accumulation of millions of nerve fibers that run across the left and right hemisphere. In addition to the corpus callosum, the anterior and posterior commissures connect the two hemispheres. The anterior and posterior commissures are often used as reference points in various brain mapping techniques and in some instances of stereotaxic surgery, since they are easily located anterior and posterior to the third ventricle.

Research on Hemispheric Asymmetry

In the 1960s and 1970s Sperry and his colleagues (see Sperry, 1974) conducted famous experiments on functional laterality. They studied patients with intractable epileptic foci in either the left or right hemisphere after the callosal fibers in these patients had been surgically severed. This procedure, called a *commissurotomy*, disconnects the hemispheres from each other (Bogen, 1985). The often dramatic differences in behavior shown by these patients after a stimulus was presented to either the left or the right hemisphere laid down much of the foundation for modern research on hemispheric asymmetry (see, e.g., Hellige, 1993).

In one case (Sperry, 1974), a patient was shown a word of a common object in either the left or right visual half-field. When shown a word like *pencil* in the left half-field and asked to name what he saw, the patient answered that he had not seen anything. When asked to use his left hand to find the object whose name was spelled out on the screen among a collection of objects placed within his reach, he correctly identified the pencil, even though he could not see the objects in front of him. The explanation for this surprising result is that the right hemisphere, which processed the information detected in the visual field, is mute, and since the patient's nerve fibers between the two hemispheres had been surgically cut, there was no way for the word-

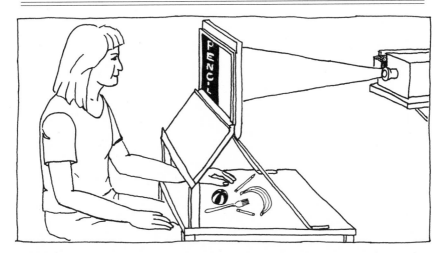

Figure 4.1. Experimental setup of an investigation of hemispheric specialization by Nobel laureate Roger Sperry and colleagues. The subject is required to pick up the object from the table that corresponds with the word shown in either the left or right visual half-field. The subject is also required to alternate use of the left and right hand.

information to reach the left, talking hemisphere. The left hemisphere literally had not seen anything, and the patient answered accordingly when asked what had been shown on the screen. The right hemisphere controls left hand movements, however, so it could direct the left hand to pick up the pencil. (See Figure 4.1.)

The Somatomotor Cortex and the Somatosensory Cortex

A major functional division of cortical areas is that between the motor and sensory cortices. It is important to remember, though, that brain areas other than cortex, like the basal ganglia and cerebellum, are also involved in motor control. The somatomotor cortex extends as a strip across the cortex between the two lateral fissures just in front of the central sulcus. If the different body structures that are controlled were drawn in position on this strip of cortex, the picture would form a functional "homunculus," meaning "little man" (see Figure 4.2).

A guiding principle for functional localization of the motor cortex is that the more finely graded motor control the cortex has over a part of the body, the larger is the area occupied by that part on the motor

Somatosensory   Motor Cortex
Cortex

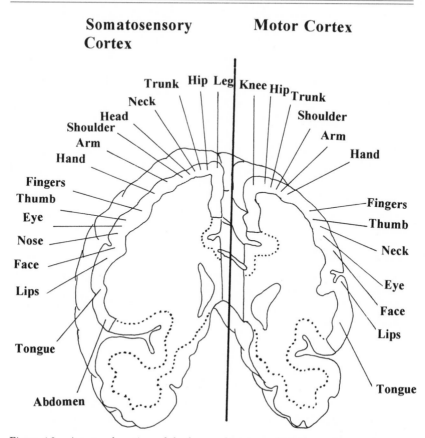

Figure 4.2. A coronal section of the human brain on which the sensory and motor cortices are laid out on the post- and precentral strip, respectively. Note that the somatosensory sectioning is located behind the motor sectioning as shown here.

cortex. For example, the thumb and the lips occupy significantly larger areas on the cortex than the trunk and the legs.

The "little man" is laid out on the motor cortex with the foot and leg tucked into the longitudinal fissure and the arm and hand following on the curvature of the cortex. The cortical areas controlling the face and mouth lie just above the lateral fissure.

The somatosensory cortex is arranged in a way similar to the motor cortex: the different body parts innervated by the sensory peripheral nerve fibers are spread out on the sensory cortical strip in a manner corresponding to the functional organization of the motor cortex. The somatosensory cortex extends posteriorly from the central sulcus a few centimeters toward the back of the head. Also like the motor cortex, the somatosensory cortex has a "somatotopic" representation (see Figure 4.2).

Contralateral Crossing

An important organizational principle in the nervous system, including the brain, is the principle of contralateral crossings, or decussations. Nerves from the left side of the body connect to the right side of the brain and nervous system, and nerves from the right side of the body connect to the left side of the brain and nervous system. For example, the left hand and fingers are controlled from the motor cortex on the right side of the brain.

The Lobes of the Cortex

The major anatomical and functional structures of the cortex are the four lobes occupying the cortical surface of the brain. These are the frontal, temporal, parietal, and occipital lobes (see Figure 4.3). Note that there are two sections of each lobe, one on each side of the longitudinal fissure.

The Frontal Lobe

The frontal lobe occupies the anterior part of the cortex, from the Sylvian fissure on the lateral side to the central sulcus in the middle of the brain. The functions of the frontal lobes are related to the organization and control of complex cognitive functions, like certain aspects of attention and language (Milner, 1964), as well as the programming and execution of motor patterns. A typical disorder after frontal-lobe damage is the inability to stop and inhibit ongoing behavior and to shift attention to other behavior (Milner, 1982). This type of disorder, called perseveration or perseverative behavior, is sometimes seen in neurological degenerative diseases, like Parkinson's and Alzheimer's disease, and in the major psychoses, like schizophrenia. Another consequence of damage (lesion) to frontal areas is the loss of expressive language. This is called motor aphasia or, if damage has been done to what is known as Broca's area, Broca's aphasia.

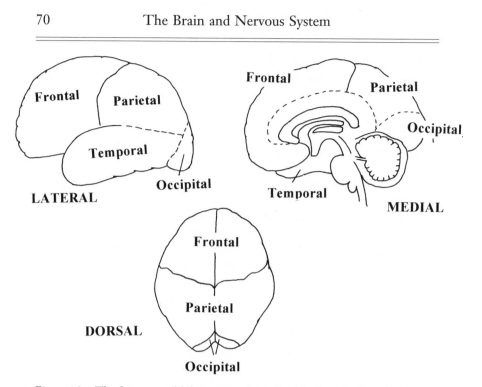

Figure 4.3. The four cortical lobes as seen from the side (lateral), the midline (medial), and behind and above the head (dorsal).

The attentional system. Using positron emission tomography (PET) imaging of changes in blood flow in different locations in the brain, Posner and Petersen (1990) identified anatomical areas in the lobes that are differentially engaged in the selection of information for focal processing. Blood-flow studies utilize a radioactive tracer that is either injected into the bloodstream or inhaled and that follows the blood to the brain. Detectors that are sensitive to the presence of the tracer in the blood that flows to the brain are placed around the scalp. When an area of the brain is actively engaged in neuronal activity, as it is when processing information, more blood is supplied to that area and consequently more of the radioactive isotope is detected at that location. Brain imaging techniques are described in more details in Chapter 13.

Using this technique, Posner and his colleagues have found a vigilance attention system involving the right frontal lobe. This system is typically engaged when a subject is instructed to "get ready" to make a rapid response after a target stimulus appears. The vigilance system, or network, is thus engaged when individuals have to maintain alertness over longer periods of time, as might be required, for example, of someone monitoring a radar screen. The frontal lobes also house an executive attention network, which comes into play when a stimulus is brought into conscious awareness (Posner and Raichle, 1994).

The Temporal Lobe

The temporal lobe is the portion of the brain inferior to the lateral fissure. It extends posteriorly along an imaginary line from the end of the lateral (Sylvian) fissure to the parieto-occipital sulcus (see Figure 4.3).

A major function of the temporal lobe is audition, and the auditory cortex is localized in the superior temporal gyrus just at the base of the lateral fissure. Other functions of the temporal lobe are the understanding of spoken language and storage of visual memories. Patients with damage to an area partially overlapping the auditory cortex (Heschl's gyrus and Wernicke's area) lose the ability to understand language. These patients retain the ability to produce spoken utterances intact, but since the brain cannot understand what it produces, the sounds these patients produce are utterly incomprehensible. Interestingly, since they retain prosodic language—that is, they speak words with normal stress and intonation—these patients can sometimes appear to be speaking normally, until one listens to what they actually say. Individuals with damage to Wernicke's area who have lost the ability to understand language often suffer from sensory aphasia, also called Wernicke's aphasia.

Medial in the temporal lobe and longitudinal to it is a structure called the hippocampus, which is related to memory and particularly to the consolidation of memory (Squire and Slater, 1978). Much research has been devoted over the last few decades to reveal the cognitive functions, such as learning and memory, associated with the hippocampus and related structures.

The Parietal Lobe

The parietal lobe occupies the major portions of the posterior part of the cortex (see Figure 4.3). It is situated between the central and parieto-occipital sulci in the anterior-posterior axis, above the lateral fissure and the imaginary posterior extension to the parieto-occipital sulcus.

The parietal lobes, with the somatosensory cortex posterior to the central sulcus, are first of all involved in bodily sensations of touch and kinesthetics. They also help to integrate sensory input across modalities, as when we both see and hear a car and perceive it as a unitary phenomenon, "a car." Disorders of parietal areas result in the inability to make tactile discriminations, called tactile agnosia. Other dysfunctions are the inability to integrate sensory input into purposeful behavior (apraxia). Posner (1988) has also shown that the posterior parietal lobe is involved in visual attention, particularly when a person is disengaging attention from one spatial location and redirecting it to another location.

Hemineglect

A fascinating phenomenon that sometimes occurs in individuals who have suffered parietal lesions, mainly lesions to the right parietal lobe, is the phenomenon of hemineglect or inattention (Heilman and Watson, 1977). The patient neglects, or ignores, the left side of his or her body and the left side of the visual field. Literally, *hemineglect* means ignoring half of something. According to the principle of contralateral crossing described above, having a right-sided parietal lesion will consequently show up as an inattention to the left side of the body and the left side of the visual space. For example, a patient with hemineglect syndrome may, when asked to dress, put only the right arm in the sleeve of a coat and leave the left sleeve hanging. When asked if there is something missing from the outfit, the patient becomes confused, sometimes frustrated. Other patients may eat only from the right side of the plate and ask for more food despite having food on the left half of the plate (see Bisiach and Vallar, 1988, for further examples). The British neurologist Oliver Sachs has excellently described the typical hemineglect syndrome in his collection of essays, *The Man Who Mistook His Wife for a Hat*.

Although the hemineglect phenomenon is traditionally considered a visual phenomenon, Hugdahl, Wester, and Asbjørnsen (1990) identified the typical extinction phenomenon to different auditory stimuli, presented simultaneously, one in each ear, as a case of auditory neglect. The patient, who had a lesion in the right pulvinar area of the thalamus in addition to a cortical lesion, failed to report hearing sound from the left ear when sounds were presented to both ears at once. However, he was able to hear from the left ear when there was no simultaneous competing input from the right ear.

This may be an indication that hemineglect is not a primary perceptual disorder but rather an inability to handle several things at the same time—that is, to attend to both visual or auditory fields at the same time, or to make rapid shifts of attention between the left and right sides. Posner and Driver (1992) have also suggested that neglect may be a dysfunction specific to the posterior, orienting, attention system, involving areas in the posterior parietal lobe. Other explanations of hemineglect propose a special dysfunction of arousal or activation in the reticular formation, which would cause a unilateral lowering of arousal to the right side of space (Heilman and Watson, 1977).

The Occipital Lobe

The occipital lobe contains the major visual areas of the brain. Visual input to the eye is projected over the visual trajectories to the occipital cortex. The occipital cortex is therefore closely associated with visual function, but recent research on monkeys (Zeki, 1978) indicates that the visual areas in the occipital cortex have a more complex structure and function than that originally suggested. The visual cortex is, for example, divided into at least four different areas (designated V1 to V4; see p. 60), each of which has different functional characteristics but is integrated in a complex network for the analysis of visual input. The V1 area is the primary visual cortex, and it is also designated as area 17 (in Broddman's terminology) or striate cortex.

The Basal Ganglia

The basal ganglia are a set of neuronal nuclei located on both sides of the third ventricle; interior to these ganglia, toward the medial portion of the brain, is the thalamus. The basal ganglia (putamen, caudate nucleus, claustrum, striatum, and globus pallidus) help to control body movements by integrating sensory and motor information from other areas of the brain. Dysfunction of dopamine activity in the substantia nigra, a locus in the mesencephalon, causes Parkinson's disease, which is characterized by tremor and rigidity in the limbs of the body.

The Thalamus and Hypothalamus

The thalamus (Figure 4.4) is divided into several nuclei and functional parts. In general, it can be considered a major relay station for information from the sensory organs. In addition, it has an important integrative function. Thus, the thalamus receives input from the somatosensory and somatomotor systems of the brain and the spinal cord. Both visual and auditory as well as somatosensory signals are gated through the thalamus: the auditory signal passes through the medial geniculate body, the visual signal passes through the lateral geniculate body, and the somatosensory signal passes through the ventral-posterior lateral nuclei, with the ventro-lateral nucleus being mainly a motor nucleus.

The hypothalamus plays a major role in the homeostatic control of bodily functions, like temperature, sex, thirst, and hunger. By controlling secretion of hormones from the pituitary, it also acts as a link between the CNS and the endocrine system. One psychologically im-

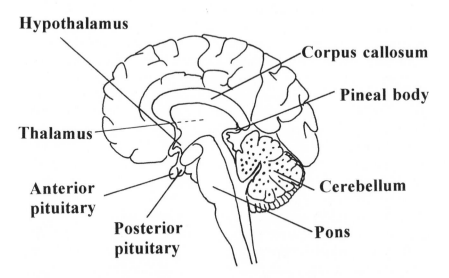

Figure 4.4. Midline sectioning of the brain, including the brainstem and medulla. Note that the thalamus is situated on both sides of the third ventricle (not shown here), along the midline of the brain.

portant function of the hypothalamus is its control of hormone secretion in response to stress. Hypothalamic control of stress reactions involves regulating hormone secretion from the pituitary gland through a fine network of blood vessels, which results in the release of the stress hormone cortisol from the adrenal cortex.

It is important to stress that although the hypothalamus regulates the release of hormones from the adrenal cortex, it is itself regulated, through feedback, by the amount of hormones circulating in the blood. A high level of cortisol in the blood stream initiates compensatory processes that act on the hypothalamus to decrease production of releasing factors that act on the pituitary. This two-way interaction to maintain internal stability is called *negative feedback* (see also p. 78).

Limbic Structures

The limbic system (from *limbus*, Latin for "border") consists of several structures, including the amygdala, the hippocampus, and the cingulate gyrus, that are sometimes included in other functional structures, like the basal ganglia or cortex. Today it is more common to refer to "limbic structures" rather than "the limbic system," since it has become evident that these structures may not make up a distinct "system" but may instead relate to many other structures and functions in the brain. The limbic structures are located between the temporal lobe and basal ganglia and have abundant connections to the hypothalamus. Traditionally, the role of the limbic structures is the control of emotion and emotional behavior, but recent research indicates that the control of emotional behavior is an intricate interplay between cortical and subcortical structures. For example, Davidson (1984) has shown that EEGs from the left and right frontal lobes can distinguish individuals as either "positive" or "negative" emotional responders.

A clinical syndrome following lesioning of temporal lobe areas and the limbic pathways is the Klüver-Bucy syndrome. A Klüver-Bucy animal cannot connect emotional tonus with sensory information. As an example, rhesus monkeys with temporal lobe lesions will eat raw meat, though normal rhesus monkeys are herbivores, and males may try to copulate with other males: what the damaged monkeys see and hear does not give rise to an appropriate emotional response. In humans, the Klüver-Bucy syndrome may be expressed as a dulling of the person's emotional life, agnosia, and an inability to separate appropriate from inappropriate behavior.

Electrical stimulation of various regions of the amygdala and the other limbic structures will elicit fear and attack behavior. The emotional function of limbic structures, and particularly of the amygdala, has recently been investigated by LeDoux, Iwata, Chiccetti, and Reis (1988), who demonstrated that classical conditioning of fear responses in the rat are mediated through amygdaloid pathways.

Further down the brain, in the mesencephalon, are the tectum (the "ceiling") and tegmentum (the "floor") of the cerebral aqueduct. The tectum consists of four "hills" arranged in two pairs, the superior and the inferior colliculus. The superior colliculus receives input from the optic nerve. The inferior colliculus connects the auditory signal to the auditory cortex in the temporal lobe.

Blood Supply of the Brain

The brain needs a continuous supply of blood, because the only fuel it can utilize is blood glucose. Blood glucose is converted to energy for the nerve cell through oxygenation, a process in which oxygen, also in the blood stream, chemically interact with glucose. This is why the brain cannot survive without an oxygen supply for periods longer than approximately 2–3 minutes before the neurons are irreversibly damaged.

Major Arteries

A network of blood vessels surrounds the cortex and the deeper fissures and sulci of the brain. The brain is supplied with blood from the internal carotid artery and the vertebral artery, both of which branch off from the ascending arc of the aortic artery from the heart. The vertebral artery enters the base of the skull and divides into several branches, including the basilar artery, which itself branches into the posterior cerebral artery, which supplies the occipital lobe and parts of the parietal lobe.

The internal carotid artery branches off into the middle and anterior cerebral arteries, supplying the parietal, temporal, and frontal lobes

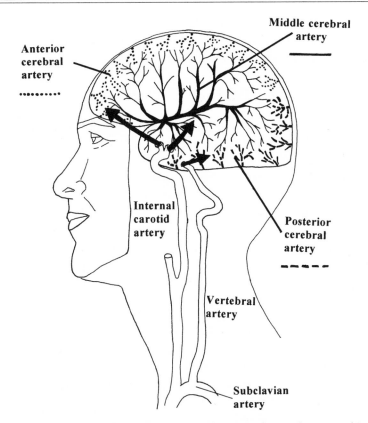

Figure 4.5. The blood supply to the brain, via the internal carotid artery and its branches, the anterior and middle cerebral arteries. The posterior cerebral artery is supplied with blood from the vertebral artery (via the basilar artery).

with blood. Most of the tissue on the lateral side of the brain is supplied with blood from the middle cerebral artery (see Figure 4.5).

Stress-Response Systems

One of the important functions of the human nervous system is to respond to situations of stress. Stress affects both bodily functions and functions in the brain. A detailed discussion of the complex definitional problems regarding stress and stress responses is beyond the scope of this book. (The interested reader may consult Hamilton and Warburton, 1979.) To simplify matters, I will present an overview of three basic "stress systems" that are potentially influenced by psychological factors: the hypothalamic-pituitary-adrenal system, the sympathetic-adrenal-medulla system, and the immune system.

The Hypothalamic-Pituitary-Adrenal System

In stressful situations, when energy mobilization is increased, the hypothalamus secretes corticotropin releasing factor (CRF). CRF acts on the anterior pituitary through the small blood vessels (also called the *vascular bed*) connecting the hypothalamus with the anterior pituitary.

The anterior pituitary, in turn, releases adrenocorticotropic hormone (ACTH) into the blood stream, which causes the adrenal cortex (located near the kidneys) to secrete several hormones, among them cortisol, a major stress hormone, into the blood stream. Cortisol influences the pituitary and the brain via a negative feedback loop, causing the pituitary either to decrease or to increase further production of ACTH depending on the cortisol level (see also p. 75).

Apart from having a generally stimulating effect in the body, including the cardiovascular system, cortisol inhibits the production of antibodies by the immune system and therefore has an anti-inflammatory effect. Interestingly, the level of cortisol in the blood stream is usually higher during sleep than during waking, which may help explain why sleep is considered to have a healing function.

The Sympathetic-Adrenal-Medulla System

Another response to stress is an increase in sympathetic activity from the autonomic nervous system, which signals the adrenal medulla to secrete epinephrine into the blood stream. This pathway, the sympathetic-adrenal-medulla system, and the hypothalamic-pituitary-adrenal cortex system described above are the two major stress-response systems (Frankenhauser, 1983). The interplay between the various stress systems may serve to increase the organism's chances for survival.

The hypothalamic-pituitary-adrenal cortex system is mobilized in situations of distress, whereas the sympathetic-adrenal-medulla system is mobilized in situations requiring effort (Frankenhauser, 1983). Henry and Stephens (1977) named the two systems the "withdrawal" system and the "fight or flight" system, respectively. In sum, whereas the hypothalamus-pituitary-adrenal cortex system is associated with low spirits and depression, as well as the effects of chronic stress, the sympathetic-adrenal-medulla system is associated with fight or flight reactions to fear or anger.

Interactions between Stress Responses

Although the two stress systems may have different physiological actions in the body, they overlap in several important respects. Recent research by Sudhir, Jennings, and Esler (1989) have shown that cortisol excreted from the adrenal cortex may enhance sympathetic nervous system activity in response to an external or internal stressor. Furthermore, Gold, Goodwin, and Chrousos (1988) have proposed that the two systems may share a common neuronal source of control, namely the paraventricular nuclei of the hypothalamus. The paraventricular nuclei may be the site where neuroendocrine responses to stress are integrated. Thus, modern research on the psychophysiology of stress emphasizes the integration and regulation of endocrine and autonomic activity by higher brain centers. The exact location and function of such brain centers, however, remain to a large extent unknown (see Checcetto and Saper, 1990, for a review of central control of autonomic function). Moreover, Svensson (1987) has suggested that the locus ceruleus, a major nucleus in the brainstem, may act as a "master director" in the central control of autonomic reactivity to stress.

The Pituitary Gland

The two parts to the pituitary, the anterior and the posterior, have different functions. The *anterior* pituitary (also called the *adenopituitary*) secretes a large range of hormones into the blood stream. In addition to the ACTH mentioned above, these include thyroid-stimulating hormone (TSH), growth hormone (GH), luteinizing hormone (LH), prolactin, and follicle-stimulating hormone (FSH). TSH is one of the hormones that help to regulate the body's basal metabolism. LH and FSH are both critical for the normal regulation of the female menstrual cycle. Prolactin stimulates lactation in the female after the birth of a baby, and GH promotes body growth. Lack of GH is related to some forms of dwarfism. It was long believed that GH was no longer secreted when an organism reached adulthood. This is not true (Guyton, 1992), although the rate of GH secretion goes down with increasing age.

Furthermore, GH secretion is increased during sleep. It has also been suggested that GH may be involved in the aging process itself: a steady, prolonged GH secretion into old age may counteract certain decaying effects of aging on the body.

From the *posterior* pituitary, the hormones vasopressin and oxytocin are secreted. Both hormones have their cellular origin in the hypothalamus. Vasopressin facilitates reabsorption of water by the kidneys, and oxytocin stimulates milk ejection during lactation. Since hormonal secretion from the posterior pituitary is neurally controlled, the posterior pituitary is also called the neuropituitary.

The Immune System and Stress

The interaction between behavior, endocrine function, and the immune system is collectively called *psychoneuroimmunology*. The immune system protects the body from foreign, "non-self" materials, or *antigens*, notably bacteria, viruses, parasites, and fungi. It also protects against "non-selfs" like transplanted organs or attacking cells like cancer cells.

The immune system consists of cells that have specialized "defense tasks" in the body. These cells originate in the bone marrow and then mature in various organs, like the thymus gland and the lymphoid system. From there, immune-system cells are released into the blood when action is needed. The most important cells in the immune system are the leukocytes, or white blood cells. Of the leukocytes, only the phagocytes and lymphocytes will be mentioned here. Phagocytes are specialized cells that engulf and literally "eat" foreign bacteria or viruses that enter the body. Lymphocytes are of two types: B cells and T cells. B cells make up the humoral part of the immune system, T cells the cell-mediated part. A *humoral* immune response is so named because the B cells secrete antibodies (proteins that attack antigens) into the blood. A cell-mediated immune response is one in which the immune cells make direct contact with the penetrated cell. B cells mature in the bone marrow, and T cells mature in the thymus gland.

O'Leary (1990) provides a wide review of research on stress and immune function.

Although the health effects of chronic stress have been difficult to prove, specific physiological consequences of depression, loneliness, and anxiety are frequently reported in the literature. Moreover, some effects of psychological factors on various disorders, such as cancer, genital herpes, and HIV infection, have been demonstrated over the last few years (see O'Leary, 1990).

Ader and his collaborators (e.g., Ader and Cohen, 1993) have proposed a classical conditioning model to account for psychological effects on immune function. By using an animal model, Ader has been able to show how immune responses can be modified by classical conditioning. His experiments involved a taste-aversion design in which saccharin-flavored water is presented to the mouse as the conditioned stimulus (CS). Simultaneously, the animal is injected with cyclophosphamide, which suppresses immune function, as the unconditioned stimulus (UCS). When the animals were re-exposed to the CS after pairings of the CS with UCS, the CS alone was sufficient to suppress their immune functioning. A description of the detailed setup with control groups in Ader's elegant studies is beyond the scope of this book, however. The interested reader should consult Ader and Cohen (1993).

A human parallel to Ader's animal model is the anticipatory nausea and vomiting seen in cancer patients undergoing chemotherapy, which is, in effect, cell-poisoning treatment. The immunosuppressive effect of the cell poison is often accompanied by rather severe nausea and vomiting that may last for hours and hours. Some patients, however, experience similar nausea and vomiting in situations associated with the treatment setting but without the treatment being given. Reports from the patients explain that "I felt nauseous when I entered the ward and encountered that typical hospital smell," or "A feeling of sickness comes over me whenever I see a nurse in uniform."

Cancer patients usually come to the hospital every fourteen days or so for treatment. For several hours the cell poison is administered intravenously, "slowly dripping" into the body. The purpose of the poison is to kill the cancer cells, but what the patient most notices are the dramatic side effects. It is not unusual for a patient to develop anticipatory nausea and vomiting after a few treatments.

Several authors (Andrykowski and Redd, 1987; Carey and Burish,

1988) have suggested that the administration of the cell poison may act as an unconditioned stimulus (UCS) that becomes paired by conditioning with the sights, smells, and sounds of the hospital environment. These environmental features may thus act as conditioned stimuli (CS) and elicit a conditioned response (CR) in anticipation of the UCS, and this CR mimics the unconditioned (UCR) response of nausea and vomiting. Interestingly, Bovbjerg, Redd, Maier, et al. (1990) found that patients with pretreatment nausea responses also showed anticipatory immunosuppressive changes. These data then confirm the animal model (Ader and Cohen, 1993) that the effects of immunosuppressive drugs can become conditioned to innocuous cues in the environment, which may later function as immunosuppressants themselves.

Relating the findings of conditioning of anticipatory side effects in

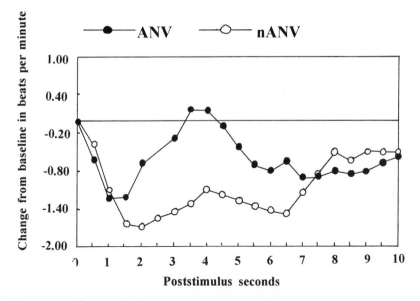

Figure 4.6.   Change in heart rate from a prestimulus baseline during 10 seconds after the presentation of a tone stimulus in cancer patients before treatment. (Recordings were made just after the patients had been diagnosed but before any chemotherapy treatment had begun.) Note the tendency toward heart-rate acceleration from the second poststimulus second in those patients that later developed anticipatory nausea and vomiting (ANV). (Data from Kvale et al., 1991, reprinted with permission from the American Psychological Association and the authors.)

cancer treatment to psychophysiology, Kvale, Hugdahl, Asbjørnsen, et al. (1991) found that psychophysiological reactivity was a "marker" of later conditioned nausea and vomiting. Studying the phasic heart-rate changes that occur in response to brief presentations of a tone through a typical habituation paradigm, Kvale et al. (1991) showed that those patients who did not habituate to the tones before any treatment was given were the ones who later (after successive treatments) developed anticipatory nausea and vomiting. (See Figure 4.6.)

This is an important study because it demonstrates that individual variability in autonomic reactivity is related to conditionability, and that more reactive patients are more prone to develop serious side effects after treatment. If the data by Kvale et al. (1991) are replicable, patients receiving chemotherapy should be screened for autonomic reactivity before being given any treatment, and those found to be at risk for developing a conditioned nausea response should, for example, be given relaxation training. A second lesson from these experimental findings is that hospital wards where chemotherapy is administered should be "exotic" in design, with unusual decor and even smells. If the "exotic" sights and smells (the CSs) are paired with the injection of the cell poison (the UCS), the patient will be less likely to encounter a similar CS in other environments and less likely, therefore, to experience the CR of nausea.

Summary

In this chapter the major structures of the brain have been introduced and the cortex and cortical functions described in more detail. The lobes of the cortex were discussed with respect to their specialized functions, including behavioral syndromes after brain lesion to particular cortical areas. The basal ganglia and limbic structures and their localization and function were outlined, and the major arteries supplying the brain with blood were named and described. The hormonal regulation of stress responses was reviewed, as was the role of psychological factors in the functioning of the immune system, particularly in regard to the classical conditioning of side effects in cancer patients.

5

The Autonomic Nervous System

The autonomic nervous system (ANS) comprises three separate systems, the sympathetic, parasympathetic, and the enteric system. The enteric nervous system is traditionally not included as a major division of the ANS, but it is generally accepted today that it is a separate system, whose main function is to innervate the gut region of the body.

Knowledge about the basic structure and function of the autonomic nervous system is important for an understanding of psychophysiology for several reasons. First, ANS effector organs, like the heart and the sweat glands, are at the focus of psychophysiology. Second, ANS activity mediates stress responses and emotional arousal, two concepts at the core of a psychophysiological approach to the mind-body interface, as well as many psychosomatic diseases.

In traditional terms, the autonomic nervous system (ANS) is considered to be an *efferent* system that controls the functioning of the heart, the gastrointestinal system, and glandular secretion. In a more strict sense, however, the ANS functions not only as a motor system but also as a sensory system: almost all visceral nerves also have *afferent* fibers providing feedback to the brain. The afferent function of the ANS resides in the sensory neurons in the dorsal root ganglion or in cranial nerve ganglia (see Loewy, 1990, for an updated overview of the ANS). The sensory neurons and nerve fibers act to feed back information to the autonomic efferent control centers in the central nervous system, which modulate the autonomic efferent outflow.

Similarly, sensory feedback from receptors in the viscera also affects the release of certain hormones. For example, vasopressin, which regulates the amount of water retention in the body, is partly under the influence of feedback from autonomic receptors.

The ANS maintains internal homeostasis by regulating the function of visceral organs within their normal ranges. For example, the beating of the heart is regulated by both the sympathetic and the parasympathetic branches of the ANS, but the two branches act in opposite directions. When the heart is beating too fast, the vagus nerve of the parasympathetic branch increases the frequency of signals sent directly to the heart muscle, which slows the beating rate. Increased sympathetic activity will increase both the heart rate and the intensity with which the heart contracts on each beat. Thus, the two major branches of the ANS act as two "gatekeepers"—one responding to decreased demands for action, the other responding to increased demands. By acting together, they uphold homeostasis in the visceral organs.

The Sympathetic System

The outflow of the sympathetic branch of the ANS has its origin in preganglionic neurons in the sympathetic ganglionic chain, which lies on both sides of the spinal cord (see Figure 5.1). This is true for most fibers leaving the spinal cord. There are, however, a few exceptions for which the sympathetic nerves travel through the sympathetic chain without synapsing—for example, the splanchnic nerves, which project to the preaortic sympathetic ganglia.

The major portion of the sympathetic outflow via the sympathetic ganglionic chain leaves the spinal cord from the T1 thoracic level to the L3 lumbar level, as is illustrated in Figure 5.1. In other words, the sympathetic fibers leave the spinal cord from the level of the shoulders down to just above the back. As mentioned above, the sympathetic system prepares the organism to take action in states of emergency, such as stress or an aggressive attack.

Pre- and Postganglionic Transmitters

The preganglionic neurotransmitter in the sympathetic system is acetylcholine (ACh), while the postganglionic neurotransmitter is norepinephrine (NE). There is, however, an important exception to this rule.

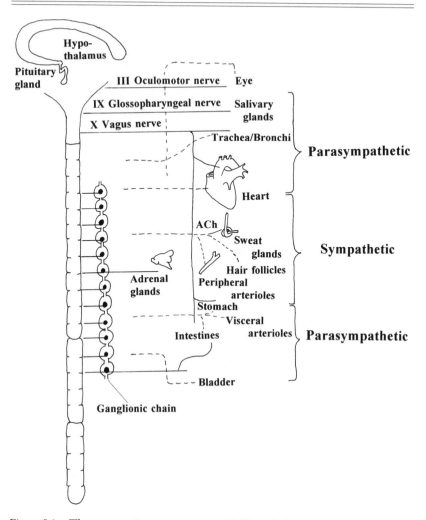

Figure 5.1. The autonomic nervous system (ANS), including the parasympathetic and sympathetic branches.

The eccrine sweat glands (see Chapter 8) in the skin are uniquely innervated only by sympathetic nerve fibers, but the postganglionic transmitter in these fibers is ACh. However, these neuronal connections are preganglionic. Recent neurophysiological research has shown that the sympathetic preganglionic neurons also utilize various neuropeptides, some of them localized in the dorsal root ganglion, as transmitters.

The Right Hemisphere and the Sympathetic System

Control of sympathetic effects on the heart and the cardiovascular system by the right hemisphere of the brain was recently reported by Hachinsky et al. (1992) in a conceptually important study. In this experiment, either the left or the right middle cerebral artery in rats was occluded, and heart rate, blood pressure, and plasma epinephrine and norepinephrine, among other variables, were monitored. The effects on the sympathetic system were clearly greater after lesions to the right hemisphere than after left-hemisphere lesions. An untested question from these findings is that patients who have suffered a right-sided cerebral stroke may be more susceptible to deadly consequences than patients with left-sided stroke. This possibility might be investigated by comparing the hospital records of patients with left- versus right-sided ischemic stroke, to determine if there are any differences between the two groups in severity of symptoms or in the progress of rehabilitation.

The Parasympathetic System

The efferent parasympathetic system is structurally similar to the efferent sympathetic system: it is organized as chains of pre- and postganglionic neurons. Some of the primary target organs with parasympathetic innervations of particular interest to psychophysiologists are illustrated in Figure 5.1.

The origin of the preganglionic parasympathetic nerves is either the brainstem or the spinal cord. Unlike the nerves of the sympathetic system, which leave the spinal cord at the thoracic and lumbar regions, the parasympathetic neurons leave the brain via the oculomotor (III), glossopharyngeal (IX), and vagal (X) cranial nerves at the base of the skull, or they exit at the bottom of the spinal cord from the last sacral roots.

The sympathetic system is sometimes referred to as a diffuse, "mass-discharge" system because it mobilizes all available energy in an emergency (Guyton, 1992); the parasympathetic system, in contrast, is a "fine-tuned" system that has more discrete effects on the different organs it innervates.

Another difference between the sympathetic and the parasympathetic system is that the postganglionic fibers in the two branches generally utilize different neurotransmitters. As noted above, sympathetic neurons mainly secrete norepinephrine in the postganglionic synapse, with the important exceptions of the cells innervating the eccrine sweat glands. In the parasympathetic system, acetylcholine is the post-ganglionic neurotransmitter. For this reason the parasympathetic sys-tem is sometimes called the *cholinergic* system. Epinephrine and norepinephrine were formerly identified as a single substance, adrena-line, whose name is still reflected in the word *adrenergic*, used to de-scribe the sympathetic system.

The Vagus Nerve

For the psychophysiologist, the vagus nerve is probably the most inter-esting of the parasympathetic nerves. The longest of all the autonomic nerves, it extends from the brainstem down to the bladder and the intestines, and it branches off to the neck, the thorax, and the abdomen on its way. *Vagus* means "wandering," and the vagus nerve "wanders" through the body.

The parasympathetic neurons where the motor component of the vagus nerve originates are located in two nuclei, the dorsal vagal motor nucleus and the nucleus ambiguus, both located at the bottom of the fourth ventricle in the medulla. These nuclei receive input from higher brain centers involving the hypothalamus and the reticular formation. It still remains to be shown exactly how vagal outflow is controlled and regulated from brain centers above the hypothalamus, and espe-cially what role is played by the cortex. This is an important issue for psychophysiology since the vagus helps to regulate heart rate and blood pressure, two major indicators of psychophysiological activity (to be discussed in later Chapters).

In an interesting recent paper, Hausken, Svebak, Wilhelmsen, et al. (1993) found that vagal tone is lower in patients with functional dys-pepsia (FD) than in healthy controls. FD is characterized by chronic stomach pain resembling the pain reported by patients with known stomach ulcers. The cause of FD is still elusive, and several sugges-tions, including psychosomatic models, have been put forward over the years. This study suggest that individuals with FD have increased gastric motility (because activity in the vagus is too low to dampen the stomach movements), which could be the cause of the stomach pain. Moreover, when put under mental stress, the FD patients experienced larger increases in motility than the controls experienced, indicating an interaction between physiological and psychological variables in the elicitation of FD pain.

Laterality Differences in Vagal Function

Porges and Maiti (1992) have suggested that the dorsal motor nucleus regulates the visceral functions of the vagus while the nucleus ambiguus deals with processes associated with emotion and communication. They thus called the branch of the vagus originating from the dorsal motor nucleus "the vegetative vagus" and the branch originating from the nucleus ambiguus "the smart vagus." Their findings should be replicated before any firm conclusions can be drawn from this rather limited study, but considering the theoretical implications if the results are corroborated, their "speculations" about the dual functions of the branches of the vagus are worth pursuing in future research.

More is known about lateral differences in vagal innervation of the heart. The right side of the nucleus ambiguus contains the origin nuclei for the vagal input to the heart. Thus, the heart is primarily innervated by the *right* branch of the vagus nerve, although there is also innervation from the left vagus. This anatomical fact has considerable significance for psychophysiology, especially for the question of how the brain controls the heart (see Figure 5.2).

The vagus innervates the heart through the sinoatrial node (SA node), which regulates the beating of the heart. Heart rate is also regulated by its own spontaneous rhythmicity and the influence of the sympathetic and endocrine systems (see Chapter 9 for further details). It appears that the atria and the atrioventricular (AV) bundle, which is located in the upper part of the heart and which transmits the nerve impulses to the bottom of the heart, are supplied with both vagal and sympathetic fibers, whereas the ventricles of the heart are supplied only by sympathetic nerve fibers. The ventricles are also influenced by the hormone epinephrine in the blood.

An important finding for psychophysiology is that the *right* vagus nerve innervates the SA node and is responsible for changes in heart rate while the *left* vagus innervates the AV node and bundle (Brodal, 1981; Schmidt and Thews, 1980). Similarly, it has been found that it is also the *right* stellate nerve of the *sympathetic* interganglionic nerve that innervates the SA node of the heart (Randall, Armour, Geis, and

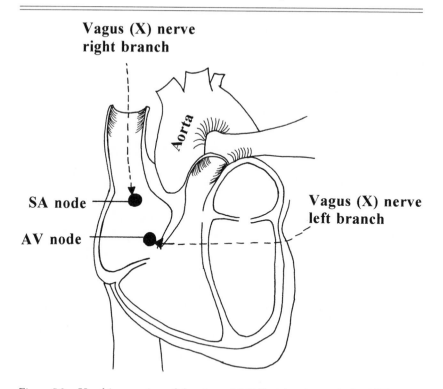

Figure 5.2. Vagal innervation of the sinoatrial (SA) and atrioventricular (AV) nodes of the heart from the left and right vagus branches, respectively.

Lippincott, 1972). Moreover, Rogers, Battit, McPeek, and Todd (1978) found a much greater effect on heart rate when the activity of the *right* stellate ganglion nerve was blocked than when the left nerve was blocked. In light of these findings, one may speculate on the extent to which psychological influences on heart rate are controlled and regulated from higher nerve centers located in the *right* hemisphere and other structures in the brain.

Laterality and the Autonomic Nervous System

An understanding of how the left and right hemispheres of the brain differ in terms of cognitive and emotional functioning may help us understand how the sympathetic and parasympathetic branches of the autonomic nervous system coordinate their control of bodily target organs. As discussed in the previous section on the vagus nerve, and as we will see in Chapter 10, there is evidence in the psychophysiological literature pointing to right-hemisphere control of heart rate. Examples of the relevant studies include Walker and Sandman (1979), which found that ERPs were larger over the right side of the brain when heart frequency changed, and Hugdahl, Franzon, Andersson and Walldebo (1983), which found that heart rate changed more in response to emotional and nonemotional visual stimuli presented to the right hemisphere than to the same stimuli presented to the left hemisphere.

A lateralized view of autonomic nervous system functioning is also taken by Shannahoff-Khalsa (1991), who used the shift in nasal-cycle dominance as a major parameter. Nasal breathing is dominant either through the left or right nostril in most individuals, and the dominant side shifts from one nostril to the other about every third or fourth hour. In another study, Werntz, Bickford, and Shannahoff-Khalsa (1987) showed that forced nostril breathing caused an increase in activation in the contralateral hemisphere, as evidenced through analysis of the EEG pattern. These authors have suggested that since the nasal cycle is regulated by the sympathetic and parasympathetic branches of the ANS, studying the lateralized shifts in nostril breathing may provide a new way of looking at laterality of the autonomic nervous system.

Lane and Jennings (1995) have recently made the interesting suggestion that not only is sudden death by cardiac failure related to emotional stress (which has been known for some time), but individual differences in hemispheric asymmetry may contribute to cardiac failure. These authors cite evidence that stimulation of the *left* sympathetic nerves to the heart increases the risk of heart fibrillation (which increases the risk for critical heart failure). They then linked this finding to other research showing that in most individuals emotional activation receives more regulation from the right hemisphere of the brain in most individuals (e.g., Silberman and Weingartner, 1986), and suggested that the minority of individuals who are left-lateralized for emotional activation may be at greater risk for cardiac failure and sudden death (see also Lane and Schwartz, 1987).

Research on Heart-Transplant Patients

Another opportunity for psychophysiologists studying the interaction between psychological processes and changes in heart function is presented by patients with a transplanted heart (Nussbaum and Goldstein, 1992; Kuhn, Davis, and Lippman, 1988). Because the sympathetic and vagus nerves cannot be attached to the new, transplanted heart, these patients lack ANS innervation of the heart. Thus, in a literal sense, heart-transplant patients have a *mind-body uncoupling*. The classic James-Lange (James, 1890) theory of emotion, which claims that an emotional feeling occurs secondarily to a bodily response, could perhaps be tested in such patients. As an example, James (1890) suggested that fear is experienced because we experience a quickening of the heart rate as a consequence of increased sympathetic tonus. James's actual claim was that the sensation of physiological changes is a necessary condition for an emotion to occur (e.g., James, 1884). This has sometimes been misinterpreted to mean that James suggested that emotions are nothing but the physiological responses (cf. Ellsworth, 1994, for an interesting discussion of James's position). In 1884 James wrote:

> My theory . . . is that the bodily changes follow directly the perception of the exciting fact, and that our feeling of the same changes as they occur is the emotion. Common-sense says that we lose our fortune, are sorry and weep; we meet a bear, are frightened and run; we are insulted by a rival, are angry and strike. The hypothesis here to be defended says that this order of sequence is incorrect, that the one mental state is not immediately included by the other, that the bodily manifestations must first be interposed between, and that the more rational statement is that we feel sorry because we cry, angry because we strike, afraid because we tremble.   (pp. 247–248)

From a psychological perspective, it should therefore be of interest to study what happens to the transplanted heart in a person facing different cognitive and emotional situations. Do these patients experience emotions in a different way after receiving a new heart? Do they show the typical deceleration and acceleration of heart rate in situations of sensory intake and rejection (Lacey, 1967)? Neuropsychological effects of heart transplantation were recently reported by Nussbaum and Goldstein (1992), who discovered consistent deficits in attention and concentration, verbal learning, and abstract reasoning. These findings suggest that there are, indeed, psychophysiological consequences of cardiac transplantation, which would argue for cognitive and other tests to be performed before heart surgery to minimize the risk of serious psychological side effects after transplantation. Hall-man et al. (1969), however, found no effect on heart rate during the cold pressor test or during the Valsalva test. From observations of the frequency of the P wave in the electrocardiogram, these authors suggested that the absence of heart-rate increase during emotional stimulation may be due to the fact that, although the SA node continues to respond reflexively, the denervation following transplantation prevents "psychological" responses from the heart.

Antagonistic Effects

The traditional view in psychophysiology and neurophysiology is that there is antagonism between the sympathetic and parasympathetic branches of the ANS, that the action of one system is counteracted by the action of the other system (e.g. Guyton, 1992). For example, while the action of the sympathetic system is to dilate the pupil of the eye, the action of the parasympathetic system is to constrict the pupil. This was the major reason Hess (1965) thought that studying changes in the eye would be a way of studying attitudes. When an individual has a positive attitude toward something, one result is the dilation of the pupils.

Similarly, the sympathetic system increases palm sweating in situations of nervousness or anxiety, and it increases the rate and force with which the heart beats in dangerous situations. The parasympathetic system, on the other hand, slows the heart and decreases the force of atrial contraction. In the skin, the sympathetic systems causes the peripheral blood vessels to constrict while the parasympathetic system causes them to dilate. The sympathetic system also has profound effects on the basal metabolism of the body—it can increase metabolism by up to 100 percent. The parasympathetic system has no substantial effect on general body metabolism.

Autonomic Space

Recent evidence seems to indicate that under certain psychological states and situations the two autonomic systems can be equally active, and sometimes also act independently of each other. This argument has been forwarded by Berntson and Cacioppo and their colleagues (e.g., Berntson, Cacioppo, Quigley, and Farbro, 1992; Berntson, Cacioppo, and Quigley, 1991). They have defined a concept of *autonomic space* in which the joint effect of the sympathetic and parasympathetic systems is translated into a functional analysis involving uncoupling, reciprocity, and coactivation.

The classical model of ANS *reciprocity* is that increased activity in one branch of the ANS is coupled with decreased activity in the other branch. As shown by Berntson et al. (1991), however, under some circumstances, for some individuals, the sympathetic and parasympathetic branches may be uncoupled from each other—that is, a change in one branch is associated with no change in the other branch.

The baroreceptor heart-rate reflex (see Chapter 9) is an example of *reciprocal control*. This reflex is controlled by vagal activity at high blood pressure, to counteract the effects of the sympathetic system and lower the heart rate, but the same reflex is controlled by sympathetic activity at low blood pressure, to increase heart frequency. It is elicited from the baroreceptors located in the internal carotid artery in the neck region. For example, when blood pressure increases, the baroreceptors will be stretched, and so they will increase their firing rate. The increased activity is interpreted in the brainstem, and corrective impulses are transmitted via the vagus nerve to slow down the beating of the heart, which lowers blood pressure.

Coactivation is demonstrated in fear responses, when the sympathetic effects on an organ are concurrent with parasympathetic effects on a functionally related organ. Table 5.1 presents some of the modes of autonomic control suggested by Berntson et al. (1991).

The concept of autonomic space may explain some of the complexities shown to exist in the control and regulation of sympathetic and parasympathetic function. An example is a study by Campbell, Kurtz, and Richardson (1992), who observed that the traditional distinction between *orienting* and *defensive* responses (see, e.g., Graham and Clifton, 1966; Chapter 7) may not hold up to recent empirical data. The traditional view holds that the orienting response (OR) is associated with cardiac deceleration and increased vagal (cholinergic) activity. The defense reaction (DR) is similarly associated with cardiac acceleration and sympathetic (adrenergic) activation of the heart. First, Campbell, Kurtz, and Richardson (1992) found that atropine, which is an anticholinergic drug, blocked the decrease in heart rate after the presentation of an auditory stimulus. This was the expected result: the typical deceleration in heart rate after presentation of a novel stimulus

Table 5.1. Modes of autonomic control.

Sympathetic response	Parasympathetic response		
	Increase	No change	Decrease
Increase	Coactivation	Uncoupled sympathetic activation	Reciprocal sympathetic activation
No change	Uncoupled parasympathetic activation	Baseline	Uncoupled parasympathetic withdrawal
Decrease	Reciprocal parasympathetic activation	Uncoupled sympathetic withdrawal	Coinhibition

Source: Adapted from Berntson et al. (1991), with permission from the American Psychological Association and the authors.

disappeared after administration of a drug that inhibited the action of the vagus nerve. However, they also found that atropine blocked the increase in heart rate that would normally follow the presentation of an aversive noise. Moreover, atenolol, a drug that slows the heart and inhibits the adrenergic functions on the heart, did not have the same effect as atropine in reducing the increase in heart rate after presentation of the aversive noise.

Cortical Control of the ANS

After a review of animal studies on the cortical control of autonomic responses, Checetto and Saper (1990) concluded that three cortical areas provide central control of autonomic function: the insular cortex, the infralimbic cortex, and the prelimbic cortex.

The insular cortex in the rat, located lateral to the basal ganglia, acts as a *visceral sensory cortex* receiving autonomic afferents. The infralimbic and prelimbic cortices are located anterior and slightly inferior to the anterior section of the corpus callosum. The infralimbic cortex, which is located close to the motor area in the rat frontal lobe, functions as the *visceral motor cortex*. The prelimbic cortex, finally, may be regarded as the *visceral premotor area*, as it receives input from limbic areas and structures but provides little motor output of its own.

Checetto and Saper (1990) concluded with a series of questions of relevance to the psychophysiologist trying to understand how a peripheral organ, innervated by the autonomic nervous system, is regulated by activity in higher centers of the brain—in other words, how the body is regulated by psychological processes. How do these three cortical sites, and others, integrate autonomic responses with behavior and cognitive or emotional activity? What are the exact localizations and structural demarcations of cortical areas responsible for autonomic function? What specific neural pathways mediate how the cortex may gain control over autonomic outflow. As we saw previously in this chapter, it is the right and not the left branch of the vagus nerve that has direct access to the main control structure for the beating of the heart (the SA node). This is an important clue for the psychophysiologist investigating how the brain exerts its sometimes dramatic control of the organs of the body, far away from the brain, and how this control is related to the functions of the mind-brain mystery.

Altered States of Consciousness

A great deal of effort has been put into the question whether different states of consciousness, like hypnosis, trance, or meditation, have unique physiological characteristics (Holmes, 1984; Wallace, 1970). Research on the effects of various forms of meditation has focused on two types of physiological changes: changes in attentional state during meditation achieved by directing one's attention either inward (as in transcendental meditation, TM) or outward (as in Zen meditation); or the reduction of physiological, or bodily, tension and stress. Changes in attentional state are usually measured by EEG recordings, particularly the effects of external stimuli on the alpha frequency. Basically, focusing attention inward should not result in alpha suppression of responses to presentations of an external stimulus, because in this situation the external world is "shut off." On the other hand, focusing attention outward should result in alpha suppression of responses to external stimuli, because in this situation the individual is "hypersensitive" to all external events.

Studies on the autonomic effects of hypnotic induction are few and difficult to evaluate because they have not focused on hypnosis per se, but rather on hypnotic suggestions. Interesting work has been done by Diehl, Meyer, Ulrich, and Meinig (1989), however. They studied cerebral blood flow in twelve subjects on and off hypnosis and found greater global hemispheric perfusion in the subjects during hypnosis than during rest. Another study in this field (Gruzelier, Brow, Perry, et al., 1984) found evidence of a shift in hemispheric laterality during hypnosis in highly hypnotizable subjects, when recording skin-conductance responses from the left and right hands. An interesting question is whether a hypnotic suggestion to ignore a stimulus, such as a tone, also will block an orienting response to that tone: do hypnotic suggestions also influence the autonomic nervous system?

Measures of lowered bodily tension and stress after meditation practice are usually based on recordings from autonomic and somatic effectors, like skin conductance, heart rate, respiration, muscle tonus. A fundamental assumption about the potential health implications of meditation seems to be linked to the mediating effects of lowered stress and arousal. A key issue, then is whether there are fundamental differences in physiological response patterns during meditation as opposed to rest. The experimental literature gives little support for a specific "meditation response" (however, see Benson, Beary, and Carol, 1974).

Two main conclusions can be drawn from the meditation studies. First, no single measure of stress seems to yield consistent effects across studies. Second, no study seems to yield consistent effects across measures (see Holmes, 1984; Becker and Shapiro, 1981). A recent paper by Telles and Desiraju (1993), however, presented evidence of an interesting differentiation among various autonomic measures during meditation practice. There were no changes in skin conductance or peripheral blood flow, but heart rate was significantly lower during mediation than under the control conditions. Moreover, there were marked differences among individuals, suggesting a dimension of individual variability that would account for a great part of the error variance. Different subjects also showed different patterns of autonomic change during the same meditative practice. Thus, a single, unitary model of autonomic effects of meditation may be inadequate to describe the physiological effects of altered states of consciousness.

Summary

The structure and function of the sympathetic and parasympathetic branches of the autonomic nervous system were reviewed. Particular attention was focused on possible lateral differences in autonomic function, and especially on right-hemisphere control of vagal output to the heart. Other psychophysiological aspects of autonomic function include changes in cardiac activity following heart transplantation and cycles of nostril dominance during respiration. Special sections were devoted to cortical control of the autonomic nervous system and to the principles of autonomic reciprocity versus autonomic space. A traditional view of autonomic functioning states that the two branches of the autonomic nervous system are reciprocal: increased activity in one branch coincides with decreased activity in the other branch. Recent research and theory of autonomic functioning argue that the two branches of the ANS can be equally active in certain situations.

III

Collecting and Analyzing Data

6

Electrodermal Activity

Most people have an intuitive understanding, or personal experience, of the tendency to sweat during times of emotional excitement or stress. In fact, sweat glands may be activated during less noticeable emotional states, as well as during the performance of various cognitive tasks. We are able to study these physiological states by recording the changes in electrodermal activity (EDA): the ability of the skin to conduct electrical current. In this chapter I will introduce the concepts of electrodermal recordings and explain how electrodermal activity is related to cognitive and emotional functions like attention and arousal; I will then discuss applications of electrodermal activity to psychopathology and clinical psychology in subsequent chapters. For more detailed reviews of electrodermal activity and measurements, see Venables and Christie (1973, 1980) and Boucsein (1992).

An older but still frequently used term for electrodermal activity is the galvanic skin reflex (GSR). Boucsein (1992) recommends that this term should not be used in reports on electrodermal phenomena for several reasons. First, it implies that the skin can be regarded as a galvanic element, a description that does not correspond with existing empirical evidence. Second, referring to physiological changes as a "reflex" implies that they are elicited automatically; to the contrary, however, electrodermal activity covers a wide range of psychological phenomena, from unconscious responses to complex cognitive processes involving attention, memory, and learning.

The human electrodermal system consists of the eccrine sweat glands, which are most concentrated in the digits and the palms of the hands, sympathetic innervation from the autonomic nervous system, and the basal ganglia-limbic-cortical control circuitry. Although a rather simple and "low-tech" technique, a recording of EDA as a function of emotional or cognitive activation is still one the most sensitive physiological indicators of psychological phenomena, both in the laboratory and in the clinic. Furthermore, recent advances in ambulatory recording techniques (see Turpin, 1985) have made it possible to measure EDA in a variety of settings, such as the work site, a traffic jam, and the classroom.

The Electrodermal Response

Electrodermal activity is recorded as changes in electrical resistance in the skin. The evidence that sweat-gland activity—and not, for example, changes in peripheral blood vessels—is responsible for electrodermal activity comes from studies showing that the electrodermal response is blocked after administration of atropine, which prevents activity in the cholinergically innervated secretory mechanisms (Lader and Montagu, 1962).

A basic assumption in psychophysiology is that the function of the sweat glands is linked to psychological factors. It is well known that the palms of the hands become moist in situations of stress and nervous tension. When a sweat gland in these areas of the body is activated, it fills with sweat (a hydrate solution of water and salt). Skin with a higher water content will conduct an electric current more easily than dry skin. Thus, a hydrated sweat gland provides *less resistance* for the passage of an electric current. Increased activity in the sympathetic nervous system will cause increased hydration in the sweat duct and on the surface of the skin. The resulting drop in skin resistance (increase in conductance) is recorded as a change in electrodermal activity.

In everyday language, electrodermal responses indicate "emotional sweating." This is in contrast to thermoregulatory sweating, or sweating as a means to regulate the internal body temperature. The final common neural pathway for electrodermal sweating is the sympathetic branch of the autonomic nervous system, probably regulated from the frontal cortex via hypothalamic-limbic pathways (Luria and Homskaya, 1970). The term *emotional sweating* is, however, misleading, since EDA also can be elicited in situations of information-processing and cognition (Siddle, 1992; Öhman, 1979a).

Endosomatic and Exosomatic Activity

EDA can be measured either as *endosomatic* or *exosomatic* activity. *Endosomatic* activity is the activity of sympathetic nerves in the skin. It measures "skin potentials," the action potentials generated by the nerve (Edelberg, 1968). Skin potentials may be *uniphasic* or *biphasic*, but all exosomatic skin-conductance responses are uniphasic. A uniphasic potential has only one deflection (positive or negative) while a biphasic potential has two deflections of different polarity (positive-negative, or negative-positive).

Wallin and Fagius (1986) have developed a technique for direct measurement of skin sympathetic activity, *microneurography*, which involves inserting a tiny microelectrode through the skin and into the underlying sympathetic nerve. Using this technique, Wallin and Fagius (1986; see also Wallin, 1981) have shown a positive correlation between bursts of sympathetic activity and the amplitude of the change in resistance measured on the surface of the skin. Direct recordings of activity in the sympathetic nerve in the skin show increased spike amplitudes in situations where an electrodermal response occurs. In other words, activity in the sympathetic nervous system is intimately linked to the elicitation of EDA.

Exosomatic electrodermal activity is the activity that can be measured from the surface of the skin. A small current is passed across two electrodes placed on the skin, and the change in the resistance of the skin to the current is recorded as a function of increased sweat gland activity. Either direct current (DC) or alternating current (AC) can be used. For DC measurements, the current is kept constant and skin resistance is measured as changes in voltage. When the voltage is kept constant, skin conductance is measured as changes in the strength of the current. The difference between skin resistance (SR) and skin conductance (SC) will be clear in a moment.

When alternating current is used, skin impedance (SZ) or skin admittance (SY) is recorded, depending on whether current or voltage is kept constant (see Boucsein, 1992, for further details). AC mode is not recommended for EDA recordings, because the time constant (time taken for two-thirds reduction of voltage amplitude) in an AC circuit will affect the amplitude of the EDA response.

Changes in electrodermal activity were first demonstrated by Feré (1888), who passed a small current through the skin and recorded conductivity while the subject was exposed to sensory stimuli. Two years later, Tarchanoff (1890) succeeded in recording potential changes directly from the skin without using an external current source. In modern literature, Feré's and Tarchanoff's pioneering work forms the basis for exosomatic and endosomatic recordings, respectively. Most of the studies discussed in this chapter will concern exosomatic recordings.

An Evolutionary Model

Psychological events influence the electrodermal system mainly in the palmar and plantar regions of the hands and feet. The signals controlling EDA probably originate in limbic structures, including hypothalamic-limbic connections, and/or in the frontal cortex (see below). Edelberg (1972) suggested that increased sweating in the hands and in the soles of the feet may be part of an evolutionary behavioral adaptation to perceived threat from the environment. (See Table 6.1.)

Edelberg (1972, see also 1973) argued that increased sweating in the hands and soles would optimize grip strength and balance in an

Table 6.1.   The biological significance of electrodermal activity.

Increased sweat-gland activity in the palms and soles of feet =
    Increased grip strength and balance (friction)

Increased grip strength and balance =
    Increased mobility (flight/fight) = Increased survival

Hydrated skin = Better protection against cuts and wounds

Thus, in a threatening situation the brain adjusts
    the hydration level in the skin via the autonomic nervous system

In a metaphorical sense, then, the skin may be regarded
    as a "first psychological defense"

Source: Adapted from Edelberg (1972).

individual fleeing from or attacking a potential aggressor. An optimal level of hydration in the skin also improves the capacity for manual manipulation or tactile discrimination. This motor-accessory role of EDA can be observed in the context of two-point tactile discrimination. Subjects are better at discriminating two adjacent tactile stimuli on the skin when hydration is high (Edleberg, 1973). Similarly, increased sweating in other parts of the body in a threatening situation makes the body surface "slippery," difficult for an aggressor to hold onto. A wet skin is also more resistant to cuts and bruises. Thus, by making it easier to hold a weapon or to climb a tree to escape a potential predator, the sweat response may have evolved as a behavioral advantage.

That modern humans still respond by increased palm sweating in situations of perceived threat and danger may thus be a psychological remnant of a highly adaptive response shown by our tree-climbing ancestors. Similarly, a phobic patient who starts sweating in the hands because the brain "misinterprets" a benign stimulus as a danger shows an irrational fear (Marks, 1969).

Electrodermal Measures

Whether it measures skin conductance or resistance, an EDA recording may register slow (in minutes), tonic changes or comparatively fast, phasic responses, which occur within seconds after a stimulus. Phasic changes also occur in the absence of a stimulus, in which case they are called nonspecific responses, or *spontaneous fluctuations* (SF). SFs are usually counted over a period of ten or twenty seconds and converted to a number of fluctuations per minute. Figure 6.1 gives some examples of electrodermal levels, responses, and spontaneous fluctuations.

The three basic modes of EDA activity—tonic levels, phasic responses, and spontaneous fluctuations—are closely intercorrelated, although they reflect different psychological processes. In some instances, the frequency of responses occurring during long stimulus exposures may be treated as the frequency of spontaneous fluctuations even though there is a stimulus present. For example, Hugdahl and Ternes (1981) recorded response frequency in opiate addicts exposed to film clips of either neutral or drug-relevant (the "cooking up" and injection of a drug) contents, in order to study the specific withdrawal symptoms of opiate addiction. Number of responses per minute was

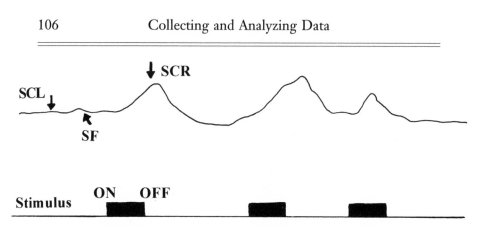

Figure 6.1. Examples of different electrodermal measures *(top)* in relation to three stimulus presentations *(bottom)*. SCL = skin-conductance level, or tonic baseline reactivity; SF = spontaneous fluctuation in the absence of an external stimulus; SCR = skin-conductance response, a phasic response to the presentation of a stimulus. Note the slight delay (approximately 1 second) of the SCR after stimulus onset.

used as a measure of the relative emotional activation elicited in opiate addicts by cues in their environment related to drug intake. The subjects showed increased response frequency (or "spontaneous fluctuations") while watching the film showing drug injections.

Tonic and Phasic Activity

The tonic activity level, that is, the baseline activity level in a subject, is believed to reflect vigilance and sustained attention, as well as heightened arousal over time (Kilpatrick, 1972). Phasic responses reflect the sudden impact a discrete stimulus may have, particularly if it is an unexpected event (Sokolov, 1963) or if it has a particular significance for the subject (Berlyne, 1958).

Phasic responses reflect both cognitive and emotional demands of a stimulus. In a recent study, Barry and Sokolov (1993) repeatedly exposed subjects to a visual stimulus and measured skin-conductance levels just before each stimulus presentation. They found that both phasic responses and tonic levels of skin conductance decreased in a similar way as a function of stimulus trials. Examples of their recordings appear in Figure 6.2.

Spontaneous Fluctuations

Spontaneous fluctuations are particularly sensitive to arousal and anxiety. For example, Lader (1967) found a positive correlation between

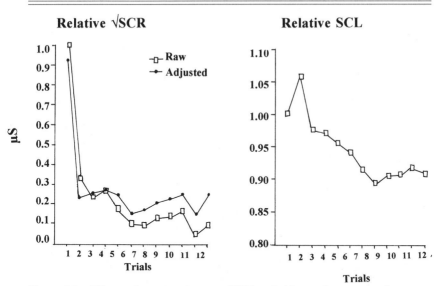

Figure 6.2. Skin-conductance responses (SCR) and skin-conductance levels (SCLs), measured in microsiemens (μS), across 12 stimulus presentations. Note that SCRs are square root corrected. (Data from Barry and Sokolov, 1993, reprinted with permission from Elsevier Science Publishers and the authors.)

subjective and objective measures of anxiety and the frequency of spontaneous fluctuations. Moreover, Hugdahl, Fredrikson, and Öhman (1977) showed that individuals high in spontaneous fluctuations were more easily conditioned to phobic stimuli, a finding that may explain why some individuals are more prone to establish a phobic reaction. In a similar vein, Kvale et al. (1991) found that cancer patients with high spontaneous autonomic reactivity more easily developed psychologically caused side effects after chemotherapy treatment.

Recovery Rate

Another measure of electrodermal responsivity is the recovery rate (Edelberg, 1970). The recovery rate is the time it takes for the level of activity being recorded to return to its prestimulus baseline after the response peak. Usually, however, it is measured as the time required for the recording to return halfway to the baseline; this is generally expressed as *rec t/2*, or the time to 50 percent recovery. Edelberg (1970) has argued that slow recovery correlates with emotionality, whereas a more rapid recovery correlates with attention and goal-directed behavior.

The Recording and Scoring of EDA Data

For most of this chapter I have been using general terms like *electrodermal activity* or *responses*. In fact, though, electrodermal recordings may be made in several different ways, and it is important to specify exactly the kind of measurement taking place in an experiment. (See Table 6.2 for commonly used terminology.)

Tonic changes are expressed in terms of *skin-resistance levels* (SRL) or *skin-conductance levels* (SCL). Phasic changes are labeled *skin-resistance responses* (SRR) or *skin-conductance responses* (SCR). Nonspecific responses, or *spontaneous fluctuations* (SF), occur in the absence of external stimulation. SFs are sometimes labeled *nonspecific skin-conductance responses* (NSSCR) if a recording of skin conductance is made.

Ohm's Law

The typical EDA experimental setup is an electrical circuit in which current passes through an electric coupler that typically contains a Wheatstone bridge, which records the resistance of the skin to the current passing between the electrodes. This apparatus, like all electrical circuits, is mathematically described by Ohm's law, $E = R \times I$, where E is the voltage in the circuitry, R is the resistance, and I is the current that flows through the circuit. The voltage is proportional to

Table 6.2. Recording parameters for tonic and phasic electrodermal activity.

	Resistance	Conductance
Tonic level	Skin-resistance level (SRL, KΩ)	Skin-conductance level (SCL, μS)
Phasic response (elicited or spontaneous)	Skin-resistance response (SRR, KΩ)	Skin-conductance response (SCR, μS)
	Spontaneous skin-resistance fluctuations (SF, fluctuations/min)	Spontaneous skin-conductance fluctuations (SF, fluctuations/min)

the current flow, and the quotient of voltage and current is a measure of the resistance to current flow in a given medium. This quotient may be written as $R = E/I$.

The reciprocal of resistance—the amount of current that would flow through the medium given a particular resistance—is the *conductance (C)*. Conductance is thus the inverse of resistance: $C = 1/R$. In modern electrodermal laboratories, conductance, rather than resistance, is the measurement of choice. The main reason for this preference is that the electrical properties of the sweat glands and the skin can be regarded as that of a population of resistors in parallel (Montagu and Coles, 1966). Resistors in parallel add inversely, which means that the inverse of the total resistance, $1/R_{tot}$, in a circuit is equal to the sum of the inverses of all individual resistors: $1/R_{tot} = 1/R_1 + 1/R_2 \ldots + 1/R_n$, which is equal to $1/R_{tot} = C_{tot} = C_1 + C_2 + \ldots C_n$. Thus, the reciprocal of the total resistance in an electric circuit with resistors adding in parallel is the same as the sum of conductances. Therefore, skin-conductance measurements, which in a way are linearly related to the number of active sweat glands, are to be preferred over skin resistance measurements. This model of the electrical properties of the skin, proposed by Montagu and Coles (1966), is illustrated in Figure 6.3.

The traditional recording unit for conductance used in psychophysiology is *mho*, which is *ohm* spelled backward (*ohm* being the unit of measure for resistance). The reversed spelling has helped students make sense of the reciprocal nature of skin-resistance and skin-conductance recordings. In recent research papers on EDA, however, the term *siemens* (S) is frequently substituted for mho. In practice, though, skin conductance may be expressed in terms of either micromhos (μmho, or 10^{-6} mho) or microsiemens (μS, or 10^{-6} S). For practical purposes of consistency between the text and figures, I will use the microsiemens as the unit of conductance.

Response Ranges

The normal variation for tonic changes in skin conductance is 1–30 μS per cm^2. The normal range of the amplitude of the phasic SCR is somewhere in the region of 0.05 to 5 μS. An important unit in all measurements of electrodermal activity is the smallest accepted phasic response. In traditional "polygraphy" this unit was set to 0.05 μS,

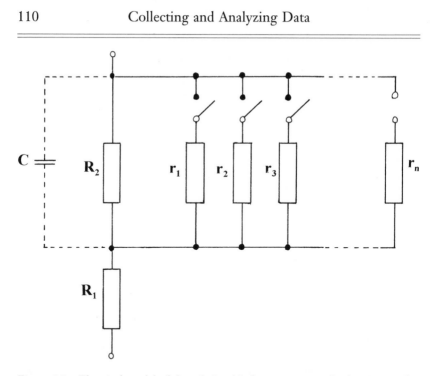

Figure 6.3. Electrical model of the relationship between sweat-gland activity and skin-conductance recordings proposed by Montagu and Coles (1966). The electrical properties of the sweat glands (r_1 through r_n) and the skin (R_1 and R_2) are like resistors in parallel in an electric circuit driven by a battery *(C)*. (Adapted with permission from the American Psychological Association.)

which usually corresponded to a distance of 0.5 mm on the polygraph chart. This was a convenient rule since it was difficult visually to identify smaller responses on the chart with any form of certainty. With modern computerized scoring programs, however, the minimum accepted phasic change can be as small 0.01 μS, or even smaller.

It should be kept in mind that all measurements may vary as a consequence of the NaCl concentration in the paste used in the skin electrodes (Hygge and Hugdahl, 1985). The electrode paste should have the same NaCl concentration as the skin: not exceeding 0.05 molar concentration. Fowles et al. (1981) have worked out guiding rules for accurate recordings. They recommend using nonpolarizable silver/silver chloride (Ag/AgCl) electrodes together with a paste having a 0.05 molar NaCl concentration, which can be made from Unibase paste and 3% saline solution mixed together.

Scoring of Phasic Responses

Phasic responses can be scored in a multitude of ways, as may be seen in Figure 6.4. Averaging responses across trials, including "zero" responses, provides an estimate of the mean *response magnitude*. Averaging without "zero responses" gives an estimate of the mean *response amplitude*. A response is measured from the deflection point to the response peak. *Response frequency* is number of responses per time unit, and *response probability* is typically scored as the number of identifiable responses in proportion to the number of trials. Thus, if there are four scorable responses on five trials, response probability is 4/5 = 0.80.

Recovery rate is usually measured as the time it takes for the record-

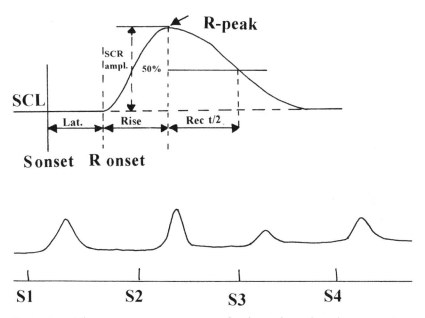

Figure 6.4. The measurement parameters of a phasic electrodermal response. At the top is one phasic response labeled with the different measurement parameters: S-onset = stimulus onset; R-onset = initiation of a skin-conductance response (SCR); SCR ampl. = amplitude of the response from base level to response peak; Lat. = response latency; Rise = rise time, the time to response peak; and Rec t/2 = half-time recovery, the time to 50 percent recovery back to base level from response peak. At bottom is a recording of several responses occurring over time; note that the responses follow the presentation of the stimuli (labeled S1, S2, etc.) after a slight delay.

ing to return from the peak value to half the displacement from the baseline. This is called the *rec t/2*, indicating time to 50 percent recovery; likewise, *rec t/4* indicates the time to 25 percent recovery. *Rise time* is the time needed for the response to reach maximum amplitude (peak) from the point of onset (the moment the response begins). *Latency* is the time from the onset of a stimulus to the initiation of the response, that is, to the point of onset. The latency of an SCR is in the vicinity of 1–2 sec, indicating the relatively slow transmission in the sweat gland and the autonomic nervous system. The *response peak* usually occurs within 1–4 sec after the stimulus is presented, and the 50 percent recovery can vary between 1 and 15 sec, but it typically occurs within 4–8 sec.

Figure 6.5 presents different examples from polygraph tracings of SCRs to two stimuli, as in a classical conditioning experiment. The first stimulus (S1) is a "weak" stimulus (conditioned stimulus, CS), the second stimulus (S2) is a "strong" stimulus (unconditioned stimulus, UCS). The blackened portion is the actual response amplitude in various measurement conventions. Note that a response may be scored only if there is a 1 sec latency from stimulus onset to response onset;

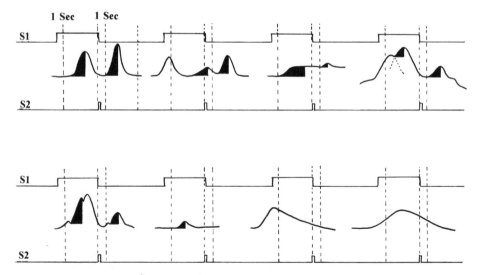

Figure 6.5. Guide to the scoring of response amplitudes in a two-stimulus (S1/S2) experiment with a long interstimulus interval. Only those responses marked with black shading are scored and included in the average.

no responses are scored for the last two trials in Figure 6.5 because this requirement was not fulfilled.

Multiple Responses

In some instances multiple phasic responses may occur within the scoring interval, or scoring "window." When there are several responses, various conventions advocate that the first, or largest, response should be scored. Lockhart (1966) noted that in experiments with two stimuli and with long interstimulus intervals between the two (more than 5 sec), three distinct responses could be observed: the first anticipatory response (FAR), the second anticipatory response (SAR), and the third omission response (TOR). The FAR is related to perceptual and attentional processes, like the orienting response; the SAR reflects a conditioned response, in anticipation of the occurrence of the UCS; the TOR also reflects learning, referring to the omission on test-trials of the UCS (Öhman, 1971). Fredrikson et al. (1993b) found that the FAR was the most internally consistent in subjects studied three weeks apart, and that the FAR is a reliable index also of classically conditioned responses. Thus, for most practical purposes, the FAR is the preferred response to register. Examples of the different responses are given in Figure 6.6.

The Palmar Sweat Index (PSI)

A recent simple but quite accurate measuring device, particularly in applied settings, is the palmar sweat index (PSI), developed by Sutarman and Thomson (1952) and recently described by Turpin and Clements (1993). The PSI has been shown to correlate significantly with both SFs and SCRs as measured by conventional recording techniques.

The PSI is a count of active sweat glands in an area of skin. A plastic impression is made of a patch of skin, perhaps a fingertip. The number of "sweat dots" on the plastic film after presentation of a stimulus, or over time, is a measure of electrodermal activity to psychologically relevant events. Because the plastic film is easily manipulated, the PSI is particularly useful in situations where conventional recordings are difficult to perform.

The PSI seems to be a sensitive measure of arousal or anxiety.

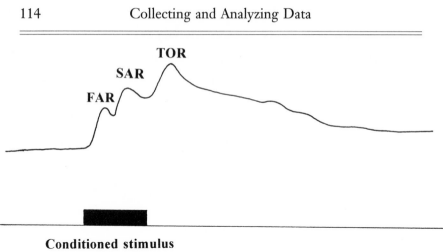

**Conditioned stimulus
(> 5 sec)**

Figure 6.6. Examples of first (FAR) and second (SAR) anticipatory responses, together with a third (TOR) omission response, recorded during an experiment involving a conditioned stimulus (> 5 sec).

Köhler, Dunker, and Zander (1992) found that the number of active sweat glands increased substantially during venous puncture in subjects donating blood; in subjects awaiting a dental exam, the PSI indicated an increase in sweating when the dentist entered the room. The highest PSI values were obtained in situations characterized as stressful.

Peripheral Mechanisms

Electrodermal responses are easily elicited from the inside (palmar) and outside (volar or dorsal) of the hand and from the sole of the foot (plantar) (Boucsein, 1992; Edelberg, 1967). However, EDA may also be elicited from the forehead (Schliack and Schiffter, 1979) and from the ankle of the foot, over the abductor hallucis (Edelberg, 1967). For most practical purposes, placing the electrodes on the second phalanx of the second and third fingers of one or both hands will yield a good exosomatic recording (see Figure 6.7). The electrode sites should not be cleaned with alcohol or with any abrasive cleaning paste, since cleaning solutions would disrupt the functioning of the sweat glands.

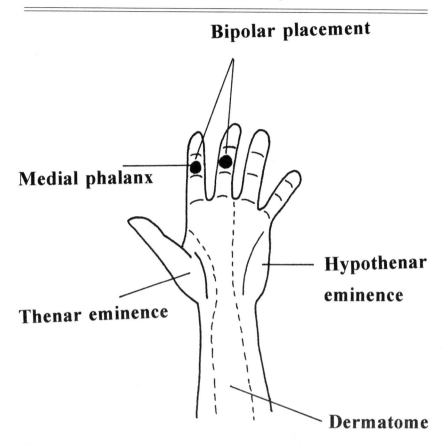

Figure 6.7.   Common positions for placing electrodes on the middle section of the second and third fingers. This arrangement ensures that both electrodes are within the same dermatome; that is, both electrodes record activity from nerves emanating from the same spinal segment.

Sweat Glands

There are two types of sweat glands located under the surface of the skin, the eccrine and the apocrine sweat glands. The apocrine sweat glands, which are found mainly in the hair follicles in the armpit and around the pubic hairs, are regulated by epinephrine in the blood stream. Because they have little effect on EDA measurement, they will not be further discussed. The eccrine glands (see Figure 6.8), which are found all over the surface of the body, are innervated via the sympa-

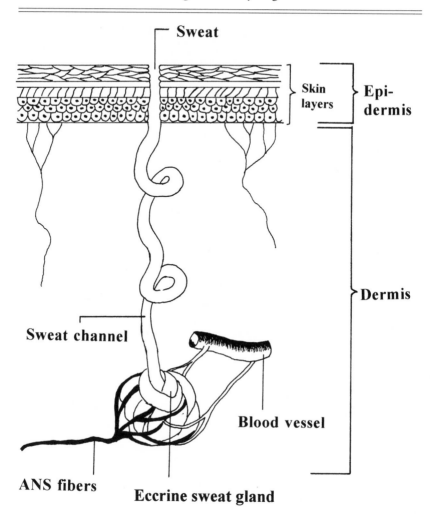

Figure 6.8.   The anatomy of an eccrine sweat gland in the dermis portion of the skin. Sweat rises in the sweat channel, or sweat duct, and hydrates the skin surface. The sympathetic branch of the autonomic nervous system (ANS) innervates the sweat gland through its nerve fibers.

thetic system, and their main purpose is the regulation of body temperature (thermoregulation).

In spite of the fact that the eccrine sweat glands are located over the whole body, they are most densely packed in the palms of the hands and the soles of the feet. The density in these two regions is in the region of 1,000 glands/cm², compared with 100–200/cm² for the trunk, legs, and arms. Although the eccrine sweat glands are innervated by the sympathetic branch of the autonomic nervous system, the postganglionic neurotransmitter is acetylcholine (ACh) (see Chapter 3). It has been suggested that myoepithelial cells, which are located in the outer layers of the skin, also contribute to the sweating response (Sato, 1977), and that they may be particularly involved in producing spontaneous fluctuations. The myoepithelial cells are affected by norepinephrine, rather than acetylcholine, and may also be responsive to circulating epinephrine, pointing to a hormonal influence on electrodermal responding.

Thus, electrodermal measurements mainly provide information about sympathetic activity, although the neurotransmitter is ACh rather than norepinephrine (NE), the common postganglionic neurotransmitter in the sympathetic nervous system.

Reabsorption Membrane

An important factor determining the magnitude of an electrodermal response is the amount of perspiration, or the level of hydration in the sweat ducts (see Figure 6.8). Edelberg (1972) assumed the existence of a membrane for the reabsorption of sweat in the epidermis; the purpose of the membrane is to regulate the level of hydration and prevent an excess of hydration on the surface of the skin. This is called the *membrane model* of electrodermal activity.

The actual level of sweat in the sweat ducts (see Figure 6.8) at a given moment determines the tonic electrodermal level. Phasic responses appear when the level of sweat in the ducts rapidly rises as a result of increased sympathetic activity at the site of the sweat gland. The hydration is, however, precisely regulated through the membrane via reabsorption and diffusion. Thus, if too much sweat is secreted and diffused, the excess sweat is reabsorbed through the duct wall via the hypothesized semipermeable membrane.

The action of the membrane is furthermore hypothesized to be timely coordinated with mental events acting on the brain and nervous system. Edelberg (1972) further assumed that the membrane is located in the epidermis and the duct wall. A plausible explanation for the action of the membrane is that the sweat gland via the sympathetic action potential depolarizes the membrane. Another explanation is that the membrane is activated in a mechanical way when the sweat duct is dilated as a result of an increased level of hydration. The dilation of the duct walls activates an absorption reflex, which quickly reduces the level of hydration in the duct. Neither of these explanations has so far been satisfactorily corroborated, and so the question of the innervation of the membrane is still unsolved.

The Poral Valve Model

In a recent paper, Edelberg (1993) revised parts of the membrane theory and replaced it with a model of *intraductal pressure*. He proposed that, because pressure builds up in the closed duct space between the sweat gland and the electrode on the skin, the pores in the skin will open up like valves and the conductivity of the duct will rise sharply, increasing skin conductance.

The value of the pressure model is that it does not presuppose the existence of a reabsorption membrane (which had never been anatomically corroborated) in order to explain rapid changes in skin conductance. Figure 6.9 illustrates the sequence of steps in a sweat response according to the poral valve model (Edelberg, 1993).

The sequence of events in an electrodermal response can be summarized as follows: At first the sweat duct is empty and its pores are closed; early filling of the duct during an electrodermal response causes an increase in conductance. Further secretion into the duct builds up intraductal pressure, which drives sweat into the deeper corneum of the skin; the increased hydration in turn causes a further increase of the conductance. At some point in time, the intraductal pressure becomes higher than the tissue pressure of the corneum. This causes the collapsed end, or surface, portion of the duct to dilate and open, increasing conductance even further. As sweat escapes out of the open duct, intraductal pressure falls below the tissue pressure, enabling the surface pores once again to close. The closing of the pores is followed by a marked drop in conductance and a consequent increase in resistance. Edelberg (1993) has suggested that this rapid shift from increased conductance to increased resistance may appear as a reabsorption response, although it is caused by the closing of the duct opening at the surface.

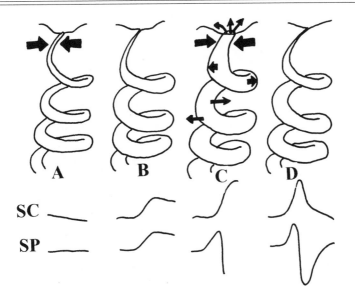

Figure 6.9. Schematic outline of Edelberg's (1993) poral valve model. At first, the ducts are unfilled and the pores collapsed *(A)*. Then secretion partially fills the ducts *(B)*. When the ducts reach the limit of capacity *(C)*, enough intraductal pressure has built up to open the poral "valve." Finally *(D)*, the release of sweat onto the skin surface reduces the intraductal pressure to the collapse point. The associated skin potentials (SPs) and skin conductance (SC) are shown at the bottom. (Reprinted with permission from Plenum Press and the author.)

Central Control of EDA

The mechanisms of control of electrodermal phenomena from higher brain centers are still to a large extent unknown. Edelberg (1972, 1973) and Wang (1964) have contributed valuable models of brain-periphery relationships in electrodermal activity. Wang (1964) found excitatory centers for the elicitation of electrodermal responses in the anterior hypothalamus and the anterior limbic and infralimbic cortices in the cat. He also recorded electrodermal responses after stimulation of the sensorimotor cortex. The reticular formation made up the major inhibitory pathways. Wilcott and Bradley (1970), in addition, found excitatory effects in the frontal cortex. Edelberg (1972) argued that areas in the hypothalamus responsible for sweat-gland hydration are influenced by limbic activity, particularly activity in the amygdala. In a recent study by Tranel and Damasio (1989), however, a patient with bilateral lesions to the amygdaloid nuclei exhibited normal electrodermal responses, making this assumption questionable.

Lateral Frontal Cortex

Areas in the cortex, the lateral frontal cortex, and the dorsolateral cortex seem to have direct influences on the electrodermal response (Bagshaw, Kimble, and Pribram, 1965; Grueninger, Kimble, Grueninger, and Levine, 1965). Moreover, Raine, Reynolds, and Sheard (1991), using magnetic resonance imaging (MRI), found a strong correlation between the amplitude of the electrodermal response and the size of selected areas in the frontal cortex. Interestingly, Raine et al. (1991) found that activity in the *left* frontal areas and the amygdala correlated better with the orienting response; the relationship did not hold for corresponding right areas. This may provide some basis for the argument that electrodermal responses are contralaterally controlled from the brain (cf. Lacroix and Comper, 1979; Hugdahl, 1984), although most findings favor the right hemisphere.

A more direct test of the neuroanatomical correlates of electrodermal responses was obtained by Tranel and Damasio (1994), who studied skin-conductance responses in patients with focal lesions in either the left, right, or both cerebral hemispheres. The patients were compared with healthy controls. The subjects were exposed to what Tranel and Damasio called "physical" and "psychological" stimuli. The physical stimuli consisted of a deep breath and a loud noise, while the psychological stimuli were ten "emotion-laden" pictures of mutilated bodies and nudes. Both categories of stimuli reliably elicit SCRs in humans. The results showed that particularly the *ventromedial frontal cortex, right inferior parietal cortex,* and the *anterior cingulate gyrus* were associated with defective electrodermal responding. This important study thus confirms that cortical areas are critical in the elicitation of a skin-conductance response. It also confirms that the control of electrodermal activity may be lateralized in the brain, particularly from the right hemisphere (right inferior parietal area). This conclusion may be valid, although the authors did not find significant differences between the left- and right-hand recordings. A closer look at their findings nevertheless reveals that, for example, the patients with left-hemisphere lesions showed larger responses on the left hand, while those with right-hemisphere lesions showed larger responses on the right hand (particularly for the physical stimuli). These results indicate that it is the contralateral hemisphere that controls electrodermal phasic activity, in an excitatory way.

Cortico-limbic Systems

From a functional point of view, central nervous control of the electrodermal system may be examined as three separate systems: he locomotor system, the orienting-activating system, and the thermoregulatory system.

The locomotor system. The locomotor system consists of premotor cortex, the pyramidal tract, and the brainstem. The main function of the locomotor system is to facilitate optimal friction of the foot against the ground and optimal hand dexterity. For the best response to danger, hydration in the palms of the hands would already be adjusted to an acceptable level (possibly through the action of the reabsorption membrane, or poral valves). Thus, the locomotor system, which links EDA to anticipation and expectation, corresponds to Edelberg's (1972) evolutionary model of the significance of the electrodermal response.

The orienting-arousal system. This system consists of the lateral frontal cortex, limbic structures (amygdala and hippocampus), and the reticular formation. As this system involves important structures for the maintenance of the orienting response (OR) and arousal, it may be called the orienting-arousal system. The orienting-arousal system is switched on in situations of focused attention or threat (via the limbic structures), boosting output from an amplification subsystem. A high level of hydration is necessary in order to protect the surface of the skin from cuts and bruises. The limbic system is mainly responsible for EDA in threatening situations. The lateral frontal cortex is important for the induction of EDA in orienting situations, when attention is focused on a novel situation. Luria and Homskaya (1970) also showed the importance of the frontal cortex for the regulation of activation, or arousal.

The thermoregulatory system. The areas of the brain important for the thermoregulatory system (the regulation of body temperature via sweating) are associated with the anterior hypothalamus. The thermoregulatory system is perhaps the least important from a psychological point of view, but the phenomenon of "cold sweating" in response to physical trauma is of interest. A trauma results in increased sweating and at the same time vasoconstriction in the peripheral blood vessels (which decreases heat loss occasioned by evaporation of the sweat). Trauma also causes increased EDA from the hands and fingers.

An Alternative Model

A more recent model of central control of EDA, proposed by Boucsein (1992), has two components: an ipsilateral system involving the hypothalamus, anterior thalamus, and cingulate gyrus; and a contralateral system involving the lateral frontal cortex, particularly the premotor cortex, and parts of the basal ganglia. (See Figure 6.10.) This model incorporates much of the three-component model discussed above into a two-component system.

In short, Boucsein's model assumes that central brain areas involved in the control of EDA act through ipsilateral influences from the limbic system via hypothalamic thermoregulatory areas, and contralateral influences from premotor cortex and basal ganglia, mainly the caudate nucleus and the putamen. Thus, the ipsilateral limbic control system is mainly responsible for EDA in emotional and affective situations, but the contralateral cortical control system is mainly responsible for EDA during orienting and cognition as well as locomotion.

One of the reasons that the issue of contralateral versus ipsilateral control of EDA has been notoriously difficult to settle in the past may be that investigators have confounded emotional tasks (ipsilaterally controlled) and nonemotional tasks (contralaterally controlled) in their definition of the stimulus. Edelberg (personal communication, May 1993) has suggested that a pure motor task, like the rubbing together of two fingers in the left and right hand, could be used to study the contralateral influences on EDA. Since rubbing two fingers in the right hand is under the control of the left motor cortex and is a nonemotional task, comparing skin-conductance responses from the left and right hand would provide unconfounded evidence of the contra- versus ipsilateral control of EDA. As will be shown below, confounding tasks for emotional versus cognitive load may seriously hamper efforts to relate the asymmetric functioning of the hemispheres of the brain to electrodermal response amplitudes in the left and right hand. Given that there are two hands to record from, and that both efferent and afferent control of the fingers and palms in the left and right hand

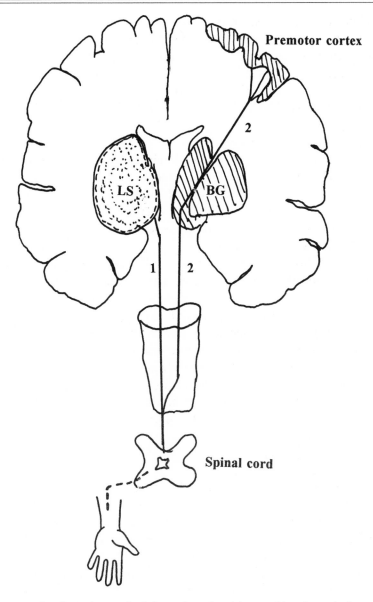

Figure 6.10.   Central control of electrodermal activity considered as a dual system, with ipsilateral and contralateral influences on activity in the sweat glands in the hand. Pathway 1 is the ipsilateral limbic system (LS), and pathway 2 is the contralateral premotor cortex/basal ganglia (BG) system. (Adapted after Boucsein, 1992, with permission from Plenum Press and the author.)

are partly contralaterally controlled from the brain, there should, at least in theory, be an ideal experimental setup for determining the asymmetric functions of the left and right cerebral hemispheres.

A conceptually similar approach was taken by Rockstroh, Elbert, Lutzenberger, et al. (1988). They argued that since most studies on bilateral EDA had used visual or acoustic tasks, the issue of hemisphere-specific stimulation might have been confounded by the fact that these tasks activate a whole range of emotional and cognitive processes, some lateralized, others not. Their experiment therefore used a sensorimotor task, with two kinds of tactile stimuli, a warning stimulus and a discrimination stimulus to which the subject pressed a lever switch. The tactile stimuli were applied either to the same hand as that used for the response or to the opposite hand. The experiment showed quite consistently that when one hemisphere was stimulated, as evidenced through EEG recordings, SCR amplitudes were larger in the hand contralateral to the more activated hemisphere.

Thus, the data by Rockstroh et al. (1988) support the conclusion that, when the confounding effects of hemisphere-specific stimulation by cognitive or emotional aspects of a task were controlled for, electrodermal responses in the hand *contralateral* to the activated hemisphere are facilitated, not inhibited. This study is thus a nice example of the general point made by Edelberg that the ipsi- versus contralateral nature of the two EDA control systems may confound the results in studies not separating sensorimotor tasks from cognitive and emotional tasks.

Hemispheric Asymmetry

The arguments regarding EDA in the left and right hand and brain asymmetry, or laterality, originated with Lacroix and Comper (1979), although they were not the first authors to have tried to link left and right hand recordings to the separate functioning of the right and left hemispheres of the brain (see, e.g., Darrow, 1937; Obrist, 1963). (For reviews of the relevant literature, see Hugdahl, 1984, 1988; see also Freixa-I-Baque, Cataux, Miossec, and Roy, 1984.) Lacroix and Comper (1979) found larger left-hand responses when the subjects performed a task involving English proverbs (a verbal task) and larger right-hand responses when the same subjects performed a task concerning the location of well-known places on a map (a spatial task).

From the literature on hemispheric asymmetry (e.g., Bradshaw and

Nettleton, 1981), an argument could be made that verbal and spatial tasks should differentially engage the left and right cerebral hemispheres, respectively. Thus, Lacroix and Comper (1979) argued that the electrodermal system was related to cortical activation through contralateral inhibition; in other words, there would be smaller responses in the limb contralateral to the more activated or engaged hemisphere. Moreover, in a separate experiment, they found that when subjects performed tasks that engaged the two hemispheres equally, any differences between the hands disappeared. However, the results by Lacroix and Comper (1979) have not been unequivocally replicated (see Hugdahl, 1984, 1988, for a discussion of the controversy that ensued after the publication of the 1979 paper).

Thus, to summarize: if there is any evidence for a link between the functioning of the hemispheres of the brain and electrodermal response amplitudes in the left and right hands, the more recent data suggest a contralateral excitatory effect (Davidson, Fedio, Smith, et al., 1992; see below), although some laboratories have found support for the contralateral inhibition model (Rippon, 1985; Skolnick, Sussman, and Gur, 1986). In any case there are still several unanswered questions. One major problem with most published studies is that the left- and right-hemisphere tasks used in the experiments differ in qualities other than laterality, as for example intensity, novelty, or difficulty.

These qualities also differentially affect cognition and activation of the hemispheres, which would confound any interpretation of the relationship between the tasks used and the magnitude of the skin-conductance response in the two hands (see Rippon, 1993, for a discussion of this issue). Unless tasks are matched on all relevant dimensions, the controversy is not likely to be solved in the near future.

Differences between the right and left hands are necessarily not the only, or even the critical, way of studying peripheral autonomic effects of the functioning of the cerebral hemispheres. In experiments using tasks that differentially activate the two hemispheres, in which comparisons across control conditions, or control groups, could be made, responses could be of similar amplitudes in the two hands as long as they differ under the critical experimental conditions. For example, if responses in both hands are increased when the right hemisphere is activated but not when the left hemisphere is activated, a cortical-peripheral link would have been established.

Rippon (1990) tried to resolve some of the inconsistencies in previous research by recording EEG and SCRs simultaneously in the same subjects. By analyzing hemispheric differences in the EEG and correlating the EEG data with the SCR data from the left and right hand, Rippon obtained a better measure of specific hemispheric activation and EDA activity. When the left hemisphere was activated, as revealed in the topographical EEG maps, there was a tendency toward larger responses in the hand contralateral to the hemisphere with the largest beta activity. In other words, there was a tendency toward larger SCRs in the hand contralateral to the more activated hemisphere (which is indicated by the increase in beta-band activity in the EEG). Thus, Rippon's findings would indicate a relationship of contralateral excitation between relative hemispheric activation and lateral SCRs. An explanation for the inconsistent results with regard to contralateral inhibition or excitation may be that the various tasks used as tests activate both the contralateral motor system and the ipsilateral arousal system in the brain (Boucsein, 1992) to varying degrees in different studies. As a result, some studies find no lateralization in EDA, others find contralateral inhibition, and still others find contralateral excitation.

Roman et al. (1989) found that electrodermal lateralization was independent of task manipulation. That is, a subject's laterality score remained constant independent of whether the left or right hemisphere was activated. In a more recent paper, the same investigators (Roman et al., 1992) found that left- and right-handed subjects exhibited opposite electrodermal responsiveness patterns: there were larger right-hand SCRs in right-handed subjects, and larger left-hand SCRs in left-handed subjects. For both groups of subjects, there was no interaction with task manipulation. Roman et al. (1992) have proposed that the direction of the response pattern is an individual "trait" independent of hemispheric activation, and that the experimenters must know each subject's response tendency before presenting hemisphere-specific stimuli or tasks, since the response direction otherwise may confound the experimental manipulation intended to expose EDA laterality.

Although evidence for unilateral differences between the hands in electrodermal recordings are observed in more recent studies, the reliability of these findings are generally low. Naveteur and Sequiera-Marthino (1990) found that right-left differences in the amplitude of electrodermal responses to a series of tone-stimulus presentations were observed in almost all subjects at the first test, but these differences did not remain consistent when the subjects were retested four times, with a week in between each test. These findings might fit an interpretation that EDA laterality is due to peripheral rather than central (hemispheric) factors (cf. Sequiera-Marthino, Roy, and Ba-M'Hamed, 1986). For example, differences in skin temperature and how the electrodes are fixed to the two hands may substantially bias the recordings.

The question of the differential involvement of the right and left hemispheres of the brain in EDA was also addressed by R. A. Davidson, Fedio, Smith, et al. (1992). They found that the EDA response profiles of epileptic patients with parts of either the right or left temporal lobe removed differed depending on which side was removed. The subjects underwent a simple auditory habituation sequence (a standard tone presented several times) and were then presented with two tones (standard and deviant) and asked to count the infrequent, deviant tones. Compared with the left-lobectomized patients, patients with right-sided lobectomies were less responsive and exhibited faster habituation. They also seemed to be less aroused than the left-lobectomized patients.

The differences were particularly evident during the tone-discrimination phase of the experiment, indicating a particular role of the right hemisphere in skin-conductance responses to more complex arousal tasks. The right-operated patients also showed significantly smaller initial responses on the left hand (contralateral to the lesion), particularly to the initial OR tone (see Figure 6.11). This would be indicative of a direct contralateral excitatory link between the right hemisphere and the left-hand EDA, since lesioning of the right hemisphere resulted in reduced SCR amplitudes and faster habituation in the left hand.

This study is important for two reasons. It shows that the two hemispheres of the brain are differentially involved in the control and regulation of arousal and orienting/habituation (first proposed by Hugdahl, Wahlgren, and Wass, 1982). And, in contrast to the prevailing idea that the major contralateral pathways are inhibitory, as originally suggested by Lacroix and Comper (1979), it suggests that the issue of bilateral differences in EDA may be mediated through contralateral *excitatory* brain-periphery pathways.

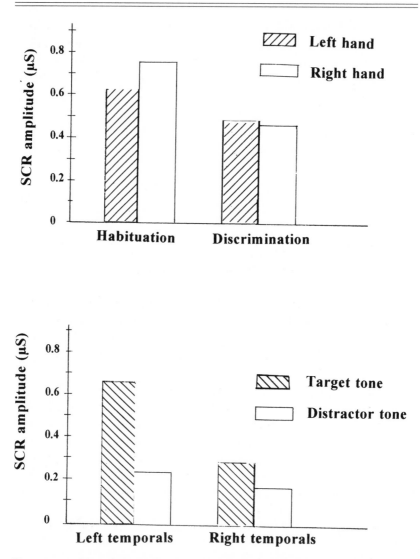

Figure 6.11. Mean SCR amplitudes *(at top)* from the left and right hands in a subject responding to an initial tone stimulus during the habituation and discrimination phases of the experiment. Mean SCR amplitudes *(bottom)* for the two groups of lobectomized patients responding to an initial target and distractor tones during the discrimination phase of the experiment. (Data from R. A. Davidson et al., 1992, with permission from Elsevier Science Publishers.)

Other Factors Influencing EDA

Since EDA is related to the thermoregulatory function of the body, recordings should be made at temperatures as constant as possible. Moreover, several studies have shown that women, although they have higher SCLs, are less reactive than men are when phasic SCRs are measured (Maltzman, Gould, Barnett, et al., 1979). Venables and Christie (1973) attributed most of the gender differences to differences in hormonal influences, given that eccrine sweating in women is related to the menstrual cycle.

The gender differences should, however, be taken with some caution, since Roman et al. (1989) found no effects of gender after regrouping subjects according to their most reactive hand (left versus right). This study is interesting in the sense that individual differences in which hand is the most reactive may override other differences in other characteristics, like gender.

Finally, some studies have shown black subjects to have lower tonic SCLs than whites, probably because of differences in the number of sweat glands in light and dark skin (see Boucsein, 1992). EDA is also attenuated during sleep and with increasing age. Muscle-relaxation drugs also attenuate EDA, probably through the action of ACh, which is the major neurotransmitter in muscle synapses.

EDA in Psychophysiological Research

A survey of psychophysiological research during the last decades shows that EDA studies have been used to investigate such different areas as orienting (Siddle and Heron, 1976; Raskin, Kotses, and Brever, 1969; Öhman, 1979a); learning and conditioning (Öhman, 1971; Prokasy and Kumpfer, 1973; Kimmel, 1967); psychopathology and personality disorders (Gruzelier and Venables, 1973; Hare and Blevings, 1975; Öhman, 1981; Zahn, Nurnberger, and Berrettini, 1989); individual differences (Crider and Lunn, 1971; Katkin and McCubbin, 1969; O'Gorman, 1983); brain asymmetry and laterality (Hugdahl, 1984; Lacroix and Comper, 1979); and cognitive neuroscience and neuropsychology (Tranel and Damasio, 1985, 1994). Applications of measures of EDA in various clinical populations are described and discussed in Chapter 8.

Summary

The electrodermal system is responsible for changes in the activity of the sweat glands, mainly in the palms and under the feet, in response to psychological events. Electrodermal activity (EDA) reflects sympathetic influences on the periphery and is thus an unobtrusive measure of arousal. Since changes in autonomic function also are closely linked to cognitive function, particularly attention and vigilance, EDA also reflects phasic changes in attentional shifts and the sustaining of attention over time. EDA has a long history as an experimental measure in psychology and is frequently used in the assessment of psychiatric disorders and brain damage.

In the present chapter, the different types of EDA are described and a possible evolutionary model of its biological utility as a response to danger is discussed. The basic electrical principles of EDA recordings are described, and detailed descriptions of techniques, scoring, and analysis of EDA data are provided. Peripheral and central physiology is discussed with a view to explaining how the brain regulates EDA in the periphery and why psychological events may have such profound effects on the sweat glands. Major anatomical systems of the brain thought to be involved in the control and regulation of EDA are presented, as are current debates over laterality and cortical and subcortical influences on EDA. The chapter ends with a brief overview of applications of EDA in psychological research and clinical practice. These topics are further discussed in Chapter 8.

7

Orienting and Conditioning

Orienting and conditioning are examples of *behavioral plasticity.* That is, both behaviors help the individual make appropriate responses to a changing environment. Orienting is a generalized response to unexpected or novel stimuli. It prepares the individual to detect and react quickly to an unexpected event. Conditioning, on the other hand, is a *learned* response. It makes the individual capable of relating two events to each other, a skill called "associative learning."

It is argued that the shifting of attention to the source of stimulation that occurs in an orienting response (OR) and the cessation of the OR upon repeated presentations of the same event over time are necessary prerequisites for learning to associate one stimulus with another. In this chapter I describe the information-processing models that explain these mechanisms. I also review and compare the theories of learning that have been proposed to account for the different kinds of classical conditioning—one type being related to unconscious, implicit, memory processes, and the other requiring conscious awareness of the stimulus contingencies.

Orienting and classical conditioning are treated in a separate chapter, rather than in the introductory chapter on psychophysiological concepts (Chapter 2), because of their central role in the history of psychophysiological research. No other constructs have had as great an impact on psychophysiological research and theorizing as orienting and classical conditioning have had.

Orienting and Habituation

The initial response on the first presentation of a stimulus is the orienting response (OR) (Sokolov, 1963; Öhman, 1979a). The OR is a kind of "surprise," and it involves a shift of attention toward the unexpected stimulus. The OR consists of a complex of sensory, somatic, EEG, and autonomic changes (see, e.g., Graham, 1973), which together interrupt ongoing behavior and increase sensory acuity. In other words, the OR facilitates sensory input to the brain (Lacey and Lacey, 1974; Siddle, 1991). In terms of information-processing models, the OR reflects passive attention to stimulus input that is amplified in the nervous system until it interrupts ongoing activity.

After repeated presentations of the same stimulus, the OR becomes smaller and smaller, and finally it disappears. The *habituation* of an organism to repetitive stimuli is one of the most powerful examples of plasticity, or "memory," in the nervous system (cf. Thompson and Spencer, 1966). Figure 7.1 reproduces a recording of typical skin-conductance responses (SCRs) to repeated presentations of a tone of moderate intensity (the nonsignal stimulus) and to the same stimulus after the tone has gained significance for the individual, through classical conditioning (the signal stimulus).

The OR was discovered by Pavlov in the late 1920s, when he was studying the conditioned response. The biological "purpose" of the OR and its habituation is obvious: to facilitate the detection of a novel threat as quickly as possible and to initiate an appropriate response. Upon repeated presentations, the event is no longer novel to the organism, and the OR loses its value as a warning response.

Habituation must not be confused with *sensory adaptation*, another phenomenon that results in response cessation after repeated stimulus presentations. Sensory adaption is a peripheral phenomenon occurring at the receptor level as a function of stimulation fatigue, which makes the receptor refractory (insensitive) to new stimulation. Habituation is a central phenomenon, probably involving cortical processing. An observation that makes this difference clear is that the OR will be reinstated also after the omission of a stimulus, because the sequence is disrupted. The sudden reappearance of the response demonstrates that the system was in fact not in a refractory state. An example is the lighthouse keeper who sleeps through a whole foggy night despite the foghorn sounding every other minute but wakes when the fuse blows and

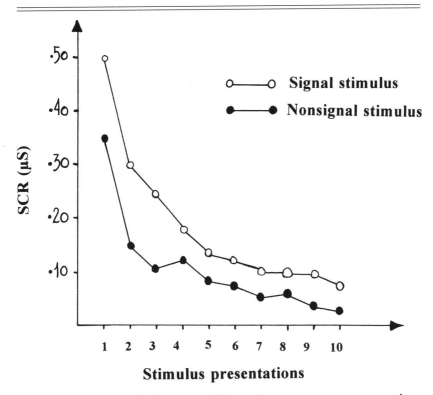

Figure 7.1. Examples of habituation of skin-conductance responses to repeated presentations (10 trials) of a nonsignal and signal tone stimulus. The SCR is measured in microsiemens (μS).

the foghorn is silenced. When the sound stops, the OR is reinstated because the sequence of stimuli "presented" to the lighthouse keeper is disrupted. Receptor refractoriness will not terminate because a stimulus suddenly is omitted in a train of stimuli.

Comparator Theories

Most modern theories of the OR and habituation are based on a "matching principle." According to this principle, an incoming stimulus is "matched" against a memory template, or *neuronal model* (Sokolov, 1963), and for every presentation of the stimulus the template is updated. With a few exceptions, the OR is elicited whenever there is a mismatch between the incoming stimulus and the template. When

the stimulus matches the template, the OR habituates. The OR is reinstated (dishabituated) if there is a change in the stimulus or in the
sequence of the presentation of stimuli (Siddle, 1991). Figure 7.2 presents a simplified outline of the neuronal model developed by Sokolov
(1960) to explain habituation of the orienting response.

In general terms, Sokolov assumed that an incoming stimulus ("input") was analyzed in the cortex and that the cortex initiates elicitation
or inhibition of the OR, depending on the status of the "neuronal
comparator" system. If there is a match between the input and the
comparator process, the OR is inhibited, and instead a learned or conditioned response (CR) may be elicited. If there is a mismatch, the
OR is elicited.

The numbers in Figure 7.2 indicate: (1) the specific pathways from
the sense organs to the cortex, (2) collaterals to subcortical structures
involving the reticular formation, (3) negative feedback from the comparator system to synaptic connections between the collaterals and the
subcortical structures, (4) ascending activating influences from the am-

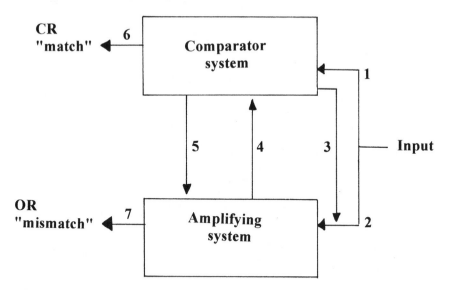

Figure 7.2. Schematic outline of Sokolov's (1963) neuronal model of the orienting
response (OR) and its relation to brain function. A conditioned response (CR)
occurs when the system finds a match between what is presented and what is currently active in the short-term memory store. (Adapted from Lynn, 1966.)

plifying system to the cortical comparator system, (5) pathways between the cortical and subcortical systems, (6) inhibition of the OR and elicitation of behaviors that coincide with the "matching process," and (7) elicitation of the OR after mismatch comparison (after Lynn, 1966).

In psychophysiological research, the electrodermal system is particularly indicative of the OR and habituation. Electrodermal responses demonstrate a dynamic interplay between a stimulus and the gradual buildup of a memory template in the brain when the stimulus is repeated. However, the OR and its subsequent habituation can also be elicited in several other response modalities, including cardiovascular, EEG, and ERP responses (see Chapters 10–12).

As argued by Siddle (1991), in a general sense, most theories of orienting and habituation can be divided into two-stage (or comparator) theories and one-stage (or noncomparator) theories. Öhman's (1979a) and Sokolov's (1963) models are both based on comparator theories. A noncomparator theory, in which habituation is explained as a change in the neuronal pathways intervening between the stimulus and the response, was suggested by Groves and Thompson (1970). These examples illustrate a common difference between the two types of theory: comparator theories are usually couched in information-processing terms, whereas noncomparator theories are usually couched in neurophysiological terms.

Allocation of Processing Resources

A central assumption of modern psychophysiological theories of orienting and habituation is that the allocation of processing resources for the elicitation of the OR is determined by a limited-resource central processing mechanism (Öhman, 1979a; Kahneman, 1973). Models operating under this assumption are collectively called *information-processing theories*. Allocation of processing resources implies, among other things, that attention is focused on the orienting task to the extent that less resources are allocated to the processing of other, simultaneous tasks.

Dawson and his colleagues (e.g. Dawson, Schell, Bears, and Kelly, 1982; Dawson, Filion, and Schell, 1989a) have investigated this topic in experiments that presented two simultaneous tasks to the subject.

Dawson et al. (1989a), for example, asked subjects to count the number of the longer of two different tones. Tones to be counted were the "task-relevant" tones, those to be ignored the "task-irrelevant" tones. The investigators confirmed that the orienting responses to the task-relevant tones were larger and less rapidly habituated than the responses to the task-irrelevant tones.

Öhman's Model

Öhman (1979a; see also Öhman, 1983) is perhaps the most imaginative advocate of linking electrodermal phenomena to cognitive processes by using the OR as a key mediating variable. A major premise of Öhman's model is that an OR is elicited whenever a stimulus causes a shift from *automatic* to *controlled* processing. Controlled processing requires the allocation of processing resources, notably a shift of attention. The model further suggests that events encountered in a familiar environment will be matched against memory templates in associative, short-term memory.

In Öhman's model there is an important distinction between automatic, preattentive processing of a stimulus and controlled, resource-limited processing. Preattentive processing leads to identification of a stimulus, but resource-limited processing implies that a limited set of the available memory store is allocated to further processing of the stimulus. Öhman furthermore labeled the available subset of the memory store the *short-term memory*. Combining these two suggestions results in a theory of orienting as follows: An OR is elicited when the automatic, preattentive processing fails to find a match for the stimulus in the short-term memory store, and it represents a request for allocation of processing resources in a central, capacity-limited channel. When the stimulus get into the capacity-limited channel, a search of long-term memory for related representations is initiated. If the stimulus matches a significant, or salient, long-term memory representation, the central channel is activated and relevant information is retrieved from the long-term memory store and activated in the short-term memory store.

As long as matches are successful and as long as the stimulus is not associated with significant other events, the stimulus will have little effect on behavior and conscious experience. Should a novel, unex-

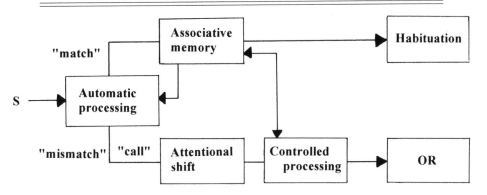

Figure 7.3. Simplified schematic of Öhman's (1979) model of orienting and habituation, based on an information-processing approach to the OR. See text for further details. (Adapted after Öhman, 1979a, with permission from the author.)

pected event occur, however, no matching template is available in the short-term memory, and this mismatch will result in a "call" for central processing resources. The demand for resources is associated with a shift from an automatic to a controlled mode of information processing for evaluating the stimulus. It is this shift from automatic to controlled modes of processing which causes the elicitation of the OR and is reflected in an increase in both tonic and phasic EDA. Öhman's OR model is shown in Figure 7.3 (adapted from Öhman, 1992).

Amplification and the OR

Another way of looking at the OR and habituation based on a cognitive-neuroscience approach is seen in Figure 7.4. In this model, a stimulus is matched against a stored template in associative memory. The amplification subsystem, involving limbic structures, boosts output from associative memory. If information activated in associative memory has emotional salience (stimulus significance), this input causes the amplification subsystem to boost the signal that is sent to higher cortical control systems, involving attentional gating.

If the signal is boosted enough, it may interrupt the execution of ongoing action plans. The amplification subsystem adds force, or valence, to the input to the cortical control subsystem.

There are two kinds of amplification valence—arousal valence and

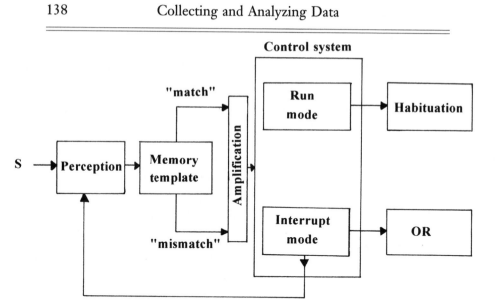

Figure 7.4. This OR model reflects a perspective that focuses on differences in modus operandi of a suggested frontal lobe control system (with *interrupt* and *run* subsystems) and amplification at the limbic level. S = stimulus input.

novelty or "surprise" valence—and it is worth distinguishing between two kinds of inputs to the limbic amplification subsystem: *arousal valence* is the emotional information associated with a specific piece of information, whereas *novelty valence* is associated with a change in the environment. Novelty-valence amplification primarily affects the orienting response. Thus, the OR reflects a stimulus input that is amplified to a level at which it interrupts ongoing activity—or, in other words, to the degree that it elicits "surprise." When a stimulus is repeated, the amplification subsystem boosts its associated action plan progressively less strongly. Habituation is thus dependent on the gradual buildup of a memory template of the stimulus, through repeated stimulus presentations, where less and less of the output from associative memory is boosted to activate the control systems in the frontal cortex.

Another dimension of orienting and habituation is the amount of significance, or *signal value*, a stimulus may have (Barry, 1982; Spinks and Siddle, 1983). A stimulus gets more signal value as a consequence of being paired with a significant unconditional stimulus (see Öhman, 1983), as a consequence of increasing arousal-valence amplification.

Cortical Control Systems

In this model (Figure 7.4) two cortical control systems for orienting behavior may be suggested. First, an *interruption* subsystem inhibits one action and allows a new action plan to be executed. The interruption subsystem operates when it receives an input that has an amplification significance higher than the ongoing plan. If, for example, you hear your child cry when you have just begun eating, the eating plan would probably be interrupted by a "go help the child" plan that was activated in associative memory and boosted by the amplification subsystem. It may be argued that the interruption subsystem is implemented in the left dorsolateral prefrontal cortex. Hugdahl and Nordby (1994) have provided evidence that the interruption subsystem relies in large part on inhibitory attentional processes, which shut down other processes, like ongoing action plans.

An OR will be elicited whenever the output from the amplification system is intense enough to interrupt ongoing action plans. The gradual buildup of the memory template will result in a corresponding decrease of the intensity of the amplification output signal, until there is a perfect match and the output signal is no longer intense enough to interrupt the ongoing activity in the control system. In this case the control system continues in the run mode, which constitutes the second subsystem, the *run* system. A continuous run mode is what characterizes habituation: there is no interruption of ongoing activity when the stimulus is presented, and no shift of attention. A sudden change in a stimulus parameter, however, would immediately disrupt the match between the memory template and the stimulus, resulting in a boosted signal from the amplification system, an interruption of ongoing actions, and a shift of attention. These processes characterize the *reinstated* orienting response, in which case dishabituation of the previously habituated OR will occur.

The control subsystems in the frontal cortex receive input from associative memory via the amplification subsystem, which is a limbic system. Thus, perceptual information may become "meaningful" because it has been matched to appropriate information in associative memory. A particularly important kind of information sent from associative memory specifies action plans. These plans are like programs in a computer: they specify a sequence of steps that can be taken to achieve a specific goal. This information is sent to control subsystems, which inhibit some plans and activate others; only activated plans actually lead the efferent subsystems to produce responses (cf. Kosslyn et al., 1995; Goldman-Rakic, 1987, 1988).

Defensive Responses

A defensive response (DR) is similar to the OR but differs with respect to the types of events that elicit it. The DR is elicited by high-intensity stimuli, which have an inherent emotional valence (Graham and Clifton, 1966). It is associated with the inhibition of sensory input and does not habituate upon repeated stimulus presentations. The DR reflects *arousal amplification*—an interruption of action plans due to increased arousal from limbic structures and the reticular formation.

A DR is usually differentiated from an OR by an analysis of cardiovascular response patterns, particularly heart-rate changes and vasomotor responses (see Chapter 10). Electrodermal activity may also vary according to the type of response, orienting or defensive, causing the activity. Edelberg (1972) suggested that palmar recordings are linked to DR, while dorsal recordings from the hand are linked to orienting behavior (OR). The reason for this distinction is the differential contributions by the sweat duct and the suggested duct membrane in orienting and defensive responses. In the cardiovascular system, DRs are characterized by an accelerated heart rate, ORs by a decelerated heart rate (Graham and Clifton, 1966).

Classical Conditioning

This description and discussion of classical conditioning is concentrated on human conditioning. Few references are made to the vast animal literature that makes up a separate branch of research on the psychology of learning.

Classical conditioning is a form of learning in which a weak sensory stimulus gains signaling qualities through repeated associations with a strong stimulus. The associative process thus transforms the weak stimulus into a conditioned stimulus (CS), which elicits a response similar to that elicited by the strong stimulus (the unconditioned stimulus, UCS). The change in behavior that follows the presentation of the UCS is called the *unconditioned response* (UCR), and the response that accompanies the temporal pairing of the CS and UCS is called the *conditioned response* (CR).

A different type of conditioning is a procedure known as *evaluative conditioning* (Martin and Levey, 1987; Baeyens, Eelen, Crombez, et al., 1992). Evaluative conditioning is a kind of referential learning, resulting from the unconscious registration of co-occurrences of neutral and valenced events. At the subjective level, it may give rise to "intrinsic" changes in CS valence. At the level of the underlying representational structure, it is based on an association between CS and UCS representations. This implies that the activation of the CS activates the UCS representation in the brain—or, put another way, that the subject "unconsciously" thinks about the UCS (Baeyens et al., 1992). An interesting feature of evaluative conditioning is that it may provide valuable new insights for our understanding of several emotional disorders, including phobias, sexual disorders, and obsessive-compulsive disorders (Baeyens et al., 1992).

Evaluative conditioning has two features that distinguish it from, for example, electrodermal differential conditioning: it appears without conscious awareness of the stimulus contingencies, and it does not extinguish after repeated presentations of the CS alone after conditioning has occurred. A typical evaluative conditioning experiment might require the subject to sort pictures of faces into those that are liked, disliked, and neutral (sorting occurs on a scale from $+100$ to -100 for very much liked to very much disliked, with 0 for the neutral faces). A subset of the neutral-rated faces are then presented together with either the most-disliked or the most-liked faces (this part of the experiment is the conditioning phase). In a third step the neutral subset is presented together with other neutral faces. The subject is then again asked to rate his or her judgment of the neutral faces. A typical result is that those faces originally rated as neutral and then presented together with the disliked faces get a lower rating when the subject is tested again after the conditioning phase. Similarly, neutral faces that were presented together with the liked faces get higher ratings.

The choice of terminology in classical conditioning reflects a "behavioristic" heritage (e.g., Spence, 1960), but the concept's origins in theories of behaviorism should not preclude its use in the study of cognitive functions, like attention and short-term memory, which mediate the building up of a learned association (cf. Öhman, 1983). Conditioning may also be a prototype for the study of brain functions involved in unconscious acquisition of knowledge (cf. Lazarus and McCleary, 1951). Classical conditioning allows for temporary behavioral and physiological adaptations to an ever-changing environment. It also plays an important role in many psychopathologies, including anxiety disorders (Seligman, 1971); in the modulation of immune-system reactivity (Ader and Cohen, 1985); in substance abuse (Stewart et al., 1984; Hugdahl and Ternes, 1981); and in placebo responses (Turkkan and Brady, 1985), just to mention a few.

Although research on classical conditioning in humans has a long history in psychology and psychiatry (Turkkan, 1989), however, little is yet known about the brain mechanisms involved in the response. For example, recent data suggest that the two hemispheres of the brain differ not only in the perceptual analysis of sensory stimuli but also in the formation of associations in memory (Johnsen and Hugdahl, 1991). In another important series of experiments, Daum and her colleagues (Daum et al., 1989, 1993) have shown rather dramatic effects of brain lesions on classical conditioning in humans. Classical eyelid conditioning was investigated in groups of patients with damage to hippocampal or cerebellar structures. Simple tone-airpuff conditioning or two-tone discrimination learning were found to be unimpaired in patients with damage to the temporal lobe, which included hippocampal lesions. Performance on a conditional discrimination task, in which reinforcement of a CS tone was contingent upon the color of a preceding light, however, was severely disrupted in this patient group. Patients with cerebellar lesions had a diminished capacity for acquiring conditioned eyelid responses during tone-airpuff conditioning, though their electrodermal conditioning seemed intact. Daum's data support neuroanatomical models of classical conditioning that relate (motor) CS-UCS associative learning to cerebellar circuitry and possibly more complex forms of conditioning to hippocampal mediation.

That non-motor conditioning may involve brain circuitries different from those involved in motor conditioning was also shown in a recent positron-emission tomography (PET, see Chapter 13) study (Hugdahl, Kosslyn, Berardi, et al., 1995), which showed increased blood flow in several areas in the frontal and temporal cortex, particularly in the right hemisphere, during extinction of a conditioned response.

Traditions in the Study of Conditioning

Among the different approaches that researchers have taken to conditioning, three basic traditions can be discerned. The first is the *reflexology* tradition, in which conditioning was seen as a tool for the study of peripheral stimulus-response (S-R) connections. This was the major behavioristic approach taken in the United States in the first two decades after the Second World War (see Kimble, 1961, for an example).

A second tradition used conditioning to study cognitive processes involved in associative learning. This is the cognitive tradition (Davey, 1987; Dawson and Schell, 1982). More recently, there has been a renewed interest within this tradition to focus on brain functions involved in conditioning.

The third tradition is called the *implicit learning tradition* because of its focus on the unconscious, automatic processes involved in human classical conditioning (Öhman, 1986; Öhman, Fredrikson, Hugdahl, et al., 1976; Lazarus and McClearly, 1951).

The Influence of Behaviorism

The behavioristic tradition is probably to blame for the neglect among Western researchers of the storage and retrieval of conditional associations in the human brain. In contrast, it may be of interest to recall Pavlov's (1927) original view of conditional learning as a theoretical tool for explaining the functioning of the cortical hemispheres. For Pavlov, studies of conditional learning provided insights into the functional properties of the nervous system, and particularly the cerebral hemispheres. This means that Pavlov looked at the CR as a result of a stimulus-stimulus (S-S) association, not a stimulus-response (S-R) association, which was later adapted as the model for associative learning among Western behaviorists (cf. Spence, 1960). Pavlov argued that when two cortical areas in the brain are excited, the areas of excitation will expand until they merge, as an excitation focus (Windholz, 1992). This theory would also hold for the case when, for example, a word is associated with a light, and then the light is paired with an UCS that elicits a CR. The CR will in this case also be elicited by the word. Pavlov called this phenomenon an "association of associations." In other contexts it has variously been labeled "higher-order conditioning" or "second-order conditioning" (cf. Rescorla, 1980).

For higher-order conditioning to occur, a CS must be paired with a UCS a number of times and then act as a UCS itself. The old CS is then presented after the new CS has been presented. A version of higher-order conditioning is semantic generalization, what Pavlov called the "second signal system." Semantic-generalization studies have shown that a response can be conditioned to the *meaning* of a stimulus rather than to the stimulus itself (Razran, 1961). For example, if a response is conditioned to the number 4, a conditioned response (CR) can be elicited also to stimuli such as $\sqrt{16}$ or 8/2. It is as if the brain is responding to the concept of "fourness" rather than to the physical stimulus. Following these lines of arguement, a recent view of classical conditioning stresses the correlation between the CS and the UCS as an important mediator of the establishment and representation of an association in the brain.

The Rescorla-Wagner Model

Rescorla and Wagner (1972) and Rescorla (1980) have argued that in order for an association to occur, the CS must provide unique information about the presence of the UCS. Another way of saying this is that the CS predicts the occurrence of the UCS. The importance of this point for the more modern views of conditioning is that concepts related to attention, expectancy, and memory are stressed, that is, an information-processing view is emphasized (cf. Öhman, 1983; Davey, 1987). A process-oriented view of conditioning also provides a basis for relating conditioning to brain function.

At the core of the Rescorla-Wagner theory is the assumption that merely pairing a CS with a UCS is not sufficient to produce classical conditioning. Instead, the establishment of a conditioned response depends on the relative predictiveness of the CS for the presence of the UCS. The CS will gain in associative value to the extent that it provides information about the occurrence (or non-occurrence) of the UCS. An example may make this clear: if for each of three presentations of the CS the UCS will also be presented, and the UCS will never be presented in the absence of the CS, the CS has 100 percent predictive value for the occurrence of the UCS. If the UCS is also presented in between and after the three CS presentations, however, the CS will have 0 percent predictive value, because the UCS occurs as often in the presence as in the absence of the CS. Thus, although the number of CS-UCS pairings remained constant (3) in the two scenarios described above, the predictive value of the CS varied dramatically.

The Rescorla-Wagner model bridges traditional conditioning and newer theories of cognitive learning, as exemplified in the learning rules used in computer simulations of neuronal networks. Consider the following equation from the Rescorla-Wagner theory:

$$\Delta V_x = \alpha_x \beta (\lambda - V)$$

The basic idea is that each subsequent CS-UCS pairing will produce smaller and smaller increments in learning, until an asymptotic level is reached. This produces a negatively accelerated learning curve. Change in the conditioned value of a CS is dependent on the CS-UCS pairings, whether the UCS is expected or not, and whether the CS has been part of other stimulus configurations in the past that have been paired with the UCS. V represents the total associative strength of all stimuli in the situation. Δ means "change," and so ΔV_x indicates the change in associative strength of stimulus x (CS). λ represents the asymptotic level of associative strength reinforced by the UCS. If $\lambda = 0$, then the UCS no longer produces any increments in associative strength on the next trial. In the example in the formula above, λ can be equated with the UCS, as x may be equated with CS. α and β are variables that affect the rate of associative change and can vary between 0 and 1. Alpha (α) represents the salience of the CS (x) and beta (β) represents the salience of the UCS. V can be both positive and negative: positive values of V correspond to conditioned excitation, while negative values correspond to conditioned inhibition.

Research Paradigms

There are a variety of different approaches and procedures to study human classical conditioning. For the purposes of this chapter, however, it will be sufficient to review two basic experimental procedures, or paradigms. A *paradigm* is a general concept covering both the independent and dependent variables and their temporal and spatial relationships within a single experiment.

The Within-Subjects Paradigm

In an experiment with a *within-subjects* paradigm, also called a "differential conditioning paradigm," each subject serves as his or her own control. Two different CSs are randomly mixed during the acquisition or associative phase of the experiment. The two stimuli are usually within the same sensory modality but differ with respect to content, shape, or pitch. One of the two CSs, the CS+, is paired with the UCS, and the other, the CS−, is not. If the response that follows the presentation of the CS+ is greater than the response following CS− presentations, conditioning is presumed to have occurred.

A potential disadvantage with the traditional within-subjects design is that the CS− may be "conditioned" to the absence of the UCS, that is, it will be learned as a safety signal. In order to circumvent this problem, a special case of the within-subjects design is to have the UCS "randomly" associated with the CS−. This means that the CS− will not predict the occurrence of the UCS, since it occurs as often without the UCS as together with the UCS, but it will not act as a safety signal either, since the UCS occasionally occurs with the CS−.

As shown in Figure 7.5, there are typically three phases of the within-subjects design: a habituation or preconditioning phase; an acquisition or conditioning phase; and an extinction or postconditioning phase. The purpose of the habituation phase is to habituate the orienting response to the CS before the conditioning proper begins. The acquisition phase is usually the pairing of the CS+ and UCS and, as a result, the acquisition of the CR. The extinction phase is typically the test phase: the researcher tests how long after the CS-UCS pairing phase it is still possible to detect differential responding to the CS+ and CS−.

The Between-Subjects Paradigm

In the standard *between-subjects* paradigm, there is a single CS and one group of subjects is presented with contingent CS-UCS pairings, in which the UCS follows the presentation of the CS. The other group receives only CS presentations, or it may receive noncontingent presentations of the CS and UCS (the CS and UCS are not paired together). For conditioning to have been demonstrated, responses in the

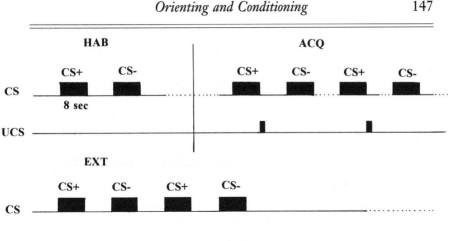

Figure 7.5. A model of differential classical conditioning in a within-subjects paradigm, during habituation (HAB), acquisition (ACQ), and extinction (EXT) phases of a conditioning experiment. The conditioned stimulus (CS) is presented for 8 seconds; the CS that is paired with the unconditioned stimulus (UCS) is the CS+, the nonpaired CS is the CS−. Conditioning is evaluated as the difference in responding to the CS+ and CS−, particularly during the extinction phase of the experiment. When the interstimulus interval is long enough (usually greater than 5 seconds), conditioning can also be evaluated with electrodermal measures during the acquisition phase.

contingent CS-UCS group should be greater than responses in the CS-alone, or noncontingent CS-UCS, group.

If an experiment is to demonstrate that conditioning has occurred, the associative process should be distinguished from nonassociative processes, like arousal and perceptual priming. For this reason an experiment should control for sensitization, or "pseudo-conditioning" (Kimble, 1961). Pseudo-conditioning occurs when the UCS primes or sensitizes a particular brain state such that the subject responds to any weak stimulus that is presented, whether it has been paired with the UCS or not. Effects of this type are controlled for in the "between-subjects" design by comparing responses in the CS-UCS noncontingent group with the CS-UCS group.

Also for the between-subjects paradigm (Figure 7.6), there are three phases: habituation, acquisition, and extinction, respectively. In general, the within-subjects paradigm is to be preferred to the between-subjects paradigm, since each subject acts as his or her own control

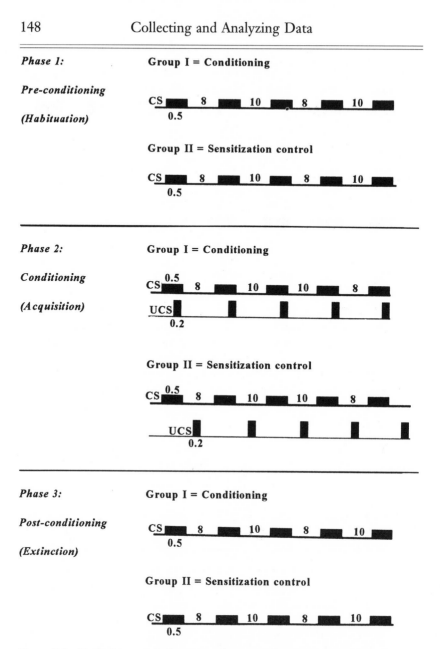

Figure 7.6. Typical setup of a between-subjects conditioning experiment. Numbers between and during CS presentations indicate examples of the interstimulus interval and stimulus duration in seconds, respectively.

and fewer subjects are required. When conditioning cannot be evaluated on a trial-for-trial basis, as when brain-imaging techniques like PET is used (Chapter 13), the between-subjects paradigm is to be preferred.

In animal conditioning experiments, CR strength usually increases as a function of the number of CS-UCS presentations (Kimble, 1961). This is not true, however, for human autonomic conditioning, where an initial increase in responding is followed by a dropoff with further pairings. The decline in response magnitudes across trials has been explained as a gradual buildup of conditioned inhibition (Kimmel, 1966) or as reduction of UCS arousal (Lykken, 1968). Figure 7.7 reproduces typical acquisition and extinction data from a human differential conditioning experiment.

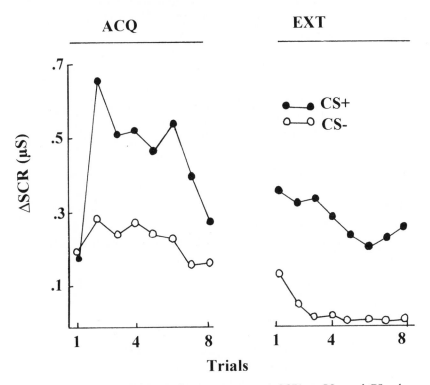

Figure 7.7.   Changes in skin-conductance response (ΔSCR) to CS+ and CS− during acquisition (ACQ) and extinction (EXT) phases of the experiment. Note that the response amplitudes to the CS+ are larger than those to the CS−, indicating conditioning.

Awareness and Classical Conditioning

A major issue in psychophysiological studies of classical conditioning is whether conditioning can occur without conscious awareness of the CS-UCS relationship. Common folklore would argue that conditioning is an automatic, nonconscious form of learning, often acquired in a single traumatic experience—as one "learns," for example, to avoid a certain road after having been in a car accident on this road. Other examples of unaware conditioning are taste aversions to foods or drinks that have made one sick and the aversion to certain smells and sights experienced by cancer patients in chemotherapy (see Chapter 4).

Despite these examples, the experimental study of conditioning has long recognized the cognitive nature of human classical conditioning (see Davey, 1987; Dawson and Schell, 1987). There is actually strong experimental evidence that conditioning is not a simple habit-learning system but that it involves complex interactions between cognitive processes, all requiring conscious awareness of the reinforcement contingencies. Instructions to the subjects that the UCS will no longer follow the presentation of the CS will help to speed extinction, although some forms of fear conditioning do not lend themselves to cognitive processing (Hugdahl and Öhman, 1977). Dawson and Schell and their colleagues (e.g., Dawson and Schell, 1987; Marinkovich, Schell, and Dawson, 1989) have employed a technique in which the CS-UCS relationship is masked and the subject has continuously to estimate the subjective probability that a certain CS will be followed by the UCS. The general finding from these studies is that conditioning does not occur prior to the moment when the subject understands that the CS is followed by the UCS, and thus that the CS has a signaling function for UCS occurrence.

Preattentive, Unconscious Conditioning

Although classical conditioning is "cognitive" in the sense that it requires the allocation of limited processing resources (Dawson and Schell, 1982), this does not mean that all conditioning is "conscious." *Cognitive* is not synonymous with *conscious*. For example, implicit memory, even though it is an unconscious process, is cognitive in the sense that it requires processing resources, though different from those devoted to explicit memory. Öhman (e.g., 1986) has developed a technique in which the CS during the extinction phase of the experiment is presented for only 30 ms and in addition also is masked by a neutral stimulus. Using this paradigm to study conditioned SCRs to happy and angry faces, Öhman has shown that differential conditioning persists during the extinction phase of the experiment, although the subject is unaware of seeing the CS.

In a more recent series of experiments, Öhman (1992) has demonstrated that both acquisition and elicitation of conditioned responses can occur unconsciously. The general procedure in these experiments was the differential conditioning paradigm, where an unconditioned stimulus (an electric shock) followed the CS+. For one group of subjects, the CSs were followed by a masking stimulus at an effective masking interval. These subjects, then, remained unaware of which of the CSs was followed by the shock. To test for conditioning effects, the CSs were presented nonmasked during an extinction series. For another group of subjects a long interval was added between the CSs and the mask, which thus allowed conscious perception of the CSs. Control groups were presented only the masks during acquisition or were exposed to random presentations of shock and CS mask, before nonmasked extinction as in the conditioning groups. The results clearly demonstrated conditioning effects to masked CSs, but only if the CS was an angry as opposed to a happy face. Thus, nonconscious, automatic conditioning effects were obtained.

Prepared Conditioning

Over the years, Öhman and his colleagues (e.g., Öhman et al., 1976) have found that normal, nonphobic subjects show greater electrodermal responses when conditioned to phobic scenes than when conditioned to neutral scenes. (For typical SCR data from these experiments, see Figure 7.8.) Electrodermal responses are "automatic" in the sense that they are normally outside of voluntary control (except, perhaps, after biofeedback training). These experimental results are an indication that biological evolutionary factors may still today influence the conditioned learning of a fear response. Prepared conditioning is used when explaining the selectivity of, e.g., snake and spider phobias. See Chapter 8 for further details.

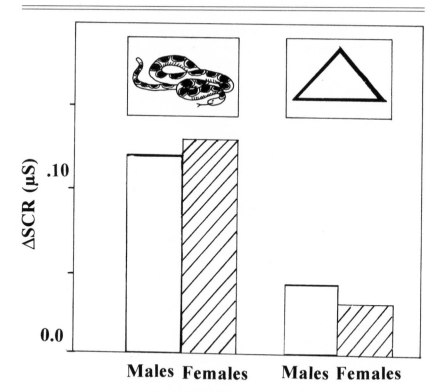

Figure 7.8. Skin-conductance changes (ΔSCR) in male and female subjects exposed to pictures of snakes and triangles (as CS+) during the extinction phase of a classical conditioning experiment. These responses illustrate the typical "preparedness effect" in human conditioning: the subjects show larger conditioned responses to potentially fearful stimuli, like snakes and spiders, than to neutral objects, like geometric shapes. See Chapter 8 for further details.

Brain Laterality and Conditioning

Hugdahl and Brobeck (1986) also found evidence for unaware conditioning in a dichotic listening experiment, but only when a verbal CS+ was presented to the left hemisphere. In a conceptually similar study, Hugdahl, Kvale, Nordby, and Overmier (1987) found stronger conditioning when a nonverbal CS was presented to the right hemisphere. Thus, it seems as if the left hemisphere of the brain conditions better to words and the right hemisphere conditions better to nonverbal and (negative) emotional stimuli. Interestingly, using a similar experimental situation as Öhman used in his studies of preattentive processes in conditioning to happy and angry faces, Johnsen and Hugdahl (1991) found that this kind of unconscious, implicit, learning occurred only when the face-CS was presented to the right hemisphere.

The Corteen and Wood (1972) Study

In a now classic paper, Corteen and Wood (1972) showed that conditioned electrodermal responses to city names, presented via earphones, could be elicited without the subject being aware of the presentation of the CS. In a first phase of the experiment, subjects received an electric shock as the UCS contingent upon the presentation of the verbal CS (the city name). During this phase, the subject's attention was directed toward the words heard in the earphones. In a second phase, a dichotic shadowing task, the conditioned words were presented in the left ear while prose passages were presented in the other ear. The subjects were instructed to attend only to the prose passages in the right ear and to ignore the left-ear input. The previously shocked city names elicited more electrodermal responses than control words when presented in the nonattended ear during the dichotic phase of the experiment.

Corteen and Wood interviewed their subjects after the experiment to make sure that they had not been aware of the city names presented in the nonattended left ear. Although postexperimental interviewing techniques may, for good reasons, be questioned as measures of awareness (see Dawson and Reardon, 1973), the results by Corteen and Wood (1972) indicate that the elicitation by a CS of a previously learned CR is possible without the subject being aware of the occurrence of the CS. This finding was later replicated by Wright, Andersson, and Stenman (1975), Dawson and Schell (1982), and Martin, Stambrook, Tartaryn, and Biehl (1984). However, Wardlaw and Kroll (1976) failed to replicate the original Corteen and Wood (1972) experiment.

What is important in the present context is the remarkable fact that previous interpreters of the discrepancy between the original Corteen and Wood (1972) study and the replication by Wardlaw and Kroll (1976) have failed to notice the procedural differences, and especially the relation of such differences to hemispheric asymmetry. Corteen and Wood (1972) presented the critical CSs in the left ear on all trials for all subjects and the prose passages in the right ear, whereas Wardlaw and Kroll (1976) *counterbalanced* CS presentations between the ears. According to my argument in the previous section, paying attention to a verbal passage presented under dichotic competition should be more effective in the right ear (initial left-hemisphere input), whereas conditioning to a shock-reinforced CS having an emotional aspect should be more effective in the left ear (right-hemisphere input). Thus, by counterbalancing the presentation of the CSs and the prose passages between the ears, it is not surprising that Wardlaw and Kroll (1976) failed to find evidence of unaware conditioning. That brain asymmetry may play a role in unaware conditioning in humans was first suggested by Dawson and Schell (1982), who found indications of a different mode of responding related to attentional shifts when the unattended words (CSs) were presented in the right ear as opposed to the same CSs presented in the left ear.

Summary

In this chapter, orienting and defensive responses and principles of human classical conditioning have been reviewed and discussed. Theories of orienting responses that focus on an information-processing perspective and memory-template models are treated at length. In particular, Sokolov's and Öhman's models of the orienting response and habituation are described and compared. A third model, framed within a cognitive-neuroscience perspective, is also described.

Human classical conditioning is described as both a cognitive learning process, requiring conscious awareness of stimulus contingencies, and as an implicit, biologically prepared process that may not require conscious recognition of the learning situation. Research paradigms are described for between-subjects versus within-subjects experiments. It is argued that classical conditioning may engage different structures in the left and right hemispheres of the brain, depending on the nature of the conditioned stimuli and the conditioning situation.

8

Clinical Applications of Electrodermal Activity

In Chapters 6 and 7, changes in electrodermal activity (EDA) have been described as evidence of changes in an individual's cognitive or emotional state. Electrodermal responses are indications of attentional processing, an aroused mental state, the processes of orienting and conditioning, and other processes. In this chapter I turn to a discussion of the applications of EDA recordings in psychological research and clinical practice. EDA data are used to explore the physiological changes that may accompany altered states of consciousness, psychopathology (both in the major psychoses and anxiety states), psychosomatic disorders, alcohol and substance abuse, and brain damage.

Altered States
Hypnosis

Hypnosis is an altered state of consciousness characterized by a shift of attention: attention may become either more focused or more diffuse, depending on the particular hypnotic induction. An individual in hypnosis is usually highly absorbed with a narrow attention span and has an ability for dissociative experiences (freeing one's mind from the body). Individuals who are highly susceptible to hypnosis also do well at making mental images and may be more "holistic" in their cognitive strategies. Using EDA, Gruzelier and Brow (1985) found that subjects in hypnosis showed faster habituation of skin-conductance responses to repeated presentations of tone stimuli than nonhypnotizable subjects. Highly hypnotizable subjects in the normal state also had lower skin-conductance levels and fewer spontaneous fluctuations than nonhypnotizable subjects. Thus, both state and trait effects were shown in the electrodermal measures.

Looking at differences between the left- and right-hand recordings as indices of relative hemispheric activation, Gruzelier and Brow (1985) found that highly hypnotizable subjects shifted from a left-hemisphere dominance in the nonhypnotic state to a right-hemisphere dominance during hypnosis (see also Gruzelier, Brow, Perry, et al., 1984). Although of potential importance regarding the underpinning neurophysiological mediators of hypnosis, the data by Gruzelier and Brow (1985) could also be indications of of a generalized relaxation response associated with lowered arousal and activation.

Unconsciousness

In Chapters 6 and 7 it was noted that electrodermal responding is primarily linked to conscious, attentive information-processing. This should not be taken to mean, however, that skin-conductance responses cannot be elicited in an automatic mode, as in an unconscious state. Bjornaes et al. (1977) showed that brain-damaged patients in coma showed signs of habituation to repeated tone presentations. Moreover, Tranel and Damasio (1985) demonstrated that patients with prosopagnosia, the inability to recognize visually the faces of familiar persons (family members or famous persons), nevertheless exhibited larger skin-conductance responses to familiar than to unfamiliar faces. Similarly, Putnam, Zahn, and Post (1990) found that patients with multiple personality disorder (MPD) had distinct electrodermal-response profiles to tone presentations when they shifted from "one personality to another." MPD patients often show strong subjective dissociations between their different "personalities," one state not being consciously aware of the other state. Despite this, electrodermal responses "followed" one state to the other, thus demonstrating unconscious automaticity in the elicitation of electrodermal responses.

Psychopathology
Schizophrenia

EDA has been used as a "marker" for schizophrenia and for differences in psychotic behavior in subgroups of schizophrenic patients (Öhman, 1981; Venables, 1983; Zahn, 1986; Dawson, Neuchterlein, and Adams, 1989b). The most robust finding with regard to EDA is the phenomenon of "nonresponding" in schizophrenic patients to the first two or three stimulus presentations (Bernstein, Frith, Gruzelier, et al., 1982), although there is considerable heterogeneity among patients. Bernstein (1970) suggested several factors, among them stimulus intensity and modality, that may affect nonresponding. Other authors have made a more direct distinction between *responders* and *nonresponders* among heterogeneous schizophrenic patients (see Öhman, 1981, for an overview). About 50 percent of schizophrenic patients are characterized by electrodermal nonresponsivity to sensory stimuli: they exhibit neither the initial OR on the first stimulus presentation nor the subsequent habituation. The other half of the patients are either normally responsive or *hyperresponsive* (a hyperresponsive shows an OR larger than normal OR and does not habituate as expected).

Venables (1983) suggested that EDA disturbances in schizophrenics are related to disturbances in limbic structures, or in the dopaminergic and cholinergic transmitters, thus linking schizophrenia to dysfunction of the structures in the central nervous system that control EDA. He also suggested that in some instances disturbances in electrodermal responding may be related to dysfunctional attentional processes in schizophrenia, linking electrodermal responding to attention through the orienting response. Although the literature is not entirely conclusive on this issue, the results point toward the theory that nonresponders are more chronically psychotic and that hyperresponsivity may be an indicator of psychotic episodes (Dawson, 1990).

Markers of Genetic Risk Factors

Another major area in schizophrenia research to which EDA measurements have been applied is in the search for risk factors for schizophrenia (e.g., Mednick and Schulsinger, 1974). Following children of schizophrenic and nonschizophrenic mothers, Mednick and Schulsinger (1974) have shown that the recovery rate of electrodermal responses to tone stimulation predicts psychiatric breakdown. A very short recovery rate may be a prognostic tool in identifying children at risk for schizophrenia.

Some studies have also found a positive correlation between risk for schizophrenia and season of birth, those being born during the winter and early spring having higher correlations with later onset of schizophrenia (Boyd et al., 1986). Explanations for this association have usually centered on a higher risk among these babies for viral infections, vitamin deficiencies, exposure to extreme ambient temperature, and the like. In a recent paper, Öhlund et al. (1990) also found that schizophrenics born in the season of excessive risk (winter-spring) were characterized by significantly lower electrodermal activity (more nonresponders) and more negative clinical symptoms than those born in the season of nonexcessive risk. The results of this study fit nicely with other reports of poorer outcome and more serious symptomatology among schizophrenic electrodermal nonresponders (e.g., Öhman et al., 1989).

Laterality in Schizophrenia

In 1973 Gruzelier reported more spontaneous responses in the right than in the left hand in institutionalized schizophrenics tested in a habituation paradigm (see also Gruzelier and Venables, 1974). This finding was followed up in another paper (Gruzelier, 1983) by the suggestion that different schizophrenic syndromes may be related to overactivation most probably in the left hemisphere and to asymmetry of limbic functioning. Flor-Henry (1969) has also reported bilateral electrodermal asymmetries in schizophrenia, arguing that the observed differences between the left- and right-hand recordings reflect a dysfunction of the cerebral hemispheres. This paper described an association between dysfunction in the left temporal lobe and schizophrenia, a suggestion that has received support in more recent studies using PET brain imaging (Chapter 14) and standard neuropsychological tests.

Specifically, Flor-Henry found that psychotic patients with predominantly schizophrenic symptoms had a high incidence of epileptic foci in the left temporal lobe, while patients with manic-depressive symptoms had a high incidence of foci on the right side of the brain. Arguing that habituation of the orienting response is associated with activity in temporal lobe and limbic structures, Gruzelier (1973) hypothesized that schizophrenic patients should be dysfunctional in OR habituation, and that there should be differences between the left- and right-hand EDA recordings. The results confirmed that there were fewer responses in the left hand in schizophrenic patients. However, Iacono (1982) and Bernstein et al. (1981) failed to show any lateral differences in skin conductance as a function of psychotic behavior, thus leaving the issue of laterality of dysfunction in schizophrenia unsettled.

Depression

Another major affective disorder is *depression*, and particularly unipolar and bipolar depression. Unipolar depression is sometimes associated with *endogenous* depression, indicating a more consistently depressive mood over time. Bipolar depression is characterized by mood swings between deep melancholia and manic behavior. Iacono, Lykken, Peloquin, et al. (1983) showed that both unipolar and bipolar depressive patients had smaller-than-normal SCRs to tones presented several times.

Thus, reduced EDA may be a marker of susceptibility to affective disorders. Interestingly, there were no differences between the patient groups and normal controls on EEG markers, indicating that there may be a specific autonomic mediator in depression. A word of caution, though: much of the research on EDA in depression is confounded by the fact that many of the antidepressant drugs are also anticholinergic, and thus central effects may be confused with peripheral effects.

Anxiety and Phobic Fears

Anxiety states correlate positively with spontaneous fluctuations of skin-conductance responses (Lader and Wing, 1964). Moreover, anxious patients continue to respond to repeated stimulus presentations; that is, they do not show the expected habituation (Lader, 1967). Some authors have suggested that the failure to habituate to repeated tone presentations among patients with anxiety disorders is related to lowered sensory thresholds for innocuous stimuli; these patients, in other words, show a defensive response instead of an orienting response (Hart, 1974).

In a series of experiments in the late 1970s and early 1980s, Öhman, Fredrikson, and Hugdahl (e.g., 1978) showed that a "phobia-like" electrodermal response could be conditioned in normal subjects who were exposed to stimuli (pictures of snakes and spiders) paired with a brief electric shock to the hand. Subjects were conditioned either to snakes and spiders or to neutral slides, like pictures of geometric shapes or flowers and mushrooms, but larger responses were elicited to the fear-relevant stimuli. The experimental situation is illustrated in Figure 8.1.

From the standpoint of traditional learning theory, the content of the conditioned stimulus, whether fear-relevant or not, should not influence the strength of conditioning as long as the CS is closely paired with the UCS in time and space (see Chapter 7). The studies by Öh-

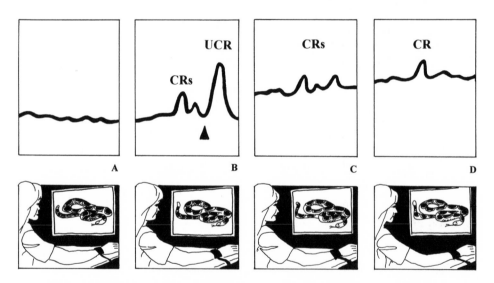

Figure 8.1. Experimental setup of the studies performed by Öhman, Fredrikson, Hugdahl, and Rimmö (1976) on prepared or phobic conditioning. There are no skin-conductance responses *(A)* late in the habituation (CS only) phase of the experiment. When the CS is followed by a shock (the unconditioned stimulus), conditioned responses (CRs) and an unconditioned response (UCR) are established *(B)*. Effects of the conditioned acquisition procedure remain on early *(C)* and late *(D)* extinction trials, when only CS presentations are made, as during the habituation phase. See also Öhman (1979b).

man and his associates showed that this was obviously not the case, a result that has implications for modern learning theories.

These experiments were inspired by the "preparedness theory" of learning originally proposed by Seligman in 1971. In contrast to traditional learning theory, the preparedness theory argued that certain behaviors were more easily learned because of an evolutionary "history" of adaptiveness. Thus, pictures of snakes were more easily associated with a brief shock (like a snakebite), than were the pictures of triangles and shock because of an evolutionary "predisposition" for the brain to associate snakes rather than triangles with an aversive event.

Clinically, phobias are directed to a limited number of events and situations. The most common phobias are the fear of open spaces (*agoraphobia*), closed spaces (*claustrophobia*), heights (*acrophobia*), small animals such as spiders (*arachnophobia*), strangers (*xenophobia*), the sight of blood and body organs (*hematophobia*). All of these "stimuli" were real dangers to our Stone Age ancestors. Open spaces lacked protective cover for hiding from predators, snakes and spiders are remnants of the large reptiles who were the natural predators of the first mammals, and strangers or outsiders might be hostile. Today, however, having the same fear of strolling through a town square as our ancestors had of the savannah is an irrational behavior. Likewise, reacting with a fall in blood pressure and fainting when looking at someone else's bleeding wound is an irrational response; the same reaction would be an adaptive response, however, to a wound of one's own, because it would prevent excessive blood loss.

Thus, it seems as if the brain, through conditioning, is sometimes deceived into misinterpreting what it perceives and reacting with the same physiological response to nondangerous situations as it must respond to real danger. Seligman (1971) suggested that perhaps there are more snake phobics than car phobics because there is a biologically based residual association that links stimuli related to potentially fearful scenes like snakes with aversive events but no association as yet that links aversive events with objects made by modern man. Marks (1981) told the story of a young girl whose hand was slammed in the door as she was stepping out of a car. At the same moment, she spotted a snake in the ditch beside the road where the car had stopped. Despite the fact that her pain was caused by the slamming of the door, she later developed a snake phobia. In terms of prepared classical conditioning, the pain caused by the slammed door was associated with the sight of the snake rather than with the car. In terms of traditional learning theory, she should have developed a car phobia rather than a snake phobia, because of the close proximity between the conditioned stimulus (the door closing on her fingers) and the unconditioned response (pain).

Psychopathy and Antisocial Behavior

A well-known observation is that psychopaths do not show elevated skin-conductance responses in anticipation of an aversive event (e.g., Hare, 1978; Raine and Venables, 1984). Lykken (1957) attributed the hyperactivity observed in psychopaths to low anxiety and arousal in situations of threat and excitement. This observation would fit the clinical view that psychopaths "lack emotional involvement" when committing a crime or when being aggressive.

Theoretically, the "cold cognition" exhibited by psychopaths committing a violent or antisocial act has been linked to an inability to exert inhibitory control of behavior (Schalling, 1978). Moreover, Fowles (1993) related EDA hyperactivity in psychopaths to the distinction between *labiles* and *stabiles* (Crider and Lunn, 1971; Katkin and McCubbin, 1969). Labile individuals show frequent electrodermal spontaneous fluctuations at rest and rapid habituation of the OR. Stabile individuals, on the other hand, show few spontaneous fluctuations and habituate poorly. Stabiles are usually characterized as having difficulty in maintaining attention over time and sustaining vigilance in boring situations. Stabiles also more easily fall asleep in monotonous situations, which is a characteristic trait also in psychopaths. The labile-stabile distinction may thus reflect individual differences in attending to and processing relevant information. Interestingly, Crider (1993) also suggested that stabiles may be antisocial, impulsive, and irresponsible, linking the concept of individual differences in electrodermal responsiveness to criminality and antisocial behavior (see also Fowles, 1993).

Alcohol and Drug Dependence

Laberg (1990) summarized his research on autonomic concomitants of cravings for alcohol and drugs and their relationship to relapse behavior. A basic assumption is that cues in the environment may become conditioned to various aspects of the physiological and psychological effects of alcohol. These cues later serve as conditioned stimuli for the elicitation of craving responses in drug-dependent subjects, leading to instrumental relapse into drinking. Thus, the change in autonomic reactivity acts as a "trigger" for drinking or drug taking.

Siegel (e.g., 1979) proposed that conditioned drug responses are opposite the effects of the drug itself (the drug acting as the unconditioned stimulus). Siegel called such opposite responses "compensatory conditioned responses." In the case of an alcoholic, a compensatory conditioned drug response is most probably aversive in effect ("hangover response"), leading to a craving for alcohol and subsequent alcohol intake. An adequate treatment regimen would therefore be to extinguish any signs of autonomic reactivity *specifically* linked to the sight, smell, and taste of alcohol cues in the environment.

A first step toward validating such a model would be to show that drug addicts have unique autonomic response patterns to drug-related versus neutral stimuli, a pattern not shared by control subjects. This has been studied by several authors (Laberg, Hugdahl, Stormark, et al., 1992; Eriksen and Götestam, 1984; Sideroff and Jarvik, 1980). The general picture is that both skin-conductance response amplitudes and number of spontaneous fluctuations were increased in drug addicts viewing short presentations of pictures with drug-related content. Interestingly, Stormark, Laberg, Bjerland, et al. (1995) showed that olfactory stimuli had an even stronger effect on alcoholics; the smell of beer, for example, elicited larger ORs in alcoholics than in social drinkers. This is an interesting study because it points to the possibility that sense modalities other than the visual may be more potent in "triggering" a conditioned craving response in a dependent subject.

Psychosomatic Disorders

As mentioned in Chapter 3, patients with specific psychosomatic disorders may have pathological autonomic regulation of, for example, gastrointestinal activity. In the case of psychosomatic ulcer, for instance, the autonomic disorder might lead to increased acid secretion in the stomach.

The notion of autonomic dysregulation in duodenal ulcer was studied by Kopp (1984). Kopp compared ulcer patients with healthy controls on a battery of auditory and visual tasks, involving word associations, color-word discrimination, and repeated presentations of brief bursts of noise. The ulcer patients had overall different electrodermal response patterns (slower SCR recovery and increased response amplitudes) that indicated enhanced sympathetic activation in ulcer patients even in situations not involving food digestion or taste stimuli.

Other Brain and Nervous System Dysfunctions

Electrodermal responses may reflect both central and autonomic nervous system dysfunction in patients with brain lesions. For example, Heilman, Schwartz, and Watson (1978) found that both skin-conductance level and skin-conductance responses were lower in patients with right-sided parietal lobe damage—this is the typical hemineglect syndrome (see Chapter 2). The failure of these patients to show adequate electrodermal responses in a situation of relatively strong stimulation (brief shocks) is an important piece of evidence for explaining hemineglect as a phenomenon of arousal as opposed to perceptual processing. The main argument is that patients with hemineglect have dysfunctional arousal systems, involving the reticular formation, which make them unable to orient and attend to certain aspects of the environment. The absence of skin-conductance responses in situations of orienting and arousal may thus support an arousal explanation of hemineglect.

Furthermore, Zoccolotti, Sabini, and Violani (1982) found that patients with left-hemisphere lesions had normal skin-conductance responses to emotional pictures, but patients with right-hemisphere lesions only showed the initial orienting response, followed by rapid habituation. This led the investigators to suggest that the right hemisphere of the brain is involved in functions of emotional arousal linked to the autonomic component of emotion and affect.

This idea was elaborated by Hugdahl and Johnsen (1993) (see Chapter 7), who suggested not only that may initial orienting and habituation to an emotional stimulus be specifically regulated from the right side of the brain, but also that emotional conditioning and implicit learning may be controlled from the same brain areas.

Oscar-Berman and Gade (1979), using electrodermal recordings, showed clear effects on autonomic functioning in patients with degenerative nerve diseases like Korsakoff's syndrome and Huntington's chorea. Iacono (1985), reviewing the literature on genetic markers for Huntington's chorea, found that among several other physiological responses, electrodermal nonresponding held promise as an indicator of this disease. There is a 50 percent probability that an offspring of a person with Huntington's chorea will develop the disease, so the search for physiological markers is an important and admirable task. Rogozea and Florea-Ciocoui (1982), similarly, showed failure to orient and habituate to a series of tones in a group of patients with encephalitic epilepsy. Their results point to the intimate relationship between electrodermal responding and the functional integrity of higher cortical functions. Boucsein, Valentin, and Furedy (1993) compared patients with Parkinson's disease with old and young normals on skin-conductance responsivity in a tone-habituation paradigm. They found that the age difference was more important than the neurological disorder when the groups were compared.

Other studies have shown that EDA can distinguish mentally retarded and autistic children from normals, once again providing evidence that skin-conductance measures may be reliable and sensitive indicators of brain dysfunctions, and not only of emotional responsivity in the autonomic nervous system. In a similar vein, Canavan (1990) has proposed that psychophysiological measurements are especially suited for the detection of those aspects of Parkinson's disease that are not so easily monitored clinically. For example, EMG recordings may be used to track muscular tremors and rigidity, and autonomic measures, like SCR, may be used for more accurate monitoring of autonomic dysfunctions that typically accompany Parkinson's disease.

Studies of electrodermal responsiveness in patients with brain lesions and brain disorders have provided important theoretical and methodological advances in the application of psychophysiological techniques in untraditional areas. EDA may be specifically linked to detailed accounts of cognitive functioning involving not only arousal but also attention, perception, and memory. Thus, by using EDA when evaluating cognitive dysfunction in patients with brain lesions, the investigator gains an arsenal of new measures to supplement the traditional neuropsychological tests.

Summary

The uses to which electrodermal responsivity may be put in clinical practice and research on diseases and disorders were discussed in this chapter. Applications of EDA measurements have been made in the field of psychopathology, including schizophrenia, depression, and anxiety. Electrodermal recordings have also been used for the study and diagnosis of other major disorders, like psychopathy, psychosomatic diseases, and alcoholism, especially in research trying to specify underlying mechanisms for a disorder. Patterns of orienting and habituation, used by researchers to localize left-hemisphere dysfunctions through recordings of responses to auditory stimuli from the left and right hands, have been used as risk markers for schizophrenia. Much research has also been directed toward the identification of electrodermal nonresponders, as an indication of vulnerability to schizophrenic episodes. EDA is used in alcohol research to assess specificity of arousal patterns in alcoholic patients exposed to alcohol-related stimuli (like a beverage advertisement). EDA measurements are also used to study psychosomatic disease and to assess the extent and localization of lesions in brain-damaged patients. The chapter also includes a discussion of EDA recordings in individuals with anxiety disorders, particularly with reference to specific phobias.

9

The Heart and Blood Circulation

Cardiovascular changes are a very common, and a very apparent, effect of changes in one's psychological state: the heart rate increases as a result of excitement, for example. This chapter will introduce the reader to cardiovascular psychophysiology by focusing on the structural and functional properties of the heart and the blood circulation. We begin with a description of the organs: the heart and the blood vessels. From there, the pathway for the circulation of blood in the body and brain is outlined, as is the nervous innervation of the heart. The methods used to make psychophysiological recordings of different cardiovascular functions, such as the electrocardiogram, are treated at length, along with examples from psychophysiological research. After this introductory material, the next chapter will turn to applications of psychophysiological techniques and methods in the study of psychological factors in hypertension, visceral perception, the Type-A behavioral pattern and heart disease, as well as cognitive processes indexed by cardiovascular parameters.

The Circulatory System

The heart can be regarded as a hollow structure divided into four different chambers: a left and a right *atrium*, and a left and a right *ventricle*

167

(see Figure 9.1). On both the left and right side, blood flows into the heart through the atrium and then into the ventricle, from which it is expelled by contraction of the walls of the ventricle. The contraction, or pumping action, of the different chambers of the heart is caused by the contraction of the heart's thick layer of cardiac muscle tissue, the *myocardium.*

Several valves between the atria and the ventricles, and between the

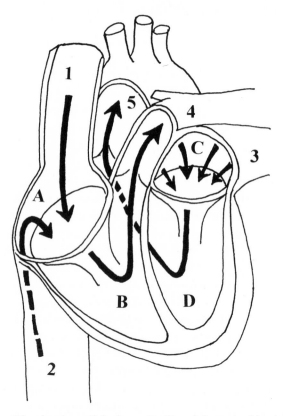

Figure 9.1.   The chambers of the heart *(A–D)* and the major blood vessels *(1–5)*. Blood that has circulated throughout the body returns to the heart via the superior vena cava *(1)* and inferior vena cava *(2)*. It enters the right atrium *(A)* and then the right ventricle *(B)*. The right ventricle contracts and expels the blood into the pulmonary artery *(4)*, which carries it to the lungs for oxygenation. Oxygenated blood returns to the heart via the pulmonary vein *(3)* and enters the left atrium *(C)* and then the left ventricle *(D)*. When the left ventricle contracts, it expels the blood into the aorta *(5)* with great force.

ventricles and the arteries, prevent the backward flow of blood. These are named for their shapes: the valve between the right atrium and ventricle is the *tricuspid valve* ("three cusps"); the valve between the left atrium and ventricle is the *bicuspid valve* ("two cusps") or the *mitral valve* (because it also resembles the Pope's hat, named in Latin the *mitra*); and the other two valves are the *semilunar valves* ("half-moons"). The semilunar valve that prevents blood from flowing back into the left ventricle once it has been ejected into the aortic artery is the *aortic valve*. The other semilunar valve, the *pulmonary valve*, prevents blood from flowing back into the right ventricle from the pulmonary artery.

Blood propelled out of the heart flows in arteries, and blood traveling back to the heart flows in veins. Between arteries and veins are networks of very small blood vessels called *capillaries*. The main vessels for the venous return of blood to the heart after it has been deoxygenated in the various tissues in the body are the superior vena cava and the inferior vena cava. The largest arteries are the *aortic*, which transports oxygen-rich blood from the left ventricle to the various parts of the body, and the *pulmonary*, which transports low-oxygen blood from the right ventricle to the lungs. The heart itself is supplied by blood through the coronary arteries that surround the heart muscle. This is called the *coronary circulation*, in contrast to the *systemic circulation* (which supplies the entire body) and the *pulmonary circulation* (which is the circulation between the heart and the lungs). When one or several of the coronary arteries becomes occluded through deposition of fatty and calcified plaques inside the vessel wall, an ischemic heart attack may result because of tissue death in the area supplied by the occluded artery. If the damage is large enough, the heart may not be able to pump enough blood to the body and brain, with death as the result. The various clinical syndromes that may result from occlusion of the coronary arteries are collectively called *coronary heart disease* (CHD).

Blood returning to the heart from the systemic circulation enters the right atrium, as noted above, through the superior vena cava and the inferior vena cava. At the same time, oxygenated arterial blood from the lungs enters the left atrium through the pulmonary vein. When the pressure in the right and left atria is high enough, the bicuspid and tricuspid valves open up and blood rushes into the right and left ventricles, respectively. A few milliseconds later, the ventricles begin contracting, forcing an increase in the intraventrical pressure. The increase in pressure soon forces open the semilunar valves, and blood is forced out into the aortic artery from the left ventricle, and into the pulmonary artery from the right ventricle. From the pulmonary artery, blood travels to the lungs, where it is oxygenated, and then back to the heart through the pulmonary vein. From the aortic "arch" (see Figure 9.1), oxygenated blood is transported to all parts of the body and brain, via the arteries and then the small capillary vessels. Oxygen is taken up by the cells and carbon dioxide, a waste product of cells, is taken up by the blood in a process of diffusion through the capillary walls. From the capillaries, deoxygenated blood flows back to the heart through the venous system, finally reaching the right atrium, and a new cycle begins.

Although both the right and the left ventricles propel blood into their respective arteries by contracting, the left ventricle must contract with much greater force than the right ventricle. That is because the left ventricle supplies blood to the entire body whereas the right ventricle supplies the much smaller area of the lungs. The walls of the left ventricle are therefore thicker and have more muscle fibers than the walls of the right ventricle.

The Sinoatrial and Atrioventricular Nodes

Inside the upper wall of the right atrium is a mass of specialized heart-muscle tissue called the *sinoatrial node*. The sinoatrial (SA) node is often referred to as the "pacemaker" of the heart because it is a major regulator of the beating frequency of the heart. The SA node depolarizes spontaneously at a rate of between 70 and 80 beats per minute (bpm). The action potentials initiated at the SA node then spread to muscle cells all over the heart. These potentials first cause the atria to contract. After a few milliseconds (see Figure 9.2), the electrical activity spreads to the *atrioventricular node*, located at the base of the right atrium in the wall between the atrium and the ventricle. From the atrioventricular (AV) node, the depolarization spreads to the ventricles through the *bundle of His*, which is a thick bundle of nerve fibers in the middle wall of the heart. At this point the ventricles contract.

The conduction of action potentials in the heart occurs in milliseconds, as shown in Figure 9.2, from the depolarization of the SA node to the depolarization of other parts of the heart. Note that the excitation spreads first to the base of the ventricles. This allows the ventricles to

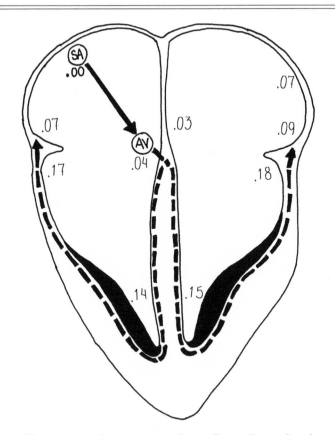

Figure 9.2. The nerve impulse is transmitted via cell-to-cell spreading from the sinoatrial node (SA) in the right atrium to the atrioventricular node (AV), also in the right atrium. From the AV, the impulse is transmitted first through the bundle of His to the apex of the ventricles, and finally to the walls of the ventricles via the Purkinje fibers. With the arrival of the impulse, the ventricles contract from the bottom up. The numbers in the figure indicate the relative delay, in seconds, in the arrival of the nerve signal from its initiation in the SA node.

contract "from the bottom up," which they must do to force blood out into the aortic and pulmonary arteries.

Innervation and Regulation of the Heart

The SA and AV nodes are innervated by the vagus nerve of the parasympathetic nervous system. The vagus nerve has an inhibitory effect on the heart: it reduces the beating frequency when it is too high with regard to metabolic and other demands. The vagus nerve has its major action in the range of 60–100 bpm. The SA node, atria, and ventricles are also innervated by sympathetic nerve fibers that have an excitatory effect: sympathetic activity increases the beating frequency, especially in the range 100+ bpm.

Regulation of heart activity is mediated through the release of acetylcholine (ACh) from the parasympathetic nervous system (vagus nerve). Sympathetic action on the heart is mediated through the release of norepinephrine at the nerve endings, which activates beta-adrenergic receptors in the SA node and in the walls of the heart. A common treatment for patients with high blood pressure (hypertension) is the administration of a drug that blocks the action of norepinephrine on the SA node, a so-called *beta-blocker*. In addition to the effect on heart rate, sympathetic action on the heart has a primary effect of increasing the force of contraction. The frequency and force with which the heart beats is also regulated by direct hormonal influences through the action of epinephrine.

The Cardiac Cycle

The beating sequence of the heart, from the time blood enters the atria until it exits through the ventricles, is called a *cardiac cycle*. A cardiac cycle is shown graphically in Figure 9.3, beginning just after a ventricular contraction, when venous blood returns to the atria. This period, the *diastole*, is the part of the cycle when the pressure in the ventricles and aortic artery is at its lowest, and blood pressure measured at this point is the *diastolic blood pressure*.

After the ventricles fill with fresh blood, the atrioventricular (AV) valves close, to prevent the blood to flow backward. This causes a rapid increase in intraventricular pressure, which soon causes the bicuspid, aortic valve to open and forces blood into the aortic arch. With the opening of the aortic valve and the rush of blood into the arch, the pressure in the aortic artery also rises rapidly, as will the pressure in the ventricle. This part of the cycle is the *systole*, and blood pressure measured at this point is the *systolic blood pressure*. When the blood has been ejected and the ventricle is almost empty, the pressure falls off and finally the aortic valve closes, to prevent blood from flowing back into the ventricle from the aorta. Then the cycle begins again.

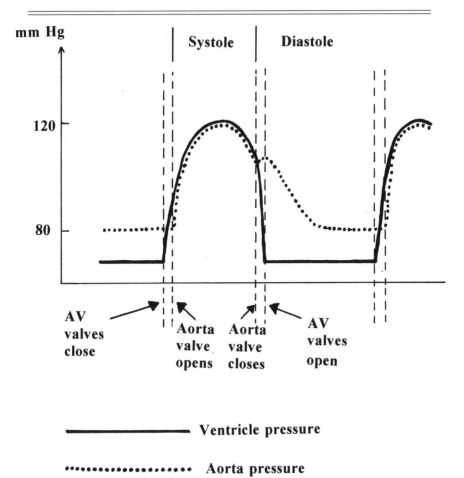

Figure 9.3.   The sequence of events in a cardiac cycle from the closing of the atrio-ventricular valves *(AV)* to their closing at the beginning of the next cycle. Blood pressure in the ventricles is indicated as a solid line, blood pressure in the aorta as a dotted line.

Cardiac Output and Stroke Volume

At rest, the heart pumps about 75–100 ml blood for every cardiac cycle. Thus, an individual with a heart frequency (pulse) of 65–70 bpm will, roughly speaking, pump 5 liters of blood per minute, or almost 3 million liters per year. The largest quantity of the body's blood at any given point in time is in the systemic circulation (80–90 percent), while the remaining volume is in the pulmonary circulation.

Cardiac output is the quantity of blood pumped by a ventricle, usually measured from the left, in one minute, and it is normally in the excess of 5 liters. The amount of blood ejected at each beat of the heart is the *stroke volume*, which, as mentioned above, is normally 75 ml, or 0.075 liters. Thus, cardiac output = stroke volume × heart rate (for example: 5.025 l/min = .075 ml/beat × 67 beats/min). During physical exercise, the cardiac output will be tripled or even more, depending on the nature of the exercise. However, the supply of blood to the brain is fairly constant, independent of exercise or resting conditions.

Cardiac output changes as both heart rate and stroke volume change. Heart rate and stroke volume are regulated by the nervous system and hormonal control, as noted above, but stroke volume is also determined by the amount of blood available for pumping. This property is described by an important principle in cardiology known as *Starling's law of the heart* (or the Frank-Starling law): "Within physiological limits, the heart pumps all the blood that comes to it without allowing excessive damming of blood in the veins." This means that if less blood is returned to the heart, as may happen after excessive bleeding, less blood will be pumped out because the heart will contract with less force. When more blood flows to the heart, the heart muscle is stretched more, with the consequence that it contracts with more force when it ejects the blood into the aortic arch. The ability to change the force of contraction in response to changes in the force of filling is also called *autoregulation of the heart*.

Recordings of Heart Activity
The Electrocardiogram

The contractions by the atria and ventricles in a cardiac cycle can be monitored on an *electrocardiogram* (ECG), a recording from electrodes on the skin of electric currents generated by the action potentials of the cardiac-muscle cells. An ECG is read from left to right (see Figure 9.4). It begins with the contraction of the SA node at the very far left. The P wave represents the spreading of contractions over the atria, reaching into the ventricles. The QRS complex, which occurs about 140–160 ms after the P wave, is the contraction of the ventricles—that is, the actual systole phase. The peak contraction occurs near the peak of the R wave; thus, the time between two consecutive R waves gives an accurate measure of the frequency with which the heart beats. Following

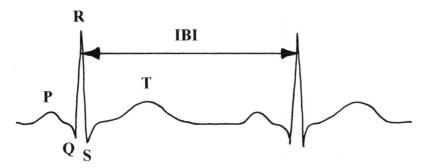

Figure 9.4. The interbeat interval (IBI) is measured as time elapsed, in milliseconds, between two successive R spikes in the electrocardiogram (ECG). The notations *P*, *Q*, *R*, *S*, and *T* denote the various phases in the contraction of the heart, as recorded in an ECG.

the QRS complex is the T wave, which represents repolarization of the ventricles in preparation for the next impulse to start a new cardiac cycle.

The time between the Q wave and the T wave is about 300 ms. Since the time between two successive R waves is about 850 ms when the heart rate is 70 bpm, the heart is in the repolarization mode longer than it is in the depolarization mode for each cardiac cycle. A simple formula for conversion of interbeat intervals (IBI), measured in milliseconds, to beats per minute (BPM) is:

$$BPM = (60 \times 10^3)/IBI$$

For example, if the IBI is 1,000 ms, the heart would have a frequency per minute of 60 bpm (60,000/1,000 = 60). Similarly, if the heart rate is 73 bpm, the corresponding IBI would be 821 ms (60,000/73). Thus, there is a reciprocal relationship between BPM and IBI: the longer the IBI, the slower the heart rate, and vice versa.

In psychophysiological research, measures of changes in heart rate as a function of stimulus presentation are usually based on the identification of successive R waves and the calculation of IBI for later conversion into BPM. In some instances, IBI rather than heart rate is used as the dependent measure, which means that the conversion into BPM may be omitted. The choice of heart rate or IBI (sometimes also called *heart period*) as the dependent measure has in most instances small effects on the results (Jennings, Berg, Hutcheson, et al., 1981), and a choice between the two should be determined by the experimental question asked. However, sometimes heart period may be a more appropriate measure—as, for instance, when the underlying physiological mechanisms that control changes in heart rate are being investigated (see the discussion below of vagal tone).

Computer technology allows for fairly accurate identifications of R waves (usually the upward slope of the R wave is used) through the use of various triggering devices. Traditionally, a hardware "Schmitt-trigger" was used, but in most current psychophysiological laboratories the triggering mechanism is part of the computer software. Software "triggers" are based on the detection of the inflection point of the R wave to the nearest millisecond. Schmitt-triggering is operated by setting a voltage level that, when it is superseded by the voltage in the R wave, "triggers" calculation of the time to the next instance when the voltage of the R wave supersedes the trigger level. A problem with the use of traditional triggers is that they may be triggered by different voltage levels relative to the peak of the R wave. Another, and more serious, problem is that the trigger sometimes may detect the T wave in the ECG instead of the R wave, thus marking off an extremely short IBI. This error is, however, often automatically corrected when computer scoring is used.

There are several different ways of placing the ECG electrodes to get a recording of the various components in the ECG (see Figure 9.5). The electrodes may be located in an arrangement known as the *standard leads*. The first standard lead, Lead I, consists of placing one electrode on the left arm and one on the right arm. Lead II is the placement of one electrode on the right arm, the other on the left leg. Lead III is the placement of one electrode on the left arm, the other on the left leg. The standard leads differ in how the polarity is selected, and Lead II produces the largest voltage, which may be important for subsequent computer analysis of heart rate and other parameters. A clinical measurement of heart activity may require that another arrangement be used: the different leads may tell the cardiologist the extent and type of damage in the heart, since abnormalities of the heart affect some leads but not others.

In addition to the standard leads, six chest leads are often used in

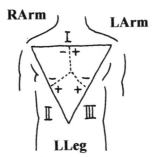

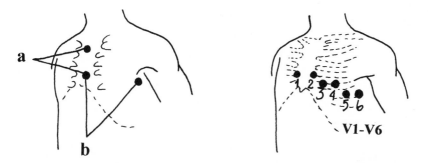

Figure 9.5. Possibilities for the placement of electrodes for recording an ECG. There are three standard leads *(top):* standard Lead I = left and right arms; standard Lead II = right arm and left leg; standard Lead III = left arm and left leg. For chest leads *(bottom right)*, the electrodes are placed across the rib cage (indicated V1 to V6). Two possibilities for bipolar chest leads are indicated *(bottom left):* two electrodes placed on the sternum *(a)*, or two electrodes placed on each side of the heart *(b)*. Bipolar chest leads are common in psychophysiology because they maximize R-wave amplitude.

routine ECG investigations. For psychophysiological studies, the most popular electrode placements are *bipolar chest leads*—for example, one electrode on the sternum, the other to the lateral left of the heart. Bipolar chest leads are preferred because they provide good R-wave amplitudes, sometimes at the expense of a detailed complete ECG curve. As noted above, however, the detailed analysis of the various components of the ECG curve traditionally is in the domain of clinical cardiology, where the focus is usually on the detection of irregularities and dysfunctions of the heart.

Impedance Cardiography

Although the measurement of R–R intervals (or IBI) is the standard technique in cardiovascular psychophysiology, new techniques, like impedance cardiography, are now available which provide noninvasive measures not revealed in the ECG. *Impedance cardiography* is a noninvasive technique for the measurement of, e.g., stroke volume, heart rate, and cardiac output. It measures the resistance (impedance), caused by blood cells, to an applied alternating current. The impedance of tissue is much less than that of blood cells. When there are more blood cells in a particular area, as when blood is ejected from the heart into the chest, the impedance of that area is smaller than when there are fewer blood cells in the area. Impedance is measured by passing a high-frequency electrical signal through the chest and recording changes in the current between electrodes placed on the chest and neck. The impedance will vary as a function of the volume of blood: it decreases with increased blood volume in the area. For measures of thoracic impedance (Kubicek, Karnegis, Patterson, et al., 1966; see also Jennings, Tahmoush, and Redmond, 1980), band electrodes are typically placed around the neck and the chest.

Measurement of different events in the cardiac cycle may be derived from measures of thoracic impedance. A pulsatile component, called the *impedance cardiogram* (ZCG), has been proposed as an index of stroke volume and cardiac output. From measures of stroke volume, values for other parameters have been calculated, including heart rate, myocardial contractility, and peripheral resistance (see Sherwood, Allen, Fahrenberg, et al., 1990, for an overview). An example of impedance cardiography, together with an ECG recording, is presented in Figure 9.6. The graph labeled dZ/dt in the figure is the first derivative of the pulsatile thoracic impedance signal that occurs during a cardiac cycle. The PCG is the *phonocardiogram*, which is a measure of the first and second heart sounds corresponding to the systole and diastole. PCGs provide important information for the measurement of systolic time intervals.

Hurwitz (1993) argued that although the theoretical and method-

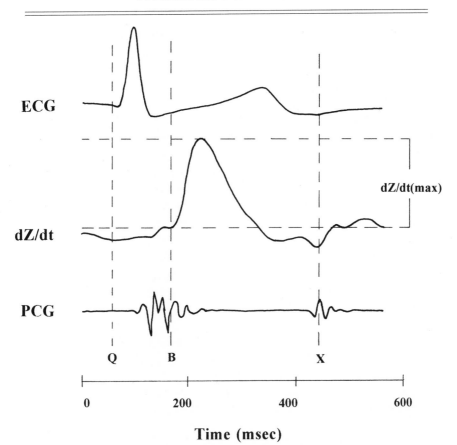

ECG

dZ/dt

dZ/dt(max)

PCG

Q   B   X

0   200   400   600

Time (msec)

Figure 9.6. Examples of an impedance cardiogram *(dZ/dt)*, a phonocardiogram *(PCG)*, and an ECG recording. (Adapted from Sherwood et al., 1990, with permission from the Society for Psychophysiological Research and the authors.)

ological bases for impedance cardiography remain somewhat controversial, and although there are instances of poor validity, the noninvasive aspects of the technique, as well as the potential applications in physiology, behavior, health, and disease, make this an interesting new technique in psychophysiology. It has, furthermore, been suggested that the cardiac impedance technique may provide a simultaneous measure of sympathetic and parasympathetic influences on the heart (Tursky and Jamner, 1982), although this is not at present generally accepted among cardiologists and cardiovascular psychophysiologists.

Heart-Rate Changes Following a Stimulus

Change in cardiac rate may be expressed either as the change in heart rate, measured in beats per minute, or as change in the heart period (HP), another term for the interbeat interval (IBI), measured in milliseconds. From now on we will be concerned only with an analysis of heart-rate change in real time. Psychophysiological investigations often compare poststimulus changes in heart rate second by second with the average heart rate during the last few seconds before the onset of the stimulus. The result is typically the tri- or biphasic heart-rate curve shown in Figure 10.5. This curve records, for 8 seconds, the second-by-second deviation in a subject's heart rate from the average heart rate during the last three prestimulus seconds. Suppose that the prestimulus heart rate was 72 bpm; then a heart rate of 70 bpm during the first poststimulus second would be plotted as -2 (70 $-$ 72), and so on for every second that heart rate is plotted.

When comparing the change in heart rate second by second from the point in time when the stimulus occurred, one is faced with the problem of weighing the relative contribution of two or more interbeat intervals occurring during the same second. A commonly used technique of weighing two or more interbeat intervals is illustrated in Figure 9.7. The stimulus occurs in the first interbeat interval (labeled a in the figure). In order to know the heart rate during the first second after the stimulus, the investigator must estimate the x_1 proportion of interbeat interval a and the y_1 proportion of interbeat interval b. The actual heart rate during the first poststimulus second is thus equal to: $(x_1 \times a) + (y_1 \times b)$. In the example in Figure 9.7, this is equal to (0.7 $\times$ 100 bpm) + (0.3 $\times$ 60 bpm) = 88 bpm, since the x_1 proportion of interbeat interval a is 0.7 and the y_1 proportion of interbeat interval b is 0.3 and heart rate is 100 bpm during interval a and 60 bpm during interval b. For the next second, the procedure is repeated, now weighting the x_2 proportion of interbeat interval b and the y_2 proportion of interbeat interval c, etc.

The Cardiotachometer

A cardiotachometer is a device that converts interbeat intervals into a continuous graphical display of heart rate. Traditionally, the cardiotachometer was installed beside the ECG amplifier in the polygraph,

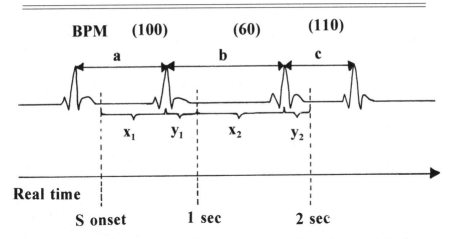

Figure 9.7. Weighted averaging of heart rate in a second-by-second analysis of changes in heart rate during stimulus presentation from prestimulus baseline average. *x* and *y* denote the proportions of two different heart beats occurring during one second. Heart rate at the first second after the stimulus may be calculated according to the following formula: $(x_1 \times a) + (y_1 \times b)$, which in the example used in this figure equals $(0.7 \times 100) + (0.3 \times 60) = 88$ bpm. In the second second after the stimulus, heart rate is $(x_2 \times b) + (y_2 \times c)$, which yields a heart rate equal to $(0.8 \times 60) + (0.2 \times 110) = 70$ bpm.

but it is seldom used today. The time between successive R waves was the input of the cardiotachometer, which graphed the data in a step-like pattern, with each step representing one heart beat in bpm (see Figure 9.8). The visual display was calibrated to cover the range of heart rates most likely to occur in a given setting. For example, the far left (or lower) end of the polygraph channel for the cardiota-chometer might be set to 50 bpm and the far right (or upper) end of the channel might be set to 100 bpm. If, for a given situation, the recording pen was moving in the middle of the polygraph channel, that would correspond to a heart rate of 75 bpm. Thus, the minimum and maximum calibrations correspond to the lower and upper limits of the cardiotachometer channel.

The upper portion of Figure 9.8 is a simplified ECG recording indicating successive R waves and the corresponding interbeat intervals (IBM) and beats per minute (BPM). The lower portion of the figure is the corresponding visual display of the cardiotachometer. It shows the actual timing of IBIs and BPMs in the ECG, providing an immedi-

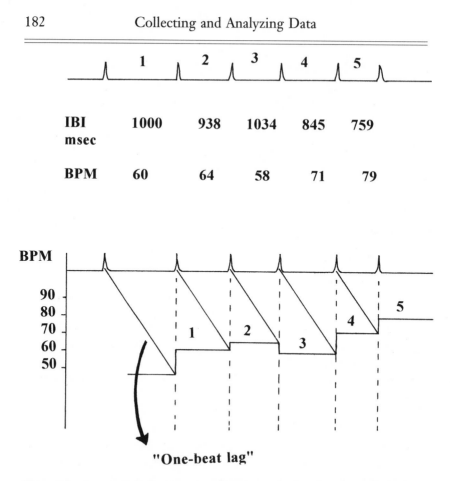

Figure 9.8. In a cardiotachometer recording, successive interbeat intervals (IBIs) are translated into heart rate in beats per minute (bpm). The upper trace shows five IBIs, with the corresponding R waves indicated as "spikes" in the ECG recording. The lower trace shows the actual cardiotachometer recording with its steplike shape for each beat of the heart. The formula for converting from IBI (in msec) to beats per minute is BPM = $(60 \times 10^3)/(\text{IBI})$. For the first IBI, for example, 60 = $(60 \times 1{,}000)/1{,}000$.

ate visual analogue in beats per minute to the spacing of the R waves in the ECG. The numbers to the left in the cardiotachometer display are the calibration scale, and the numbers in the middle of the display (1–5) correspond to the respective IBIs in the ECG. Note that the display of the "first" heart-rate measurement in the cardiotachometer occurs during the second IBI in the ECG, and so forth. This is the "one-beat lag" in data recording, which occurs because a stroke of the heart must first occur before it can be read by the cardiotachometer and must therefore be displayed after a delay of one beat in real time.

Vagal Tone and the Relationship between Respiration and Heart Rate

The effect of vagus-nerve activity on the heart, or *vagal tone*, is typically estimated from the *respiratory sinus arrhythmia* (RSA). RSA is a naturally occuring correspondence between variations in the respiratory rate and the timing between successive R waves in the ECG. It is used as a derived measure of respiratory-cardiac interactions, particularly the fluctuations in heart rate that coincide with respiration. As such, it is also a measure of vagal influences on the heart and, hence, a fairly accurate estimate of parasympathetic control of heart rate (Berntson, Caccioppo, and Quigley, 1993; Porges, 1986; Grossman and Svebak, 1987; Grossman, 1992).

It has long been known that vagal excitation of the SA node is weakened, or almost absent, during inspiration. This is evidenced by the short intervals between R waves (that is, between heart beats) during inspiration. During expiration, R–R intervals become longer, and heart rate decreases. This *arrhythmia*, or variability, in heart rate corresponds with the phase of respiration. If the vagal influence on the heart is pharmacologically blocked with atropine, which inhibits the action of the vagus nerve, heart-rate variability is reduced. Hence, the variability in heart rate between inspiration and expiration is believed to reflect the degree of vagal influence on the heart at any point in time in the cardiac cycle. Measures of RSA, or similar estimates of the respiratory-cardiac interrelationship, are thus sometimes referred to as studies of heart-rate variability (Porges and Byrne, 1992) or vagal tone (Porges, 1986).

There is currently some controversy regarding the most accurate method of quantifying RSA. One method is to record the shortest R–R interval, corresponding to inspiration, and the longest R–R interval, corresponding to expiration (Grossman and Svebak, 1987). Another is to use filtering techniques yielding time-series data of interbeat intervals, or heart periods, that reflect the beat-to-beat variability of the heart rate (Porges, 1986); a measure of RSA is then extracted from the overall heart-rate variability (HRV) in different ways (Porges, and Byrne, 1992; Byrne and Porges, 1993). The details of the arguments need not concern us here. It may suffice to say that Porges (1986) has argued that analysis of heart-rate variability through RSA/vagal tone is a reliable measure of parasympathetic influences on the heart, although Grossman (1992) cautioned that this may be so only when variations in respiratory patterns between individuals are corrected for. These influences are regulated from higher cortical centers and are related to cognitive and emotional events. Porges and Byrne (1992) have further argued that if vagal tone is an index of the functional status of the nervous system, then individuals with greater vagal tone would exhibit a greater range of competent behaviors. Similarly, medical complications that compromise the nervous system should result in an attenuation of vagal tone. For example, in studies of newborn infants, Porges (1988) found that healthy neonates with high vagal tone were less irritable. Others (e.g., Richards, 1988) have found that infants with higher vagal tone take a longer time to look at novel stimuli and that they habituate more rapidly to tone stimuli than do low-vagal-tone infants.

Heart Rate Power Spectrum Analysis

Heart rate power spectrum analysis (HRPSA) is a relatively new technique in psychophysiology based on an analysis of R–R intervals that has shown some promise in discriminating between parasympathetic and sympathetic effects on the heart within the same measure (see Porges and Byrne, 1992; Grossman, 1992). This, however, is also the subject of debate and controversy (Pagani, Lombardi, Guzetti, et al., 1986; Weise, Heydenreich, and Runge, 1987). It does seem to be agreed upon, though, that HRPSA is a reliable technique for assessing vagal, parasympathetic influences.

HRPSA is one of several techniques for analyzing heart-rate variability, or oscillations. The oscillations in heart rate have been shown to fall in three principal spectral peaks: a high-frequency component peaking around 0.2–0.4 Hz; a mid-frequency component peaking around 0.05–0.1 Hz; and a low-frequency component peaking around 0.04 Hz. In a simplified way, the high-frequency component has been considered a quantitative assessment of sinus arrhythmia, and found to be sensitive to vagal influences on the heart. The mid-frequency component may be considered a quantitative measure of the effect of the sympathetic nervous system on the heart (Pagani et al., 1986), and the low-frequency peak represents activity of both the sympathetic and parasympathetic divisions. This is, however, not agreed upon by all psychophysiologists. Some argue that the mid-frequency peak may be an index of sympathetic influences on the SA node only if vagal influences can be statistically removed (Weisz, Szilagyi, Lang, et al., 1992). It should also be noted that slow changes in heart rate (in the region of 0.05 Hz) may be related to body temperature rather than to direct influences of autonomic activity. Pagani et al. (1986) showed that the mid-frequency peak increased with enhanced sympathetic influences on the heart, and decreased after sympathetic activity was blocked by beta-receptor drugs. See Berntson, Cacioppo, and Quigley (1993) for further details on HRPSA.

HRPSA is a technique for displaying the distribution of the variability in the heart-rate signal as a power density spectrum using Fourier analysis. Figure 9.9 is an example of a graph of the different frequencies obtained after analysis of heart-rate variability over time.

Weisz et al. (1992) used the HRPSA technique in a study of hemisphere differences and heart-rate variability. Subjects were viewing a blinking light-emitting diode (LED) with either the right or left eye while heart rate and respiration were recorded. Weisz et al. (1992) argued that viewing with the left eye would activate the right hemisphere more, and vice versa. They found that the amount of heart-rate fluctuations in the mid-range frequency (0.07–0.13 Hz) was dependent on the hemisphere activated, and particularly linked to right-hemisphere activation. Thus, the authors concluded that the results had shown a right-hemisphere sympathetic effect on the heart.

Although these results are pioneering and interesting, because they relate lateralized cortical control of autonomic activity to heart rate, a caution regarding the unilateral stimulation is necessary. Monocular viewing does not necessarily involve a unique unilateral stimulation, since each eye has input to both visual cortices in the occipital lobe. In order to show unilateral stimulation of one hemisphere with visual stimuli, the visual half-field (VHF) technique (McKeever, 1986) is usually employed, meaning that the eyes are fixated on a point in the middle of the visual field while visual stimuli are briefly flashed either to the right or left of the midpoint fixation. If the presentation is brief enough to prevent eye movements, this technique will ensure that only

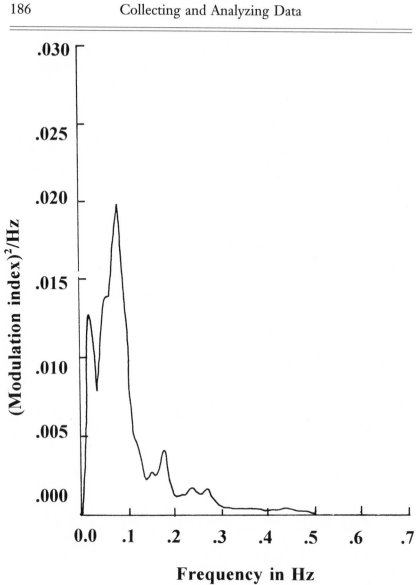

Figure 9.9.   Heart rate power spectrum analysis (HRPSA), or power density spectrum, with three peaks in the lower, middle, and higher portion of the spectrum. The different peaks in the power density spectrum are thought to reflect the activity of the sympathetic and parasympathetic branches of the nervous system.

the contralateral hemisphere is initially stimulated, although the information will reach the other hemisphere within a few milliseconds due to callosal transfer.

Anxiety Disorders and HRPSA

In a clinical application of spectral analysis of heart-rate variability, Friedman, Thayer, Borcovec, et al. (1993) found that patients with frequent panic attacks had reduced heart-rate variability but increased heart rate. Interestingly, patients with a phobia for blood showed an opposite pattern of responses when confronted with a stressor: increased heart-rate variability and reduced heart rate. These findings underscore the clinical utility of HRPSA as a measure of autonomic indices of psychopathology. The results are also pertinent to the discussion of stimulus-response specificity in Chapter 2.

T-wave Amplitude

The T-wave amplitude (TWA) of the ECG was suggested by Heslegrave and Furedy (1980) as an index of sympathetic action on the heart. In a later paper, Furedy and Heslegrave (1983) cited evidence that direct manipulation of sympathetic nerve impulses to the heart can result in attenuation or even inversion of the T-wave amplitude. The TWA was, however, put into question as an index of sympathetic activity by Schwartz and Weiss (1983), who argued that TWA is not consistently influenced by stimulation or blockade of the cardiac sympathetic nerves. Thus, the evidence has been questioned that TWA discriminates between the different receptors in the heart that are sensitive to sympathetic activity. The TWA has not been widely used in psychophysiological research over recent years, and it has not gained acceptance in general physiology as a valid measure of nervous control of the heart. A different measure, suggested by Verrier and Nearing (1994), is the analysis of repetitive patterns of T-wave amplitude *variation*, called *T-wave alternans*. T-wave alternans are suggested to be an index of vulnerability to cardiac failure.

Chaos Theory and Heart Function

Goldberger (1991) has suggested that the application of nonlinear dynamics and chaos theory to the analysis of regularities and irregularities of heart frequency may yield valuable information not otherwise seen in traditional mathematical models of cardiovascular function. Chaos theory is closely related to the concept of fractals, which is a geometric concept of irregularities hidden in regular and smooth geometric curves and shapes. A straight line may not be so smooth: if it is looked at with a microscope, it will show wrinkles and irregularities, with smaller wrinkles on the larger ones, and so on.

The use of fractal theory to analyze the irregularities of heart beats has added a new dimension to the analysis of ECG tracings in cardiovascular arrhythmias. For example, sudden death due to cardiac arrhythmia was long believed to occur because the beatings of the heart became chaotic and irregular. However, Goldberger and his associates have shown that the heart rates of patients just before sudden death are periodic and nonchaotic, whereas the variability of the *normal* heart follows algorithms predicted from fractal and chaos theory. The applications of chaos theory and nonlinear dynamics to cardiovascular functions are just beginning, and more research is needed before we may draw more firm conclusions about their relevance in psychophysiological research and cardiovascular practice.

Blood Flow and Blood Pressure

The flow of blood in a vessel is determined by the pressure exerted by the flow divided by the resistance of the vessel to the passing blood. That is: blood flow = pressure/resistance. Similarly, pressure = blood flow × resistance. The arterial pressure is thus determined by the product of cardiac output and total peripheral resistance. For flow calculations, the mean pressure is used. Arterial pressure includes both the diastolic pressure, which is the lowest pressure in the cardiac cycle, and the systolic pressure, which is the highest pressure in the cardiac cycle. The diastolic pressure normally varies between 80 and 90 mm Hg, while the systolic pressure varies between 120 and 140 mm Hg. A blood-pressure reading is usually expressed as the systolic pressure above the diastolic pressure, or as 120/80, to take an example. Women usually have lower blood pressure than men.

The *mean arterial pressure* (MAP), an important measure of the functional status of the cardiovascular system, is defined as the difference between the diastolic and systolic pressures plus 1/3 of the diastolic pressure. It is expressed in this way because the diastole lasts a little bit longer than the systole. The MAP is, though, an approximation, and the integral of pressure might be a better measure. The different concepts and equations related to the hemodynamics of the cardiovascular system are shown in Table 9.1.

Auscultation

Auscultation is the standard technique for measuring blood pressure. An inflatable cuff with a pressure gauge is wrapped around the upper arm of the patient or subject. A microphone is inserted in the cuff above the brachial artery, and a stethoscope is attached to the microphone. The cuff is then inflated so that it occludes the circulation of blood in the artery and no Korotkoff sounds may be heard in the stethoscope, indicating that blood is no longer circulating through the brachial artery. (The Korotkoff sounds are caused by the "murmurs" that circulating blood gives rise to when its flow is turbulent.) The cuff is then slowly deflated until the the sound of blood flow is heard again in the stethoscope. At this point the corresponding reading, in mm Hg, on the pressure gauge indicates the systolic blood pressure. The cuff is then deflated even more, until blood is circulating freely (without turbulence) and the sounds disappear. The pressure reading

Table 9.1. Important concepts and definitions in cardiovascular psychophysiology.

Blood flow = Pressure/Resistance

Pressure = Flow × Resistance

Cardiac output = Quantity of blood pumped by the left ventricle into the aorta per minute = Stroke volume × heart rate

Arterial pressure = Cardiac output × Total peripheral resistance (TPR)

Diastolic pressure (DP) = Lowest pressure in the cardiac cycle

Systolic pressure (SP) = Highest pressure in the cardiac cycle

Mean arterial pressure (MAP) = $\left(\dfrac{SP - DP}{3}\right) + DP$

Stroke volume = Amount of blood pumped by the heart into the aorta at each stroke at this moment is the diastolic blood pressure. Modern blood-pressure devices usually have a built-in, automatic inflation device that inflates the cuff at regular, programmable intervals so that several readings can be taken on the same subject over reasonably short time spans. See Hassett (1978) for a description of various blood-pressure techniques in psychophysiological research.

Pulse Transit Time

Pulse transit time (PTT) and carotid *dP/dt* (Obrist, Light, McCubbin, et al., 1979) are two measures of the rate of change in blood pressure when blood is ejected from the left ventricle. These measures are not so often used today in psychophysiological research and clinical practice. It has also been questioned whether PTT should be considered a valid measure of blood-pressure change. Both methods measure the time it takes for the pulse from the peak of the R wave to reach a certain point at a distance from the heart. Traditionally the distance between the heart and a sensory device (a piezoelectric transducer) placed over the carotid artery was measured, but pulse transit time is mostly assessed with impedance techniques today. Carotid *dP/dt* is a measure of the relative change *(d)* in pressure *(P)* in relation to change in time *(dt)*. The subject wears a neck collar to which the piezoelectric pressure-sensitive device is attached.

A measure closely related to PTT is pulse wave velocity (PWV), which is the time it takes for the pulse to travel between two peripheral recording sites, rather than the time between the heart beat and the arrival of a pulse at a peripheral site. The PWV measures the speed of a wave traveling along the viscoelastic wall of the blood-filled vessel, using, for example, a photoplethysmographic sensor (Jennings and Choi, 1983).

Measures of pulse transit time or pulse wave velocity are considered to index sympathetic influences on the heart: increased sympathetic influence on the heart will lead to increased contractility and stroke volume, resulting in decreased time for the pulse to reach the sensing device on the carotid artery. Obrist et al. (1979) assessed cardiovascular activity by measuring PTT during the resting state and following three stressors: a cold pressor test (immersion of the subject's hand or arm in cold water), a sexually arousing movie, and electric shock. Pulse transit times covaried with changes in systolic blood pressure but not so consistently with changes in diastolic blood pressure. Using invasive techniques, Steptoe, Smulyan, and Gribbon (1976) also found highly significant correlations between the pulse, measured as the radial pressure pulse, and blood-pressure changes in response to various stressors (e.g., mental arithmetic and isometric exercise).

Plethysmography

Plethysmographs record the change of blood flow, typically in one of the digits or in the skin on the forehead, by measuring the volume of blood in the blood vessels monitored. There are both phasic and tonic changes in peripheral blood flow. Phasic changes are the beat-to-beat fluctuations that occur in blood flow for each stroke of the heart; these are changes in *pulse volume* or *pulse amplitude*. Tonic changes, over longer periods of time, are measured as changes in *blood volume*. Figure 9.10 gives examples of fluctuations in blood volume, pulse amplitude,

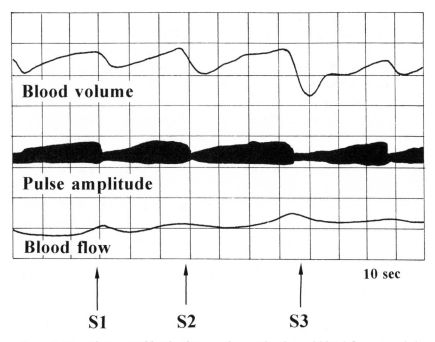

Figure 9.10. Changes in blood volume, pulse amplitude, and blood flow, recorded peripherally (e.g., from a digit) during three stimulus presentations *(S1–S3)*. (Adapted from Hassett, 1971.)

and blood flow in response to repeated presentations of a brief auditory stimulus. An increase in pulse amplitude indexes dilation of the peripheral blood vessels *(vasodilation)* and is caused by sympathetic inhibition. A decrease in pulse amplitude is caused by constriction of the blood vessels *(vasoconstriction)*, and this in turn is caused by increased activity in the sympathetic nervous system.

Although the experiment is almost never replicated, Sokolov (1963) used plethysmographic recordings in the fingers and on the forehead to distinguish between orienting (OR) and defensive (DR) responses to sensory stimuli. Both OR and DR result in vasoconstriction in the digits, because the blood vessels in the digits are innervated only by the sympathetic nervous system. On the forehead, however, the OR results in vasodilation, and the DR results in vasoconstriction, suggesting parasympathetic and sympathetic effects, respectively.

A standard way of measuring vasodilation and vasoconstriction through plethysmography is to apply a light-emitting diode and a sensor on each side of, for example, the thumb. This is called *photoplethysmography*. Sometimes the light source and the sensor are placed adjacent to each other and light that is scattered back from the measured area is detected by the sensor (cf. Jennings and Choi, 1983). Infrared light emitted from the source is recorded by the sensor, whose signals are transmitted to the amplifier and polygraph (or computer). The amount of light reflected to the sensoring device is dependent on the amount of blood flowing in the peripheral vessels. Blood absorbs light, so the more blood there is in an area, the less light will be reflected from that area. Pulse-amplitude changes are usually measured as a percentage change from prestimulus amplitudes for a predetermined number of successive pulses.

Other methods of estimating blood-volume pulse or volume flow are impedance plethysmography and Doppler flowometry. *Impedance plethysmography* measures changes in blood volume in an area by measuring changes in electrical resistance in that area (see Jennings, Tahmoush, and Redmond, 1980). Blood is an ionic solution capable of conducting an electric signal. Impedance is a measure of electrical resistance to alternating currents. When there is an increase in blood volume in an area, the resistance to current flow (impedance) decreases. With impedance plethysmography, inferences about corresponding changes in blood volume in the vessels under study are made from increases or decreases in the impedance of the vessels.

Doppler flowometry is a measurement of the velocity of blood flow by acoustical monitoring. Modern Doppler devices detect ultrasonic echoes reflected from blood cells in vessels. Directing ultrasonic energy at a blood vessel makes it possible to record the speed of blood cells in a blood vessel. Thus, Doppler flowometry is a measure of flow velocity rather than of blood volume (cf. Jennings et al., 1980).

Plethysmographic recordings are often used in clinical psychophysiology—for example, in the study of migraine attacks and Raynaud's disease. *Migraine attacks* are often biphasic: they start with a profound vasoconstriction of the forehead vessels, which is followed by a painful vasodilation of the scalp arterioles. The monitoring of migraine attacks with plethysmography has provided important insights into the nature of this disorder. Biofeedback training—either to control a migraine attack after a change in skin temperature (which is correlated with vasodilation and vasoconstriction), or directly to prevent vasodilation—has sometimes proved helpful to patients.

Similarly, patients who experience extreme vasoconstriction, so-called vasospasms, in the fingers in response to an exposure to cold have benefitted from biofeedback training based on plethysmographic recordings. Extreme vasospasms, as in *Raynaud's disease*, have been found to covary with mental stress. It is speculated that the physiological etiology of this condition involves dysfunctional sympathetic regulation of the peripheral blood circulation. Common pharmacological substances change the vasculature. For example, smoking has been shown to affect the peripheral resistance, sometimes causing rather dramatic peripheral vasoconstriction.

Control of Blood Pressure

The precise control and regulation of blood pressure is one of the major requirements of life, since dramatic changes in blood pressure may have serious effects, such as causing tissue death in the heart and the brain. Excessive blood pressure is a major risk for heart and brain infarcts, as well as for brain hemorrhage or bleeding following the rupture of a blood vessel supplying the brain. Loss of blood supply to the brain leads to brain damage, known as stroke, and possibly death.

The control mechanisms involved in blood-pressure regulation can be grouped into three major categories: nervous control through the baroreceptor reflex; renal control of body fluids (filtering by the kid-

neys); and hormonal control acting through water retention or depletion (the hormonal system also has nervous components). Among
psychophysiologists, nervous control has been most studied, as will be
explained in some detail below. The hormonal mechanism involves
the release of the hormone angiotensin, which causes the kidneys to
retain water and the small blood vessels to constrict. Both of these
effects will result in an increase in blood volume and blood pressure.

The *baroreceptors* are pressure-sensitive receptors located where the
common carotid artery, the major supplier of blood to the brain,
branches into the internal carotid artery. They are part of a tissue ag-
gregation in the wall of the artery called the *carotid sinus*. When the
pressure increases in the internal carotid artery, pressure will also be
increased on the carotid sinus, with the result that the baroreceptors
will increase their firing frequency.

Figure 9.11 outlines the means by which the baroreceptor reflex acts
to regulate blood pressure within normal limits. Although conceived
of as a reflex with internal homeostatic control, baroreceptor activity
is also controlled centrally and under psychological influences. When
aortic pressure rises, the baroreceptors will increase their firing rate,
signaling to the brain that the pressure is higher than normal. This
system is responsible for the tonic control of blood pressure. In an
emergency situation, other control mechanisms, such as the release of
angiotensin II, will rapidly change blood pressure.

The carotid sinus is innervated by cranial nerves *IX* and *X*, the glossopharyngeal and vagus nerves, respectively. The glossopharyngeal
nerve is an afferent nerve that connects with vasomotoric center
(VMC) in the pons in the lower medulla. The VMC is under cortical
influence as well, which may explain why psychological factors can
influence the adjustment of blood pressure and heart rate.

Sensors in the VMC "detect" increased activity in the glossopharyngeal nerve and sends impulses back to the SA node through the vagus
nerve to slow down the beating of the heart. When the heart rate slows
down, the cardiac output will be reduced, further reducing the overall
arterial pressure. This, finally, causes the baroreceptors to stop their
rapid firing, and the system comes to a new equilibrium. Thus, the
baroreceptor reflex is a nice example of a homeostatic feedback mechanism, whereby the brain and the body interact in complex ways to
keep the internal environment within normal physiological limits.

As is also shown in Figure 9.11, when blood pressure drops below

Diencephalon

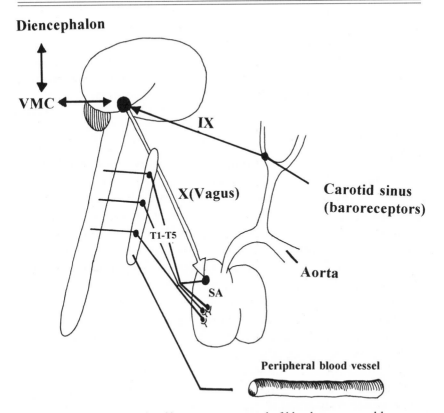

Figure 9.11. The principle of baroreceptor control of blood pressure and heart function. Baroreceptors located in the carotid sinus in the internal carotid artery signal to the vasomotoric center *(VMC)* in the lower brain stem to either increase or decrease heart frequency through the action of the two branches of the autonomic nervous system. Cranial nerves IX and X supply parasympathetic innervation to the heart. Thoracic nerves T1–T5 supply sympathetic innervation from the spinal segments T1 to T5. The peripheral blood vessels have alpha-adrenergic receptors that make the smooth muscle of the vessels respond with constriction to the presence of norepinephrine. Blood vessels of the heart have beta-adrenergic receptors that respond to the presence of epinephrine.

acceptable limits, the sympathetic nervous system and the vagus nerve will act on the ventricles and the SA node to increase heart rate and contractility in order to increase cardiac output and the pressure. The sympathetic system in addition causes the peripheral vessels to constrict, which also has the effect of raising blood pressure.

Baroreceptor Stimulation

The baroreceptors in the carotid sinus in the internal carotid artery may be mechanically stimulated from the outside by adjusting pressure to the neck (Eckberg, Kifle, and Roberts, 1980; Dworkin, 1988; Rau, Elbert, Geiger, et al., 1992; see also Elbert, Tafil-Klawe, Rau, et al., 1991). This technique requires that a cuff that is connected to an air pump be placed around the neck. Rau, Pauli, Brody, et al. (1993) have shown that a brief external suction applied to the cuff during the systole of the cardiac cycle has potent stimulatory effects on the baroreceptor firing, whereas the application of a similar pressure pulse during the diastole inhibits baroreceptor firing. Thus, by adjusting the pressure in the neck cuff during the systolic or diastolic phase of the cardiac cycle, the baroreceptors may be "artificially" manipulated in or out of phase with the cardiac pressure pulse. Rau et al. (1993) found that shifts in the EEG in the frontal areas of the cortex were smaller during baroreceptor stimulation than during inhibition. Thus, their data provide some evidence for the claim made by Lacey and Lacey (e.g., 1970) that cortical activity was influenced by changes in cardiac pressure, through the changing firing rate of the baroreceptors. Interestingly, baroreceptor stimulation has also been shown to increase pain thresholds in borderline hypertensives.

Summary

In this chapter we have looked at the heart and the major blood vessels, and how blood is pumped from the heart to the different parts of the body, including the brain. Various measures of cardiac activity, including the ECG, and blood pressure were then introduced. Finally, psychological influences on the cardiovascular system were described and specific methods for recording psychophysiological changes in the cardiovascular system introduced.

10

Cardiovascular Psychophysiology

This chapter offers detailed examples of physiological changes in the cardiovascular system in response to different psychological stimuli. It focuses on the effects of behavioral and cardiovascular reactivity on heart disease and hypertension, especially the Type A construct. Research on visceral perception and heart-beat detection will also be described. In addition, research on changes in heart rate during cognitive processing is discussed, in particular the work of John Lacey and Paul Obrist.

Cardiovascular Reactivity

Individuals display considerable variation in their cardiovascular reactions to stressful stimuli, also known as *stressors* (see Fredrikson and Matthews, 1990; Manuck, Kasprowicz, and Muldoon, 1990; Sherwood and Turner, 1992, for overviews of cardiovascular reactivity). Some people react to stressors with marked elevations of heart rate and blood pressure, especially individuals with a history of hypertension or with hypertension in their family; hypertensives have strong reactions, for example, to the cold pressor test (Manuck and Krantz, 1986). There is great interest not only in the nature of these reactions but also in a second, related issue: whether phasic changes in cardiovascular functioning to external stressors may be *predictive* of hypertension or coronary heart disease (CHD) in an individual. Recent research has shown

197

that offspring of hypertensive individuals show elevated cardiovascular reactions to laboratory stressors, such as mental arithmetic tasks in which the individual may be required to count backward from 100 in steps of 7.

Cardiovascular reactivity has been defined by Matthews (1986) as a deviation of a cardiovascular response parameter from a comparison or control value that results from an individual's response to a discrete, environmental stimulus. This definition has a disadvantage in that it is a definition of a response; it does not address the key issue of individual differences in reactivity, which was the root of psychophysiologists' interest in the concept in the first place. Manuck et al. (1990) suggested that the observed reaction could not be predicted from knowledge of the variability that exists in the parameter under study or among the same individual(s) in the absence of an external stimulus. For the purposes of this book, cardiovascular reactivity will be defined as an *acute and relatively rapid change in a cardiovascular parameter as a function of the presentation of a stressor.*

As pointed out by Lovallo and Wilson (1992), however, reactivity is never directly observed—it is indirectly inferred by observing differences between persons in their responses to specific tasks and provocations. In order to infer that a person is hyperreactive, the investigator must make comparisons of the individual's responses and compare those with responses observed in a reference group.

According to Lovallo and Wilson (1992), there are three ways in which *hyperreactive* individuals can be identified. Subjects may be randomly recruited and tested with standard laboratory provocation tests, like mental arithmetic tasks, immersing an arm into cold water (the cold pressor test), or a speech stressor. Those individuals producing the largest change in response (from baseline) may be considered hyperreactive. This has the drawback that reactivity is typically measured only in response to a single task, and only once in the laboratory. The experimental situation is also artificial in comparison with real life challenges and stressors. The second method requires that the same individuals be retested with the same stressors at a later time, which would provide a measure of the reliability of the results. Still, this approach has the disadvantage that it will not be helpful in identifying those individuals that will be hyperreactive to a range of different stressors, which is the most likely real-life challenge. The third approach, therefore, measures an individual's responses to repeated tests with different stressors, in order to obtain both test-retest reliability scores and a measure of the generalizability of the hyperreactive response pattern seen in the laboratory to the range of stressors encountered in real life. Typical cardiovascular responses are changes in mean output of blood from the heart during one minute and changes in the resistance of the peripheral blood vessels due to vasoconstriction (see Figure 10.1).

The classic concepts of stimulus-response specificity and response stereotypy that were described in Chapter 2, emphasize individual differences in baseline physiology, and physiological reactivity brings up the important question of what hyperreactivity is measured against. If two individuals differ in their baseline reactivity, within normal ranges, the larger response seen in one individual to a stressor may not necessarily represent a hyperreactive response, since his or her baseline reactivity was higher to begin with. In psychophysiological experiments, therefore, a resting baseline measure is taken against which the *change* in response magnitude during or immediately after the application of the stressor may be calculated.

It should be remembered, though, that what constitutes an "abnormal" or "hyperreactive" response cannot be determined in advance, since no criteria have been established for hyperreactive cardiovascular functioning, except that the individual must deviate from other individuals tested under similar conditions.

Cardiovascular Stressors

Typical stressors used to test cardiovascular reactivity include the mental arithmetic task mentioned above, the Stroop task, the cold pressor task, and various motor tasks, like hand-grip or reaction-time tests. The Stroop task is named after Stroop (1935), who found that asking subjects to identify the color of the ink of words that spell out the name of a color was quite difficult if the color of the ink and the color spelled out by the word differed. For example, a subject exposed to the word RED written in blue ink and required to name the color of the ink as fast as possible would make more errors and take a longer time than he or she would if asked just to name the color-word. The *Stroop interference effect* is a very robust empirical phenomenon, causing stress and frustration in almost every subject. The cold pressor task also elicits a strong reaction: it involves putting the hand and arm in

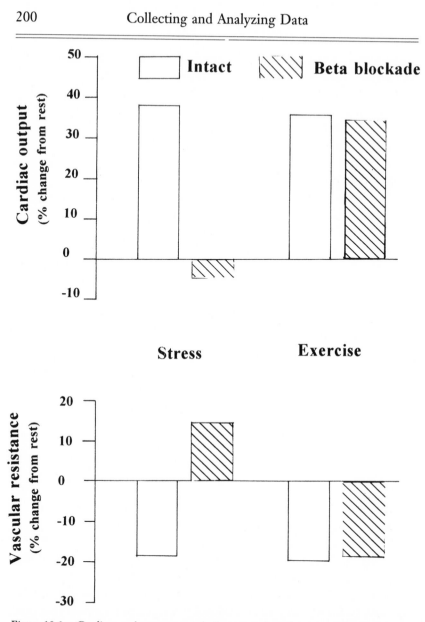

Figure 10.1. Cardiovascular responses during stress (aversive reaction-time task) and exercise (bicycle). Responses are shown for subjects whose sympathetic inner-vations are intact and for subjects following beta-adrenergic receptor blockade. Both cardiac output *(top)* and the resistance of peripheral blood vessels *(bottom)* are influenced by stress and exercise under both normal (intact) and modulated (blockade) conditions. (Data from Sherwood and Turner, 1992, with permission from Plenum Press and the authors.)

ice water for as long a time as possible, which is a truly stressing experience.

Manuck et al. (1990) reported a mean increase in heart rate from a baseline value of 68 beats per minute (bpm) to 89 bpm during the Stroop task. A commonly used index of heart-rate reactivity is to correlate heart rates between the baseline condition and the task condition, and to calculate the difference between the actual heart rate during the task and the heart rate that may be predicted from the regression line for a given subject sample under the same conditions. This is called the *residual variability*. The advantage of the residual variability score over other quantifying measures is that it provides a score of change to the stressor which is "baseline-free." In the case where a residual variability score cannot be calculated, Manuck et al. (1990) advocated the use of multiple measures of baseline performance in an analysis of covariance to evaluate the specific contribution of the stressor on the cardiovascular parameter under study.

Stressors can be characterized, according to Obrist (1976), depending on whether they involve active and passive coping tasks. *Active coping tasks*, or stressors, usually require active engagement and the demonstration of some skill. Typical active coping stressors are mental arithmetic tasks and other neuropsychological tests, like Raven's matrices, which is a test of general reasoning ability, or the Stroop test, which is a test of attentional switching. *Passive coping tasks* are the cold pressor test and other vigilance tests. (See also p. 224.) Other typical stressors are speech stressors (such as speaking in front of a crowd), mirror tracing (drawing over a sketch seen only in a mirror), or the experience of "ischemic pain," caused by a cuff placed around the upper arm and tightened to produce a temporary blocking of blood flow.

In general, it has been found that individual differences in cardiovascular reactivity to a stressor are consistent over time and between individuals. That is, an individual with a large-magnitude reaction to a particular behavioral task will tend to show a similar reaction also on later test occasions. An important question, of course, is the extent to which laboratory-induced changes may be generalized to everyday life. Although some promising studies have been done, more research is needed to clarify the relation between experimentally detected reactivity and reactivity outside of the laboratory.

In one study, Matthews, Manuck, and Saab (1986) showed that heart-rate and blood-pressure changes in response to a mental arithmetic task in the laboratory could predict how these same measures changed in a real-life stress situation, giving a public speech. Although the data, shown in Figure 10.2, indicated that heart rate and blood pressure immediately prior to and after the speech were higher in the "high-reactors" than in the "low-reactors," the change in cardiovascu-

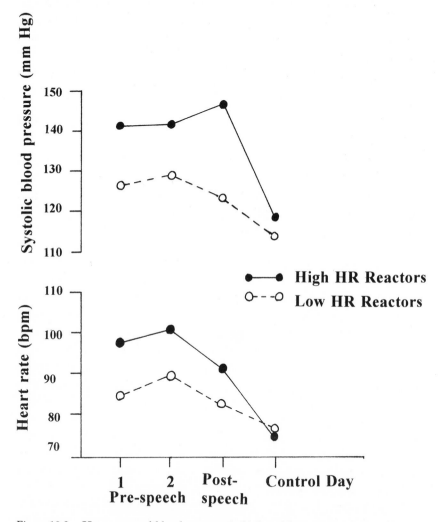

Figure 10.2. Heart rate and blood pressure in high and low reactive individuals before, during, and after delivering a classroom speech. The "Control Day" data were collected on a separate occasion, when subjects were not scheduled for presentation. (Adapted from Manuck et al., 1990, with permission from the authors.)

lar reactivity from Test 1 to the Control Day test was about equal. Thus, in contrast to what may intuitively have been expected, the high-reactors did not respond with larger change to the speech provocation than did the low-reactors. Although some data reinforce the conclusion that laboratory-induced cardiovascular reactivity can generalize to the real-life situation, most reactivity studies have utilized tasks and situations that are not similar to the stressors we encounter from one day to another in our jobs or at home.

Hypertension and Heart Disease
Essential Hypertension

Hypertension is a clinical condition of chronically elevated blood pressure. There are many different forms of hypertension, some having known pathophysiological or neurogenic causes; an example is renovascular hypertension, caused by a disorder of kidney function. For the psychophysiologist interested in behavioral medicine, the most important type of hypertension is *essential hypertension*, so called because there is no known, or accepted, physiological or neurogenic explanation. Essential hypertension has long been suspected to be accelerated by exaggerated psychophysiological reactivity, which ultimately produces permanent cardiovascular changes and stable high blood pressures. In their meta-analysis of the literature on an association between essential hypertension and cardiovascular reactivity, Fredrikson and Matthews (1990) concluded that "relative to normotensive controls, essential hypertensives exhibited large blood pressure responses during all stressors" (p. 30). The difference between the groups was significant for both diastolic (DBP) and systolic (SBP) blood pressure as well as for heart rate. An interesting observation was that the difference between normotensive and hypertensive subjects was largest for passive as compared to active stressor tasks. This finding fits well with the argument often made that it is the degree of a person's control over a situation, and particularly perceived control, that determines the degree of excessive physiological responding.

It has frequently been suggested that the pathophysiologic mediator between responses to behavioral stressors and essential hypertension is excessive sympathetic nervous system activation. Goldstein (1983) reported increased plasma levels of norepinephrine among hypertensives, indicative of a dysfunctional sympathetic system. A finding by

Conway (1984) indicates, though, that the increased responsiveness in hypertensive subjects to a stressor may not be a uniquely psychological phenomenon, since the blood-pressure responses during physical exercise are exaggerated, in comparison with those of normotensive controls.

Reactivity Models

Manuck et al. (1990) proposed four models of a potential association between heightened cardiovascular reactivity to a stressor and essential hypertension. The first may be called a "risk-factor model." In this model, enhanced reactivity is only indirectly related to hypertension through the acting of another (unknown) factor that causes both enhanced reactivity and hypertension. Thus, enhanced reactivity is seen only as a predictor, or risk factor, for hypertension. The causing agent(s) may be dysfunction of centers in the central nervous system that regulate cardiovascular functions, for example, or changes in the vasodilator function of the peripheral blood vessels that would increase blood pressure.

The second model is a direct-cause model, in which hypertension is believed to be caused by enhanced cardiovascular reactivity. It has been suggested that prolonged and sustained exaggerated response to stressors may finally lead to structural changes in the dynamic adjustments of the peripheral blood vessels (e.g., Folkow, Grimby, and Thulesius, 1958). Few experimental studies fully support the direct-cause model.

The third model, the diathesis-stress model, assumes that an individual with a propensity to overreact with increased heart rate and blood pressure in situations of an external stressor will not become hypertensive unless he or she is subject to other, more long-lasting, negative social events, like frequent stressful life events. The diathesis-stress model also assumes a role for individual characteristics not directly linked to the pathophysiology of the cardiovascular system, such as personality and stable behavioral traits. This is an important extension of the overall model, since it opens up the possibility that both psychological "markers" and social "markers" (for example, the degree of social support in a person's life) may affect one's chances of developing hypertension.

A common argument is that individuals with repressed hostility (Alexander, 1950), or with a general tendency to repress feelings, have a tendency for more vigorous physiological reactions. Crown and Marlow (1964) have developed a scale, the Marlow-Crown Social Desirability Scale, that measures the extent to which individuals repress negative feelings in order to be "socially desirable." Thus, in the present context, the Marlow-Crown scale is a measure of repressive coping, that is, coping with an undesirable aversive situation by denying or repressing one's thoughts and emotions.

The fourth model is concerned with the additive effects of several independent but potential risk factors. This is the effect-modification model. Manuck et al. (1990) provide the hypothetical example that both physiological and familial factors may be related to hypertension in an interactive way, so that neither factor alone may cause hypertension; instead, the joint action of both factors may be required to establish a physiopathologic condition.

Neuropsychology of Hypertension

Although it is primarily seen as a physiological disease, indirectly or directly caused by psychological factors, essential hypertension may also have consequences for psychological functioning. It has repeatedly been reported in the literature that essential hypertension has effects on cognitive performance: memory, perception, psychomotor functioning, and particularly for attention and abstract reasoning (see Waldstein, Manuck, Ryan, and Muldoon, 1991, for an overview). Some studies (e.g., Elias, Robbins, Schultz, and Pierce, 1990; Farmer, Kittner, Abbott, et al., 1990) indicate that these neuropsychological effects remain even after controlling for the effects of medication and other confounding variables, like age, sex, and psychiatric disorders. An important observation in the review by Waldstein et al. (1991) was that hypertensive patients did not show a decline in cognitive performance as a consequence of the duration of hypertension. This suggests that the inferior performance of hypertensive patients on tests for neuropsychological functioning is secondary to their elevated blood pressure and not part of a general dysfunction of higher cortical processes, as may be seen in the typical neurodegenerative diseases like Parkinson's disease or Huntington's chorea. Thus, whatever the causes for the cognitive dysfunction in hypertension, they are probably not linked to a more general decline in cognitive performance.

The neuropsychology of hypertension, linking peripheral disease states to dysfunctional cognitive processing, is a new area of research that should receive more support in the future. The interaction between the central and peripheral nervous systems is probably a key link in the final understanding of how psychological factors enter into the chain of causal factors leading to a pathophysiologic response. The study of neuropsychological correlates of peripheral dysfunction is also important from the perspective of basic research; as argued in this book, the future of psychophysiology lies in its explanation of the interaction of central and peripheral nervous activity. This is similar to saying that both a psychophysiological and neuropsychological approach will be necessary to unravel the intricacies of the mind-body problem.

Coronary Heart Disease

Coronary heart disease (CHD) is a major cause of death in the industrialized countries. An understanding of how psychological and behavioral factors may increase the risk of CHD is therefore of paramount importance not only for psychophysiology and behavioral medicine but also for cardiology and medical practice in general. The term *CHD* will be used in the present chapter to refer to a variety of heart problems: myocardial infarction, ischemic heart disease, and atherosclerotic heart disease. In the typical CHD case, the arteries supplying the heart with oxygenated blood are clogged, with the result that heart tissue is damaged by the inadequate supply of oxygen.

The "clogging" of the arteries, or *atherosclerosis*, occurs when fat is deposited inside the artery, on the vessel walls. A myocardial infarction is the end result of a series of physiological processes that starts with the buildup of *atheromatous* plaques inside the walls of the blood vessels. The atheromatous plaque has a core of cholesterol and other fatty products covered by scar tissue. Their presence in an artery can lead to insufficient delivery of oxygen to the heart muscle. The plaque may eventually completely, or partially, block the blood vessels. When this happens the result is ischemic pain, or *angina pectoris*, usually radiating from the left side of the chest out to the left arm. If the ischemia continues, and the damage to the heart tissue is so great that the heart can no longer pump enough blood, a heart attack or myocardial infarction occurs.

The reason for the buildup of atheromatous plaques inside the artery wall is not completely known, but it is believed to be caused by damage to the inner lining of the artery. This in turn causes the accumulation of lipid in the vessel wall and then proliferation of new aggregations of cells inside the artery, which block the passage of blood.

The classic risk factors for developing atheromatous plaques are high blood pressure, smoking, and a high cholesterol level in the blood. According to Keys (1966), however, the three classic risk factors do not account for more than about 50 percent of the variance for developing CHD. They cannot accurately predict which individuals will have a heart attack and which will not. It is therefore clear that other factors may increase the risk for CHD. One of the possible risk factors that has been studied is a behavioral trait known as the Type A personality, which will be discussed shortly. Another line of research involves a possible association between reactivity and the amount of lipids in the blood.

Cardiovascular Reactivity and Lipid Levels

Several recent studies have reported an association between serum lipid levels and cardiovascular reactivity (e.g., Stoney and Matthews, 1988). Although the results are far from consistent (McCann, Veith, Schwartz, et al., 1988), an association between increased cardiac activity in response to mental stressors and serum cholesterol levels would constitute an important mediating factor in understanding how the mind may have significant effects on the functioning of the heart.

Lipids and lipoproteins play important and well-established roles in the etiology of CHD, and in particular in the etiology of the atherosclerotic process whereby the inner lining of the blood-vessel wall becomes clogged with lipid plaques. Most recent data seem to indicate that increased lipid levels are correlated with changes in resistance of the peripheral blood vessels rather than with cardiac activity (van Doornen, Snieder, de Geus, et al., 1993). Thus, the question of changes in serum lipid levels as a function of hyperreactivity to stressors is still open, indicating that the common stress-related mediator in CHD is yet to be identified.

The Type A Behavioral Pattern

In the mid-1950s, two cardiologists, M. Friedman and R. H. Rosenman, mailed a questionnaire to active businessmen in the San Francisco bay area, asking them to indicate what habits characterized people they had known who had suffered a heart attack. A clear majority of the answers mentioned extreme competitiveness, an intense rush to meet deadlines, and an attitude of urgency concerning time.

These first observations, together with a matched cohort study (Friedman and Rosenman, 1959) led to the proposal of a specific behavioral disposition, or trait, called the *Type A behavioral pattern*. The Type A pattern was characterized as a tendency to be expressive in speech, hypervigilant and restless, rushed for time and impatient, hard-driving and competitive, ambitious, hostile, and aggressive.

During the 1960s and 1970s several large-scale studies compared the incidence of CHD in men and women characterized as Type A versus Type B personalities. The most well-known of these studies, the Western Collaborative Group Study (WCGS) and the Framingham Heart Study, both showed that there was an elevated risk for myocardial infarction and/or angina pectoris in Type A individuals when other risk factors, like smoking and high blood pressure, were controlled.

The two main approaches to the measurement of Type A behavior are the structured interview (SI), which was developed by Friedman and Rosenman during the early studies on Type A, and self-report questionnaires, of which the Jenkins Activity Survey (JAS) is a common method. A third method is the Framingham Type A scale, which is a twenty-question inventory based on the interviews performed in the Framingham Heart Study.

An interviewer using the SI technique is more focused on *how* subjects answer questions about their behavior than what they answer. Rapid, single-word answers given at an accelerated pace would be clear signs of Type A behavior, although the answer in itself might not indicate impatience. The SI, which requires a skilled and well-trained interviewer, is intended to elicit information on the subject's (1) drive and ambition, (2) competitive, aggressive, and hostile feelings, and (3) time urgency.

The JAS self-report survey contains about fifty items similar to the questions used in the SI. A typical question from the JAS is: "When you listen to someone talking and this person takes too long to come to the point, do you feel like hurrying him along?" A typical Type A answer would be "Yes, very often," while a Type B answer would be "No, almost never." Examples of the JAS and SI are given in Tables 10.1 and 10.2.

Table 10.1. Questions from the Jenkins Activity Survey (JAS) for identification of Type A individuals.

Question	"Type A" answer	"Type B" answer
Have you ever been told that you eat too fast?	Yes, often	No
When someone takes too long to come to the point during a conversation, do you feel like hurrying him along?	Frequently	Almost never
How is your temper nowadays?	Fiery, hard to control *or* Strong but controllable	Almost never get angry
Do you ever set deadlines or quotas for yourself at work or at home?	Yes, once a week or more often	No

An excellent review of the literature on Type A behaviors up to 1981–1982 was prepared by Matthews (1982, p. 293), who concluded that the Type A behavioral pattern is "firmly established as a risk factor for coronary heart disease, although it is not well understood from a psychological perspective." Part of the failure to understand the psychological basis of Type A behaviors may have been the failure to measure it in a comprehensive way. As Matthews (1982) points out, a global rating of Type A says little about individual behavior. Some individuals may have a high Type A score because they show signs of hostility or aggression even if they answer questions in a slow way. Others may seem hurried and have expressive speech, although they show no signs of hostility.

Another reason it is difficult to explain the Type A individual may have been the slight overlap between the various measures used to identify Type A behavior: the SI seems to identify as Type A people who display a general responsivity to provocative situations, whereas the JAS seems to classify as Type A those with a rapid pace of living.

Several studies have tried to relate Type A behavior to pathophysiology, in particular to increased levels of epinephrine and norepineph-

Table 10.2. Questions from the Type A Structured Interview (SI) for a male respondent.

I would appreciate it if you would answer the following questions to the best of your ability. Your answer will be kept in the strictest confidence. Most of the questions are concerned with your superficial habits, and none of them will embarrass you. (Begin taping now.)

Your code number is _____.

1. May I ask your age?
2. What is your job here at _____?
   (a) How long have you been in this type of work?
3. Are you SATISFIED with your job level?
   (a) Why? Why not?
4. Does your job carry HEAVY responsibility?
   (a) Is there any time when you feel particularly RUSHED or under PRESSURE?
   (b) When you are under PRESSURE does it bother you?
5. Would you describe yourself as a HARD-DRIVING, AMBITIOUS type of person in accomplishing the things you want, OR would you describe yourself as a relatively RELAXED and EASY-GOING person?
   (a) Are you married?
   (b) (If married) How would your WIFE describe you in those terms: as HARD-DRIVING and AMBITIOUS or as relaxed and easy-going?
   (c) Has she ever asked you to slow down in your work? Speed up?
   (d) (If no) NEVER?
   (e) How would SHE put it in HER OWN words?
   (f) Do you like to get things done as QUICKLY as possible?
6. When you get ANGRY or UPSET, do people around you know about it?
   (a) How do you show it?
   (b) Do you ever pound on your desk? Slam a door? Throw things?
7. Do you think you drive HARDER to ACCOMPLISH things than most of your associates?
8. Do you take work home with you?
   (a) How often?
   (b) Do you really do it?
9. Do you have children? (If no children: Have you ever played with small children?) With your children, when they were around the age of 6 and 8, did you EVER play competitive games with them, like cards, checkers, Monopoly?
   (a) Did you ALWAYS allow them to WIN on PURPOSE?
   (b) Why or why not?
10. When you play games with people YOUR OWN age, do you play for the FUN of it, or are you REALLY in there to WIN?

rine, blood pressure, and sympathetic nervous system activity (Matthews, 1982). In general, it has been shown that Type A individuals exhibit elevated levels of stress-related physiological responses. An interesting observation is that Type A's tend to respond with greater blood-pressure changes than Type B's when unconscious during a coronary by-pass operation (Krantz, Arabian, Davia, et al., 1982). This may suggest that the Type A behavior is mediated by excessive sympathetic responsivity, and that this may be a constitutional factor of Type A behavior. There is little evidence in the literature that the Type A behavior has a genetic origin, however, and Krantz and Manuck (1984) found little evidence in the literature of a strong correlation between globally defined Type A behavior and physiological hyperreactivity, with the possible exception of increased levels of systolic blood-pressure reactivity.

Sex Differences

Interestingly, most of the early studies of Type A were on males—there were relatively few investigations of female Type A behavior. One may perhaps speculate whether this "sex bias" in the research on Type A has its counterpart in a similar "bias" in the society at large that the typical Type A behavior is a hallmark of the successful and striving young *male* executive. In a recent study, Lawler, Harraldson, Armstead, et al. (1993) found that hostility and anger (components in the Type A construct) were associated with greater diastolic blood-pressure changes in males than in females. In another study (Lawler and Schmied, 1992), however, it was found that Type A women who were retested after five years showed more signs of illness and increases in blood pressure.

Although women rate Type A men as more socially attractive than Type B men, men rate Type B women as more attractive than Type A women. This is important for two reasons: first, it shows how a potentially disease-promoting behavior may be socially reinforced in modern society, and second, it shows that this behavior actually may relate to basic psychological and social mechanisms in courting and dating behavior.

Some studies have found that whereas male Type A's are more physiologically reactive than their Type B counterparts, this is not the case for females (Frankenhaeuser, Lundberg, and Forsman, 1980). These results have not been replicated in other studies, however.

Overall, the data show that the Type A behavioral pattern may be expressed differently in women than in men—that is, have a physiological profile different from that seen in Type A men. More recent studies have also found that age and work experience may play a role in the difference between the sexes in how Type A behavioral traits are expressed. The older, more experienced executive women tend to have response patterns similar to those of their male counterparts. This indicates that the Type A response profile may be shaped by environmental contingencies, such as work experience (Frankenhaeuser et al., 1980).

Type A Behaviors in Children

Children, too, may be characterized as Type A (Matthews and Jennings, 1984), although it is unclear whether Type A children reveal similar physiological reactivity as adult Type A's. In one study, Lundberg (1983) found that Type A children 3–6 years of age showed greater task-induced changes in systolic blood pressure than did Type B children (cf. Jennings and Matthews, 1984).

Modification of Type A Behavior

A critical issue in all discussions of Type A behavior and its relation to coronary heart disease is whether Type A behavior can be altered once it is identified as a prominent part of the daily behavioral repertoire of an individual. Alteration of Type A behavior may protect healthy individuals from the risk of CHD, but it is perhaps even more important for Type A individuals who have suffered a heart infarct to try to lower the risk of having a second infarct by altering their behavior. A large-scale intervention study was initiated in 1977 by Friedman, Thoresen, et al. (1984) on more than eight hundred patients who had suffered myocardial infarction. The patients were randomly enrolled into two groups: a control group of 270 patients who received group cardiologic counseling, and an experimental group of 592 patients who received counseling therapy intended to change Type A behavior in addition to the cardiologic group therapy. Change in Type A behavior was measured by means of three types of questionnaires and a structured interview.

The experimental group of patients were exposed to various cognitive and emotional restructuring techniques that focused on typical Type A behaviors. This kind of therapy might be described by a metaphor: Life is like driving a car, and it is important to identify exaggerated emotional and physiological reactions to critical "traffic" situations; the patients were taught how to change from driving in "the fast lane" to driving in the "slow" lane, how to avoid getting impatient or hostile when caught in a traffic jam. Treatment methods included lectures, demonstrations, and readings, which were intended to provide a theoretical rationale for the program, as well as instructions and practice exercises for developing competence and skills in alternative behaviors. Alternatives to a Type A way of living and thinking were spelled out through videotapes, diagrams, and the like.

There was a significant difference between the rate of recurring CHD symptoms in the control (counseling) and experimental (intervention) groups. The cumulative three-year recurrence rate was 7 percent in the intervention group and 23 percent in the counseling-only group. The difference between the groups was mainly caused by a lesser incidence of nonfatal infarctions in the intervention group. Thus, the data by Friedman et al. (1984) showed that Type A behavior can be altered through psychological intervention, and that changes in behavior may have significant implications for the recurrence of fatal CHD.

Recent Developments in Type A Research

The Type A concept generated a vast amount of research during the 1970s and first half of the 1980s. This was accompanied by great enthusiasm for using psychological intervention to modulate Type A behavior and, subsequently, to reduce the risk of a heart infarct. As was the fate of biofeedback training a decade earlier, however, the Type A concept and its importance for CHD have lost research "momentum." It is rare nowadays to see a poster or a symposium on "Type A" at psychophysiological meetings and conferences.

Miller, Turner, Tindale, et al. (1991) reviewed the literature up to 1990–1991 and concluded that the trend toward null findings in research on Type A behavior has been so consistent in recent years "that the participants at the 1987 annual meeting of the Psychosomatic Society questioned the relevance of the whole Type A concept" (p. 469). These null results are for the most part the outcome of studies using fatal heart infarcts as the disease criterion. Thus, a direct link between global Type A behavior and death by CHD may be questionable today, although Matthews (1988) argued that "the occurrence of some failures to replicate does not justify abandoning the concept" (p. 383).

There may be many reasons for the decline in research interest in Type A during the last couple of years. One is probably the failure to replicate many of the promising results that came out of psychophysiological laboratories in the 1970s. Booth-Kewley and Friedman (1987) reanalyzed the data on the correlation between CHD, Type A, and other psychological factors and found that Type A behavior does not in itself increase the risk of CHD; only if Type A behavior is accompanied by depression or anxiety does the risk increase.

Another important dimension in the meta-analysis performed by Booth-Kewley and Friedman (1987) was that, in addition to depression, anger and hostility seemed to account for the largest portion of the shared variance between Type A and CHD. This is an interesting observation, since it shifts the focus away from the Type A behavioral pattern as a global construct to subcomponents that make up the overall pattern. Thus, an important distinction in recent research on Type A is the difference between global and component analyses of the construct. The subcomponents anger and hostility have increasingly been the focus in research on the psychological predictors of CHD. Taken together, the data by Booth-Kewley and Friedman (1987) showed that the JAS component that relates most strongly to heart disease was hard-driving and competitive behavior.

Thus, the subcomponents in the Type A behavioral pattern that best predict CHD are hostility/aggression and competitiveness, in addition to other psychological factors such as depression and anxiety. This conclusion was supported in a recent commentary by Ray (1991) on a review of Type A and B behaviors by Ivanesivich and Matteson (1988). Ray argued, after a review of the literature, that the Type A construct may be a false trail and that researchers instead should focus on those subcomponents that have been shown to correlate with CHD, notably aggression/hostility. Ray (1991) furthermore made the argument that although there is a coronary-prone personality trait, hostility, the most commonly used measure of Type A, the JAS, does not reliably measure it. Rather, the JAS measures a mixture of traits that should best be studied separately. It may be added that in a study in which the subcomponents were considered separately, Svebak,

Knardahl, Nordby, and Aakvaag (1992) found that the hostility/irrita-
bility components of the Type A construct correlated positively with
release of catecholamines, including dopamine, while increased cortisol was associated with high dysphoria, or distress.

Visceral Perception and Heartbeat Detection

An area of research that has gained increased popularity over the last
decade is the possibility of self-perception of cardiac events, particularly whether individuals can detect their own heartbeats (see Katkin,
1985; Jones, 1994, for overviews). Interest in this area may be traced
to Brener's (1974) theory of how an individual might gain control of
visceral, or autonomic, events and enhance self-perception through
operant biofeedback training. A possible clinical implication might
have been that subjects who were able to detect their heartbeats also
may gain more from biofeedback training. Furthermore, actual
physiological responses overall have shown little intercorrelation
with subjective evaluations of physiological activity measured with the
Autonomic Perception Questionnaire (APQ) (Mandler, Mandler, and
Uviller, 1958). This may have prompted an interest in developing
more objective measures of the relationship between subjective experience of and actual change in a physiological parameter.

The APQ is a self-report questionnaire that solicits information
about physiological reactions in various situations. It has frequently
been used in studies of autonomic disorders, like Raynaud's disease
(Hugdahl, Fagerström, and Brobeck, 1984). Typical items are "Face
becoming hot," which may be answered from "no change" to "very
hot"; "Hands becoming cold"; or "Mouth becoming dry." Hugdahl
et al. (1984) showed that patients with Raynaud's disease, which is
characterized by spasms in the small blood vessels in the fingers and
hands in response to cold, also experience dramatic vasoconstriction
in response to stress.

In a more general sense, research on heartbeat detection can be
linked to the debates in the 1920s among William James and Walter
Cannon over whether an emotion is experienced as a consequence of
the perception of visceral change (see Chapter 1). Moreover, as
pointed out by Katkin (1985), Schachter and Singer's (1962) classic
study on the influence of cognitive appraisal in emotional experience
also relates to the issue of autonomic perception. Schachter and Singer

explicitly argued that the perception of one's own physiological arousal preceded the cognitive attribution of the cause for increased arousal. Thus, research on heartbeat detection has both theoretical and methodological implications for theories of emotion and for behavioral medicine, including such issues as vulnerability to visceral disorders, fear and anxiety, and personality traits.

Methods and Paradigms

In a typical heartbeat detection experiment (Katkin, 1985; Whitehead, Drescher, Heiman, and Blackwell, 1977), subjects are presented with two different tones (S+ and S−) that are timed to cardiac events. The S+ tone is delayed 100 msec from each upslope of the R spike in the ECG. The S− tone is presented after a longer delay, or at varying intervals. Thus, for each heartbeat there are two tones, the task of the subject being to discriminate between the S+ and S− tones. The presentation of S+ at about 100 msec after the upslope of the R spike will coincide with the contraction of the ventricles. If the subject tries to use respiratory or muscle manipulations to "pace" heartbeats, both the S+ and S− stimuli will be affected. Similarly, if the subject has no sense of his or her heartbeats, the two stimuli will be indistinguishable (Katkin, 1985).

A variant of the tone-delay paradigms used by Katkin and Whitehead is the tracking paradigm developed by Schandry (1981; Weitkunat and Schandry, 1990). Schandry had subjects count their heartbeats silently during time intervals varying in length. The onset of each interval was signaled by a tone, and the subject reported his or her heartbeats after each interval. An interesting finding with Schandry's technique is that subjects who scored high on measures of anxiety and emotionality were better at detecting their heartbeats. Thus, at least at the extremes, there seems to be a correlation between subjective experience of emotion and actual increase in a physiological parameter.

In an experiment by Katkin, Morell, Goldband, et al. (1982), subjects were presented with randomized sequences of S+ and S− tones. All subjects were tested for a baseline measure, and then some subjects received feedback training (which involved informing subjects of the accuracy of their perceptions). All subjects were then tested for a second time. Subjects were also screened for electrodermal lability, which

is a measure of the frequency of spontaneous skin-conductance fluctuations (see Chapter 6). Electrodermal lability has previously been
shown to correlate with perceptual discriminability (Hastrup, 1979).

The results of this experiment are shown in Figure 10.3. (Note that
the y-axis measure, $2\arcsin\sqrt{p(A)}$, is an approximation of d', which is
the standard measure of perceptual sensitivity.) The labile subjects
who also had biofeedback training were most accurate at detecting
their heartbeats. Most of the other subjects were poor detectors, a
conclusion also shared by Jones (1994). In subsequent studies, however, Katkin and his group have shown that this experiment's results
may have been confounded by a variety of other variables, notably sex
of the subject and hemisphere dominance preference. In one study,
only the male subjects showed significant effects during the feedback
training phase.

Right-Hemisphere Mediation

Individuals who are characterized as right-hemisphere dominant are
also better at heartbeat perception. Hantas, Katkin, and Reed (1984)
divided subjects into hemisphere-dominant groups depending on their
scores on a lateral eye-movement task (LEM). The LEM task requires
that subjects answer questions regarding verbal and nonverbal relations. The experimenter records the subjects' lateral eye movements
when reflecting on and answering the questions. Some individuals
consistently move their eyes to the right when reflecting on a verbal
task or question (for example, "Give a synonym for the word *prehen-
sile*") and move them to the left when reflecting on nonverbal, spatial
questions ("Are the stars on the American flag in the upper or lower
part of the flag?"). According to the theory of LEMs (Ehrlichman and
Weinberger, 1978), eye movements to the right are indicative of left-
hemisphere activation, while eye movements to the left are indicative
of right-hemisphere activation.

Hantas et al. (1984) showed that subjects who moved their eyes left
were more accurate at detecting their heartbeats than those that moved
right. Recently Katkin has suggested that the perception of cardiovascular events are mediated through cardiac afferents to the right side
of the brain, a suggestion that is supported by other data showing a
possible unique relationship between the right hemisphere of the brain

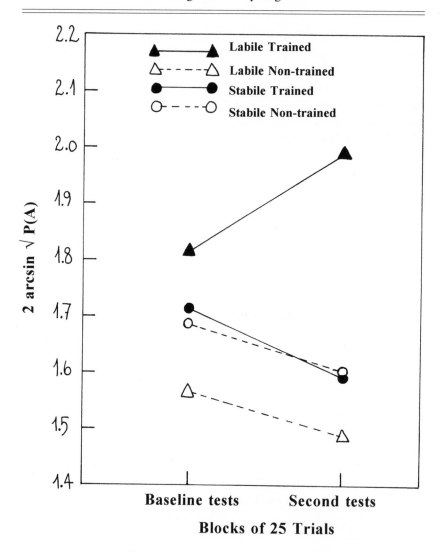

Figure 10.3.   Perceptual sensitivity for detection of one's own heartbeat, for trained and untrained subjects. (Data from Katkin et al., 1982, with permission from the Society for Psychophysiological Research and the authors.)

and cardiovascular function (Walker and Sandman, 1979; Hugdahl, Franzon, Andersson, and Walldebo, 1983).

Another test of the mediation of autonomic, or visceral, perception is the study of patients with transplanted hearts, also recently suggested by Katkin. Patients with transplanted hearts do not have the normal autonomic innervation of their hearts, since it is impossible to reconnect the nerve fibers to the implanted heart. If these patients are as accurate as normal subjects in detecting their heartbeats, the mediation surely must occur through means other than autonomic afference from the heart to the brain. (See also Chapter 5.)

Fitness Levels

In another study on heartbeat detection, Jones and Hollandsworth (1981) investigated whether physical fitness level and physical exertion would affect the ability to discriminate heartbeats. The rationale for the study was the previous observation that athletes may have a superior ability to perceive their internal physiology and to maximize physical resources partly through this ability. Jones and Hollandsworth (1981) found that fitness level positively correlated with cardiac perception, but only for the female subjects, and physical exertion had an effect only when heart rate was substantially increased above resting baseline. The results were therefore partly at odds with the findings by Katkin's group, who found the male subjects to be superior perceivers. Maybe the rather extreme conditions at which the athletes were compared (markedly raised heart rates) could account for some of these differences.

Recent Trends

More recently, researchers in autonomic perception have started to investigate whether an ability to detect one's heartbeat may be of use in treating clinical disorders. These researchers are extending previous findings of a relationship between, for example, anxiety levels and accuracy of heartbeat perception. A second line of research is studying interactions between the autonomic and the central nervous systems; an example is the use of ERPs and other EEG measures to determine how cardiac and brain events are correlated (e.g., Koriath and Lindholm, 1986).

Cardiovascular Responses and Cognitive Processes

Changes in heart rate as an autonomic concomitant of cognitive processes have a long tradition in psychophysiology. This is perhaps especially true for studies of attention and vigilance (see Jennings, 1986, for an overview). A typical paradigm for studying attention and vigilance is to present a tone to which the subject orients. The presentation usually results in an initial cardiac deceleration, sometimes followed by an acceleration and a second deceleration.

Information Processing

Cardiovascular cognitive psychophysiology is often framed within an information-processing perspective. Information processing is a general concept for modeling the sequence of events from the presentation of a stimulus to the execution of a response; a simple example would resemble a flow chart (see Figure 10.4). A stimulus is first registered in the perceptual system, which is an automatic process. If the stimulus requires further processing, higher-order features are encoded, a process that involves an active memory search for matching of the presented stimulus with what is stored in memory. This step requires allocation of processing resources and a shift of attention to the incoming stimulus. This is called *controlled processing*, in contrast to *automatic processing*, which requires only perceptual analysis. In order for a response to be executed, it must first be selected; in other words, some response tendencies should be inhibited and others should be facilitated if a rapid or accurate response is to be made. Finally, the response is executed.

We will return to the information-processing model after the following introduction of some basic concepts and terms, which are intimately linked to the work of the Laceys and Paul Obrist.

Sensory Intake and Environmental Rejection

John and Beatrice Lacey (e.g., Lacey, 1967; Lacey and Lacey, 1974) proposed that changes in cardiovascular function facilitated or inhibited cortical processing. The essence of their theoretical argument was that increases or decreases in the beating of the heart could have a causal influence on cognitive efficiency. As a metaphor, it could be

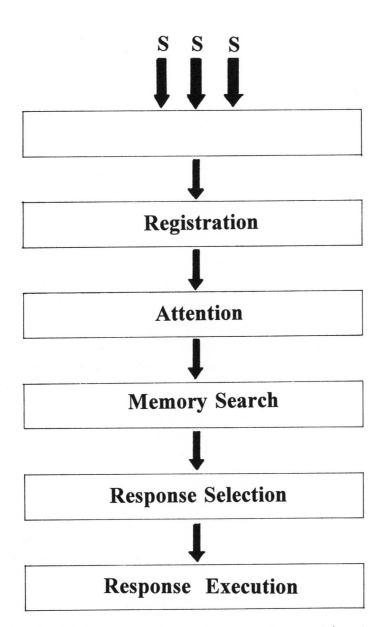

Figure 10.4. The input-output sequence of events according to an information-processing perspective, from stimulus activation to response execution.

said that the Laceys' model is a "cognitive" analogue to William James's model of the role of bodily processes in emotional experience. Both argued that the registration by the brain of a change in a physiological system in the body is instrumental in shaping a particular psychological construct.

Specifically, Lacey et al. (1963) suggested that stressful mental activity, like counting backward by subtracting numbers, increased (accelerated) heart rate, which in turn caused a state of *environmental rejection*. Environmental rejection is a "shutting off" of sensory stimulation through temporary cortical inhibition, caused by increased firing of the baroreceptors in the carotid artery in the neck (Chapter 9). The baroreceptors are sensitive to increases and decreases in blood pressure to the brain; they increase their firing when blood pressure rises, as it does when heart rate increases. When there is a decrease (deceleration) in heart rate, the cortex would be facilitated to process new stimuli, a situation which Lacey called *sensory intake*.

Lacey focused the theory of intake and rejection on cardiac-cycle effects. During the S–T and T phases, late in the cardiac cycle, aortic pressure is peaking (see Chapter 9 for details of ECG phases). This means that baroreceptor activity is maximal, and the cortex relatively inhibited. During the T–P and P phases, early in the cardiac cycle, however, aortic pressure is at its lowest, with cortical activation being at its highest (see Hassett, 1978, for further details). If one assumes, as Lacey did, that reaction times (RTs) should reflect cortical activation, then RTs near the diastolic phase of the cardiac cycle (the T–P and P phases) shoud be shorter than RTs during the systolic phase (the S–T and T phases). Thus, sensory intake should correspond to shorter RTs, while environmetal rejection should correspond to longer RTs.

The pattern of heart-rate acceleration during environmental rejection and deceleration during sensory intake resembles the cardiovascular response patterns that follow the presentation of defensive and orienting stimuli, respectively (Chapter 7). The connection between the cognitive concepts of rejection and intake and the emotional and attentional concepts of defense and orienting responding has been elaborated in detail by Graham and Clifton (1966) and Graham (1973).

The traditional view of a reciprocal autonomic relationship in orienting (OR) and defensive responses (DR)—which presumes that parasympathetic activity activates the OR and sympathetic activity the DR—has recently been questioned. Using the concept of autonomic space (Chapter 5) to explain various modes of reciprocal and nonreciprocal activation of the two branches of the autonomic nervous system, Berntson, Boysen, and Cacioppo (1991) argued for the recognition of multiple determinants of autonomic state and multiple modes of autonomic control. The two branches are not simply the opposite of each other, and any autonomic effect underlying heart-rate changes in response to environmental stimuli should be analyzed in terms of the multidimensional autonomic space.

The late Paul Obrist, who conducted postdoc research with John Lacey, argued that the phasic changes in heart rate exhibited during intake and rejection were probably only a reflection of differences in metabolic needs in these situations. In a situation characterized by sensory intake, the individual probably is quiet and attentive to the outer world, and so the decrease in heart rate reflects the lowering of muscle tonus and metabolic demands. Similarly, heart-rate acceleration during mental arithmetics, which is a situation characterized by Lacey as "rejection of the outer world," may only mean that the individual tenses the body's muscles while trying to solve a difficult problem.

Cardiac-Somatic Coupling

Obrist (1981) termed this association between heart rate and metabolic demands the *cardiac-somatic coupling*. In other texts it is frequently referred to as the cardiac-somatic relationship. A key notion in Obrist's thinking is that of the close relationship between the functioning of a physiological system, like the cardiovascular system, and the biological demands on that system. For this reason we may characterize Obrist as a "psychobiologist" more than a classic psychophysiologist.

An interesting but often neglected feature of Obrist's experimental work (see Obrist, 1981) was his use of the classical conditioning paradigm in his exploration of the intricate relationship between behavior and physiology. In his 1981 book, Obrist tells the fascinating story of how he and his colleagues tracked down the explanation for the counterintuitive observation that the animal subjects' heart rate *decelerated* after the presentation of the conditioned stimulus (CS), while they were waiting for the occurrence of the aversive unconditioned stimulus (UCS). All major theories of emotion and activation at that time predicted heart-rate acceleration at this moment, because of the arousal and anxiety being built up in the anticipation period in the CS–UCS interval. Obrist determined that the heart-rate deceleration was accompanied by somatic quieting, as if the dogs were passively waiting for the aversive UCS. This response is called *passive coping*, during which the heart is thought to be under parasympathetic (vagal) control. The opposite occurs—heart-rate acceleration—in situations of instrumental conditioning. This is called *active coping*, during which the heart is under sympathetic control (Obrist, 1976).

It is tempting to draw a parallel between Obrist's work on active and passive coping and Seligman's (1975) theory of *learned helplessness*. Learned helplessness is a syndrome of "giving up" in the face of uncontrollable circumstances, of not striking back and fighting against the odds. Learned helplessness is thought to cause depression in some instances, as the typical "giving up" behavior is often displayed by depressed people. Learned helplessness was first observed in classical conditioning of dogs, in dogs that seemed to "give up" and not learn an instrumental avoidance response after having been exposed to uncontrollable electric shocks. The phenomenon of learned helplessness thus shares several important features with the behavior seen in passive coping as it was defined by Obrist (e.g., 1981).

An important aspect of the foregoing discussion is that the classical conditioning experiment provides a "vehicle" or paradigm for studying the mediating mechanisms in complex behavior-physiology relationships. Unfortunately, the behavioristic movement after the Second World War, particularly in the United States, has left many students indifferent to, and today probably also ignorant of, the richness of psychological processes in the typical classical conditioning paradigm (see Chapter 7). Classical conditioning is not a passive stimulus- response paradigm; it involves the study of complex cognitive functions involving perceptual, attentional, and memory processes (Hugdahl, 1987).

The Triphasic Heart-Rate Curve

The heart-rate curve is a record of cardiac responses. An example is a record taken during an information-processing sequence from stimulus input to the execution of a response, such as the performance of a reaction-time task requiring the subject to press a button in response to a stimulus (see Figure 10.5). The initial deceleration (D1) is associated with the cognitive processes of focusing attention and orienting to the stimulus. The acceleration (A) is related to emotional aspects of the stimulus, as in a classical conditioning situation, or to internal processing, as suggested by the concept of environmental rejection proposed by Lacey (1967). Coles and Duncan-Johnson (1975) suggested that the accelerative component is related to the signal function

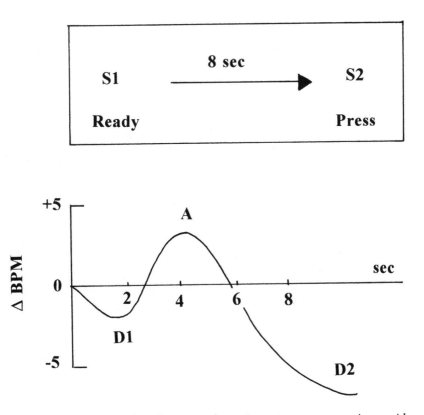

Figure 10.5. Typical triphasic heart-rate change in response to an experiment with a two-stimulus paradigm (S1–S2) and a long interstimulus interval. The subject is required to get ready after the first stimulus and to press a response button after the second stimulus. Heart-rate change first decelerates *(D1)*, an indication of an orienting response (OR) to S1; then it accelerates *(A)*, an indication of internal processing; and then it decelerates again *(D2)*, an indication of anticipation and expectancy of the S2. The A component is sensitive for emotional reactivity and defensive responding (DR).

of the first stimulus in a two-stimulus paradigm, where the first stimulus is a "warning" stimulus to get ready for a rapid response to the second stimulus. Thus, the accelerative component has been related to both emotional and cognitive processing. The second deceleration (D2) is related to anticipation or expectancy of a second stimulus. Anticipation of a second stimulus is a common feature of a reaction-time paradigm, where a first stimulus warns the subject to get ready and the second stimulus (occurring a few seconds later) signals the subject to press a button as fast as possible.

The form of the cardiac response depends on the intensity and onset time of the stimulus. The rapid onset of an auditory stimulus causes an accelerated HR response as compared with the the response to a slower-onset stimulus. The rapid onset causes a *startle reflex*, which also involves eye blinking and subtle changes in the skeletal muscles. Similarly, a more intense stimulus will also cause acceleration in the response. Figure 10.6 shows examples of HR acceleration in response to a rapid-onset white noise as compared with the response to a slower-onset tone, both of similar intensity. As is also seen in Figure 10.6 (lower panels), the peak of the D2 "wanders" with the length of the interstimulus interval.

Venables (1991) proposed that heart-rate deceleration is coupled to an "open attentional stance" whereas acceleration is related to a "closed attentional stance." He gives as an example the responses of male students to different stimuli: when shown a picture of an attractive girl, heart rate decelerated; but when asked to solve anagrams, heart rate accelerated. The concepts of open and closed attentional stance are similar to the notions of "sensory intake" and "environmental rejection" (Lacey, 1967) and to the difference in heart-rate responses to orienting (OR) versus defensive (DR) response stimuli (Graham, 1973).

Attention and Heart Rate

Brief changes in heart rate typically follow significant events that involve shifts of attention. A "shift" of attention is a multifaceted concept referring to the change that occurs when alertness is narrowed and heightened on some aspects of the environment to the expense of reduced attention to other aspects.

Focusing one's attention usually involves mental effort and the allo-

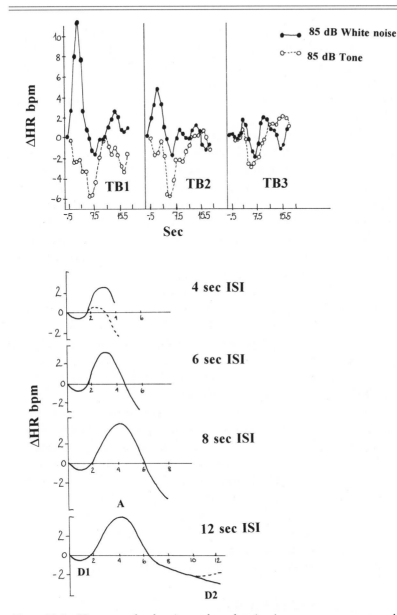

Figure 10.6. Heart-rate deceleration and acceleration in response to a tone and to "white noise" *(upper panel)*. The graphs labeled *TB* give data for the trial blocks (i.e., average change across a block of trials). (From Graham, 1973, with permission from the author.) The lower panel shows how the shape of the deceleratory and acceleratory components depends on the interstimulus interval (ISI). (Data from Bohlin and Kjellberg, 1979, with permission from Lawrence Erlbaum and the authors.)

cation of "executive" processing resources, processes that may require the use of extra energy, in terms of increased blood flow and metabolism, for processing the attended events. Thus, a resource-allocation perspective on attention may explain why there is a sudden change in cardiovascular parameters when one is responding to a novel, unexpected stimulus.

Cardiac responses recorded when a subject is in an attentional situation may be indicators of attention, or they may facilitate attention, or they may act as regulators of attention. Jennings (1986) proposed that cardiac decelerations that occur following unexpected OR stimuli and while waiting in anticipation of an expected event, as happens in a reaction-time situation, are examples of attention indicators. Arousal may act to facilitate attention in the sense that high arousal may make the individual hyperalert to rapid shifts of attention to relevant aspects of the environment. Arousal states may thus induce a cardiovascular response that facilitates shifting of attention.

However, an extremely high level of arousal may actually interfere with the ability to shift attention. The well-known Yerkes-Dodson law states that the relationship between arousal and performance, if graphed, would resemble an inverted U. Extremely high *and* low arousal states are associated with lower levels of performance than are expected during intermediate arousal states.

In addition to these effects of attention on cardiovascular activity—facilitation and interference—attention may inhibit some forms of cardiac responding. Jennings (1992) reported that in subjects "waiting" in anticipation of the imperative stimulus in a two-stimulus reaction-time paradigm, there is both inhibition of competing responses and facilitation of expected responses. During the anticipation of the RT stimulus, competing responses are inhibited while the planned RT response to the stimulus is facilitated. Heart-beat timing is delayed as part of this inhibitory set. The vagus nerve is activated, which then hyperpolarizes the sinus node cells, delaying, or "inhibiting," the heart beat.

Schizophrenia and Heart Rate

Steinhauer et al. (1992) showed that schizophrenic patients did not show the predicted anticipatory cardiac deceleration preceding a tone stimulus, indicating that schizophrenic patients differ from control subjects in the way they process simple perceptual-motor input. A possible reason for the failure of schizophrenics to exhibit cardiac deceleration may be high resting-level activity in the sympathetic nervous system, which may counteract the effect of the vagus nerve on the heart.

An alternative explanation may be that the cortical control system, which both regulates the cognitive and autonomic response patterns to an unexpected tone, may be dysfunctional in schizophrenics. This possibility is supported by the results of a study by Yokoyama et al. (1987), who found that patients with damage to the right-hemispheric areas of the brain did not show the predicted deceleration in heart rate during a standard orienting task.

Motivation and Heart Rate

Heart rate also changes with level of motivation. In an experiment that presented subjects with a simple continuous motor task, Fowles (1983) found that heart rate is specifically linked to increases in appetitive motivation. The subjects were to press a button adjacent to whichever of five lights (arranged in a semicircle) was lit. Pressing the button turns the light off. Another light comes on randomly when the subject presses a central button, and the task continuous until the subject is told to stop. The subjects were provided with information about their successes and failures and given a monetary reward for successful completion of the task.

Fowles suggested that there is an *appetitive motivational* system that is activated in simple reward-seeking situations like the described continuous motor task and that heart rate may be significantly linked to appetitive motivation, while, for example, the electrodermal system is more influenced by an *aversive* motivational system. Applying the model of separate appetitive and aversive motivational systems, Fowles's (1988) proposal that various forms of psychopathology may be understood in terms of being too much driven by either system may be consistent with much of the clinical literature. Moreover, it may be speculated whether psychopathy, which may be defined as a lack of engagement, also may be related to a dysfunctional balance between an appetitive and aversive motivational system, the effect of which would be a kind of emotional "vacuum" so often seen in psychopathy.

Brain Asymmetry and Heart-Rate Responses

Typically, a deceleration of the heart rate is observed in classical conditioning just prior to UCS onset after CS–UCS pairings (cf. Obrist, Webb, and Sutterer, 1969). The typical cardiac response is the multiphasic decelarative-accelerative-decelerative pattern described above. Several papers have reported a right-hemisphere effect in cardiac responding in conditioning experiments, although the investigators have started from different theoretical and empirical positions. A common finding, though, in most of these studies is that phasic changes in cardiac activity in response to external stimuli may be uniquely related to right-hemisphere activation.

First of all, in 1979 Walker and Sandman recorded event-related potentials (ERPs) separately from the left and right hemispheres when their subjects exhibited spontaneous changes in heart rate over time. The most interesting finding from the point of view of the present discussion was that ERPs recorded from the right hemisphere were different from the ERPs recorded from the left hemisphere when heart rate changed. Walker and Sandman (1979, p. 727) concluded that "changes in heart rate are reflected more clearly in the right hemisphere than in the left." This finding was followed up in another study (Walker and Sandman, 1982), where it was demonstrated that ERPs recorded from the right hemisphere, but not from the left hemisphere, were different in amplitude during systole and diastole of the cardiac cycle. Walker and Sandman (1982, p. 524) thus concluded from their studies that "the relationship between the heart and the brain is lateralized, and this factor has not been considered in behavioral studies."

Following the suggestions by Walker and Sandman (1979, 1982), Hugdahl and his co-workers (Hugdahl, Franzon, Andersson, and Walldebo, 1983) reported a relationship between heart rate and the brain similar to that found by Walker and Sandman. The important thing is, however, that Hugdahl et al. (1983) took a different approach from the previous studies. Thus, whereas Walker and Sandman demonstrated differences in electrophysiological activity between the hemispheres when heart rate and blood pressure were "manipulated," Hugdahl et al. demonstrated changes in heart rate when the left and right hemispheres were separately "manipulated." Hugdahl et al. (1983) presented verbal and spatial visual stimuli initially only to the left or the right hemisphere with the visual half-field (VHF) technique. The stimuli were flashed for 200 msec, either to the left or the right hemisphere. In three consecutive experiments, heart rates were found to accelerate, with a peak 4 sec after CS onset, only when the right hemisphere was initially stimulated (See Figure 10.7). Thus, while Walker and Sandman recorded cortical activity as the dependent variable and cardiac activity as the independent variable, Hugdahl et al. (1983) reported similar results although they recorded cardiac activity (the dependent variable) when cortical activity (the independent variable) was manipulated.

Working from yet another perspective, Katkin and his co-workers (Katkin, 1985; Hantas, Katkin, and Reed, 1984) have reported that the right hemisphere may be uniquely involved in autonomic perception, and especially in heartbeat detection. (This work is described above, in the discussion of visceral perception.) This has also been demonstrated by Davidson, Horowitz, Schwartz, and Goodman (1981), who found that left-hand finger tapping (regulated by the right hemisphere) is closer in time to the preceding R wave in the ECG than were right-hand finger tappings (regulated by the left hemisphere). Thus, the findings by Katkin of a right-hemisphere superiority for heartbeat perception are supported by the data produced by Davidson et al. (1981), which demonstrated the possibility of special interoceptive abilities of the right hemisphere. Similarly, in a theoretical paper devoted to an analysis of hemispheric differences in the control and maintenance of attention, Jutai (1984) convincingly argued for a right-hemisphere dominance of attention and arousal on the basis of the available empirical literature. Jutai argued further that the empirical data concerning the dominance of the right hemisphere in attention and arousal is most intriguing when cardiac activity is used as an indicator of attentional and arousal behavior.

Furthermore, Yokoyama, Jennings, Ackles, et al. (1987) failed to observe anticipatory heart-rate changes in a reaction-time task in patients with lesions to the right hemisphere. Findings like these may further be illuminated by the observation that it is mainly the right branch of the vagus nerve that innervates the sinoatrial node of the right atrium (Brodal, 1981). (See also Chapter 5.)

Summary

This chapter has reviewed some important concepts and research findings relating cardiovascular functioning to psychological processes

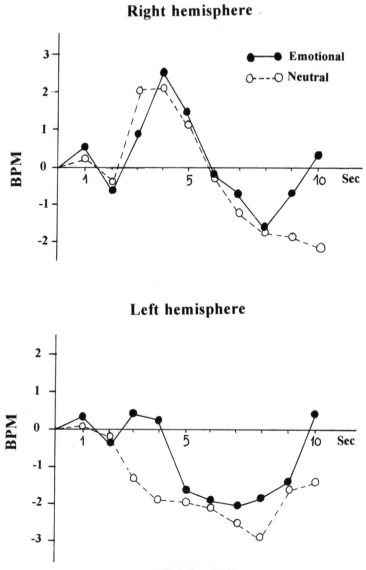

Figure 10.7. Changes in heart rate during stimulus presentations of emotional and neutral pictures. The pictures were presented either to the right or left hemisphere of the brain, through the visual half-field technique. Heart-rate acceleration was more pronounced when the stimuli were presented to the right hemisphere. (Data from Hugdahl et al., 1983, with permission from the publisher.)

and traits, such as stress and personality patterns. Cardiovascular reactivity was described, as were the methodological and conceptual pitfalls that must be avoided when defining an increase in cardiovascular reactivity.

The Type A behavioral pattern has generated a large amount of research over the last twenty years, linking, among other things, anger and hostility to increased risk for myocardial infarction. This chapter reviews the research on Type A and offers criticisms of some of the results generated within current paradigms.

Perception of visceral phenomena, and particularly one's own heartbeat, is described here as an important new area of cardiovascular psychophysiology. This chapter ends with a review of cognitive processes that are reflected in cardiovascular functioning. A special section is devoted to the "triphasic heart-rate curve," which is characterized by an initial deceleration, acceleration, and a second deceleration in situations of anticipation and expectancy. The Lacey-Obrist arguments on cardiovascular cognitive psychophysiology were discussed, along with hemispheric differences in control of heart rate and attentional and motivational effects on heart rate.

11

The Electroencephalogram

The electroencephalogram (EEG) is a recording of the difference in electrical potential between various points on the surface of the scalp. The rhythmic pattern of an EEG wave is generated by cyclical changes in the membrane potentials of underlying nerve cells. These cyclical changes are probably caused by synchronizing impulses from a corticothalamic neurogenerator, which establishes corticothalamic "current loops" that produce synchronous neuronal activity in the cortex.

The potentials recorded in the EEG come from the cortex, and particularly the large pyramidal cells in layers IV and V of the cortex. A pyramidal cell might be considered a dipole whose axes are perpendicular to the surface of the cortex (Cooper, Osselton, and Shaw, 1974). In this model, a current dipole, which is an approximation of the currents caused by sources and sinks in many neurons, gives rise to a localized flow of current when the neurons and their axons depolarize.

Nunez (1981) has provided a somewhat different view on what an EEG represents. According to Nunez, the EEG records the interaction of cortical neurons by means of action potentials. The neurons of the cortex have a hierarchical columnar organization, with different types of neuronal cells at different cortical depths. There are six layers of cells in the cortex, designated layer I to layer VI from the cortical surface inward. Nunez postulated that neurons in one column of the

234

cortex interconnect with neurons in another through short-range intracortical fibers or through long-range association fibers (which link distant areas of the cortex, such as the anterior and the posterior parts). The recordings that Nunez calls *wave phenomena*—that is, standing waves—occur when action potentials travel along association fibers connecting cortical regions over some distance. This explains why EEG frequency is much more sensitive to changes in long-range (association) connections than to short-range (intracortical) connections.

When electrodes are placed on the scalp, the EEG will reflect the activity of large groups of neurons being synchronously depolarized. It is therefore important to keep in mind that the EEG is not particularly sensitive to focused activity in narrow regions of the cortex. This is further emphasized by the fact that the voltage signal picked up by the EEG electrodes has been conducted from the source through a conductive fluid medium, through the bony structure of the skull, and then through the scalp to the electrode.

This chapter will provide a framework for understanding EEG recordings and their applications in studies of activation, sleep, and hemispheric asymmetry, with a focus on the different waveforms in the normal EEG and quantitative techniques for describing EEG waves. Practical guidelines for recording the EEG signal are provided throughout the chapter. Chapter 12 discusses potential changes in the EEG in response to stimulus presentations, so called event-related potentials (ERPs).

Recording the EEG Signal

EEG patterns are wavelike, and their analysis is based on measurements of the frequency and amplitude of the waves. Visual inspection is the simplest way of characterizing the waveforms but, because different observers may have different opinions, it is not a scientifically reliable method. In clinical practice, though, visual inspection is standard procedure for identifying the distinctive patterns of serious disorders, such as an epileptic seizure.

For scientific purposes, the EEG signal is best described by decomposing it into sinusoidal waveform components, each with a certain frequency and amplitude. In a sinusoidal wave, the electrical potential (voltage) goes up and down around a resting baseline level in cycles.

(The example shown in Figure 11.1 illustrates two cycles.) One cycle is the change in voltage from resting baseline in a positive, then a negative, and then again a positive direction, until it returns to the baseline.

The peak-to-baseline amplitude is the magnitude of the deflection from baseline to maximum in one direction. The peak-to-peak ampli-

Sinusoidal waveform

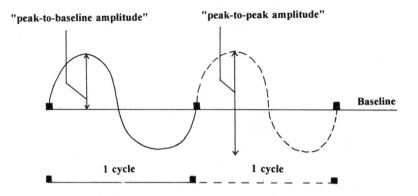

EEG signal

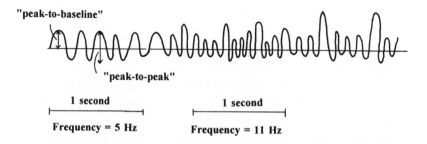

Figure 11.1.   A sinusoidal wave with two cycles *(top)* and an EEG signal *(bottom)* with many cycles. Amplitude = displacement from baseline, frequency = cycles per second (in Hertz, Hz).

tude is the magnitude of the deflection between two peaks. The frequency of a sinusoidal signal is the number of cycles per second, measured in hertz (Hz) or kiloherz (1,000 Hz). A frequency of 5 Hz thus means five cycles in one second.

The EEG signal is picked up by tiny electrodes, usually placed on the scalp but sometimes implanted in the cortex or hippocampus. EEG electrodes are typically plated with gold or silver–silver chloride in order to prevent the buildup of electrode potentials during a recording session. The signal from the electrode is then amplified before it is written out on polygraph paper (as the standard EEG machines do) or stored on a computer for subsequent analysis (as modern research laboratories do). The EEG signal is in the microvolt range ($\mu V = 10^{-6}$ volt), much smaller than the ECG signal, which is in the millivolt range ($mV = 10^{-3}$ volt). Typical amplitudes are 30–50 μV for alpha waves and 10–20 μV for beta waves.

The International 10–20 System

The locations on the scalp for EEG electrodes have been standardized since 1958 (Jasper, 1958) in the so-called International 10–20 system. The system uses four reference points: the inion (the small bump at the back of the head), the nasion (the small cavity just at the base of the nose), and the left and right preauricular points (the tiny cavities above and behind each ear). The electrodes are placed on the scalp as shown in Figure 11.2, at points 10 and 20 percent of the distance of the lines from the nasion to inion and from the left to the right preauricular points.

As a general rule, the capital letter in each electrode location (F, T, P, O, C) refers to the cortical lobe—frontal, temporal, parietal, and occipital—or the central sulcus, respectively. Odd numbers refer to locations on the left side of the scalp, even numbers to locations on the right side. A full 10–20 montage involves nineteen EEG leads, which usually are supplemented with two recording leads of eye-movement recordings. Thus, a common full-scale EEG recording montage involves twenty-one recording channels, but many modern EEG and ERP laboratories use as many as 32, 64, or even 128 recording channels (e.g., Gevins and Bressler, 1988). A large number of recording channels is commonly used for functional analysis of brain electrical activity mapping (BEAM), which is described below.

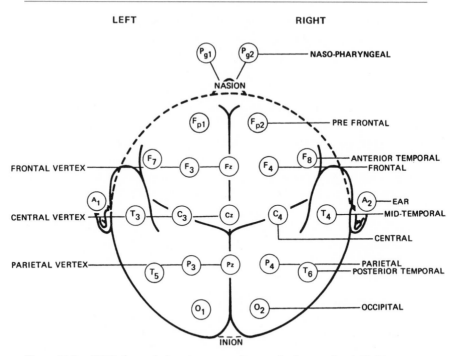

Figure 11.2. EEG electrode locations according to the International 10-20 System.

The EEG Laboratory

Figure 11.3 illustrates the layout of a standard EEG system, with pre-amplifiers, amplifiers, filters, FM tape recorder for data storage, and computer analysis. Note that only two leads, or channels, are being recorded, though most laboratories today use more than two leads. Many laboratories have also bypassed the FM tape recorder for storage of data in favor of off-line analysis. It is common now for the raw data to be stored directly on the hard disc on the computer or on various optical-disc storage devices.

Monopolar and Bipolar Recordings

A *montage* is a specific arrangement of electrodes. The nineteen electrodes in the 10–20 system may be connected together into various

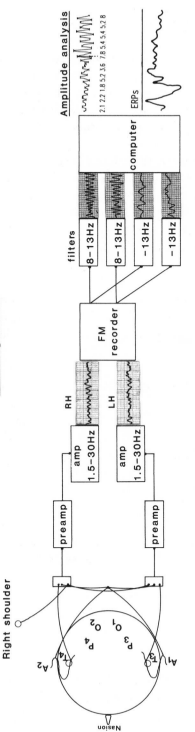

Figure 11.3. A typical EEG laboratory, with the subject to the left and examples of EEG recordings to the right. Only two electrode leads are shown here, but the principle is the same when more leads are added. RH = right hemisphere, LH = left hemisphere, amp = amplifier. The settings for the filters are only examples of possible settings.

montages, and standardized electrode montages are typically used in clinical EEG diagnostics.

Leads may be arranged to form monopolar or bipolar montages. In a bipolar montage, each recording channel is connected to two scalp electrodes, both of them being active. In a monopolar montage, also called the *common reference method*, one electrode is active and the other one (or two electrodes connected together—see below) acts as a reference electrode.

Typical arrangements for the reference electrode(s) are the "linked-ears" and the "linked-mastoids" arrangements. A linked-ears reference is made by connecting together two electrodes at points behind the ears (A_1 and A_2 in Figure 11.2) and using the connected electrodes as a common reference for the active electrode(s). A linked-mastoids reference is made by connecting together two electrodes placed on the mastoid muscle on the side of the neck and using this as the reference point. The reference electrode(s) should not be affected by the EEG signal from the scalp. Some authors have used the tip of the nose as the reference point, since it is further "away" from the brain. In addition to reference electrodes, a ground electrode, connected to earth, may also be used.

It is important to keep in mind that there is probably no area on the scalp, or the face, that is an absolute "zero" reference. All reference placements mentioned above will be affected by some neuronal activity. This is partly because of the problem of volume conduction, the fact that the electrical signal is conducted in a fluid-filled medium. (For more details, see the discussion in Chapter 12 on artifacts in electrical signals from the brain.) Selecting the reference electrodes is a complex problem, especially since there is no "absolute" reference point anywhere on the body surface. As will be discussed in more detail below, the use of a linked-ears arrangement as a reference in studies of EEG asymmetry may actually attenuate and abolish any effects of differences at homologous EEG sites across the hemispheres. Furthermore, noncephalic reference placements may pick up heart and muscle activity that could interfere with the EEG signal.

Filters

The EEG signal is usually filtered before being recorded in order to reduce "noise" and enhance the frequency components that are of interest. All standard EEG amplifiers have different filter functions built in. A typical instruction in psychophysiological research may be to filter out frequencies above 30 Hz and below 5 Hz, although the actual figures vary tremendously, depending on the research agenda and the available equipment. Today digital filters are included as part of the software in the EEG computers used to analyze the signal.

It should be remembered that setting the high- and low-frequency filters at a certain value does not mean that all frequencies within the accepted range are unaffected by the filter or that all other frequencies are ignored by the amplifier. Filters may differ in sharpness, which means that they attenuate the signal at certain frequencies lower and higher than the filter setting. How close to the filter setting the filter actually attenuates the EEG signal is determined by the sharpness of the filter.

Artifacts

The EEG signal may be affected by various types of *artifacts*, or interference. For example, the EEG may record 60 Hz interference from the main power line in the laboratory, or eye movements or heartbeats may change the signal recorded at the scalp. Alpha waves are particularly sensitive to whether the eyes are closed or open, and eye blinks may make EEG waves resemble event-related potentials.

A frequent artifact in EEG recordings is muscle activity (see Pivik, Broughton, Coppola, et al., 1993, for an excellent discussion of artifacts in EEG recordings), which is especially troublesome because the frequency spectrum of the electromyographic (EMG) signal is very broad, covering most of the EEG bands. Thus, filtering the EMG signal will in many instances not help the researcher, since doing so may filter out large aspects of the EEG signal as well. Alternatively, setting the low-pass filter at, say, 40 Hz in order to filter out frequencies above 40 Hz will not help, since EMG activity will also be recorded in the frequency range below 40 Hz. Muscle activity is especially problematic when the subject has to perform cognitive or emotional tasks during the recording, because subjects concentrating on these tasks will probably not be relaxed and immobile. Pivik et al. (1993) suggest methods for statistically separating muscle activity from EEG recordings.

The time constant of the low-pass filter may also affect the recorded signal, which requires the EEG psychophysiologist to have some understanding of basic electronics and electricity. The *time constant* (TC) is the time it takes for an AC signal to fall two-thirds of its initial amplitude. There is an inverse relationship between the lower cutoff frequency for the low-pass filter and the time constant, such that a cutoff frequency of 0.16 Hz corresponds to a time constant of 1.0 sec, a cutoff frequency of 0.027 Hz corresponds to a time constant of 6 sec. On some amplifiers the time constant is provided as a switch, while on others the low-pass frequency filter settings are provided. Conversion between time constants and cutoff frequency is given by the equation: $TC = 1/(2\pi F)$, where F is the lower cutoff frequency.

EEG Rhythms

EEG recordings will vary in frequency and amplitude when the individual being recorded is engaged in different cognitive or emotional activities. These differences have been noted since the introduction of the technology: Hans Berger, the Austrian psychiatrist who in 1929 suggested that "wavelike" electrical activity could be recorded from the human scalp, recognized that the "waves" tended to change in frequency and amplitude with the state of the organism—higher frequency and smaller amplitude in states of arousal, very large amplitudes and slow frequencies in sleep.

Berger furthermore observed that when the individual was at rest and relaxed, rhythmic wave sequences were generated at about 10 Hz, but when the individual became alert, this rhythm disappeared and was followed by a new, higher frequency varying somewhere between 15 and 50 Hz. Berger called the "relaxing" waves *alpha waves*, and the "alertness" waves *beta waves*. The occurrence of alpha and beta waves, respectively, in states of relaxing drowsiness and alertness is one of the major characteristics of the EEG. Figure 11.4 depicts the four most typical EEG waveforms: alpha, beta, theta, and delta.

The alpha rhythm. The alpha rhythm is a regular, but not always sinusoidal, waveform with a characteristic 8–12 Hz frequency of mid range amplitudes varying between 10 and 150 microvolts (µV). Alpha is most easily recorded from occipital-parietal regions and can be driven by opening and closing the eyes. Opening the eyes attenuates the alpha wave, and closing the eyes enhances alpha occurrence. The alpha rhythm is probably generated by multiple processes in the posterior part of the brain (Shagass, 1972). Cohn (1948) advanced the view that there were two source generators in each hemisphere and that a change of dominance of the activity of one hemisphere relative to the other would give rise to movement of a single focus of EEG activity. It is further suggested that an alpha wave recorded from the scalp is the average signal of the activity of several generators deep in the brain tissue.

The alpha wave is also typically attenuated or blocked during arousal or cognitive activity. As previously mentioned, the blocking of alpha over one hemisphere when a subject is engaged in a particular cognitive activity has traditionally been used as an index of hemispheric differences in the performance of that particular task. The reason for this is that an absence of alpha waves from an area would indicate greater cortical activation in that area. However, conclusions about specific localizations of cortical activity based on the presence or absence of alpha activity in an EEG should be made with some caution, since the EEG does not have a particularly good spatial resolution.

The spontaneous alpha rhythm is typically recorded at occipital leads and is of similar amplitude over both hemispheres, although it may sometimes be of slightly higher amplitude in the right hemisphere. As can be seen in Figure 11.4, a characteristic feature of alpha is that it waxes and wanes over time.

The beta rhythm. The beta waveform is typically of higher frequency and smaller amplitude than the alpha (from 14 Hz and up, usually lower than 25 μV in amplitude). A simple rule of thumb regarding the relation between frequency and amplitude is that as the frequency increases, amplitude generally decreases, and vice versa.

Beta activity occurs over most parts of the scalp, often with frontal predominance, although posterior dominance may also occur. It is most often associated with increased activation and arousal. Since the alpha wave is absent when the individual is aroused and beta activity is recorded, this state is called *alpha desynchronization* or *alpha blocking.*

The theta rhythm. Theta waves are slow, high-amplitude waves with frequencies between 4 and 7 Hz. They have a variable distribution over the scalp, depending on the age and degree of alertness of the subject. The normally occurring theta has, though, a more posterior than anterior localization. Theta waves are considered to co-occur with vascular changes that accompany increasing age.

The delta rhythm. Delta waves are predominant during later sleep stages, when the subject is in deep sleep (see below), although this pattern of activity decreases with increasing age. The waves have vari-

Alpha (α)

Frequency: 8 - 12 Hz

Amplitude: 10 - 150 μV

Location: Occipital/parietal regions

Attenuated on eye opening   **Eyes opened**

$P_z - O_1$ ⎍⎍⎍⎍⎍⎍⎍⎍⎍⎍⎍⎍⎍⎍⎍⎍⎍⎍⎍⎍⎍⎍

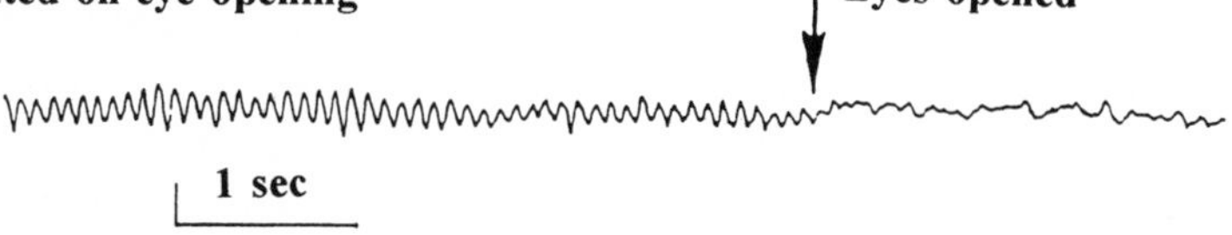

⌐ **1 sec** ⌐

Waxing and waning of alpha

$P_z - O_1$

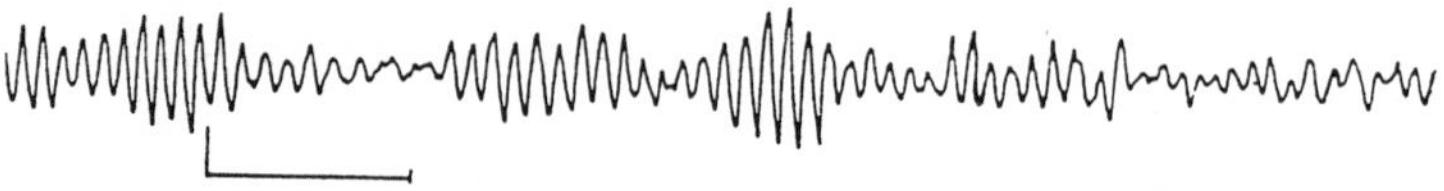

Beta (β)

Frequency: 15 Hz and up

Amplitude: Up to 25 μV usually, but higher at times

Location: Typically frontal regions, but also posterior dominant

$F_4 - F_2$

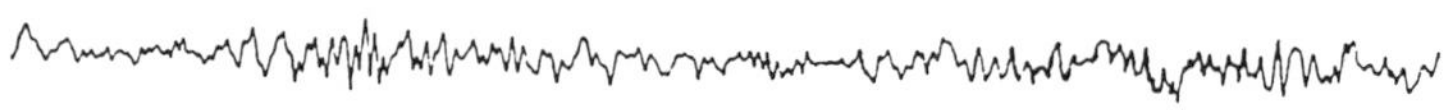

Figure 11.4.   Four types of EEG waves. (Adapted from Craib and Perry, 1975, Beckman Instruments.)

Theta (Γ)

Frequency: 4-7 Hz

Amplitude: Variable

Location: Variable

T$_z$ - C$_z$

Delta (δ)

Frequency: 3 Hz or slower

Amplitude: Variable

Location: Variable

C$_z$ - P$_z$

1 sec

able high amplitudes and very slow frequencies, from 3 Hz and slower. Delta waves are considered signs of brain abnormality if they occur frequently in the awake state. In general, slow waves below 8 Hz should be rare or absent in the EEG of a normal awake individual.

Analytic Techniques

The EEG signal can be analyzed by reference to the time or the frequency domain of the signal. Time-domain analyses are based on measures of the amplitude, such as correlational analyses, in which the amplitude of the signal is averaged over time, independent of signal frequency. Frequency-domain analyses are based on measurements of the frequency of the signal, as in power spectral analysis. Examples of each type of analysis are provided below.

Amplitude Analysis

A simple way of performing an amplitude analysis is to determine the mean amplitude. The investigator first determines a "scoring interval," perhaps 10 seconds after the presentation of a stimulus. The next step is to measure all peak-to-peak amplitudes within the scoring interval and convert the summed amplitudes to mean amplitude. Figure 11.5 illustrates an exercise in amplitude analysis across a 5-second scoring interval.

As an alternative, the investigator might first "rectify" the EEG signal. In a recording that has been rectified, all deflections of the signal point in only one direction. With the signal in this form, the investi-

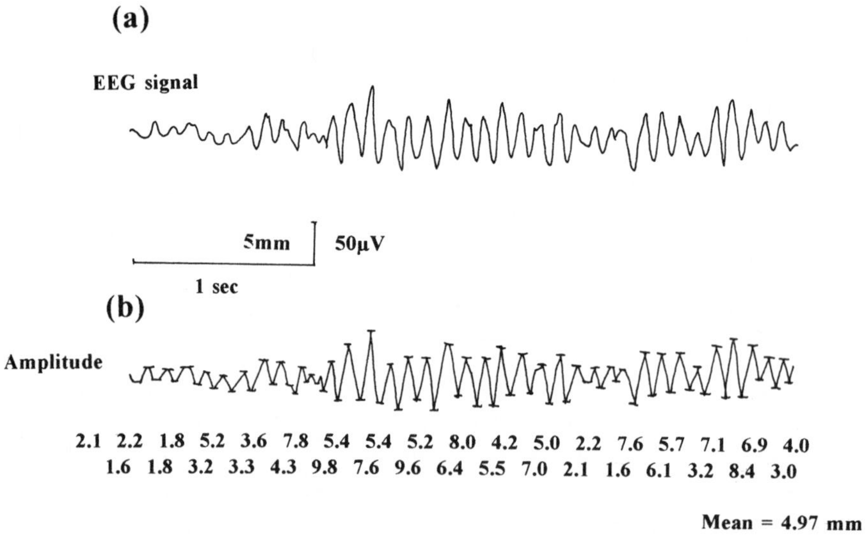

Figure 11.5. For EEG amplitude analysis, the peak-to-peak amplitudes of the waves in an EEG signal (as in *a*) are outlined and measured (as in *b*). The amplitudes are then summed and averaged across the scoring interval. (Adapted from Cooper, Osselton, and Shaw, 1974, with permission from Butterworth and Co., London, U.K.)

gator can then mathematically integrate and average the rectified amplitudes.

Correlational Analyses

Another type of amplitude analysis is correlational analysis. Correlational analyses are calculations of the degree of similarity between two EEG signals occurring at homologous sites on the scalp (see Cooper, Osselton, and Shaw, 1974). Theoretically, the degree of similarity between two signals may be expressed as a correlation coefficient. By multiplying two homologous signals together, the cross product of each pair is obtained, and the cross product is integrated and summed in order to obtain the covariance and correlation coefficient of the signal pair. Two signals may have a large covariance because they are similar in shape, but a large covariance can also be obtained because of large amplitudes in the individual signals. This problem is usually avoided by normalizing the covariance function by dividing the covariance by the square root of the product of the variance of the two signals. The normalized covariance is the correlation coefficient. Correlational methods, as stand-alone methods, are less frequently in use today than previously, after the introduction of power spectral analyses (described below).

Cross-correlation techniques are used to analyze signals that have similar patterns but that are recorded from different locations on the scalp. For example, alpha frequencies that occur over parietal brain areas may be delayed by 30–50 msec after the corresponding alpha waves at more anterior, frontal leads. Although this delay can be expressed as both phase and time differences, time differences are less complex mathematically. Cross-correlations provide information about similar activity recorded at the two leads and the time delay between the signals, so common patterns of activity are emphasized while dissimilar activity is suppressed (Gevins, 1987). An example of cross-correlation is a comparison of the EEG signals from two homologous (similar) sites on the left and right hemisphere, which might detect lateral asymmetries in EEG function across the two cortices of the brain. If two signals are similar in shape and frequency but have different time lags at different locations on the scalp, this pattern may indicate independence of underlying neuronal generators for this particular wave frequency.

Auto-correlation analysis is a comparison of the EEG signal with a time-shifted version of itself. The time delay can be as short as 5–10 msec. Auto-correlation techniques are primarily used to detect periodicity in the EEG signal. An example is the "waxing and waning" of the alpha frequency across time in a single EEG channel. The occurrence of alpha bursts at regular time intervals may be detected by auto-correlation. See Figure 11.6 for an example of an auto-correlation graph.

The mathematical principles behind cross- and auto-correlations are similar, but the auto-correlation technique compares epochs of the same signal while the cross-correlation technique compares epochs from two different signals.

Power Spectral Analysis

Frequency analyses are far more common than amplitude analyses, and Fast Fourier Transform (FFT) is one of the most common techniques. The FFT technique determines the *power spectrum* of an EEG signal, sometimes called a *frequency spectrum*, by separating the signal into its specific sinusoidal and cosine waveforms, a procedure called *spectral analysis*. The mathematical operations involved in FFT analysis are beyond the scope of this book. The resultant frequencies are graphed on an *x-y* plot, called a *power spectrum plot*, as relative amplitude for each frequency component.

For research purposes, the EEG signal may be filtered to get rid of unwanted frequencies (like interference from 60 Hz energy sources) before being subjected to a power spectral analysis, or Fourier analysis, to separate the relative contribution of the different frequencies in the signal. The result is plotted as the "power" or intensity for different frequencies by multiplying amplitudes by frequencies. Figure 11.6 shows a typical EEG signal recorded during rest in an adult individual and the resulting power spectrum. Note the maximum power in the frequency region 8–12 Hz, which corresponds to the alpha wave band usually recorded from occipital leads during rest.

Coherence Analysis

Coherence analysis is a technique in the frequency domain, although the method in itself is a correlational one. Coherence analysis involves

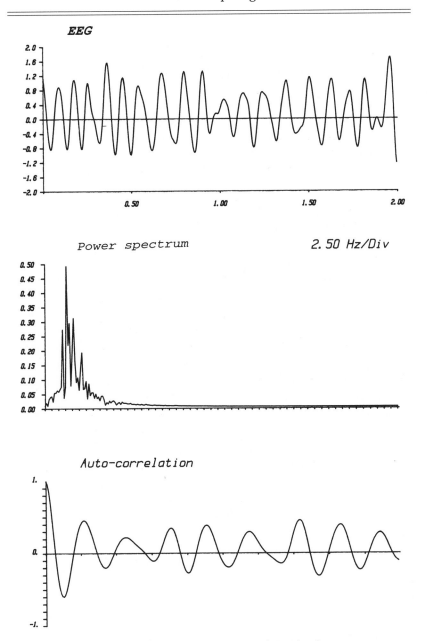

Figure 11.6. Frequency analysis of a raw EEG signal *(top)* by the power spectrum *(middle)* and auto-correlation *(bottom)* methods. (Courtesy of Lars Bäckström, Uppsala University, Sweden.)

the computation of Pearson's product-moment correlation coefficients between various EEG leads, which provides a measure of correlation at each frequency. Coherence is a measure of the relatedness between two EEG signals frequency by frequency. A high correlation coefficient thus indicates that two signals are similar in frequency, and that the activation patterns under these two electrodes are symmetrical. Coherence analyses are typically used in EEG studies of hemispheric asymmetry.

Topographical Mapping of EEG Activity

Brain electrical activity mapping, or *BEAM* (Duffy and McAnulty, 1985), is a new technique for analyzing EEG signals that has already yielded interesting results. It involves the simultaneous analysis of either EEG frequencies or ERP amplitudes at many electrode locations. Each electrode voltage, at any point in time, is given a digital value. The corresponding values at areas between the electrodes are "estimated" with various forms of mathematical interpolation, using data from the three or four nearest electrodes (see Itil, Mucci, and Eralp, 1991, for a comprehensive description of the BEAM technology). Other terms frequently used to denote BEAM technique are *brain mapping* and *EEG topography* (Pivik et al., 1993).

The result is a "map" of the scalp showing different values corresponding to the frequencies and amplitudes in the EEG or ERP signal. These values are then "color-coded" so that a color map of the cortex may be produced, with some colors (green or red) indicating areas of

➤

Figure 11.7. A topographic map of brain activity made from electrophysiological data. (Data for this map provided by ERP waves, which are derived from an EEG signal; see Chapter 12 for details.) Individual ERPs are recorded at the electrode locations indicated *(A)*. Mean voltage values are calculated for each location *(B)* for the interval beginning 192 msec after the stimulus (indicated by the vertical line in *A*). The head region is treated as a 64 × 64 matrix *(C)*, resulting in 4,096 different spatial domains (pixels). Each domain is assigned a voltage value by linear interpolation from the three nearest known points. Finally *(D)*, the raw voltage values are fitted to a discrete-level equal-interval intensity scale matched to the appropriate pixel, and the images are displayed in a gray scale (or can be converted to a color scale). (From Duffy and McAnulty, 1985, reprinted with permission from Little, Brown, and Company, Boston, MA.)

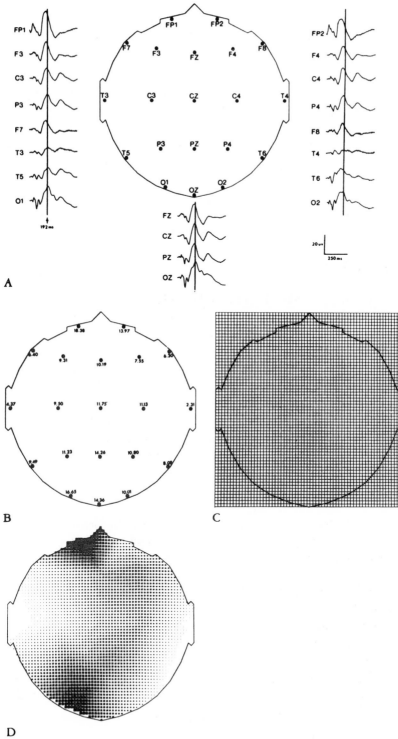

higher EEG frequencies, other colors (dark blue or white) indicating areas with lower frequencies. By relating the different frequencies in the EEG, or the amplitudes in the ERPs, to brain activity levels, the BEAM technique may thus map the spatial localization of cortical activity to a given stimulus at a given point in time.

BEAM maps can be upgraded at specific intervals, such as every 500 msec, to provide a series of brain maps over time. These may be presented in a display to show how EEG activity in certain areas of the brain may shift localization as a particular stimulus is processed or as a task is solved. The principle behind the BEAM technique is illustrated in Figure 11.7 (from Duffy and McAnulty, 1985).

Clinical BEAM Diagnosis

John, Prichep, Friedman, and Easton (1988) have developed a clinical diagnostic system that compares the BEAM profiles of normal control persons with the BEAM profiles obtained from individuals with different psychiatric disorders. They used computed values for the standard normal distribution (z scores) of the relative power in different EEG frequency bands (alpha, beta, theta, and delta), and each BEAM map represents the difference in relative EEG power after Fourier analysis between the diagnostic groups and the normal control group for each frequency band. The researchers noted a large decrease in activity among subjects with alcoholism and dementia relative to the control data.

BEAM in Psychopathology

The BEAM technique has been used to study the brain activity of individuals with various learning disabilities, including dyslexia (Duffy and McAnulty, 1985). The BEAM maps of children with learning disabilities, for example, show deviations of EEG features from the predicted normal range. Dyslexic children tend to have less variability in their BEAM topographic distributions. They also tend to have more alpha activity over the left hemisphere, a possible sign of reduced activity in the left (language-specialized) hemisphere. Furthermore, Buchsbaum, Hazlett, Sicotte, et al. (1985) found that administration of benzodiazepines to anxiety patients altered frontoparietal and occipital alpha distribution, in the direction of increased alertness. These findings reveal the usefulness of BEAM topographical mapping for investigating clinical disorders, in this case to identify cortical areas involved in anxiolytic drug action.

Although the BEAM technique is an interesting development of standard EEG technology, it should be remembered that it does not represent a new recording technique—it is simply a new way of plotting EEG and ERP data. Thus, a BEAM map is a more efficient way of displaying data produced by familiar recording technologies. An exception is the mapping technique for event-related covariances (ERPs) developed by Gevins (e.g., Gevins and Bressler, 1988), in which event-related potentials are mapped on the cortex from a large number of EEG channels. BEAM also has the advantage that it can show changes in EEG patterns across cortical sites with time, as noted above. This is a new and important addition to standard EEG and ERP analyses.

An important distinction must be made between BEAM maps and other models of brain activity; because BEAM maps resemble "pictures" of the brain, some researchers or clinicians may regard them as anatomically similar to MRI or PET scans, which are based on actual blood-flow changes (see Chapter 13 for a description of MRI and PET). For one thing, BEAM maps are usually created from data from a restricted number of EEG leads, and they have far less spatial resolution than, for example, an MRI scan. Furthermore, the use of similar color-coding principles in BEAM and PET maps may actually mislead the researcher to interpret effects in the BEAM image that are certainly not present.

The Electroencephalogram in Psychophysiology

The electroencephalogram is a record of a person's psychological state. As noted above, deviations from the normal EEG patterns for both frequency and amplitude may indicate pathology, most notably the occurrence of epileptic seizures. Some of the more typical and frequent EEG wave rhythms, for both normal and abnormal psychological states, are listed in Table 11.1.

EEG patterns are also useful for studying psychophysiological states and events. In classical psychophysiology, the EEG is most typically associated with studies of sleep stages (Dement and Kleitman, 1957), activation theory (Lindsley, 1960), and classical conditioning (Jasper and Shagass, 1941), although it has been used as a brain correlate of

Table 11.1. Description of EEG waveforms and corresponding scalp locations and psychological states.

Type of waves or rhythm	Frequency per second (range)	Amplitude or voltage (V)	Percent of time present	Regional or diffuse	Region of prominence or maximum	Condition when present	Normal or abnormal
Alpha	8–12	5–100	5–100	Diffuse	Occipital and parietal	Awake, relaxed, eyes closed	Normal
Beta	18–30	2–20	5–100	Diffuse	Precentral and frontal	Awake, no movement	Normal
Gamma	30–50	2–10	5–100	Diffuse	Precentral and frontal	Awake	Normal, sleep deprived
Delta	0.5–4 0.5–4	20–200 20–400	Variable Variable	Diffuse Both	Variable Variable	Asleep Awake	Normal Abnormal
Theta	5–7	5–100	Variable	Regional	Frontal and temporal	Awake, affective or stress stimuli	Normal (?) Abnormal
Kappa	8–12	5–40	Variable	Regional	Anterior and temporal	Awake, problem solving?	Normal
Lambda	Pos. or neg. spike or sharp waves	5–100	Variable	Regional	Parieto-occipital	Visual stimulus or eye opening	Normal (?)
K-complex	Pos. sharp waves and other slow pos. or neg. waves	20–50 50–100	Variable Variable	Diffuse Diffuse	Vertex Vertex	Awake, auditory stimulus Asleep, various stimuli	Normal (?) Normal
Sleep spindles	12–14	5–100	Variable	Regional	Precentral	Sleep onset	Normal

Source: From Lindsley (1960), with permission from Academic Press and the author.

almost every mental faculty, from personality (Henry, 1965) to intelligence (Kreezer, 1940). As early as 1944, however, Lindsley concluded that there was little empirical evidence to support the notion that EEG patterns could measure the intelligence of an individual.

In more recent psychophysiological research, EEG has been used to separate functions in the left and right hemispheres of the brain (Galin and Ornstein, 1972; Gevins, Schaffer, Doyle, et al., 1983), to characterize stable individual traits in positive and negative emotionality (Davidson, 1992), and to indicate hypnotic susceptibility (Morgan, MacDonald, and Hilgard, 1974), just to mention a few examples. EEG is frequently used in clinical neurological and psychiatric practice as an invaluable diagnostic tool for identifying functional disorders. For epileptic patients, for example, implanted EEG electrodes in the brain can give advance information that a seizure is about to start.

Activation Theory

Lindsley (1960) used associations between EEG waveforms and behavioral patterns, ranging from deep coma to strong emotional excitement, to describe a "behavioral continuum" going from lower to higher forms of awareness and consciousness. The EEG pattern served as a cortical correlate to the behavioral pattern, and it, too, was graded according to a "continuum" of activation and awareness.

The activation theory was quite influential during the 1960s and early 1970s, but it fell more or less into disrepute after studies by Lacey (e.g., 1967) suggested that different physiological measures changed in opposite directions from changes in behavioral activation. For example, as mentioned in Chapter 2, whereas an EEG moves through a gradual continuum of change from coma to rage, heart rate decreases in response to highly activating but nonaversive stimuli, but increases in response to aversive stimuli.

Hypnosis

The search for EEG concomitants of hypnosis and hypnotic susceptibility has traditionally been focused on two phenomena: the search for changes in brain activity during hypnosis, either as a state or as a trait phenomenon; and the search for shifts in hemispheric asymmetry during hypnosis, as mediating brain "markers" or "footprints" of hypnosis (MacLeod-Morgan and Lack, 1982; Morgan, MacDonald, and Hilgard, 1974). Although several promising findings have been reported, particularly that hypnosis may involve a general shift of hemispheric activation to the right hemisphere, a more critical analysis of the data reveals that neither search is unequivocally confirmed. It should be clear, though, that EEG effects of hypnosis are frequently observed and that they are probably a unique kind of "brain footprint" of the state of hypnosis.

It is problematic, however, that some studies report large differences in EEG activity between individuals with low and high susceptibility to hypnosis, and between hypnosis and the waking state, while other studies fail to find any differences at all. One disturbing fact may be that both slow and fast EEG frequencies are reported to covary with hypnosis. Since the alpha band (8–12 Hz) is a marker of a relaxed state and the beta band (>15 Hz) is a marker of an activated state, it is unsatisfactory that effects of hypnosis have been reported both in the alpha and beta ranges.

Another methodological problem is that only one or two EEG leads are used in many studies. Since many studies differ in their placement of the electrodes, differences in outcome between studies may thus be due to the different types of activity recorded at different cortical sites. For example, it has been shown that alpha power increases at occipital but not at central and frontal leads as subjects moved from waking to hypnosis. Thus, an experiment that records only from central or frontal areas will miss changes occurring at other electrode leads during hypnosis.

Hemispheric Asymmetry

Differences in EEG frequency over the left and right hemispheres of the brain have traditionally been taken as an indication of functional differences in processing ability between the hemispheres for various cognitive tasks. Briefly, reduced alpha power of one hemisphere, or parts of a hemisphere, relative to homologous sites over the other hemisphere is a sign of increased activity in that hemisphere. Since alpha power is related to resting state, a decrease or blocking of alpha over a certain region of a hemisphere during the performance of a specific task indicates that this region is more activated by this task than is the homologous region in the opposite hemisphere.

A problem with EEG frequency analyses of hemispheric asymmetry is that the spatial specificity of any EEG electrode is poor. The recorded frequency under one electrode on the scalp could, in principle, be generated at many local sites, possibly even from the other side of the corpus callosum. In other words, increased power over the cortex in one hemisphere may be generated by many local sources at different cortical sites. However, some studies have shown significantly reliable consistency of task-related asymmetries in the EEG over time. Ehrlichman and Wiener (1979), for example, demonstrated that the right to left differences in the alpha frequency band remained stable over two separate test occasions for four verbal and four spatial tasks.

A classic study of the EEG-frequency index of hemispheric asymmetry is the study by Galin and Ornstein (1972), who had subjects either write a letter from memory or solve Koh's Block Design (a spatial test from the WAIS intelligence test battery). To complete the Block Design, the subject must arrange a collection of different-colored cubes to match a two-dimentional sketch. In terms of hemispheric asymmetry theory, writing a letter is a language-related task that should activate the left hemisphere, and solving the Block Design test is a visuospatial task that should activate the right hemisphere. In line with the predictions, Galin and Ornstein found that posterior alpha wave was suppressed over the left hemisphere when the subject engaged in the letter-writing task, and it was suppressed over the right hemisphere when the subjects engaged in solving the Block Design test. In a critical examination of EEG studies of alpha asymmetries, Gevins, Zeitlin, Doyle, et al. (1979) made the important argument that noncognitive factors—stimulus characteristics, limb and eye movements, and the subject's ability and effort—may have affected the EEG patterns and contributed to the observed asymmetries. For example, writing a letter from memory involves unilateral hand movements in addition to cognitive processing. Hand movements may affect the EEG on the side contralateral to the writing hand, but this effect would be unrelated to the cognitive effort involved in verbal behavior.

In two experiments using tasks similar to those used by Galin and Ornstein (1972) and others who had observed alpha asymmetries, Gevins et al. (1979) tried to separate cognitive from noncognitive factors. In their second experiment, no motion of the limbs was required and stimulus characteristics were better controlled. After having analyzed the results of their studies, Gevins et al. (1979) concluded that "it is likely that the EEG patterns that discriminated between the tasks of experiment 1 were due to intertask differences in efferent activities, stimulus characteristics, or performance-related factors, rather than to cognitive differences. These experiments offer no support for the idea that lateralized EEG differences in different tasks reflect cognitive processes, as has previously been suggested" (p. 667).

Despite the critique of Gevins et al. (1979), several more recent papers have used EEG recordings to investigate the functional specialization in the brain for verbal and spatial tasks so often observed in other response modalities (see, e.g., Chapter 2). Papanicolau, Loring, Deutsch et al. (1986) concluded that left-hemisphere beta enhancement, rather than alpha suppression, is associated with unilateral activation of the left hemisphere during the performance of linguistic tasks. Thus, this study suggests that the beta frequency may be more sensitive than alpha blocking as an index of lateralized hemispheric function in the execution of cognitive tasks. However, following up on these findings, Davidson, Chapman, Chapman, et al. (1990a) again found evidence for a genuine alpha-suppression effect in posterior EEG leads during a word-finding (verbal, left-hemisphere) and dot-localization (spatial, right-hemisphere) task. Their recordings showed greater power suppression in the hemisphere putatively most engaged in task processing—that is, reduction of alpha waves over brain areas putatively engaged in processing of a specific task.

An important feature of the study by Davidson et al. (1990a) is that these authors were careful to match their verbal and spatial tasks psychometrically. They also chose tasks for which they had reliable performance data along with the EEG data, in order to relate differences in EEG asymmetries to differences in performance asymmetries. Furthermore, they showed that using the linked-ears arrangement for the EEG leads may produce an attenuation of existing asymmetries, for the leads may act as a shunt across the head and result in reduced asymmetries being detected between homologous EEG sites on the left and right hemispheres. In order to solve this problem, Davidson et al. (1990a) used a computer-derived equivalent to the linked-ears reference locations that did not involve physical linking of the two ears during the recording. In some recent studies from Davidson's laboratory (personal communication), it is obvious that physically linking the ears does not attenuate the magnitude of the asymmetry, but other problems may arise with linked-ears reference leads. The most impor-

tant one for studies of laterality is an asymmetry in electrode impedance of the two ear electrodes. Since the ear leads are linked together
prior to their input to the EEG amplifier, any disparity in impedance
between the two ears will have an effect on the effective location of
the reference, which in turn can affect the recorded asymmetry over
the hemispheres. Another critical point to remember, particularly with
regard to the use of the beta band to study asymmetries, is that these
frequencies are dramatically affected by muscle activity, and this interference has not always been carefully controlled in studies of beta
asymmetries.

To sum up: more recent findings have shown robust differences in
posterior alpha asymmetries produced by well-matched verbal and
spatial tasks, and particularly if care is taken to control for irrelevant
factors, such as task and subject demands and limb movements.

EEG asymmetry analysis was also used in a study of hemisphere
differences in sleep and dreaming (Ehrlichman, Antrobus, and Wiener, 1985). This study addressed the popular claim that sleep and
particularly dreaming is mediated by a shift to right-hemisphere activation as processing for the "rationality" performed by the left hemisphere during waking decreases. In contrast to popular claims,
Ehrlichman et al. (1985) found no evidence of a shift toward more
right-sided activation during sleep, and particularly not during dreaming, than during the waking state.

Emotionality and Approach-Avoidance

In another series of studies, R. J. Davidson and his group (reviewed
in Davidson, 1993) have investigated individual differences in resting
EEG and emotional reactivity as subjects viewed filmclips depicting
various positive and negative emotional scenes. Subjects with greater
right-sided frontal activation (lower alpha power) were also the ones
who rated filmclips designed to elicit fear and disgust more negatively.
Thus, subjects with more right-sided activation in their EEGs also
subjectively rated the filmclips as more negative and aversive. The opposite was found for subjects with greater left-sided EEG activation
at rest. These subjects rated the filmclips designed to elicit happiness
and amusement more positively than did the subjects with greater
right-sided EEG activation.

From these studies, and others, Davidson has argued that anterior left and right EEG asymmetry may predict affective behavior along an approach-withdrawal dimension: greater left-sided activation seems to be associated with approach behavior, greater right-sided activation with withdrawal behavior.

EEG Asymmetry and Psychopathology

Differences in left- and right-hemisphere EEG patterns have been identified in recordings from individuals in different psychopathological states, particularly schizophrenia. Merrin, Fein, Floyd, et al. (1986) found that reduced alpha power over the right hemisphere in premedicated schizophrenic patients, indicating overactivation of the left hemisphere, shifted toward normal alpha levels after treatment with neuroleptics.

Davidson (1993) reviewed several studies from his laboratory showing how individual differences in anterior EEG asymmetry during resting may predict dispositional mood, affective reactivity, and psychopathology. In one study, subjects were screened for depression using the Beck Depression Inventory (BDI). Subjects with high scores on the BDI had less left frontal activation, according to a power spectral analysis of alpha EEG, than did subjects with low scores on the BDI.

In order to separate state effects from trait effects—that is, whether the decreased left frontal EEG power in depressed subjects is a marker of the state of depression or a marker of a trait that predisposes the subject to episodes of depression—Henriques and Davidson (1990) compared the EEGs of remitted depressive patients with those of healthy controls. All of the remitted depressives were functioning normally at the time of testing and showed no signs of depression, although each had a lifelong history of psychopathology. Interestingly, the remitted depressives showed the same decrease in left frontal EEG activation as the acutely depressed subjects screened with the BDI. Thus, Davidson (1993) concluded that an asymmetry in frontal EEG alpha power may be a state-independent marker of individual differences in vulnerability to depression.

Sleep and Dreaming

Although the ultimate function of sleep is not known, brain activity during sleep is clearly different from brain activity during waking. The frequency of the EEG signal is reduced and amplitude increased in sleep, leading to a kind of synchronization in the EEG. Sleep also seems to be related to energy conservation, for "whatever benefits sleep may accrue for tomorrow, one clear function is to conserve calories for today" (Hobson, 1990, p. 372).

Sleep is essential for health and life. Rechtschaffen, Bergman, Everson, et al. (1989) have shown that animals that are deprived of sleep will lose weight and, if kept awake for extended periods of time, will die even if they are adequately fed. Recent findings (Kreuger, Walter, Dinarelli, et al., 1985) have also revealed a link between sleep and immune system function: risk of infection increases after extensive sleep loss. This may explain why people often get colds or other common infections after a long journey, for example.

Sleep also has effects on cognitive functions, like learning, attention, and memory, although the empirical evidence has sometimes been inconsistent. Recent findings, though, indicate a decline in affect and cognitive performance after sleep loss (Mikulincer, Babkoff, Caspy, and Sing, 1989).

Hobson and McCarley (1977) proposed a neurophysiological theory of sleep and dreaming that entailed a demodulation of the adrenergic neurons in the brain during sleep and an increase of cholinergically driven activity. This "activation-synthesis" theory attempted to explain sleep in physiological terms, as the shutdown of the norepinephrine system during sleep, and particularly during those periods known as *REM sleep*.

That the EEG changes rather dramatically during sleep has been known since the 1930s, although it was in 1953 that Aserinsky and Kleitman first made the revolutionary discovery that rapid eye movements (REM) occurred regularly, with about 90-minute cycles, during a night's sleep. The eye movements, furthermore, seemed to occur when subjects were dreaming (Dement and Kleitman, 1957).

The REM periods were associated with EEG waves that resembled the wave pattern seen in the awake, resting state, and REM sleep during Stage 1 is therefore also called *paradoxical sleep*. In addition to changes in EEG patterns and REM cycles during sleep, loss of muscle tonus is also a typical characteristic of sleep.

A typical psychophysiological sleep laboratory is therefore equipped with apparatus for recording brain activity (EEG), eye movements (electrooculogram, EOG), and muscle tonus (elelctromyogram,

EMG). Mamelak and Hobson (1989; see also Ajilore et al., 1995) have recently devised a simple, home-based recording system that the subject can wear in his own bed. The system (NightCap) consists of a piezoelectric sensing device that is taped to the eyelid and a movement detector attached to the forehead (see Figure 11.8). The piezoelectric sensor detects eye movements during the night and stores a record of these movements in a small computer memory under the pillow for later transfer to a host computer. In a similar way, the movement detector detects gross movements and stores that data on the computer memory too.

From EEG recordings, four stages of sleep have been identified during a good night's sleep (see Figure 11.9). A fifth stage is the REM stage mentioned above. Since REM epochs can occur during several of the other stages, however, one usually talks about four sleep stages and refers to the REM stage as a qualitatively different, or fifth, stage.

The awake state is characterized by a mixture of alpha and beta waves. When the individual closes his or her eyes and relaxes in order to sleep, alpha frequencies start to dominate. When the individual then actually falls asleep, the alpha waves are replaced by low-amplitude, high-frequency EEG waves mixed with slower waves (2–7 Hz).

When the subject falls deeper into sleep, there is a shift in the EEG pattern to slower frequencies with higher amplitudes *(theta waves)*. This is Stage 2 sleep, and it is characterized by the occurrence of K complexes and sleep spindles, large negative and positive deflections in the EEG together with bursts of high-frequency activity.

As the subject continues to sleep, there is a progressive change in the EEG, as *delta waves*, with larger amplitudes and slower frequencies, form. The EEG during Stage 3 sleep contains about 20–50 percent delta waves, and during Stage 4 sleep it contains more than 50 percent delta waves.

After a full cycle of sleep is completed, Stage 1 through Stage 4, a person shifts back and forth through the different stages of sleep. Typical REM episodes occur at intervals of about 90 minutes; non-REM (NREM) episodes occur during all four stages. Stages 2, 3, and 4 are sometimes also called *slow-wave sleep* because of the predominance of delta waves, particularly during Stages 3 and 4. Stages 3 and 4 are analogously sometimes also referred to as *delta sleep* or *deep sleep*.

Dreaming usually occurs during REM sleep, and an individual will have a much more vivid memory of a dream if awakened in REM than in NREM sleep and asked to recall the content of the dream. Crick

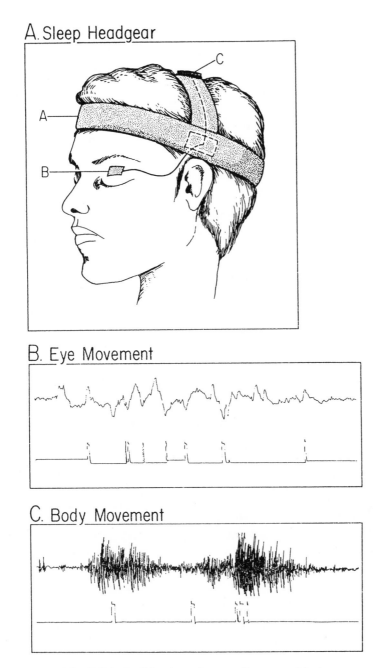

A. Sleep Headgear

B. Eye Movement

C. Body Movement

Figure 11.8. The "NightCap" headgear for recording eye and body movements during sleep. Sensing devices are fitted to the eyelid and the top of the head *(A)* to record eye movements *(B)* and gross body movements *(C)*. (From Mamelak and Hobson, 1989, reprinted with permission of the authors.)

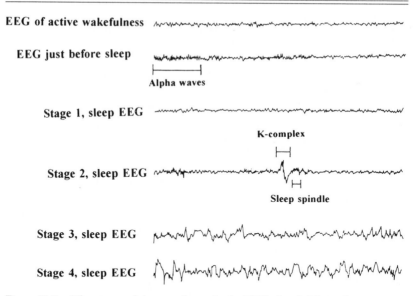

EEG of active wakefulness

EEG just before sleep

Alpha waves

Stage 1, sleep EEG

K-complex

Stage 2, sleep EEG

Sleep spindle

Stage 3, sleep EEG

Stage 4, sleep EEG

Figure 11.9. The stages of sleep as shown in the EEG signal. The waking state is characterized by alpha activity in the EEG and/or by a low-voltage, mixed-frequency EEG, frequent occurrences of beta activity. Stage 1 sleep: low-voltage, mixed-frequency EEG with much 2–7 Hz activity. Stage 2 sleep: presence of sleep spindles (bursts of waves with 12–14 Hz) and/or K-complexes (bursts of high-voltage spikes) on a background of low-voltage, mixed-frequency EEG. Stage 3 sleep: 20–50 percent of epochs with high-amplitude delta waves (2 Hz or less). Stage 4 sleep: delta waves occurring in more than 50 percent of epochs.

and Mitchison (1983) have suggested that we dream because the brain needs to "forget," to get rid of neuronal connections that are no longer necessary—dreaming as a kind of "unlearning." Hobson (1990), on the other hand, suggested that dreaming is what happens when the noradrenergic system in the brain is "shut down" and there is just random neuronal input to the brain (see the discussion above of Hobson and McCarley, 1977). Thus, Hobson (1990) tries to explain dreaming in neurophysiological terms, in sharp contrast to Freud, who proposed that dreaming releases the anxieties and worries built up during the day.

Summary

In this chapter the principles of the electroencephalogram were described, and an overview was given of the use of EEG in psychophysiological research on activation theory, sleep and dreaming, hypnosis, emotionality, and hemispheric asymmetry. Particular emphasis was put on a review of the use of EEG to define different stages of sleep. Recording procedures, including electrode montages, filter settings, and controls for artifacts, were also described. Finally, some of the major analytical techniques for interpreting the EEG recording were discussed, including power spectral analysis and various correlational techniques. A separate section was devoted to the recently developed BEAM technique, a "brain mapping" technique based on the EEG signal (see Chapter 13 for mapping techniques based on other physical features of the brain).

12

Event-Related Potentials

An event-related potential (ERP) is a change in an EEG recording from the scalp that is related to the occurrence of an external or internal stimulus. The ERP is an "answer" from the brain that is "time-locked" to the stimulus or event—that is, the potential either coincides with or follows the stimulus after a brief delay. ERPs used to be called *evoked potentials*, but since they occur as a consequence of an event it is better to refer to them as "event-related." Furthermore, ERPs may occur in the absence of a stimulus, as when an expected event is omitted in a train of stimuli, or they may precede voluntary motor responses, and in these cases the potentials are not "evoked" by stimuli. ERPs are generated by the brain through extracellular potentials associated with the activity of groups of neurons firing in synchrony.

Psychophysiological research on ERPs is the fastest growing subfield of psychophysiology. Many different components of the ERP signal, and possible meanings of these components, have been identified over the last thirty years. ERPs are used not only in basic research on brain functions and cognitive processes, but also in clinical practice to identify disorders of cognitive and affective functioning. Some of the components of ERP recordings will be described in more detail below. Excellent reviews of the components and their psychological meanings are Näätänen (1992), Squires and Ollo (1986), Hillyard and Hansen (1986), and Donchin, Karis, Bashore, et al. (1986).

266

The ERP Signal

ERPs were first reported by Davis in 1939, who found that there was a relatively large negative response in the EEG about 100–200 msec after each presentation of an auditory stimulus. Although Davis could see the response by visual inspection, most ERPs are too small to be observed after a single-trial, although there are exceptions to this rule. For most recordings, the ERP signal must be averaged. The principle of *signal averaging* is illustrated in Figure 12.1.

When two sinusoidal signals that are completely out of phase with each other are added together, the result is a "zero signal," or a straight line. The summed average of sinusoidal signals that occur randomly with regard to each other tends to be just such a straight line. Signals that have an invariant time relationship to a repeated stimulus, however, tend to "sum," or build up, over time. In the case of ERPs, the time-invariant relationship of the response to the stimulus makes it possible to extract the response from the EEG background through signal averaging.

Signal averaging was pioneered by Dawson (1954), who superimposed EEG traces succeeding each stimulus presentation for a short period of time. Since the EEG amplitudes occur randomly in the traces, with signals out of phase with each other, and since the ERP is time-locked to the stimulus, only after averaging will the ERPs "stick out" from the background EEG, if enough trials are used. Signal averaging, in effect, is the enhancement of a portion of the EEG after each stimulus is presented. An example of signal averaging with sixteen stimulus presentations is shown in Figure 12.2. Although signal averaging is the rule in almost all ERP research, some components of the ERP complex are so large that they *can* be observed on a single trial. The first presentation of a completely unexpected auditory stimulus may produce quite large ERPs that can be identified by visual inspection.

Artifacts

Although signal averaging is rather straightforward, ERPs are subject to a range of artifacts that may confound or obscure the recordings. There are many sources of ERP artifacts, including the ECG, muscle tension, electrode sources, eye movements, and blinks probably pre-

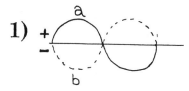

2) EEG

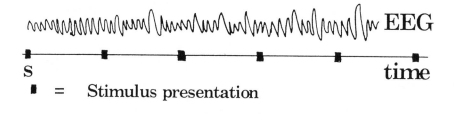

s   time

▮ =   Stimulus presentation

3) ERP   averaging

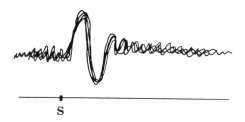

s

Figure 12.1.   The principle of ERP averaging. If two sinusoidal waves (like EEG waves) that are out of phase with respect to their positive and negative amplitudes are superimposed *(1)* and the two signals (*a* and *b*) are summed, the result is a "zero-amplitude" signal. If an EEG signal is recorded after repeated stimulus presentations *(2)*, the EEG waves will be randomly out of phase with respect to each other and thus sum toward "zero" (as shown in *3*). The ERP will be nonrandom with respect to each stimulus presentation, however, and thus sum to a positive and negative deflection when the repeated EEG samples to the stimulus are "added" (averaged) on top of each other (also shown in *3*).

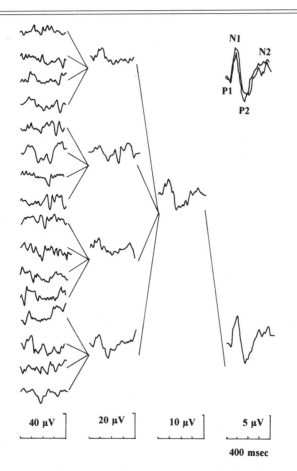

Figure 12.2. Successive ERP averaging to an auditory stimulus. (Note that negativity is recorded as the upward direction.) In the first column are the responses to a brief tone burst in 16 trials recorded at the vertex (C_z). In the second column, four groups of 4 responses have been averaged together to make a total of 4 responses from the original 16. The third column shows the average of all 16 responses. At the bottom of the fourth column is an average of 64 responses to the same tone burst, for comparison with the average to 16 responses in the third column. At the top of the fourth column are two averages of 32 responses, with ERP components indicated. (Adapted from Picton, 1980, with permission from Wiley and Sons and the author.)

sent the most interference. Eye movements and particularly blinks give rise to large potential shifts in the EEG, particularly at anterior and frontal electrode placements. There are basically two ways of handling eye-movement artifacts: rejection and correction. For example, all potential shifts in an EEG lead that exceed a preset value (e.g., 50 or 100 μV) might be automatically discarded from the ERP average. In some instances, however, as when only a few trials can be obtained, there may be too few trials left for an adequate average to be computed if trials are rejected because of interference from artifacts. In that case, mathematical algorithms are used to remove, or correct, the contribution of eye movements to the average (see Brunia, Moecks, Berg-Lenssen, et al., 1989). ERP recordings should therefore be complemented with simultaneous recordings of horizontal and vertical eye movements through, for example, electrooculography (see Chapter 14). It is recommended that horizontal and vertical eye movements be recorded on separate channels, but if this is not possible, a combined EOG measure may be derived by placing one electrode above the eye and the other electrode at the outer canthus of the eye.

Brain and Source Generators

Within certain limitations, ERPs may be considered brain correlates of mental operations. Moreover, from the distribution of ERP components over the scalp, the underlying regional brain activity may be inferred. This is, however, no easy task, since the same ERP deflections may be caused by almost any number of different source generators in the brain that act in linear fashion. This is called "the inverse problem" (Wood, McCarthy, Squires, et al., 1984), and there is no unique solution to it (see also the discussion of magnetoencephalography in Chapter 13). Part of the problem is that the inside of the skull is a volume-conducting space, conducting source-generator activity in many directions. ERPs represent electric fields that are generated by the flow of current when a large number of neurons are simultaneously activated. Electrical activity picked up by an electrode on the outside of the scalp, however, may not have its origin in the brain tissue directly underneath the electrode. If magnetoencephalography (MEG), which picks up the small magnetic fields generated by a dipole source in the brain (Hämäläinen, Hari, Ilmoniemi, 1993), is employed at the same time as the ERPs are recorded, some of the problems inherent in localizing the source of the ERPs may be overcome.

BESA Analysis

In an attempt to decompose the recorded ERP waveform into its underlying multiple dipole source potentials, Scherg (e.g., 1989) have developed a method of analyzing multiple time-varying dipole sources localized within a spherical head model that are mapped onto a magnetic resonance image (MRI) of the brain. Their technique, *brain electric source analysis* (BESA), is a sophisticated mathematical method for linear summation of multiple dipolar fields generated by multiple restricted brain regions.

Advantages and Limitations

Despite the problems inherent in determining the source generator of an ERP in the brain, ERPs have several distinct advantages, the major one being the good temporal resolution. Measuring ERPs time-locked to a stimulus event make it possible to probe information-processing in the brain on a very minute time scale, in the range of milliseconds. In principle, it is possible to follow the time course of the processing of a stimulus in the brain, from the initial sensory registration to the preparation and execution of a motor response. ERPs are typically used to infer brain activity related to cognitive processing, including sensory memory (Näätänen, 1992), attention (Hillyard, 1993), and stimulus probability (Duncan-Johnson and Donchin, 1977).

ERP Components

The recording of ERPs requires the same equipment as recordings of EEG, with the important addition of a signal-averaging device or computer software for averaging. A simplified example of the different ERP components is given in Figure 12.3.

ERP components may be classified with respect to the *polarity* of the waveform, whether it is positive or negative. In Figure 12.3 positive waveforms have an upward deflection and negative waveforms have a downward deflection. It is customary in the ERP literature, however,

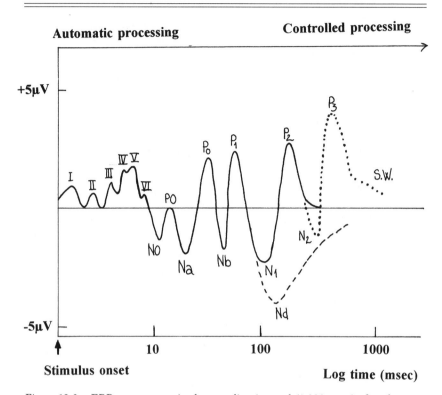

Figure 12.3. ERP components in the sampling interval (1,000 msec) after the presentation of a stimulus. This example is from an EEG recording of responses to an auditory stimulus of moderate intensity. Note the logarithmic *x*-axis. S.W. = slow wave activity. (Adapted from Hillyard and Kutas, 1983.)

to display negativity upwards, and positivity downwards, directly opposite to common conventions in mathematics. All figures, with one exception, in this chapter are drawn with positivity up. Figure 12.4 is a typical laboratory recording of ERP components occurring during 1,000 msec after the stimulus.

Components may also be classified with respect to *latency*, that is, the latency in msec when a certain component deflection occurs in relation to a stimulus event. A third classification is the *ordinal number* of a component following a stimulus. Components are numbered in accordance with their appearance after the stimulus: for example, the first negative-going deflection after the brainstem potentials is called the N1 (or N100, because it typically appears with a latency of about 100 msec after the stimulus).

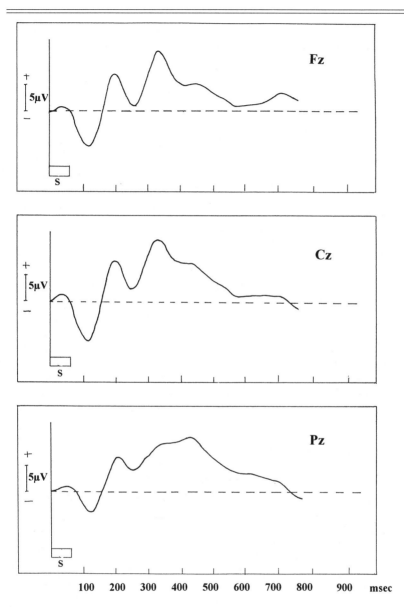

Figure 12.4. Laboratory recordings of the later components (N1, P2, and P3) recorded at three electrode leads (F$_z$, C$_z$, and P$_z$). These components occur 100 msec and more after the stimulus has been presented. Each horizontal grid is 100 msec.

Components may, finally, be classified after their distribution on the scalp. For example, the typical P3, or P300 (Sutton, Braren, Zubin, and John, 1965; Sutton, 1979), has its maximum amplitude over the vertex (Cz) and parietal midline (Pz) of the scalp.

Definitions of ERP Components

Most textbooks use the term *ERP component* to denote both the deflections and curves recorded at the scalp site, and the underlying source generator. Näätänen and Picton (1987), however, have made a distinction between the recorded positive and negative peaks and the underlying cortical activity, calling only the latter an ERP component. In their own words:

> We define an EP "component" as the contribution to the recorded waveform of a particular generator process such as activation of a localized area of cerebral cortex by a specific pattern of input . . . Whereas the peaks and deflections of an EP can be directly measured from the average waveform, the components contributing to these peaks can usually be inferred only from the results of the experimental manipulation."" (p. 376)

Thus, according to Näätänen and Picton (1987), the recorded ERP waves should not be called components but rather deflections, peaks, or averages.

This definition may be compared to the definition of an ERP component given by Donchin, Ritter, and McCallum (1978), who said that an ERP component was "a source of controlled, observable variability." This definition describes an ERP in terms of observable, recorded electrical activity, whereas Näätänen and Picton (1987) stressed the importance of linking the component with its localized physiological activity within the brain and with the generator process.

An ERP component is thus the contribution of this generator process to the observed, recorded waveform. Peaks, deflections, and averages do not represent any unitary brain events but instead, as discussed above, consist of the summed result of many different components whose electrical activity affects a single recording electrode. Different statistical methods, like principal-component analysis (PCA) or waveform subtraction, may be applied to disentangle the underlying components from the surface waveforms. For the sake of simplicity, and to concur with common terminology in the ERP literature, in this book I will refer to both waveform deflections and true brain components as "components."

Prestimulus Potentials

Another way to classify ERP components is to separate those components that occur before a stimulus from those components that occur after the stimulus. Most of the discussion so far has been concerned with ERPs that follow a stimulus, but some components are characteristics of brain events that precede a stimulus.

Contingent Negative Variation

The contingent negative variation (CNV) (Walter, Cooper, Aldridge, et al., 1964) typically occurs in the waiting period between a warning stimulus and an imperative stimulus, when the subject is anticipating an event. Figure 12.5 shows the increase in cortical negativity that occurs just before the execution of a motor response; this increase is different from the large and narrow N1 response that occurs following the presentation of the "get-ready" stimulus. This is also called the *readiness potential* (Kornhuber and Deecke, 1965). If the interval between the warning and imperative stimulus is long enough, the CNV may be decomposed into two components: a sensory component (also called the "O wave"), reflecting the effect of the warning stimulus; and a motor or readiness component, reflecting the anticipation of the second, imperative stimulus (Loveless, 1983).

The CNV and movement-related potentials have been studied extensively by Brunia and his collaborators over the years (see, e.g., Brunia, Haag, and Scheirs, 1985). Brunia and co-workers usually employ a fixed foreperiod reaction-time paradigm, with a warning stimulus alerting the subject to get ready and an imperative stimulus requiring the subject to make the motor response, usually pressing a button held in the hand. By minute measurements of CNV and the readiness potential, Brunia has been able to trace the information processing and response preparation that goes on in the warning foreperiod. Specifically, Brunia and Vingerhoets (1980) recorded CNV simultaneously with bilateral electromyography (EMG) from the calf muscles preceding a plantar flexion of the right foot. The EMG over

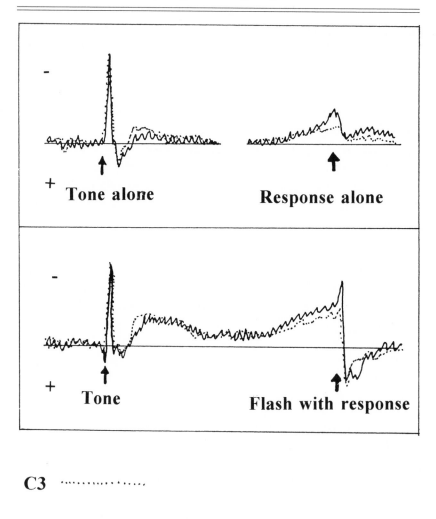

C3

C4 ————————

Figure 12.5. Typical Contingent Negative Variation (CNV) recording in a two-stimulus paradigm. The first stimulus (tone) is a warning stimulus for the subject to get ready. The second stimulus (flash) is a signal to respond. C3 and C4 are two leads along the central midline of the scalp. (Note that negativity is up in this figure.) (Adapted from Rohrbaugh et al., 1976, with permission from the American Association for the Advancement of Science and the authors.)

the right side of the muscle increased systematically over time, the largest EMG values being observed when the motor-preparation wave of the CNV reached its maximum just before the release of the response.

Lateralized Readiness Potentials

More recently, Coles (e.g., 1989) has shown that the readiness potential, elicited when the subjects waits to respond after a warning stimulus, is lateralized over the motor cortex. Coles has shown that as the subject prepares to execute a motor response by squeezing a hand-held dynamometer, a negativity develops that is maximum at the scalp electrodes contralateral to the responding hand. Coles (1989) has suggested that this negative potential reflects response activation. An example of this kind of activation is shown in Figure 12.6, where the readiness potentials are recorded from the left (C3) and right (C4) central scalp locations. By subtracting the potentials recorded at the contralateral electrode from the potentials recorded at the ipsilateral electrode for right- versus left-hand responses, the lateralized readiness potential can be derived.

Slow Potential Shifts and Biofeedback

Birbaumer and his coworkers (e.g., Elbert, Birbaumer, Lutzenberger, and Rockstroh, 1979; Rockstroh, Elbert, Birbaumer, and Lutzenberger, 1982) have demonstrated that CNV-like potential shifts occur in a 6-second interval when subjects are instructed to enhance brain negativity or positivity voluntarily. The task is a biofeedback task in which the subject is provided with a visual display that conveys information about cortical potential shifts in the subject. By changing the information on the screen when the subject produces larger cortical negativitity, Birbaumer and his colleagues have shown how operant conditioning of CNV-like potentials is possible (see also Birbaumer, 1977).

Exogenous versus Endogenous Components

A distinction is usually made between "exogenous" and "endogenous" components (Donchin, Ritter, and McCallum, 1978). Exogenous components usually occur within the first 100–200 msec after the stimulus; endogenous components occur later, from 100–200 msec and up to 500–1000 msec.

Exogenous components reflect the first neural processing of the physical characteristics of a stimulus. Moreover, they are obligatory responses to the stimulus, and the magnitude of the response is not dependent on the cognitive processing of the stimulus. These responses are called "exogenous" for just this reason—they are derived from "outside" the subject. Subjects in an experiment designed to tap exogenous components are typically asked to remain passive while stimuli are presented over and over again. Common experimental situations designed to elicit the early exogenous components are "photic driving" and "checkerboard reversals." Examples of exogenous components are the so-called brainstem potentials (see below).

Endogenous components, on the other hand, are elicited in complex experimental situations and often require active participation from the subject. They involve higher cognitive processes like attention or memory. Typical examples of endogenous components are the P3 component and the just-described CNV. Endogenous components are so named because they are driven from "inside" the subject—they are not obligatory to the physical characteristics of the stimulus. Their elicitation will depend on the nature of the information-processing requirements in the stimulus task. For example, the endogenous components occurring in the time interval between a warning stimulus and an imperative stimulus in a reaction-time experiment is dependent on

Figure 12.6. Examples of lateralized readiness potentials. Shown at top are idealized scalp-recorded brain potentials from the left (C3) and right (C4) scalp sites in a warned reaction-time task when subjects know in advance of the imperative stimulus the hand to be used to execute a correct response. WS = warning stimulus, IS = imperative stimulus. As subjects prepare to execute a movement, a negativity develops that is maximum at scalp sites contralateral to the responding hand. The asymmetry in these potentials is illustrated by subtracting the potential recorded at the scalp site ipsilateral to the movement *(middle)*. Then, the difference potentials for left- and right-hand movements are averaged to yield lateralized readiness potentials *(second from bottom)*. The lowermost panel shows the response activation phenomenon that Coles (1989) has suggested is reflected in the lateralized readiness potential. (Adapted from Coles, 1989, with permission from the Society for Psychophysiological Research and the author.)

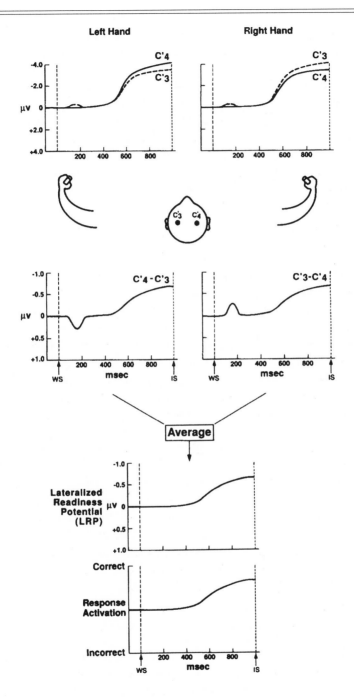

the subject's processing of the warning stimulus and anticipation of and preparation for the imperative stimulus, as reflected in the typical CNV.

Although endogenous ERP components have their distinct topographical scalp distributions—usually the larger responses are recorded at central and parietal leads—their corresponding dipole sources may not be close to the electrode with the maximum amplitude (Donchin, Karis, Bashore, et al., 1986). Some evidence exists that these components may have a subcortical origin in the hippocampus (Halgren, Squires, Wilson, et al., 1980).

Exogenous Components
The Auditory Brainstem Potentials

The auditory brainstem potentials (ABR) are seven deflections in the ERP signal occurring in the first 10 or 12 msec after the delivery of a click to the ear (Picton, Stapells, and Campbell, 1981). The seven waveforms are numbered I–VII (see Figures 12.3 and 12.7). The first deflection (wave I) reflects activity in the eighth cranial nerve, which is the hearing nerve. Wave II reflects activity in the cochlear nucleus, although this is not unambiguously agreed upon. Waves III–V reflect activity in the pons, the lateral lemniscus, and the inferior colliculus. Waves VI–VII involve activity in the medial geniculate body, although it has been questioned whether these waveforms are true brainstem responses, and that they also reflect thalamocortical activity (Vaughn and Arezzo, 1988).

ABRs are typically not studied by psychophysiologists, but they are important tools for diagnosing the source of various hearing deficits. ABRs are easily elicited with short auditory clicks. In neurology, ABRs are frequently used to identify tumors localized at the brainstem level. The ABR is also abnormal in patients with multiple sclerosis (MS), and several studies have shown how ABRs may be used in the diagnosis of MS (reviewed in Squires and Ollo, 1986).

Middle-Latency Components

After 10–12 msec, ABRs are replaced by the so-called middle-latency components (N0, P0, Na, Pa, Nb). These waveforms, which include both positive and negative deflections, are the first signs of activity in

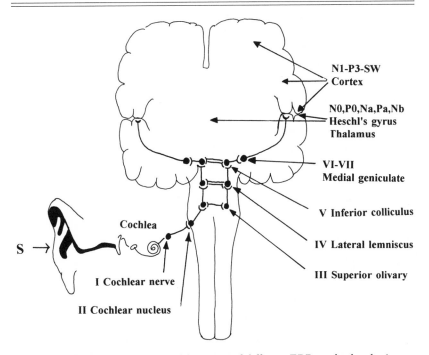

Figure 12.7. Suggested anatomical locations of different ERPs and other brain potentials recorded in response to an auditory stimulus. The components I to IV have a brainstem localization and a latency of 1–12 msec. The components N0 to Nb have their focus at the thalamic/auditory cortex level and a latency of 12–50 msec. The late components N1-P3-SW have their origin in the cortex and a latency of 100–1,000 msec. SW = slow wave activity.

the auditory cortex involving the Heschl's gyrus. The middle-latency waves are also related to thalamic activity.

Long-Latency Exogenous Components (N1 and P2)

From 100 msec and up to 200–300 milliseconds after the auditory stimulus, long-latency exogenous components, notably the N1 and the P2, are detected. These components are called *transient* since they share characteristics with endogenous components. In the auditory modality, the N1 usually peaks at about 100 msec, and it is therefore also called the N100. This is a relatively large waveform that is almost invariantly elicited to repeated presentations of auditory stimuli. The P2 has its peak around 180–200 msec after the stimulus and is therefore also designated the P200.

The N1 may be preceded by a small deflection, the P1 component, with a peak at about 50 msec. The P1, N1, and P2 components have somewhat longer latencies in the visual modality, but their interrelationships remain constant. The auditory N1 is most likely generated in the primary auditory cortex in the temporal lobe (Vaughn and Ritter, 1970). The N1 and P2 components share a great deal of overlap in how they are elicited by external stimulus conditions, although their scalp distribution is somewhat different. Thus, both the N1 and P2 may be considered to reflect neuronal activity generated in the superior temporal lobe involving the auditory cortex.

The N1 Attention Effect

The N1 component is related to selective attention, so, in a more restricted sense, it is not exclusively an exogenous component. It shares features with the later endogenous components. The N1 is related to processing negativity, an additional endogenous component (see below).

In a now classical study, Hillyard, Hink, Schwent, and Picton (1973) asked subjects to ignore tones presented to one ear while they were attending to tones of a different frequency presented to the other ear. The N1 component recorded by the vertex (Cz) electrode was enhanced for stimuli presented to the attended ear. This study solved a problem for early ERP studies, pointed out by Näätänen (1967): since stimulus sequences were presented in a predictable and fixed sequence, it was possible for the subject to prepare for the presentation of a stimulus.

The N1 effect observed by Hillyard et al. (1973) had an early latency of about 50 msec in some instances and was thought to reflect an early selection process in selective attention. It is generally believed to index Broadbent's (1971) concept of the stimulus-set mode of attention. Broadbent suggested that attention is related to a process that passively admits sensory input from a maintained set over the attended channel rather than to a process that requires active discrimination of each individual stimulus (Loveless, 1983).

The N1 component elicited in response to a brief auditory stimulus is one of the best-known ERP components. Näätänen, Alho, and Sams (1985) suggested that the N1 actually consists of two components, one emanating from the auditory cortex, the other perhaps not specific to any modality, since it may also be elicited by visual stimuli. Later it was suggested that it actually consists of three subcomponents. The amplitude of the N1 increases with increases in the interstimulus interval (ISI), up to about 10 sec. Its peak latency is also affected by the length of the ISI. The typical N1 effect observed by Hillyard et al. (1973) is illlustrated in Figure 12.8.

The N1 Neural Substrates

The neural substrates, including the dipolar magnetic field, of the N1 (N100) component of the ERP and the typical "N1 effect" observed by Hillyard and his co-workers (see Woldorff et al., 1993) have been identified through the use of magnetoencephalography techniques (see Figure 12.9). These "maps" locate the principal source generator for the N1 attention effect over the temporal cortex involving the primary auditory cortex.

The N2 Component

Negative deflections that occur around 200 msec after the presentation of a deviant stimulus in a train of stimuli are labeled "N2." As will be discussed in more detail below, the earlier deflection (N2a) share common features with the so-called mismatch negativity (MMN) deflection. A later deflection (N2b) is one of the endogenous components discussed in a later section of this chapter. The N2b is triggered by an auditory change in a train of stimuli, and particularly when the subject is attending to the deviant stimulus. The distribution of the N2b over the scalp is broad, resembling the distribution of the modality-nonspecific N1 component (Nätäänen, 1992).

The P2 Component

Closely related to the N1 is the P2 component, or deflection. Although they typically occur together in the auditory modality, the two components can be dissociated from each other. Furthermore, their scalp

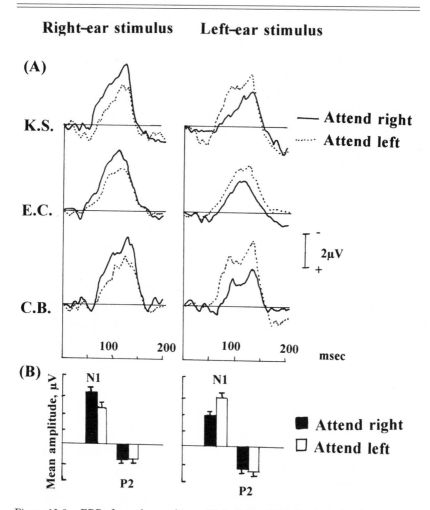

Figure 12.8. ERPs from three subjects (K.S., E.C., C.B.). Each tracing is an average of 1,024 stimulus presentations to each ear under attend-right *(solid line)* and attend left *(dashed line)* conditions. The bar graphs show the mean and standard error for group data (10 subjects). Note that negativity is up. (From Hillyard et al., 1973, with permission from the American Association for the Advancement of Science and the authors.)

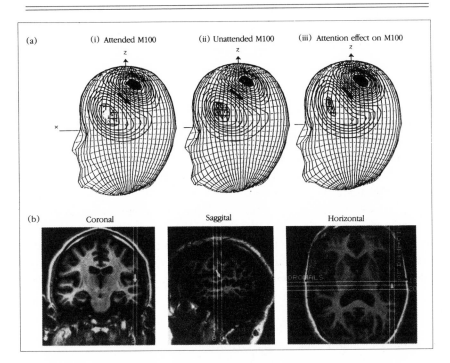

Figure 12.9. Magnetic-field distributions *(a)* for the M100 component (same as N100m in Figure 13.7) elicited by right-ear tones in a dichotic listening experiment. Separate mappings are shown for the M100 elicited by attended tones, unattended tones, and the "attention effect," which is the subtracted differential between the attended and unattended responses. These mappings show a dipolar field with magnetic field lines emerging from the head superiorly and entering inferiorly. The arrows indicate the direction and schematic positioning of the single equivalent dipole sources that were calculated to best fit these surface ERF distributions. Below, MRI scans indicate the calculated location of the best-fit dipole sources for the subject shown in *(a)*. The dipoles for the attended M100, the unattended M100, and the differential M100 attention effect were all situated within millimeters of one another in the auditory cortex of the supratemporal plane (location of the arrow). (From Hillyard, 1991, reprinted with permission from the author.)

distributions also differ (Näätänen, 1992): the N1 is maximal over the vertex (Cz) of the scalp, whereas the P2 is not so focally localized.

Mismatch Negativity

The mismatch negativity (MMN) deflection can be thought of as a cortical concomitant of the orienting response (OR) to change, as it also involves the gradual buildup of a memory template. Thus, MMN is a form of sensory memory and it is generated by a discrepancy between the memory trace representing the precise physical features of the previous stimuli and the sensory input from the deviant stimulus (Näätänen, 1990). Research on the MMN component is intimately linked to the work of the Finnish psychophysiologist Risto Näätänen (see Näätänen, 1992, for an excellent summary), although others have also made substantial contributions (see, e.g., Hillyard et al., 1973, regarding the N1 effect).

Stimulus Deviance and Passive Attention

Mismatch negativity may involve a passive attentional shift that occurs when there is a mismatch between what is currently represented in short-term memory and the properties of a presented stimulus. Thus, in contrast to the N1-P2 complex, the MMN wave is considered a response to stimulus deviance, in terms of physical characteristics. The scalp distribution of the MMN is modality-specific, particularly for the auditory modality. The MMN occurs around 100–250 msec after the presentation of a deviant stimulus against a background of more frequent stimuli, while the subject either ignores the stimuli or perform some task related to them.

The MMN is a negative waveform that occurs in response to deviant stimuli imbedded in trains of more frequent stimuli. The task of the subject is typically not to attend to the stimuli but to engage in some other, distracting activity. For example, as in the experiment whose results are shown in Figure 12.10, the subjects might be presented with blocks of auditory stimuli consisting of a standard stimulus of 1,000 Hz on 80 percent of the trials and a deviant stimulus of a slightly higher frequency (between 1,004 to 1,032 Hz) on 20 percent of the trials. In this experiment, the interstimulus interval was kept at 1 sec,

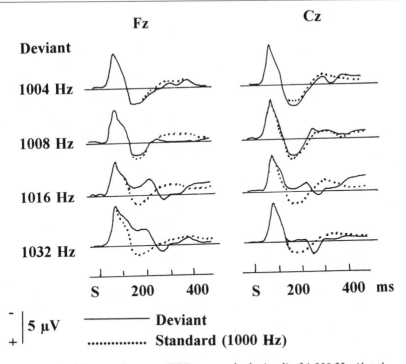

Figure 12.10.   The grand average ERPs to standard stimuli of 1,000 Hz *(dotted line)* and deviant stimuli *(solid line)* of 1,004, 1,008, 1,016, and 1,032 Hz. Eighty percent of the stimuli were standard stimuli and 20 percent were deviant stimuli. (Data from Sams et al., 1985, reprinted with permission from Elsevier Science Publishers and the authors.)

and the subjects were distracted from the stimuli by reading a book (Sams, Paavilainen, Alho, and Näätänen, 1985).

The MMN response to the deviant stimulus is usually derived from a difference-waveform. A *difference-waveform* is obtained by subtracting the ERP waveform in the infrequent, deviant condition from the corresponding waveform in the frequent, standard condition. See Figures 12.13 and 12.14 for examples of difference-waveforms. The MMN thus appears as a negative deflection that typically starts at about 100 msec after stimulus delivery and lasts until 200–250 msec after the stimulus. The largest MMNs were elicited to the 1,032 Hz deviant stimulus, which suggests that the magnitude of the MMN is related to the degree of physical deviance between the standard and deviant stimuli.

Automatic Deviance Detection

Originally, the MMN was believed to indicate automatic analysis of the physical characteristics of a stimulus and to be elicited whenever there is a mismatch between a "neuronal memory model" and the presented stimulus. The automatic nature of the MMN is somewhat controversial, however, since the deflection is smaller when it is elicited in hypnotized subjects instructed to ignore all tones being presented (Helge Nordby, University of Bergen, unpublished results). If MMN is completely automatic and dependent only on the physical characteristics of the stimulus, instructing subjects in hypnosis to ignore all stimuli should have no effect on the MMN's amplitude. One must conclude, therefore, that the MMN is influenced by attention, at least under certain experimental conditions.

In another study, Nordby, Roth, and Pfefferbaum (1988) demonstrated that the MMN could be elicited also to temporal stimulus changes: for example, having the standard and the deviant tones similar except that the deviant is shorter in duration. Nordby et al. (1988) found that MMN was also elicited by stimulus-repetition effects.

MMN and Memory

MMN is a rather robust empirical phenomenon, and it has been related to a variety of stimulus situations and experimental conditions: the spatial origin of a stimulus, memory, phonetic change, partial omission, sleep effects, and drug effects. Näätänen (1992) suggested that MMN is generated by a memory process that registers the stimulus change, which would indicate a kind of memory representation of the standard stimulus (Näätänen, Paavilainen, and Reinikainen, 1989). An alternative explanation is that the MMN is a response to a difference between sequentially presented stimuli and is generated by activation of new afferent neuronal elements corresponding to the frequency of the deviant stimuli. These neuronal afferents will remain responsive over the course of an experiment because the interstimulus interval between the deviant and the standard stimuli is long in comparison with the interval between the consecutive standard stimuli (Näätänen, 1992).

Visual ERPs

Visual ERPs (VERPs) differ from auditory potentials in that they consist of fewer waves. Visual ERPs are typically elicited in response to light flashes, as in "photic driving" experiments, or to patterned stimuli, as in the "checkerboard reversal" paradigm. This paradigm is the presentation of white and black squares that reverse in position every second or half-second. The VERPs are recorded at each reversal of the checkerboard; that is, whenever the squares change position, there is a trigger pulse to the EEG recording channel instructing the computer "to start sampling" for the VERP.

The most prominent VERP is a large positive potential that occurs at approximately 100 msec after the squares change position. The visual P1 (P100) is usually largest over the occipital cortex, although the distribution varies with stimulus conditions, including the luminance, contrast, and spatial frequency of the visual stimuli used. Typical VERPs elicited in response to the checkerboard paradigm are seen in Figure 12.11.

The latency of the visual P1 is typically prolonged in patients with multiple sclerosis (Halliday, McDonald, and Mushin, 1973), and this fact is often used in neurological practice to diagnose the disease. P1 latency prolongation occurs also in other neurodegenerative diseases, like Parkinson's disease and Huntington's chorea (see Squires and Ollo, 1986, for an overview).

Visual Attention and the Cuing Paradigm

In a recent series of studies, Mangun, Hansen, and Hillyard (1987) and Mangun, Hillyard, and Luck (1993) have shown facilitation of the early P1 component in studies of selective attention to spatial localizations. These studies are based on the so-called attention-cuing paradigm in selective attention (e.g., Posner and Driver, 1992). The standard Posner paradigm is illustrated in Figure 12.12.

A trial usually begins with the presentation of two rectangles on the computer screen while the subject is fixating the center cross. One of the rectangles suddenly becomes brighter (represented in Figure 12.12 as a double line). On half of the trials the left rectangle becomes brighter, on the other half of the trials it is the right rectangle. The

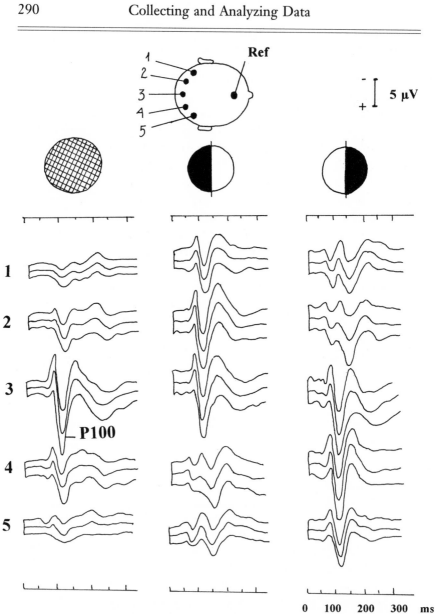

Figure 12.11. Examples of visual ERPs to three different black-and-white stimuli, recorded from 5 different electrode locations (indicated at top). Note the large visual P100 component at about 100 msec after stimulus presentation. (Adapted from Squires and Ollo, 1986, with permission from Oxford University Press, Inc., and the authors; originally adapted from the work of McCarthy and Wood.)

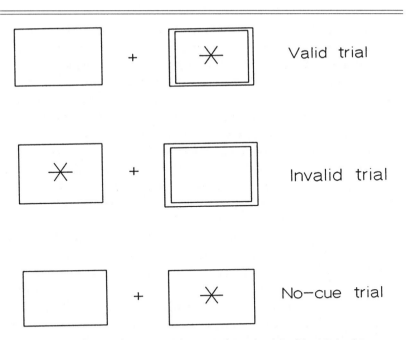

Figure 12.12. The visual attention cuing paradigm developed by Michael Posner employs the presentation of different display for valid, invalid, and no-cue trials. Typically, reaction times are prolonged on invalid trials.

brighter rectangle acts as a cue to attract the subject's attention to its spatial location without moving the eyes. This is called *explicit cuing*. After a short delay of a few hundred milliseconds, an asterisk appears in either the illuminated or the other rectangle. The task of the subject is typically to press a button as fast as possible when the asterisk appears. The asterisk is thus a target stimulus that follows the cue stimulus in this reaction-time (RT) task.

Those trials in which the asterisk appears inside the illuminated rectangle are the valid trials, the others invalid trials. In addition, control trials in which no cue is given are interspersed among valid and invalid trials. Valid trials are more frequent than invalid trials.

The typical behavioral finding is that RTs are faster on valid trials and slower on invalid trials, in comparison with the no-cue control trials. Posner (e.g., Posner and Petersen, 1990) has suggested a series of elementary mental operations in order to explain the orientation of attention to the cued target. When the target occurs in a spatial location different from that of the cue, shifting attention to the target involves interrupting ongoing activity, moving attention to the new location, and re-engaging attention at the target's spatial location. Usually, there is a behavioral advantage for the cued location over the uncued location, with shorter RTs to targets presented at the cued location and longer RTs to targets at the noncued location. These effects are called *attention facilitation* and *attention inhibition*, respectively.

The attention-cuing paradigm is frequently used in studies of selective attention. It has also been employed in clinical settings to study disorders of attention in schizophrenic subjects (Posner, Early, Reiman, et al., 1988) and in patients with parietal-lobe damage (Posner, Walker, Friedrich, et al., 1987).

There are several different variants of the Posner paradigm. In a variant used by Mangun et al. (1987), for example, a centrally placed arrow pointing either to the left or right visual half-field was used as the cue. This is called *implicit cuing*. The target to which the subject pressed a button was a vertical bar flashed inside a rectangle or square display. A valid trial was defined as a trial in which the light flash appeared inside the rectangle at the location to which the arrow pointed, invalid trials as those in which the light flash appeared at the opposite side of the location to which the arrow pointed.

The RTs showed the typical Posner effect, but there were also significant effects for the early N1 and P1 waves of the ERP, occurring at 170 and 110 msec, respectively. These effects are illustrated in Figure 12.13, for left-field target presentations. The P110 and N170 components shown in the figure were larger in the valid condition than in the invalid condition. Increased amplitudes during invalid trials were seen for the P3 component at about 350 msec, a finding that has later been replicated by Hugdahl and Nordby (1994).

Sensory Gating

The increased amplitudes of the long-latency exogenous P1 and N1 components suggest a gating of early sensory-evoked activity in the visual pathways. The findings by, for example, Mangun et al. (1987) thus support Posner's suggestion that providing the subject with information of the probable spatial location of a target stimulus will result in selective facilitation of sensory processing. In addition, Hugdahl and Nordby (1994) suggested that the enhanced P3 amplitude they

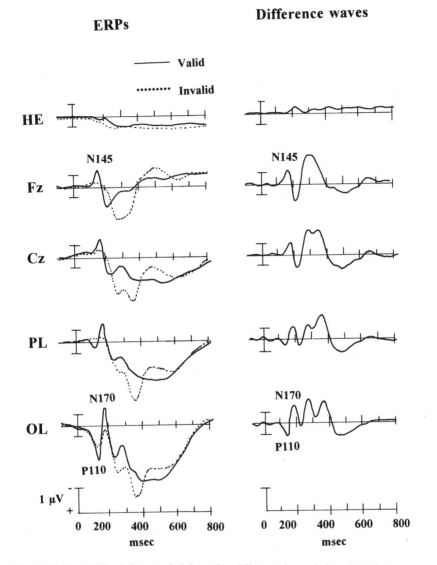

Figure 12.13. ERPs *(left)* recorded from five different electrode locations during responses to invalid and valid left visual field cue trials in the Posner attention cue-target paradigm (the cue was an arrow pointing to either the left or right side). Difference waveforms *(right)* are produced by subtracting the invalid from the valid ERP waves. Note the early components around 100–200 msec for recordings made under the valid condition, indicating attentional facilitation. (Data from Mangun et al., 1987, reprinted with permission from Elsevier Science Publishers and the authors.)

recorded after presentation of invalidly cued targets, and the distribution of the P3 mainly over central and frontal areas, may reflect the interrupt/disengage processing in the frontal cortex on invalid trials.

Somatosensory ERPs

Somatosensory exogenous ERPs are typically recorded as responses to nerve stimulation. For example, an experiment might require a brief electric stimulation to the median nerve of the arm. A whole range of very early waves can typically be seen after nerve stimulation, such as the N10, P15, and N20/P30 waves (which occur from 10 to 30 msec after stimulation). These waves probably reflect transmission in the somatosensory system from the brachial plexus nerve at the spinal cord level, over the thalamus, to the somatosensory cortex posterior to the central sulcus.

40 Hz ERPs

Patients who have received anesthetic drugs, such as benzodiazepine, sometimes show a 40 Hz component ERP to auditory stimulation. The 40 Hz ERP consists of two to four periodic occurrences in the 40 Hz range (Galambos, Makeig, and Talmachoff (1991). It disappears during states of deep anesthesia, including unconsciousness, and it has been suggested that this component is an indicator of the presence or absence of awareness (Kulli and Koch, 1991).

Endogenous Components
Processing Negativity

Processing negativity (PN) is considered an endogenous component (Näätänen et al., 1978) generated by a cerebral process that is different from the process that generates the exogenous N1 component. A typical experimental setup for the study of PN presents subjects with four types of tone stimuli that differ along two dimensions (e.g., pitch and location), each having two levels (e.g., left- vs. right-ear presentation, or high vs. low pitch). The subject may be instructed to try to detect the high-pitch tones presented in the left ear. Thus, the subject is instructed to actively attend to some features of the stimuli. The result is larger negativity in the response to the attended tones in the left ear than in the response to the right ear. The moment in time when the left- and right-ear ERP waveforms deviate from each other is interpreted as the time by which attentional filtering must have occurred. Hansen and Hillyard (1980) named the greater negativity that occurs in response to the attended tones than to the unattended tones the *negative difference* (Nd). Hansen and Hillyard (1980) also made the argument that there may be two topographically distinct portions of the processing negativity, or negative difference waves—a frontocentral component and a frontal component occurring later. The earlier, frontocentral portion of the Nd component may be similar to the "classic" N1 attention effect described earlier, having a gating function.

The P3 Component

The P3 component is a large positive wave that peaks around 300 msec after presentation of a stimulus when the subject is actively attending to that stimulus. The P3 may also be elicited when a stimulus is novel or surprising, as when an unexpected tone of a different pitch is interspersed among repeated presentations of another, more frequent tone. The P3 is thus closely linked to the orienting response (see below) and requires that attention be directed toward the stimulus.

Because the P3 occurs around 300 msec after the stimulus, it also called the P300. Specifying a time latency as implied in the names P300 or P345, however, implies a specific latency, while the name P3 is less specific but does specify that it occurs around 300 msec after the stimulus. The P3 is probably the most "researched" wave of all ERP components. It was discovered in 1965 by Sutton, Braren, Zubin, and John, who recorded ERPs following the presentation of stimuli that altered between the visual and auditory modality. Subjects had to guess the sensory modality, and a large, late, positive wave was recorded after both visual and auditory stimuli when they were presented in the unexpected modality. The P3 is thus modality-nonspecific.

Information Delivery and Stimulus Probability

Sutton et al. (1965) suggested that the critical feature of P3 elicitation was *information delivery*. That is, an infrequent or unexpected stimulus contains "more information" to the subject than a frequent and expected stimulus that merely "confirms" what was expected or known. Information delivery is thus inversely related to *stimulus probability*, in the sense that the less probable an event is, the larger is the information delivery.

In later research, stimulus probability became the major variable for eliciting the P3 wave. The most typical experimental paradigm is the *oddball paradigm*, a presentation of two tones that differ in pitch and probability. One of the tones, often referred to as the "frequent" or the "standard" tone, has a probability of occurring during each trial of 80–90 percent, while the other tone, as the "infrequent" or "target" tone, occurs with only 10–20 percent probability and is randomly interspersed among the more frequent standard tones.

The P3 is observed as a large positive deflection following presentation of the target stimulus (see Figure 12.14). The deflection is particularly apparent when the subject is actively attending to the infrequent tones, as one might be if instructed to count the "odd" stimuli. Note also that the classic P3 elicited in the oddball paradigm is maximal at parietal lead over the cortex.

The optimal condition to elicit a large P3 is 10–20 percent probability of stimulus occurrence. Duncan-Johnson and Donchin (1977) recorded ERPs in an experiment employing a typical oddball paradigm that varied both which stimulus was the target and the probability of occurrence. The critical feature in this experiment (see Figure 12.15) was stimulus probability, irrespective of whether the tone was the standard or the target. However, Polich (1990) demonstrated that the length of the interstimulus interval (ISI) affects the P3 independently of stimulus probability. By gradually increasing the ISI from 2 to 10 sec, Polich (1990) demonstrated that the P3 amplitude in response to the infrequent stimulus was larger only for the shorter ISIs.

Context Updating and the OR

The brain generators of the P3 are not completely identified, but at least some aspects of the P3 seem to be generated in the hippocampal region (although some would disagree). In a general sense, since the hippocampus is closely related to memory and memory processes, some authors have claimed that the P3 is also associated with memory and learning, particularly context updating (Donchin, 1981).

The dependence of the P3 on stimulus probability, with larger P3 amplitudes elicited by improbable events, links the P3 to the orienting

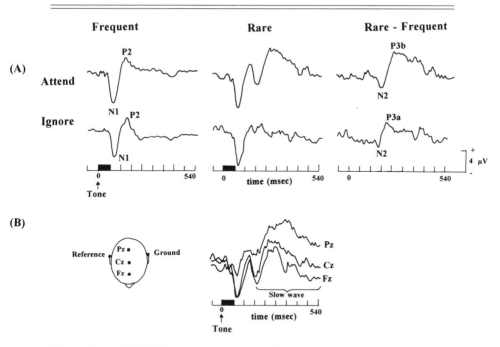

Figure 12.14. P300 (P3) components recorded in an experiment employing the typical oddball paradigm, with frequent and rare tones. At right are the difference waveforms, for which the ERPs to the rare tone are subtracted from the ERPs to the frequent tone. The upper waveforms were recorded while the subject is instructed to attend to the rare tone, the lower ones while the subject is instructed to ignore the rare tone. (Data from Squires and Ollo, 1986, reprinted with permission from Oxford University Press and the authors.)

response (OR) and the neuronal model (see Chapter 7). An OR interpretation of the P3 requires that P3 be elicited to novel, surprising stimuli and that it decline in amplitude over a number of trials (habituation). The first requirement, elicitation by unexpected events, is a typical feature of the P3. Regarding the second requirement, however, common folklore in ERP research has it that P3s can be elicited repeatedly over numerous trials with no obvious habituation. It is therefore interesting to contrast this common belief with a recent study by Polich (1990), who found a decline in P3 amplitude when comparing early with later trial blocks. Moreover, Donchin, Heffley, Hillyard, et al. (1984) argued that when the subject receives the stimulus passively the P3 also habituates over trials.

Donchin (1981) suggested that the P3 reflects the updating of working memory and named this change to the memory *context updating*. Subjects are presumed always to have a subjective expectancy, or "schema," that guides their responses to future stimuli. When an unexpected stimulus upsets this expectancy in subjective context, the schema in working memory is updated to enable the subject to act appropriately on the stimulus. In other words, the P3 is elicited whenever the subjective model of the environment has to be changed because new relevant information is being delivered with the stimulus (Donchin and Coles, 1988).

The view that the P3 component is related to context updating in working memory is not exclusive of an OR explanation, since it is possible to interpret the OR within the theoretical perspective of context updating.

P3-latency

The latency of the P3—that is, the time to its peak amplitude from the presentation of a stimulus—is not determined by the same parameters that determine P3 amplitude. Donchin and Coles (1988) suggest that P3 latency reflects the duration of stimulus evaluation: the longer it takes for a subject to evaluate the novelty or significance of a stimulus, the longer the latency. P3 latency is typically prolonged in certain neurodegenerative disorders, as Alzheimer's disease (see Squires and Ollo, 1986).

P3a and P3b

The P3 may in most cases be regarded as a single, unitary waveform elicited in response to improbable events, in particular when the sub-

---

Figure 12.15. Effects of varying the stimulus probability in the oddball paradigm with two auditory stimuli. The task of the subject was to count the number of the high-frequency tone in a session. ERPs were recorded from Pz. Note that the P300 component is largest when the subjects are asked to attend to (count) the stimuli and when there is a fairly large discrepancy between the probabilities for the attended and ignored stimuli. (Data from Duncan-Johnson and Donchin, 1977, reprinted with permission from the Society for Psychophysiological Research and the authors.)

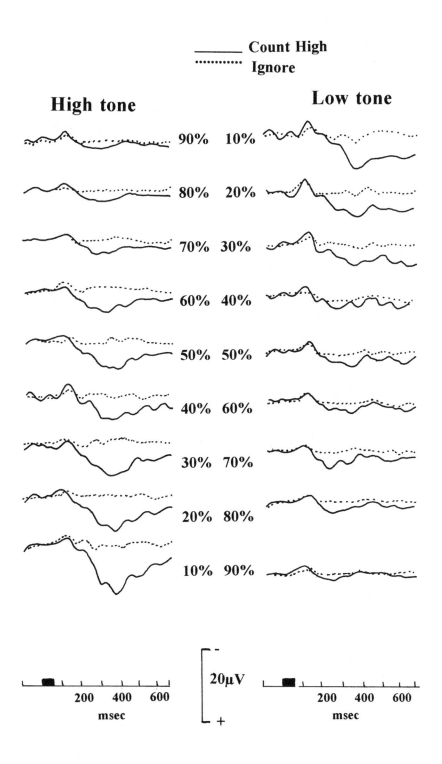

Count High
Ignore

High tone

Low tone

90%   10%

80%   20%

70%   30%

60%   40%

50%   50%

40%   60%

30%   70%

20%   80%

10%   90%

200 400 600
msec

20µV

200 400 600
msec

ject has to pay close attention to the occurrence of the less frequent events. However, Squires, Squires, and Hillyard (1975) observed that the P3 actually consists of two distinct waveforms, P3a (with a latency around 250 msec) and P3b (with a peak latency around 300 msec).

The P3a has a more frontal scalp distribution, whereas the "classic P3b" distribution is more parietal. It has been suggested that the P3a "registers" a mismatch between the current memory template and the incoming stimulus—that is, the P3a would act as an attention switch, focusing attention to the deviant stimulus—while the P3b reflects more elaborate processing, involving active discrimination and action preparation. The P3a and P3b waveforms often overlap in subjects actively attending to stimuli during an oddball task, making it difficult to distinguish between them. P3a shares features with the MMN (see above) in that both are related to deviations in the physical characteristics of the stimulus (Näätänen, 1992). They differ, however, in the sense that MMN also may be elicited without subjective awareness of the stimulus deviation. The P3a is therefore a more genuine endogenous component than the MMN.

Figure 12.16 gives schematic representations of the P3a and P3b waveforms. Note the difference in scalp distribution between the two waveforms, with the P3a being maximal over the central and frontal areas while the P3b has a more posterior scalp distribution.

Psychophysiological Implications of the ERP
Clinical Applications

The features of ERP waveforms may be affected by various psychological disorders. Table 12.1, for example, lists the amplitudes and latencies of P3 waveforms elicited by the oddball paradigm in subjects with different clinical disorders (see Squires and Ollo, 1986, for further details). As a general rule, P3 latency is prolonged in individuals with disorders related to the aging process, particularly various forms of dementia, such as Alzheimer's disease, and degenerative disorders, such as Parkinson's disease. Note also that the latency is prolonged in elderly individuals not affected by such disorders.

P3 amplitudes are reduced in patients in whom various psychopathologies, such as schizophrenia and depression, or alcoholism have been diagnosed. It is, however, unclear whether these reductions reflect a direct cortical correlate of psychopathology, or whether they

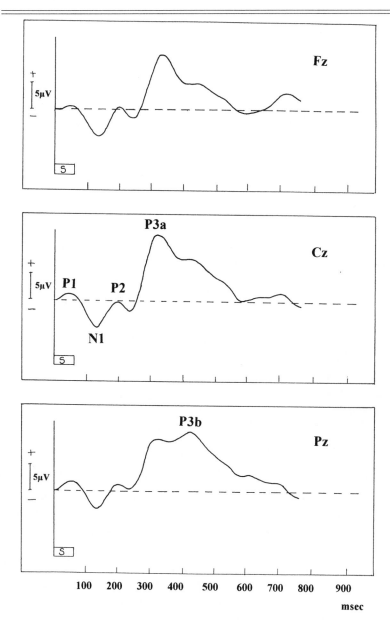

Figure 12.16. Development of the P3b component over the parietal lead, with P3a over the central lead. The distinction between P3a and P3b is difficult to make for recordings from frontal leads.

Table 12.1.   P3 latency prolongation and P3 amplitude reduction in clinical groups with diminished mental function.

Effect on P3 wave	Clinical Diagnosis	References
Latency prolongation	Normal aging	Pfefferbaum et al. (1980b)
		Syndulko et al. (1982)
	Dementia	K. Squires et al. (1980)
		Syndulko et al. (1982)
	Head trauma	K. Squires et al. (1980)
	Retardation	N. Squires et al. (1979)
	Alcoholism	Pfefferbaum et al. (1979)
		Skerchock and Cohen (1981)
Amplitude reduction	Alcoholism	Begleiter et al. (1980)
		Porjesz et al. (1980)
	Schizophrenia	Verleger and Cohen (1978)
		Roth et al. (1980b)
	Depression	Goodin et al. (1978b)
		Litzelman et al. (1980)

Source: Adapted from Squires and Ollo (1987), with permission from Oxford University Press and the authors.

are secondary phenomena due to reduced activation and motivational drive in schizophrenic and depressive patients. P3 amplitude reduction is also observed to some extent in persons affected by dementia.

ERPs, and particularly the P3 amplitude, have been linked to claims of a biological mediation of alcoholism (Elmasian, Neville, Woods, et al., 1982; Begleiter, Porjesz, Bihari, et al., 1984). Both these papers reported that young males with a family history of alcoholism showed attenuated P3 amplitudes to both auditory and visual stimuli. Thus, P3 amplitude seemed to be a "marker" of risk for alcoholism in sons of fathers who were alcoholics. Both studies noted a significant reduction of the P3 amplitude between subjects with a family history of alcoholism and the controls (subjects with no family history of alcoholism). After the initial reports of a link between P3 amplitude and alcoholism, several investigators tried to replicate the original findings but with varying success. For example, Polich and Bloom (1988) found no systematic relationship between P3 amplitude and family history of alcoholism. In a recent literature survey and meta-analysis, however, Polich, Pollock, and Bloom (1994) concluded from the studies reviewed that individuals with a family history of alcoholism demon-strated smaller P3 amplitudes than individuals without a family history of alcoholism. Moreover, a possible reason for the failure of some in-vestigators to replicate these findings may be what the authors called "moderator variables"—that is, differences in age, task difficulty, and stimulus modality across studies.

Language Processing

Although deviant, unexpected events are associated with mismatch negativity (MMN) and the P3 amplitude, some unexpected events, such as the presentation of incongruent semantic information, elicit late negative potentials around 400 msec, the N400 wave (Kutas and Hillyard, 1980). The N400 is lateralized to the right hemisphere and is maximal over the centroparietal scalp regions.

The typical paradigm used to elicit the N400 waveform is a reading task: the subject is asked to read a sentence whose last word is semanti-cally incongruent with the rest of the sentence, thus creating a "sur-prise" effect. The words are presented serially on a screen, and the subject must read the words one by one at a fixed rate. An incongruent sentence, for example, may read: "The pizza was too hot to cry." The N400 amplitude is related to the degree of incongruity, possibly re-flecting the existence of a specific cortical processor of semantics.

Related to the studies on N400 by Marta Kutas is ERP research on linguistic processing in congenitally deaf subjects (Neville, Kutas, and Schmidt, 1982). This research has determined that the late negative wave is not asymmetrically distributed in deaf adults, which may indi-cate a difference in cortical organization of language function in deaf and hearing subjects.

Word Repetition and Recognition Memory

In a conceptually similar study to that of Kutas and Hillyard (1980), Rugg (1985) also found a negativity around 400 msec after the presen-tation of words that had been primed by previous presentation or through semantic association. Rugg (1985) recorded ERPs when sub-jects performed a lexical decision task (deciding whether a string of letters briefly flashed on a screen is a word or not), in which a propor-tion of the words were either semantic associates or repetitions of the preceding word. RTs were faster to the second item of pairs that were associated, as well as to repeated words that had been primed by the preceding word. The ERPs to the semantic primes were larger than those to targets, with a maximal negative peak amplitude around 400–450 msec after the stimulus was presented.

In several more recent studies (e.g., Rugg and Nagy, 1987, 1989; Friedman, 1990), it has been shown that repetition of a word in a string of words yields larger negative N300 and positive P300 responses after the first presentation of a word than after the repetition of the word. The "old versus new" effect could be either an enhancement of the P3 following the new item or a reduction in negativity in the response to the recognized items in the word string. Some authors have argued that the sustained positive wave during repetition priming to the second presentation of a word is different from a late P3; this sustained wave is labeled P600 since it occurs around 600 msec after the repeated word is presented.

A typical recognition-memory experiment (e.g., Friedman, 1990) involves presentations of blocks of around fifty words for about 300 msec on a screen at intervals of 2 sec. A certain number of nonrepeated words are presented between the first and second presentation of the repeated word. Subjects are instructed to respond "old" or "new" for each word seen on the screen by pressing one of two buttons as quickly as possible. ERPs to the new and old items are then separately averaged. Interestingly, the old-new effect in the ERPs was independent of whether the subject correctly identified a previously presented item as "old" or not. Thus, there is a dissociation between subjective awareness memory and cortical processes involved in this kind of recognition memory. In a recent paper, Dool, Stelmack, and Rourke (1993) reviewed the N400 literature with specific reference to dyslexia and dyslexic children. In general, dyslexic children have smaller N400 amplitudes than control children. This difference may indicate difficulties in semantic processing of words and problems in accessing words.

ERPs, Sleep, and Hypnosis

ERPs generated during sleep and during various sleep stages have been extensively studied (see Chapter 11 for a description of sleep stages). Summarizing the findings in the literature, Shagass (1972) concluded that the latency of the ERP becomes longer as an individual progresses into deeper sleep stages, with the exception that ERPs during REM sleep are similar to those during the waking state. Overall, the data suggest that ERPs do occur during sleep, indicating a specific response from the brain to an external stimulus that the subject is not consciously experiencing.

Since then, other studies have shown that the auditory ERPs during REM differ from the corresponding potentials recorded during the waking state. A recent study from our laboratory (Nordby, Hugdahl, Stickgold, Brønnick, and Hobson, unpublished) showed that negative slow-wave shifts to the infrequent stimulus presented in the oddball paradigm (passive condition) during REM sleep differed from the potentials recorded during both non-REM sleep and the waking state. Frequent and infrequent stimuli were presented to the subject before going to sleep, during non-REM periods, during REM periods, and after awakening in the morning. Stimuli were 75 dB tones that differed in frequency and that were presented with 80 and 20 percent probabilities for the frequent and rare tones, respectively.

In this experiment REM versus non-REM periods were identified through recordings obtained by the Nightcap procedure developed by Allan Hobson and colleagues (Mamelak and Hobson, 1989). This procedure utilizes a piezoelectric sensor attached to the eyelid to detect eye movements while the subject sleeps. The main results (see Figure 12.17) were larger P2 responses to the infrequent stimulus during sleep than during waking, and particularly during REM sleep. Moreover, there was a profound negative slow-wave shift at about 500–700 msec after the deviant stimulus in REM sleep.

The question of whether instructions to a subject in a hypnotic state either to block or to enhance perceptual sensations also alter brain potentials has received mixed empirical support. Early studies (Shagass and Schwartz, 1964) found that hypnotic suggestions had no effect on responses to somatosensory stimuli, nor did instructions to "dim" or "make brighter" a visual stimulus have any effect (Beck, 1963). However, more recent studies have shown significant reduction of the P3 amplitude elicited in responses to visual stimuli when subjects in hypnosis were instructed to imagine a cardboard box blocking their view of the monitor presenting the stimulus (Spiegel, Cutcomb, Ren, et al., 1985; see also Spiegel, 1991).

Interestingly, the P3 attenuation that followed hallucinatory blocking of the visual field was more pronounced over the right hemi-

Wake

Pre-sleep

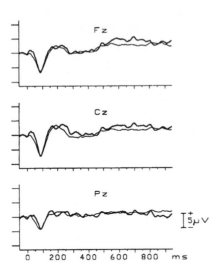

Post-sleep

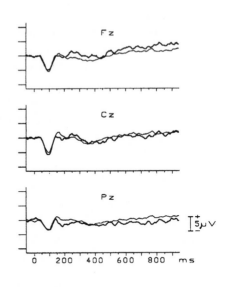

Sleep

NREM   ### REM

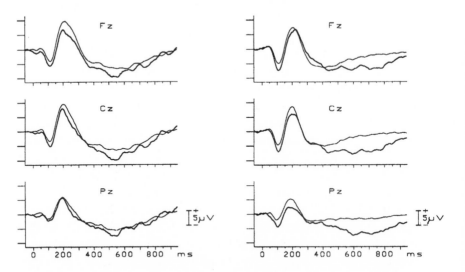

Figure 12.17. ERP responses to tones in an experiment using a passive oddball paradigm during wake and REM and NREM sleep. Note the profound N1-P2 complex and the slow-wave negativity during sleep, and particularly during REM sleep, indicating a kind of hypervigilance during REM sleep.)

sphere, possibly indicating a right-hemisphere activation shift in hypnosis. No blocking effect was observed in nonhypnotizable subjects. Spiegel (1991) also reported similar P3 reduction in responses to somatosensory stimuli when the subjects in hypnosis imagined that their hand was becoming cool and numb. In addition to the P3 reduction, there was also reduction of the early P1 component, suggesting an early filtering, or gating, mechanism in the sensory modality.

Summary

Figure 12.18 presents a highly schematized and simplified view of some of the later exogenous and endogenous components of event-related potentials (ERPs) that traditionally have attracted the interest of psychophysiologists. Early components of the ERP (those to the left on the horizontal axis, which represents time) probably reflect automatic, nonvolitional kinds of processing. The later components reflect active, controlled engagement on behalf of the subject and attention switching as the "gatekeeper" into a controlled mode of processing. The cognitive processes listed under the different ERP waveforms represent a continuum of more automatic processes, from the comparison of the physical features of stimuli involved in mismatch negativity (MMN) to higher-level cognitive processing, such as the detection of semantic incongruities reflected in the N400 component. ERPs have good temporal resolution—changes that occur in just milliseconds can be detected—although their spatial resolution—the exact localization of the source generator in the underlying brain tissue—is poorer. A major challenge to future research in ERP psychophysiology is to identify and localize the source dipoles that give rise to the various scalp-recorded ERP waveforms.

ERPs are a noninvasive measure of localized cortical activity in response to external (or internal) triggering events. An example used often in this chapter is the presentation of an unexpected auditory stimulus against a background of recognized, familiar tones. ERPs provide important information about central nervous system (CNS) activity in conjunction with psychological events. In this respect ERPs complement other psychophysiological measures that are focused on the activity of the automatic nervous system (ANS), like electrodermal or cardiovascular measures. ERPs and autonomic measures typically

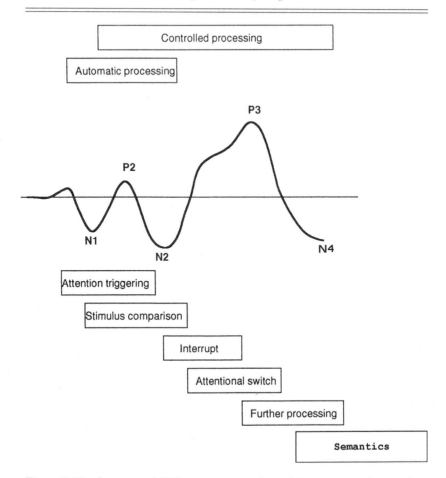

Figure 12.18. Summary of ERP components and cognitive processes, illustrated on a continuum from automatic to controlled processing. (Courtesy of Helge Nordby, University of Bergen.)

operate on different time scales (see also Chapter 1), however, with ERPs operating in the range of milliseconds and electrodermal responses operating in the range of seconds. It is sometimes difficult, therefore, to obtain simultaneous CNS and ANS measures within the same experimental setting. This integration of CNS and ANS measures is, however, important for the future development of psychophysiological knowledge.

13

Brain Imaging Techniques

In this chapter I review some of the new imaging methods for direct visualization of brain functions. The different imaging techniques provide a "landscape" of the brain by "lighting up" areas of increased neuronal activity during cognitive and emotional provocation. The imaging techniques have thus revitalized the old issue of the localization of function in the brain, a topic much debated during the last century in psychology and behavioral sciences.

Today brain imaging techniques are most often noninvasive in the sense that brain activity is detected from the outside of the scalp by sensing devices, most of which detect changes in the blood flow or metabolic demands in underlying tissues. However, sometimes a radioactive isotope is injected in the blood stream. These new techniques provide unique opportunities to study the living human brain *in vivo* at the systems level. They can demonstrate functionally specialized areas activated in the brain in response to sensory, motor, cognitive, and emotional stimuli, with certain areas in the brain specialized for specific types of neuronal activity. Thus, in a general sense, brain imaging techniques allow us to take a "localizationist" perspective on brain function. For example, using functional magnetic resonance imaging (fMRI), McCarthy, Blamire, Bloch, et al. (1993) found specific activation of areas in the left dorsolateral prefrontal cortex when subjects were asked to generate a verb to match a substantive that was presented to them.

Although these new techniques have shown tremendous promise in localizing task-specific activation in the brain, the correlation of increased blood flow in an area of the brain and mental activity does not give information about the location of the underlying neuronal activity that causes the increase in blood flow. Different areas of the brain may be active in a number of different mental functions, and an association between a certain brain area and cognitive function does not preclude the possibility that other areas also contribute to the function in question. Some areas may be activated during a cognitive function while other areas at the same time may be inhibited. In traditional blood-flow measurements, inhibition or deactivation of neuronal activity is not as easy to detect and monitor as activation or neuronal facilitation, although hypometabolism is detected with the positron emission tomography (PET).

Brain imaging techniques cover a range of "imaging modalities"—some techniques measure regional changes of blood flow in the brain, others measure the glucose metabolism in brain cells, and still others measuring an induced voltage signal caused by protons in the brain after they have been exposed to high-frequency radio impulses. Still another technique is the recording of magnetic fields from various locations at the scalp, so-called magnetoencephalography (MEG). The different imaging modalities "see" different things in the brain and are thus differentially sensitive to different aspects of brain function. The choice of an imaging method may depend on three characteristics of the technique: its temporal and spatial sensitivity, selectivity, and contrast (Clinthorne, Leahy, Mareci, and Moses, 1992). The *sensitivity* is a function of the imaging machine and is related to its efficiency to detect what the researcher wants to see. For example, the sensitivity of a PET scan is related to the spatial resolution of the imaging machine—how well it can detect small, narrowly localized, differences in activity between adjacent brain areas. The *selectivity* of the imaging technique is related to how well the technique can distinguish activity from the random background noise that is always present. The *contrast* of the image is related to the physical range of the activity being imaged in the brain. If, for example, the distribution of blood flow to a specific area of the brain would be the same in both normal and psychotic states, the contrast of blood-flow techniques would be quite low for distinguishing psychotic states from normal states with respect to brain function.

Another distinction among the different techniques that must be borne in mind is the difference between *functional* and *structural* imaging. The PET technique, for example, records levels of activity and produces an "image" of the *function* of different areas of the brain. In contrast, the clinically more common computed tomography (CT), an X-ray technique, or magnetic resonance imaging (MRI) techniques produce an image of the different anatomical *structures* of the brain. Traditional functional images do not automatically show the precise anatomical locations of the functional changes. Such images are re-sampled and superimposed onto sample anatomical images. The new technique of functional MRI, however, presents the co-registered structural and functional information in a single examination.

The different brain imaging techniques discussed in this chapter are gaining increasing popularity in all branches of behavioral sciences, not only in psychophysiology. To mention just a few examples of the uses to which imaging techniques have been put: particular emphasis has recently been placed on the imaging of complex cognitive processes, like attention (e.g., Posner, 1993) and mental imagery (Kosslyn, Alpert, and Thompson, et al., 1993), and the imaging of psychopathological conditions, like schizophrenia (Gur and Pearlson, 1993). See Posner and Raichle (1994) for an excellent introduction to brain imaging.

Positron Emission Tomography

In positron emission tomography (PET), a radioactive tracer is injected into the blood stream and follows the blood to the brain. Coincidence detectors that are sensitive to the presence of the tracer in the blood are placed around the skull. When an area of the brain is engaged in neuronal activity, as when it is processing information, more blood is supplied to that area. The increase in blood supply will be sensed by the PET detectors since more of the radioactive tracer will be concentrated in that area.

A *PET scan* is a computer-generated picture of the brain in which areas of different levels of activity are presented in different colors. Red in the PET scan traditionally denotes high levels of activity, while blue areas denote low levels of activity. See Figure 13.1 for black-and-white examples of PET images of subjects performing cognitive tasks related to seeing, hearing, or generating words. If PET images are made while subjects complete a series of tasks of increasing complexity, the images of tasks of lower complexity can be subtracted from the images of tasks of higher complexity. In this way, the specific activation of a brain area by a sensory, cognitive, or emotional task can be shown on the PET scan by subtracting the nearest background activity. PET subtraction images are often based on a statistical method called Statistical Parametric Mapping (SPM) (Friston, 1994). SPM images are, e.g., made up by computing a t-test for each pixel between the two conditions for which the subtraction is made. The t-statistic images may be normalized to z-scores, and significant differences between the two conditions may be displayed in different colors in the overall PET subtraction image.

Metabolism versus Blood-flow Studies

PET imaging can be used to measure either the distribution of blood flow to various regions of the brain or changes in glucose utilization by the brain cells. The neurons in the brain are unique in the sense that they use only glucose, transported in the blood stream, as "fuel." Other cells in the body can, for example, also use lipids as energy. Glucose is used together with oxygen in the metabolic process in the brain cells.

When a brain cell is active it needs more energy—or, put another way, it has a greater metabolic demand—and consequently more glucose will be supplied to that area. In a PET blood-flow study, an isotope of oxygen, ^{15}O, is usually the radioactive compound used as a tracer, but in a PET metabolism study, 18-F-fluoro-2-deoxyglucose (^{18}F-FDG) is often used as the radioactive compound. FDG is a compound that when labeled with the radioactive positron-emitting isotope ^{18}F mimics the action of the naturally occurring glucose in the blood stream. The brain cannot fully metabolize FDG, however, and so the tracer compound accumulates in the brain tissue. Thus, monitoring the ^{18}F-FDG tracer, and the emission of positrons, in various brain regions produces an estimate of localized metabolic rate and activity in those brain areas (see Raichle, 1986, for an excellent overview).

The most popular method for the study of regional cerebral blood flow is to inject radioactively labeled water into the blood stream. The tracer used is oxygen-15 (^{15}O), which is a radioactive isotope of oxygen that emits positrons (as FDG does) when it reaches the brain. The regional blood flow parallels the regional glucose consumption in the brain (see Hartshorne, 1995). Thus, more positrons will be emitted from the radioactive water in an area of increased glucose consumption. Blood flow will therefore also change with activation and stimulation of brain cells.

Positron Emission and Photon Annihilation

PET is a quantitative method for measuring radioactivity (gamma rays) from radioactive isotopes that emit positrons during radiation (thus the name positron-emission tomography). A positron has a short reach in the brain tissue after it is emitted (a few mm), after which it is annihilated by colliding with an electron to form two, back-to-back high-energy photons. When the positron is annihilated, the two high-energy photons are separated by 180°. It is these 180°-separated photons that are detected by the coincidence sensing devices. The more active a brain area is, the more glucose is needed by the neurons. This will result in increased blood flow in the area, and increased delivery of radioactive water in the case of $_{15}$O studies, with the consequence that more positrons are emitted in that area.

Because of the time required for the decay of the radioactive isotopes, an ^{18}F-FDG PET study cannot be repeated within 40–45 minutes, but an ^{15}O study has a turnaround time of about 10 minutes. In terms of spatial and temporal resolution, PET blood-flow (^{15}O) measurements have better temporal resolution (30–60 sec) than FDG measurements but somewhat less spatial resolution (both measurements provide spatial resolutions of a few millimeters). Too many PET scans should not be made on the same subject because of the risk to health from ionizing radiation. This risk should not be exaggerated, however, since the radiation a subject accumulates over 7–10 consecutive scans is about equal to what an airline stewardess receives after 1.5 years of flying.

PET data are typically translated to a brain atlas coordinate system, using, for example, the midline between the anterior and posterior commissures as references (e.g., Talairach and Tournoux, 1988). With this procedure, the PET functional data can be "mapped" onto brain anatomy.

Subcortical Imaging

PET technology can be used to image both cortical and subcortical functions. The PET technology also allows for "imaging" of concentrations of neurotransmitters in different brain regions. For example, PET images have demonstrated the depletion of dopamine in the region of the substantia nigra in Parkinson's patients, thus confirming other studies relating dopamine deficiency to Parkinson's disease.

Pet Imaging and Anxiety

Recently, Fredrikson, Wik, Greitz, et al. (1993a), using the blood-flow PET technique, found that snake-phobic subjects showed elevated blood flow in the posterior, visual regions of the brain when they were exposed to a short videotape containing snakes. It therefore seems as if phobic anxiety lowers the sensory thresholds, yielding a kind of "supersensitive" visual system in order to spot the feared phobic stimulus as soon as possible.

The data reported by Fredrikson et al. (1993a), however, do not entirely match other PET findings with anxiety patients. Reiman, Raichle, Butler, Herscovitch, et al. (1984) found the largest increases in blood flow in the vicinity of the pole of the temporal lobe during panic attacks, whereas Johanson, Risberg, Silverskiold, and Smith (1986) reported the largest changes in the left fronto-orbital region of the brain. To complicate matters even more, the data by Reiman et al. (1984) were later withdrawn because the results could have been caused by jaw movements by the subject, which give rise to PET changes similar to those reported in the study. Thus, the issue of brain-function changes during exposure to emotionally laden stimuli and during panic attacks is not settled.

It may be worthwhile to note that PET images obtained during teeth clenching are similar to those obtained during a panic attack (Drevets, Videen, MacLeod, et al., 1992). Thus, the data by Reiman et al. (1984) may have been confounded by extracranial muscle activity, which is a common clinical observation during an anxiety reaction.

An interesting difference between Johanson et al. (1986) and Reiman et al. (1984), on the one hand, and Fredrikson et al. (1993a), on the other, is that Fredrikson et al. looked at brain blood flow in patients with specific phobias while the others studied blood flow in patients with generalized anxiety. Patients with specific phobias may, in addition to experiencing an increase in emotional arousal, undergo a change in their perceptual search patterns when encountering feared situations. Thus, there may be a lowering of the perceptual thresholds in individuals with specific phobias during a fear response, not seen in those with generalized anxiety. It is a well-known clinical phenomenon that, for example, spider-phobic individuals "visually search" every corner of a room upon entering the room, if they suspect that there may be spiders inside. This hypervigilant perceptual state in a phobic individual may have a direct cortical correlate in the occipital, visual cortex, as suggested by the data by Fredrikson et al. (1993a).

Attention and PET Imaging

Posner and Petersen (1990; see also Posner and Driver, 1992) concluded from a review of many studies that selective attention is related to neural activity in three different attentional systems, each with its own distinct functional localization. These three attention networks (Posner, 1992) are: the anterior attention network, involving the left frontal cortex and the anterior cingulate gyrus; the posterior attention network, involving the parietal cortex and parts of the thalamus; and the vigilance network system, involving the right frontal cortex.

The *anterior attention network* is involved in the detection of targets in situations where target stimuli, to which the subject makes a response, are mixed with other stimuli that may act as cues to signal the onset of a target. This network is also involved in the control of streams of thought in a more general sense, and in the semantic analysis of language. Posner (1992) reviewed studies on how word meaning and semantics relate to attention and brain function, suggesting that the anterior attention system, involving in particular the left prefrontal cortex, plays an important role in semantics. The anterior cingulate gyrus in the longitudinal midline in the frontal cortex is also critical for processing of visual stimuli. As an example, the anterior cingulate gyrus becomes active when subjects monitored a list of words for animal names. The subjects were asked to keep track of how many animal words there were in the list. In this naming experiment, the semantic area of the left dorsal prefrontal cortex and the anterior cingulate gyrus were activated, as seen in PET blood-flow scans, indicating that these areas are critically involved in attention to semantic targets.

The second network is the *posterior attention network*, which is involved in orienting attention to a spatial location and to the analysis of the visual form of a word (but not to the semantic analysis of the meaning of the word). The posterior system is thus related to extraction of the visual features of a stimulus. As also mentioned in Chapter 4, the posterior attention system involves the parietal lobe, the pulvinar area of the thalamus, and the superior colliculus in the midbrain. After studying the attention deficits produced by lesions in these and other areas of the brain, Posner (1992) has hypothesized that these areas are activated in a brain "circuitry" for the shifting of visual spatial attention. Cognitive operations are carried out by the parietal lobe, which prepares for a contralateral shift of attention. The midbrain superior colliculus has the major responsibility for carrying out the shift. The thalamic pulvinar area, finally, locks attention in place at the spatial location of focus (Posner, 1992).

The *vigilance attention system* involves the right frontal lobe and is typically engaged when a subject is instructed to "get ready" to make a rapid response, as in a reaction-time task. The vigilance system, or network, is thus engaged when individuals have to maintain alertness over periods of time, as, for example, one must do while monitoring radar screens.

A recent paper by Pardo, Fox, and Raichle (1991) suggests that while patients with right frontal lesions cannot maintain alertness following a warning stimulus, patients with similar lesions on the left side can. Thus, there is an important asymmetry in how the right and left frontal lobes exert control over vigilance and alertness.

PET and Language Processing

PET blood-flow studies have proved useful in understanding brain activation in language processing. Figure 13.1 shows examples of PET scans produced by subjects hearing words, passively seeing words, pronouncing words that were heard or seen, and generating new words from a series of heard words (Petersen, Fox, Posner, Mintun, and Raichle, 1988). Forty words were presented during one minute through earphones and on a computer screen. In the first "baseline" condition, all subjects just sat in front of the computer screen without any stimulation while blood flow was measured. In the "hearing words" and "seeing words" conditions, 40 words were presented at a rate of about every 1.5 sec. Blood flow during the baseline condition was then subtracted from blood flow during the stimulus conditions. The results showed blood-flow changes in the posterior/superior tem-

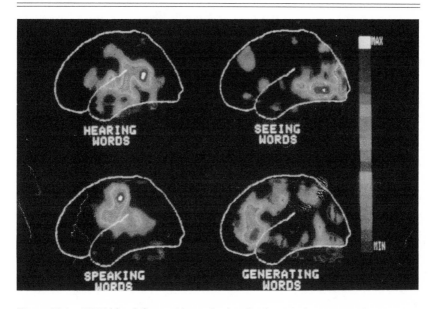

Figure 13.1. PET blood-flow evidence for localized cortical activation during various language tasks. Hearing words activates areas adjacent to Wernicke's area in the temporal lobe. Seeing words produces activation primarily over occipital areas. Speaking words activates the precentral motor cortex, and generating words activates areas in the frontal lobe and anterior cingulate. Areas in light grey and white indicate more activation. (Photo courtesy of Marcus Raichle, Washington University, St. Louis, Missouri.)

poral lobe when subjects were hearing the words and in the occipital lobe when subjects were seeing the words. The subjects were then asked to pronounce aloud a similar number of words. Subjects pronouncing the words showed specific activity in the frontal cortex, particularly in the motor cortex (of both hemispheres). In the final stage of the experiment, the subjects were asked to generate a verb for every noun word they saw on the screen or heard and to say the verb aloud. This condition thus added a semantic component to the task, that is, the subjects had to access the meaning of the words before they could pronounce them. This activated areas in the frontal lobe (anterior cingulate), but also in the temporal lobe and cerebellum. Thus, PET studies of language processing have revealed an interesting dimension from the sensory areas of the brain to the frontal areas when subjects engage in cognitively more demanding tasks (see also Posner and Raichle, 1994, for an easy accessible review of PET blood-flow studies in cognition).

Mental Imagery and Perception

The notion that imaging an object activates the same brain areas as actually seeing the same object was recently demonstrated by Kosslyn, Alpert, Thompson, et al. (1993) in a series of PET blood-flow studies on mental imagery. In one experiment, subjects either visualized letters in grids and decided whether an X mark flashed onto the grid would have fallen on the "imagined" letter, or they saw actual letters on the grids and decided whether the X mark fell on each letter. In-

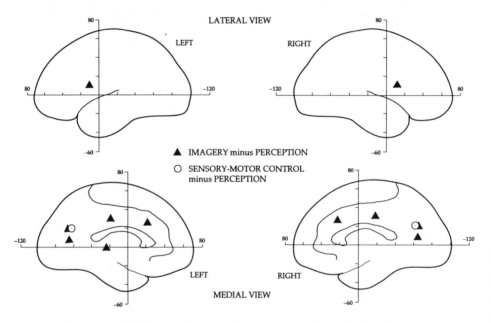

Figure 13.2. Patterns of brain activation as detected with the PET technique during mental imagery. The left and right hemispheres are seen from the lateral and medial views. Triangles represent the loci of significant increases in activity in the imagery task relative to the perception task. The circles represent the loci of significant increases in activity in the sensory-motor control task. The tick marks on the axes specify 20 mm increments relative to the anterior-posterior commissures. (From Kosslyn et al., 1993, reprinted with permission from MIT Press and the authors.)

terestingly, area 17 in the occipital cortex was activated during the mental-imagery task as it was during the perception task. Some of the results are shown in Figure 13.2.

Posner (1993) recently reviewed PET studies showing how visual color stimuli, for example, or moving targets activate the same prestriate areas in the human brain as have been determined by cellular recording to be activated in the monkey brain.

SPECT and rCBF

SPECT stands for *single photon emission computed tomography*. This technique is similar to PET but it involves injection of a biologically active, radiolabeled drug, typically technetium-isotope (HMPAO). SPECT is good for functional imaging of subcortical structures of the brain. The HMPAO isotope gives only a static image of the function in a brain region, like a snapshot of the brain at a certain point of time.

The HMPAO ligand (a radioactive tracer carried in the blood stream) passes the blood-brain barrier and is taken up at receptor sites in the brain, where it stays for hours. Thus, the HMPAO SPECT provides an image of activated cells in the brain at the moment in time when the radioactive ligand is taken up by the receptor. The reason for this is that the HMPAO radioactive tracer is rapidly taken up by the brain (within minutes) and converted to a meso-isomer that is trapped inside the brain (Hartshorne, 1995).

Blood-flow studies with the ^{133}Xe technique, often also referred to as *regional cerebral blood flow* (rCBF; see Risberg, 1986), have a turn-around time of about 10 minutes, after which the tracer is "washed out." During this time, so-called scintillation detectors outside of the skull will detect changes in radiation occurring at various regions in the brain, thus providing a continuous measure of changes of regional brain function. The rCBF technique was pioneered by Lassen and Ingvar (e.g., 1961), but more recently it has been extensively applied to psychophysiology and neuropsychology by Risberg (see Risberg, 1986, for an overview). Using the [133]Xe rCBF technique, for example, Risberg, Ingvar, and their colleagues have shown the regional distributions of blood flow in the brain during various mental processes. They have studied memory and reasoning (Ingvar and Risberg, 1965); hemispheric asymmetry (Risberg, Halsey, Wills, and Wilson, 1975), and organic dementia (Risberg and Gustafson, 1983).

A common finding with the rCBF technique is the "hyper-frontal" syndrome, reported originally by Ingvar. The hyper-frontal syndrome is an increase in blood flow in the frontal regions of the brain at rest. A particular area that is hyperactive during resting is the dorsolateral frontal cortex, a region that is critical for higher cognitive functions, like attention and vigilance (see the discussion of attention and PET studies, above). Ingvar has suggested that the hyper-frontal syndrome is related to the anticipation of motor action performed by the frontal lobes; that is, the frontal areas of the brain have a role in planning and advance "monitoring" for the execution of actions.

In an interesting study on brain laterality, Risberg et al. (1975) found larger increases in blood flow in the right hemisphere for a visual perceptual test (Street test), while there were larger increases in the left hemisphere during a verbal reasoning test. The main finding when rCBF has been used to study brain activity in patients with dementia, such as those with Alzheimer's disease, is reduced blood flow in parietal, posterior regions. Another major finding is that the degree of blood-flow reduction is positively correlated with the severity of symptoms.

Subtraction Technique

Because changes in brain metabolism, as seen in the PET, are small (in the order of 5–20 percent), it is difficult to show changes directly in a single display. In order to highlight blood-flow changes that occur specifically in one stimulus condition, simple image-processing techniques have been employed to scale and perform pixel-wise subtraction of series of images. As an example, a PET image for the processing required for "saying displayed words out loud" (see Figure 13.1) may be derived by subtracting from the image recorded while the subject was "seeing" the same words without saying anything. The areas that are lit up during the "speaking words" condition after subtraction of those areas that are activated by only "seeing" the same words would thus be the brain areas of interest for "saying words."

A basic assumption behind the subtraction technique is that only a single feature is added from one condition to another, which means that after subtracting one condition from another, any differences between the two images must be due to this single feature. In the PET literature, there are variants of the "single-feature" assumption, as in higher-order subtractions, that is, subtracting already-subtracted images from each other. A typical use of the subtraction method is a comparison between a reference or baseline condition and an active condition in which a new cognitive process is added to the cognitive processes present in the reference condition.

Although subtraction is an attractive method, one may be concerned whether only a single feature is different between any two conditions (see Demonet, Wise, and Frackowiak, 1993, for a critical analysis of the subtraction technique). A baseline defined as the passive resting condition, with minimal sensory stimulation and mental activity, may be too underspecified from a cognitive point of view and artificial from a physiological point of view (cf. Demonet et al., 1993). Activity recorded from one subject under these conditions may furthermore not be reproducible in another subject. As an example, a subject asked to say out loud the words seen on a screen, after he or she has seen the same words previously but without saying anything, may experience increased arousal in addition to whatever processing is required to say the words. The subject, in other words, may get nervous when asked to speak. In this case, then, *two* features would differ between the baseline "seeing words" and the experimental "saying words" conditions, speaking and arousal. A subtraction of images would not tell which of these two factors has caused the difference between the PET images.

An example of image subtraction is presented in Figure 13.3, which reproduces rCBF data from the study by Johanson et al. (1986). The image to the left is a map of blood flow occurring at the detector sites during a resting condition. The middle panel shows the distribution of blood flow during the anxiety-provoking condition, and to the right is a picture of the difference in blood flow after the left image has been subtracted from the middle image.

Functional Magnetic Resonance Imaging

The newly developed technique of functional magnetic resonance imaging (fMRI) (Kwong et al., 1992; Belliveau, Kennedy, McKinstry, 1991; see also Cohen, Noll, and Schneider, 1993; De Yoe, Bandettini, Neitz, et al., 1994) can be used to monitor changes in blood flow and blood volume in the brain within a couple of hundred milliseconds, and with better spatial resolution than the PET. However, fMRI so far offers poorer selectivity; that is, fMRI requires a higher signal-to-

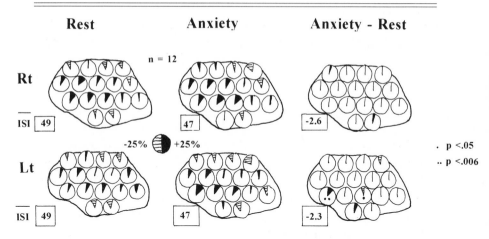

Figure 13.3. Regional changes in blood flow as determined by the xenon-rCBF technique during rest and anxiety provocation for the right (Rt) and left (Lt) hemispheres. The maps to the far right show the resulting activity when the blood-flow pattern during rest is subtracted from pattern during provocation. Note the increased activation level in the lower frontal and temporal areas during anxiety. (From Johansson et al., 1986, with permission from the authors.)

noise ratio in order to get a good image. Functional MRI has a spatial resolution of about $2 \times 2 \times 5$ mm³, depending on the magnetic field strength. Whole brain areas as well as specific loci can be assessed and displayed within an anatomical framework. Functional MRI is also noninvasive in the sense that no radioactive tracers are injected into the subject.

The traditional magnetic resonance imaging (MRI, not fMRI) is a *structural*, not a functional, technique. In other words, it maps the anatomical structures of the brain rather than the location of brain activity. It is a technique for detecting area of high tissue contrast for the purpose of scanning the anatomy. The individual is placed in a strong magnetic field, in which protons in the brain take a certain equilibrium state. High-frequency radio pulses are then used to put the protons in, for example, the brain into a state of unrest. When the protons are put out of the magnetic alignment of 90°, a voltage is induced in a coil surrounding the head, or part of the head. A magnetic gradient is applied to the core magnetic field. The gradient allows spatial information about the positions of the protons to be recorded, thus generating a high-contrast image of brain structures. The image in an MR scan is a map of the hydrogen distribution, mostly in the form of water. The excitation and re-emission of the hydrogen protons is sensitive to the local environment of the hydrogen atom, thus, an MRI scan can be used to differentiate various types of brain tissue, which will show up on the scanned image.

The newer fMRI, in contrast to MRI, is a technique for assessing *function* in the brain. Thus, it belongs to the family of functional imaging techniques. The functional MRI technique is based on the different magnetic properties of oxygenated (arterial) and deoxygenated (venous) blood. When subjected to certain gradient echo pulse sequences, oxygenated blood provides a stronger MR signal than deoxygenated blood, and it is the difference in signal intensity between hemoglobin in its oxygenated and in its deoxygenated state that provides the contrast in the fMRI image. In other words, during cognitive activation there will be local vasodilation in areas of the brain where neurons are more active, and the supply of oxygenated blood will exceed their metabolic need. This will show up on the MR image as a high-intensity signal covering the region of the brain with increased activity.

The signal in the fMRI scan may be described by the BOLD phenomenon (*blood oxygenation level dependent* contrast). Localized increase in neuronal activity causes increased metabolic rate (as seen in the PET). This also causes local vasodilation in the blood vessels and increase in blood volume in the area. Paradoxically, the increase in blood flow is larger than the metabolic-rate increase (the *Fick principle*). The excess of oxygenated blood will be drained through the small veins surrounding the activated area. Since oxygenated blood provides a stronger MR signal than deoxygenated blood, the activated neuronal area will show up as a contrast on the MR scan. The brain thus uses anaerobic metabolism in instances of increased mental activity—metabolic rate is increased but not the consumption of oxygen. Sequences of radiofrequency pulses are used to create an MR image: they excite and refocus the protons that are aligned in the magnetic field. Each pulse sequence has its own characteristics for generating a particular MR image.

Functional MRI has good spatial and temporal resolution, and it may therefore be a better technique for monitoring of function in the living brain than the PET technique, which has a limited temporal resolution. Since fMRI can be performed on standard MR machines, the fMRI technology does not require huge investments in equipment, as is the case for the PET technology. Some fMRI studies have achieved temporal resolution in the millisecond range and a spatial resolution in the mm range, allowing for studies of rapid changes in blood flow in certain regions of the brain as a consequence of mental activity. The intensity of the signal in the fMRI setting is dependent on the strength of the magnetic field (measured in tesla). Typically, a 1.5 tesla magnetic field and gradient echo pulse sequences are used in fMRI studies. A special pulse sequence is used to produce echo planar imaging (EPI), which significantly reduces the scan time. This makes it possible to acquire several scans of the brain within short time intervals (under a second). Short-interval scans are important when physiological activity (such as blood-flow change) in the brain is monitored. Once again, it is important to keep in mind that it is the interaction of magnetic field strength and the applied pulse sequence that determines the signal intensity (and hence the contrast between activated and nonactivated areas in the brain) in fMRI. Thus, applying optimally developed pulse sequences in a medium-strength magnetic field (e.g., 1.0 tesla) may provide results as good as those obtained from a 1.5 tesla machine operating with nonoptimal pulse sequences.

Applications of fMRI

Applications of fMRI in studies of psychology and physiology are not very frequent today, but given that the technique is noninvasive and that MR machines are used in many clinical settings, they will no doubt increase in scope and number over the coming years. Among the available examples are the following: Kwong et al. (1992) determined that 8 Hz photic stimulation (pulsating light) activates the occipital calcarine sulcus. Cohen et al. (1993) reported clear laterality effects of right versus left visual half-field stimulations with patterned stimuli. The main result of this experiment was a profound increase in signal intensity over the contralateral visual cortex after unilateral stimulus presentations in either the left or right half-field. Moreover, Connelly, Jackson, Frackowiak, et al. (1993) found increases in blood flow over the motor cortex after repeated finger-to-thumb movements of the hand. Finally, DeYoe, Bandettini, Neitz, Miller, et al. (1994) showed that the position of a visual stimulus in the visual field activated unique areas in the visual cortex.

Figure 13.4 is an fMRI image of the occipital cortex of a human brain during a response to photic stimulation. Note the increase in neuronal activity in the occipital cortex when the photic stimulation is on, and the decrease in signal intensity when the stimulation is off. The image was produced at the Haukeland University Hospital, Bergen, Norway, using a standard MR machine with a 1.0 tesla magnetic field. The advantage of the fMRI technique, as can be seen in Figure 13.4 (from Lundervold, Ersland, Gjesdal, Smievoll, et al., 1995), is that both detailed anatomical information in the subject (left panel) and co-registered functional information (right panel) related to primary visual processing are acquired with the same technology.

Processing and Analysis of the MR Signal

In addition to the subtraction techniques previously described, Bandettini, Jesamanovicz, Wong, and Hyde (1993) suggested that a cross-correlational technique be used (see Chapter 11 for a general discussion of cross-correlational techniques). The MR signal from each voxel (three-dimensional pixel) is compared (that is, correlated) with an ideal reference signal that represents the stimulus conditions. For example, the light ON and OFF conditions in Figure 13.4 may be represented by an alternating square-wave that goes "on" and "off." Ideally, the MR signal should follow the stimulus waveform, increasing during the ON condition and decreasing during the OFF condition. Because of artifacts, however, the MR signal will not perfectly match the stimulus waveform, and the degree of matching is represented as a correlational coefficient between the stimulus waveform and the waveform described by the MR signal during the different stimulus conditions.

MR Spectroscopy

The MRI technique can also be used to monitor small concentrations of certain amino acids, like aspartate and glutamate, in specified regions of the brain. These amino acids are putative neurotransmitters, and it is therefore of great interest to be able to monitor their concentrations in the brain (see Chapter 4). This kind of monitoring is called *MRI spectroscopy*. The technique is usually performed on brain tissue extract or animal preparations. Changes in amino acid concentration

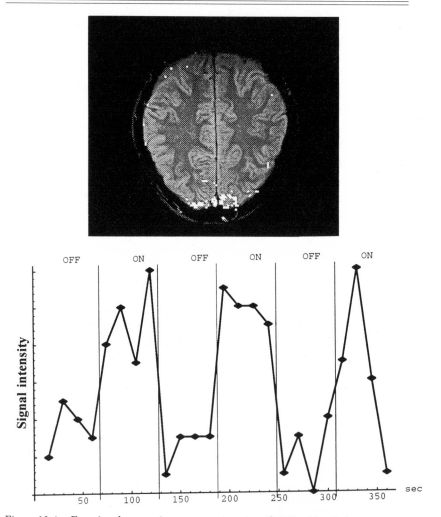

Figure 13.4. Functional magnetic resonance imaging (fMRI) of local changes in
blood flow in the occipital cortex (white areas in the left-hand figure) mapped
directly onto an MRI anatomical scan (right-hand figure) recorded during presentations of 60 sec intervals of darkness (OFF) and 8 Hz flicker-light stimulation (ON).
The left-hand scan shows the difference in blood-flow activation between the OFF
and ON conditions. The bottom graph shows relative increases and decreases in
blood flow as a function of light stimulation versus darkness. (Data from Lundervold et al., 1995, used with permission from Gordon and Breach Science Publishers
and the authors).

in various regions of the brain are, in principle, possible to follow for periods of time (hours) in the living animal (and human).

Magnetoencephalography

Magnetoencephalography (MEG) is the recording of weak magnetic fields produced by brain currents (Kaufman and Williamson, 1986; Hari and Ilmoniemi, 1986; Hari, 1990, for reviews). It is treated as a brain imaging technique rather than as a type of ERP recording because most recent MEG methods provide a "map" of activity over the whole cortex. The whole-head MEG technique has recently been made possible by the development of a 122-channel magnetometer instrument (Ahonen, Hämäläinen, Kajola, et al., 1992) (see Figure 13.5).

The major advantage of the MEG technique is that it is more accurate than EEG recordings are in localizing current sources in the brain. The sources that are detected by the MEG are mainly only cortical in origin, and the generator has to be tangentially oriented to the skull in order to provide a maximum MEG response. The reason for this is that magnetic fields are perpendicular to electric fields. This means that MEG measures mainly the activity generated from cortical fissures. MEG thus detects tangentially oriented dipoles; it is not able to detect radially oriented dipoles.

The MEG technique makes it possible to differentiate between signals from various cortical regions with good spatial and temporal resolution. Another advantage is that it does not require the use of reference electrodes (recall from Chapter 11 that the choice of optimal reference location is a source of controversy in EEG studies). It cannot be emphasized too much that MEG is the superior technique for dipole localization in the brain. Thus, whenever possible, ERP localizations should be corroborated by recordings of MEG.

SQUIDs

Since the magnetic field signal is very weak, only about a few billionths of the strength of earth's magnetic field, MEG recordings require superconducting devices in order to pick up the tiny magnetic signal. Superconduction, the flow of a current against very little resistance, is now possible only in materials that have been cooled almost to abso-

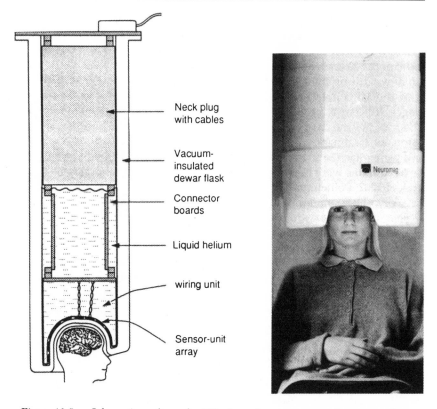

Labels on schematic:
Neck plug with cables

Vacuum-insulated dewar flask

Connector boards

Liquid helium

wiring unit

Sensor-unit array

Figure 13.5. Schematic outline of a 122-channel magnetometer instrument for recording of magnetoencephalography (MEG). The subject's head is surrounded by a sensor-unit array that picks up the magnetic fields generated by brain activity. The tube-like helmet is filled with liquid helium in order to achieve superconducting properties for detection of the small magnetic fields. (Courtesy of Professor Mikko Sams and the Group of the Low Temperature Laboratory at the Helsinki University of Technology, Finland.)

lute zero (approximating a temperature of $-273°$ Centigrade or $-460°$ Fahrenheit). The skull is therefore surrounded by detectors that are immersed in liquid helium, which provides a superconducting medium. The signals are first picked up by a superconducting flux transformer and are then sensed by sensors known as *superconducting quantum interference devices* (SQUIDs).

Some laboratories have 20–30 SQUID sensors covering the head. The Low Temperature Laboratory in Helsinki, Finland, has developed MEG recording equipment consisting of 122 detectors (Hämäläinen, Hari, Ilmoniemi, Knuutila, and Lounasmaa, 1993). Figure 13.6 is an example of a recording of magnetic evoked responses to repeated presentations of tones to the subject's right ear.

Event-Related Fields

MEG responses, or event-related magnetic fields (ERFs), look quite similar to ERPs and are also averaged across stimulus presentations. The magnetic N100 response over the temporal auditory cortices appears in Figure 13.6 as a relatively large deflection compared with responses from other areas of the brain.

Although MEG is usually claimed to be more accurate at locating source generators, there is some controversy in the literature as to the validity of this statement. Cohen (1991) argued that "the MEG offers no significant advantage over the EEG in localizing a focal source . . . its principal use is not in localization but in its ability to see more specific information than EEGs can" (cited in Crease, 1991, p. 375). It may be of interest to note that Cohen was the first to record magnetic fields from the brain (Cohen, 1968), in a procedure that produced a magnetic equivalent to the EEG alpha wave.

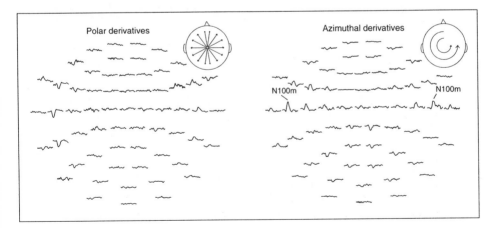

Figure 13.6.   Examples of evoked magnetic fields recorded with a 122-channel device when 50 msec tones were presented to the subject's right ear once every 4 sec; scalp viewed from above. Strong magnetic N100m responses are seen over the left and right auditory cortices. (Courtesy of Professor Mikko Sams and the Group of the Low Temperature Laboratory at the Helsinki University of Technology, Finland.)

Applications of MEG

MEG is today applied in a variety of clinical and experimental settings, including studies of epilepsy and stroke as well as sleep and speech disorders (see Hämäläinen et al., 1993). Another major research area is the study of selective attention, in which MEG has been instrumental in localizing the various source dipoles for mismatch negativity (MNN) and attentional shifts in ERP research (see Näätänen, 1992, for further examples).

Responses to auditory stimuli have also been studied with the MEG technique. Any abrupt, unexpected noise evokes a typical magnetic ERF around 100 msec after the sound (the N100). The localization of the N100 source depends on the parameters of the stimulus, for example, tone frequency. This indicates that the human auditory cortex has a tonotopic organization (different frequencies are processed in different temporal areas). An interesting feature of the auditory evoked magnetic field to brief auditory stimuli observed by Mäkelä, Ahonen, Hämäläinen, et al. (1993) is the asymmetry observed over the hemispheres, with some subjects showing larger contralateral than ipsilateral N100 responses.

The earliest cortical response to an auditory click occurs 19 msec after the stimulus, and the generator is localized deep inside the sylvian fissure in the posterior temporal auditory cortex. Magnetic responses to a 400 msec noise burst are seen in Figure 13.7. Note the slower P200 deflection after the N100 response, and also the magnetic response to the cessation of the stimulus.

MEG recordings may also be used to obtain visual ERFs from the occipital areas of the brain. Studies have been performed with alternating checkerboards but also with face stimuli. In the latter case, areas outside of the primary visual cortex were also activated after the presentation of the face stimulus, thus indicating that more complex processing accompanies the presentation of socially relevant visual stimuli (Lu, Hämäläinen, Hari, et al., 1991).

In another recent study, Woldorff, Gallen, Hampson, et al. (1993) used a 37-channel magnetometer to study selective attention to auditory stimuli presented to the left and right ear. Subjects listened to sequences of rapidly presented tones in one ear while ignoring tones of a different pitch in the other ear. The tones that were attended to evoked larger magnetic brain responses (in the 20–50 msec and 80–

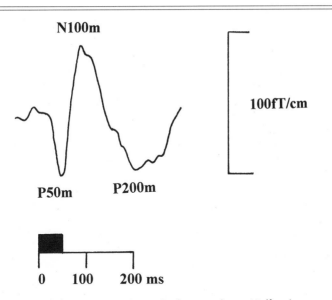

Figure 13.7. Typical magnetic response (in femto-tesla, or 10^{-15} tesla, per cm), measured close to the subject's auditory cortex, as a function of time. The signal was evoked by a 50 msec tone (illustrated by the black bar on the time axis). The magnetic response to a auditory stimulus consists of: a small, P50m peak at about 50 msec; a prominent peak, N100m, at about 100 msec; and another peak, P200m, at about 200 msec (*m* labels a magnetic waveform to separate it from the corresponding electric ERP component, which is always designated without the *m*). (From Ahonen, Hämäläinen, Kajola, et al., 1992; courtesy of the Group of the Low Temperature Laboratory at the Helsinki University of Technology, Finland.)

130 msec range) than were evoked by the unattended tones in the opposite ear. Using source localization techniques together with magnetic resonance imaging (MRI) for structural information, the authors localized the source generators in the auditory cortex on the supratemporal plane of the temporal lobe. This study showed that selective attention can affect processing of an auditory stimulus as early as 20 msec after the stimulus is presented. The authors interpreted their data to mean that there is "early selection" of auditory attention in the brain that regulates the auditory input and subsequent perceptual and cognitive analysis at later stages in the information-processing chain of events. These findings nicely corroborate previous results obtained from ERP studies of auditory selective attention that detected early ERP components in the responses to attended cues (see Chapter 12).

The McGurk Effect

Sams, Aulanko, Hämäläinen, et al. (1991) used the MEG technique to investigate audiovisual interaction in speech perception. They were interested in what happens when visual information about speech is in conflict with the actual speech sounds heard—when, for example, one sees someone on a TV monitor making one sound, *ka*, but hears the sound as another, *pa*. In this case, the perception of the sound is *ta*. This illusion, called the "McGurk effect" (McGurk and MacDonald, 1976), is a powerful demonstration of how visual perception is integrated with the auditory system in complex perception, as in speech perception.

MEG responses are different when visual perception and auditory perception are concordant than when they are discordant; that is, a waveform appears around 200 msec after discordant stimuli that does not appear after concordant stimuli. Thus, visual information might enter into the auditory cortex and result in a different brain response depending on whether the visual information is in conflict with the auditory information.

Summary

The newly developed "imaging" technology for the study of regional changes in brain activity as a consequence of sensory stimulation or mental activity was reviewed in this chapter. Various techniques for measuring local changes in blood flow in the brain were described and discussed, particularly positron emission tomography (PET), SPECT, and ^{133}Xe regional cerebral blood flow (rCBF) measurements. A special section was devoted to the method of functional magnetic resonance imaging (fMRI), which measures blood-flow changes in the brain with standard magnetic resonance machines and which provide good temporal and spatial resolution in one measurement. Temporal resolution has been a problem with the PET and rCBF techniques, and especially when the object of the study is cognitive activity occurring in the millisecond range. The last section of the chapter was devoted to a closer look at still another technique, the magnetoencephalograph (MEG), which records tiny magnetic fields that are created by neuronal activity. The MEG technique has a great advantage in localizing the source of neuronal activity (a dipole) that is detected as scalp-recorded magnetic responses.

14

Skeletal Muscles, Eye Movements,
and the Respiratory System

In this chapter I review the ways in which studies of the activity of muscles—the skeletal muscles, the muscles of the eye, and the respiratory system—are employed in psychophysiology. Muscle activity attracts a great deal of attention in psychophysiology. So far, somewhat less interest has been shown in the muscle systems discussed here (though electromyography has long played an important role in psychophysiological studies). Researchers today are following many promising leads in these areas of psychophysiology, however, and we may expect more activity in the future.

The Electromyogram
Striated Muscles

The muscles of the body may be grossly categorized as of two types, the smooth muscles and the striated muscles. The smooth muscles make up much of the internal organs that are innervated by the autonomic nervous system (see Chapter 5). The striated muscles, which are innervated by the somatomotor nervous system, make up the major skeletal muscles that are under voluntary control. The focus in this chapter is on the striated muscles. A striated muscle consists of a large number of individual muscle fibers arranged in bundles (see Figure 14.1). Each muscle fiber has a sensitive area, the endplate, on which axons from the spine terminate. This is the connection between the nervous system and the muscle system, and its function is similar to that of the synaptic junction in the central nervous system. For this reason the connection between muscle fiber and endplate is called the *neuromuscular junction.*

A nerve impulse traveling from the motor cortex over the pyramidal motor nervous system causes calcium ions to flow into the axon terminal, which in turn affects the release of acetylcholine (ACh) from the axon terminal when it reaches the endplate on a muscle fiber. ACh is the major neurotransmitter in the motor system, and it is present in all striated muscles. ACh activates the cell membrane in a muscle fiber, which generates the action potentials that make the muscle contract. ACh is then broken down by acetylcholinesterase, allowing the muscle to relax after it has been contracted. There are two basic kinds of muscle contractions: isometric (the muscle "pulls" at the muscle joints without getting shorter when it contracts) and isotonic (the muscle is shortened when it contracts).

The axon of a motoneuron innervates from 100 to 1,000 different muscle fibers. All muscle fibers that are innervated by the same motoneuron are collectively grouped together as a single *motor unit.* All motoneurons that end on the same muscle make up a *motor pool.* Striated muscles are controlled from the brain via the pyramidal somatomotor nervous system (see Chapter 3), which is named for the cell assemblies in the medulla consisting of large, pyramid-shaped cells.

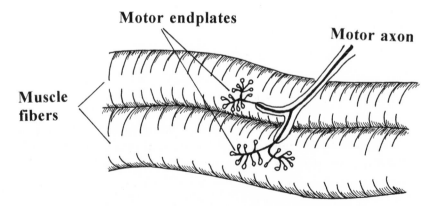

Figure 14.1. Muscle fibers with neural innervation (motor axon and motor endplates). (Adapted from Milner, 1970.)

Recordings of Muscle Activity

The electromyogram (EMG) is a recording of action potentials generated when the fibers of a muscle contracts. The amplitude and frequency of the EMG signal in most situations have a positively linear
relation to the strength of the contraction of the muscle. EMGs are
usually surface recordings, though some are made by inserting needle
electrodes into the muscle. Surface recordings may be related to the
activity of several muscles and muscle groups, even when the experimenter has been careful to place the electrodes over a specific muscle.
Guidelines for psychophysiological studies using EMG recordings can
be found in Fridlund and Caccioppo (1986).

The EMG signal is in the μV region, and EMG recordings normally
put the same demands on amplifier and filter devices as the EEG does.
A typical EMG recording can vary between 10 and 1,000 Hz in frequency, although for most practical purposes a range between 40 and
400 Hz will be sufficient. The EMG amplitude can vary between 100
to 1000 μV, although amplitudes as small as 2–4 μV can be observed
when the muscle is kept resting, as in deep sleep.

An EMG is typically recorded using the *bipolar technique*. That is,
both of the recording electrodes are placed over the recorded muscle,
and both are active with regard to the ground electrode. The closer
the electrodes are placed to each other, the more precise is the recording with regard to single motor units. Precision about the activity of
the motor unit is gained, however, at the expense of information from
the muscle as a whole. A common electrode placement in psychophysiological EMG recordings is over the frontalis flexor muscle in the
lower arm (see Figure 14.2). An example of a typical EMG recording
made during muscle tension and relaxtion is presented in Figure 14.3.

Analysis of the EMG Signal

Common techniques for quantifying an EMG signal are *rectifying* and
signal integration. To rectify an electrical signal means to align the positive and negative spikes in a single direction, usually by displaying the
downward, negative spikes upwards. A rectified signal is seen in Figure
14.4.

After rectifying, the area under a particular part of the curve is computed by signal integration. The area to be integrated depends on

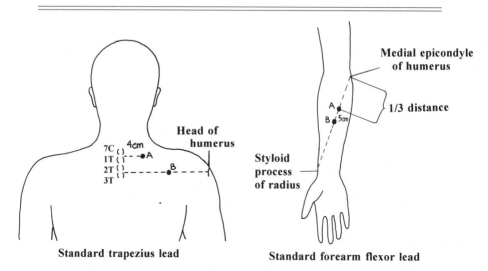

Figure 14.2. Typical electrode locations for EMG recordings from the neck (using the seventh cervical and first three thoracic vertebrae as markers) and forearm. (From Lippold, 1967, with permission from Elsevier Science Publishers.)

whether the researcher is interested in a response that is time-locked to an event or in spontaneous activity over time. The logic is that the larger the amplitudes, and the higher the EMG frequency, the larger the integrated area under the rectified curve will be. A variant of signal integration is *criterion integration*. This means that the integrated voltage is compared with a preset voltage level called "the criterion." Whenever the integrated voltage reaches the criterion level, the computer marks a spike on the screen. After the experiment, the experimenter can simply count the number of "marked spikes" and from that make an estimate of EMG activity during the session.

Psychophysiological Studies

In a general sense, the most direct means of communication between the "inner" and "outer" environment of an individual is through the muscles and the efferent motor system. Not only do muscle tensions occur in response to physical motor demands; they are also intimately linked to emotional and cognitive activation—that is, muscles are sensitive to changes in internal states and moods. Recordings of muscle activity are therefore relevant in many situations: physical motor dys-

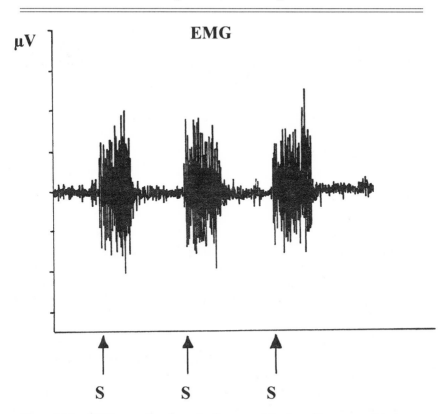

Figure 14.3. EMG recording from the forearm while the subject tenses (black bursts of activity following the clench, indicated by *S*) and relaxes the fist.

function, chronic pain, anxiety disorders, and stress. Muscle tensions caused by stress and anxiety are also a major psychosomatic disorder, affecting the work and social lives of thousands of individuals.

Psychophysiological studies of muscle activity have a long history; experiments have been made, for example, on muscle tension as the subject waits to respond to a signal stimulus (Davis, 1940), on the increase in muscle activity in the chin, lip, and tongue during "silent reading" (McGuigan, Keller, and Stanton, 1964), and on the activity of single motor units during classical conditioning (Basmajian, 1977). Perhaps the most well-known application of psychophysiological studies of muscle activity is operant learning, or biofeedback learning (see Andreassi, 1989, for a selective overview), which has been used to gain control of involuntary muscle tensions. Other well-known examples

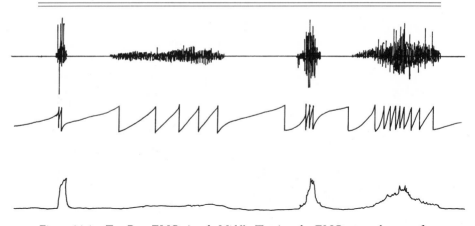

Figure 14.4.   *Top:* Raw EMG signal. *Middle:* Tracing the EMG power by use of a cumulative-resetting integrator; the power accumulates up to a pre-set μV criterion, where the value is re-set to zero, and cumulation up to the criterion starts again, etc. *Bottom:* Tracings of EMG μV power by estimates of the size of the area under the curve in successive 20-msec periods. (Courtesy of Sven Svebak, University of Bergen, Norway.)

of the use of studies on muscle activity in psychotherapy are relaxation training and systematic desensitization. Both these techniques have been applied with success to the treatment of anxiety disorders, including phobias and obsessive-compulsive disorders.

Electromyographic recordings of muscle activity were used by Malmo (e.g., 1975) to study EMG gradients, the increase in muscle activity during the solution of a mental or motor task. Malmo (1975) interpreted this increase as a form of "motivated behavior"; that is, the more the EMG gradient changed during a task, the more "involved" or motivated the individual was in the task. Thus, EMG gradients may be seen as a psychophysiological correlate of task absorption. Malmo's suggestion was partially supported by a study by Svebak, Dalen, and Storfjell (1981), in which the researchers found that the EMG gradient was steeper during a difficult than during an easy tracking task, suggesting "deeper" involvement in a difficult task.

A major application of psychophysiological recordings of muscle tonus is in sleep research and clinical practice. The absence of muscle tonus is a key marker of the deeper sleep stages (see Chapter 11), particularly during dreaming. Measures of EMG during facial expressions have been used in important studies of emotion. For example, subtle changes in the muscles controlling the cheeks in a smile occur in subjects viewing pictures of happy-looking faces (Dimberg, 1982, 1990) or imagining pleasant thoughts (Schwartz, Ahern, and Brown, 1976). Moreover, Vaughan and Lanzetta (1980) showed that facial-muscle activity could be vicariously conditioned in a subject looking at a "model" subject grimacing as if in great pain.

In an attempt to validate the claim that certain muscles of the face are specifically involved in different facial emotions, Tassinary, Cacioppo, and Geen (1989) placed EMG eletrodes over different but closely related muscles in the face while subjects were instructed to make different expressions. For example (see Chapter 2), two areas in the eyebrow region were selected to assess the specificity of the corrugator muscle as an index of negative facial expressions (such as an angry look), while four recording areas were selected in the area of the mouth to assess the claim that the zygomatic muscle(s) is specifically involved in positive facial expressions (such as a smile). The authors also had a smaller subsample of the subjects return to the laboratory for a second recording, thus assessing the reliability of the obtained recordings. The results clearly demonstrated that certain recording sites located over specific facial muscle regions are more sensitive and valid indices of particular facial actions than other nearby sites. This study is important for two reasons: it is one of the few studies that have tried to locate the specific focus or site of facial-muscle activity related to emotion and affect, and it showed that EMG responses are maintained over time, thus indicating a certain degree of reliability of EMG measures (see also Dimberg, 1990).

Muscle Activity and Cognition

EMG has also been used as a peripheral concomitant of cognitive activity, although the use of other psychophysiological measures, like heart rate, ERPs, and electrodermal activity (see Andreassi, 1989), to study cognition is much more common. Jennings, Averill, Opton, et al. (1970) reported increases in muscle tension immediately after a warning stimulus was presented in a two-stimulus reaction-time paradigm. The muscle tension was followed by quieting later in the foreperiod, just before the presentation of the second, imperative stimulus. Jennings (1992) discussed this finding in relation to a response-inhibition model of interaction between the central and autonomic nervous systems (see Chapter 10).

EMG measures are frequently used in studies of motor preparation, which require subjects to wait before responding. These peripheral measures are then compared with central measures, such as ERPs, to investigate how the central nervous system integrates cognitive function, like attention, with preparations to respond to the "go" stimulus (see Brunia, 1993, for an excellent treatment of this topic). Brunia (1993) also provides a model of how the thalamus gates subcortical motor information to the cortex.

In a series of studies related to muscle activity and mental processes, McGuigan (e.g., 1978) has shown that there are specific changes in the musculature of the speech muscles and writing-arm muscles during silent language processing, such as silent reading or other "silent" language tasks.

Perhaps the most programmatic research on the relation between muscle activity and information processing is the work by John Cacioppo and his colleagues (e.g., Cacioppo and Petty, 1981). One of Cacioppo's main arguments is that mental processes are accompanied by muscular activity in focal sites, typically at sites in the musculature required for "acting out" one's thoughts. In a related discussion Cacioppo and Petty (1981) argue that "amplitude of somatic responses decreases as the distance of measurement from these focal sites increases" (p. 441). This is also called the *Davis principle* (Davis, 1939). Thus, EMG responses are good indicators of mental activity, particularly when they are used to monitor the efferent link between information processing and behavior. Moreover, when the focus of interest is on a specific area of the body, such as facial emotional expressions, EMG recordings from the face area would be "close in distance" to the focus of mental activity and would therefore have increased amplitudes. In a now classic study, Davis (1939) had subjects perform a mental arithmetic task and memorize nonsense syllables. The subjects exhibited increased EMG activity in the arms during the mental arithmetic task but not during the nonsense syllables task. They reported feeling an urge to write during the arithmetic task. Davis made the inference that while the subjects performed mental arithmetic the focus of muscular sites was at the recorded area, but while the subjects memorized nonsense syllables the focus was somewhere else on the body.

Cacioppo and colleagues, elaborating on the Davis principle, stated that inhibitory as well as excitatory changes in skeletomuscular activity can characterize psychological processes, and that changes in muscle activity are patterned both spatially and temporally. This means that EMG activity patterns from several muscle groups may have characteristic patterns both over time and across muscles. An example of EMG patterning was a study (Cacioppo and Petty, 1979) in which the subject was instructed to determine whether a word was self-descriptive (a self-reference task) or whether it was printed in upper-case letters (an orthographic task). The study was performed with a paradigm developed in cognitive psychology and called "an orienting task paradigm" (not to be mixed with the orienting response described in Chapter 7). In the orienting task paradigm, the subject is signaled by a cue to focus on a specific aspect (called a *trait adjective*) of the stimulus in order to solve a problem. Examples are "Does the following word rhyme with ——?" or "Is the following word similar in meaning to ——?" In the Cacioppo and Petty (1979) study, a trait adjective was presented after each question that was either printed in upper- or lower-case letters and that was either self-descriptive or not. It was assumed that the self-reference task required that more linguistic associations be allocated and activated in order to solve the task than were required in the orthographic task. Following the Davis principle, it was predicted that EMG activity of the speech muscles would be greater during the self-reference task than during the orthographic task. Such a differentiation should not occur in muscle groups not related to linguistic processing. EMG was recorded from the lip and from the forearm. The results confirmed the prediction, in that muscle activity was greater from the lip electrode than from the forearm electrode. That is, muscle activity was focused on the area that was closest to the site or source of cognitive activity, and activity decreased at greater distances from the site of processing. This finding was later replicated in numerous studies in Cacioppo's laboratory using different paradigms and different stimuli (see Cacioppo and Petty, 1981, for an excellent review).

The Electrooculogram

The electrooculogram (EOG) is a technique for recording a wide range of eye movements, including saccadic movements, smooth pursuit and smooth compensatory movements, nystagmus, and blinking (Schackel, 1967).

Saccadic eye movements are the rapid movements of the eyes when they shift from one fixation point to another. Saccadic eye movements have a latency of about 200 msec, a matter of some importance in visual studies of brain asymmetry using the visual half-field technique (VHF). The VHF technique involves presenting a stimulus to only one visual half-field in order to activate the contralateral hemisphere of the brain (see McKeever, 1986). The stimulus should be brief, shorter than the normal saccadic latency, to guarantee unilateral stimulus presentation. If the eyes shift position during stimulus presentation, through a saccade, both visual half-fields may contribute to the visual input to the brain. A fixation lasts for about 250–1,000 msec, whereafter the saccade jerks the eyes to the next fixation position.

Smooth pursuit eye movements are the movements of the eyes as they follow a moving object in space. *Smooth compensatory movements* are adjustments that the eyes reflexively make with respect to passive movements of the body. Examples of EOGs of saccadic and smooth pursuit movements are given in Figure 14.5.

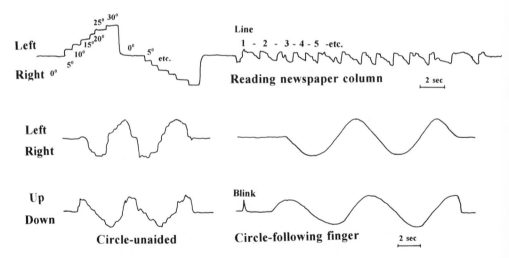

Figure 14.5. Saccadic and pursuit eye movements to the left/right and up/down recorded while subject is fixating points at 5° intervals reading, blinking, and following a finger moving in a circle. Note the typical step-like eye movements made as a reader comes to the end of a line. (From Schackel, 1967, with permission from Elsevier Science Publishers.)

Nystagmus is the continuous, more or less rhythmic oscillations of the eyes that prevent images from remaining stationary on the retina. Nystagmic movements may be pendulatory (movement of equal speed and amplitude in both lateral directions) or jerky and slow (movement in one direction, followed by rapid saccadic return) (Schackel, 1967).

Blinking has a duration of about 200 to 400 msec and may happen at intervals ranging from 1 to 10 sec, with large variations, since blinking is also under voluntary control. Recordings of eyeblinks are frequently used in studies of startle reflexes, as will be described at some length below.

Recording Techniques

There is a difference in standing electrical potential between the front and back of the eyeball, the front of the eye being positive with respect to the back of the eye. The electric field created by the standing potential moves as the eye moves, and electrodes placed on the sides (or above and below) of the eyes will subsequently detect the changing

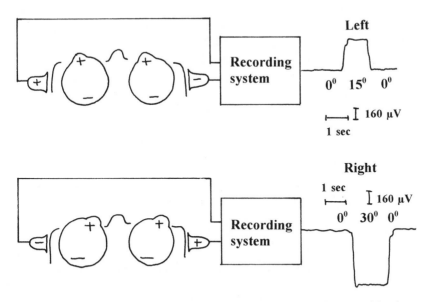

Figure 14.6. Electrooculograms (EOG) record voltage differences caused by the movement of the fronts of the eyes (positive) and the backs of the eyes (negative) in the proximity of the recording electrodes (one positive, one negative). (From Schackel, 1967, with permission from Elsevier Science Publishers.)

potential fields as a change in direct current (DC) potentials, which are recorded on polygraph paper or computer. This is the electroocu-logram. Schackel (1967) compared this setup (see Figure 14.6) with a small battery. As the eyes rotate, the poles of the "battery" move nearer to or away from the respective electrodes on the skin, causing the change in the DC potential.

Using DC recordings for an EOG means that the pen deflections on the polygraph channel will indicate either positive or negative change in potential, and the pen deflections will be linearly related to the amplitude of the movements of the eyes. It should be kept in mind that EOG signals are small in magnitude, in the μV range, as is the case for the EEG. Schackel (1967) recommended that amplifiers be calibrated to enlarge deflections to about 20 μV per degree of eye movement.

A problem with DC recordings is the slow drift of the pen during the recording. This is, however, a much smaller problem than the dif-ficulties caused by the time constant in AC recording techniques. The time constant (TC), discussed in Chapter 11, is the time it takes for an AC signal to fall two-thirds of its initial amplitude, and is related to the lower cutoff frequence (F) by the equation $TC = 1/(2\pi F)$. If the eyes move in one direction and then return to their original posi-tion, an AC recording may actually show that the eyes have not only returned to the original lateral position but have actually swung over in the opposite direction. This is because the time constant tends to "return" the pen back to where it was positioned with a certain speed before the eye movement occurred. If this happens before the eye has moved back to the original position, the polygraph will move the pen across the "zero" midline, erroneously indicating that the eye has "moved" in the other direction. Good EOG recordings can be achieved with an upper cutoff frequency of 40 Hz.

EOG electrodes (preferably 1 mm in diameter) may be placed at the outer and the inner canthus of the eye, or above and below the eye. Horizontally placed electrodes will detect lateral eye movements, while vertically placed electrodes will detect movements up and down in addition to eyeblinks. If only one amplifier channel is available for the EOG, one electrode can be placed on the outer canthus of the eye and the other above the eye. In this situation, both horizontal and vertical (blinks) eye movements will be detected within a single record-ing channel. This is, however, at the expense of not knowing which type of eye movement occurred at the pen deflection, since deflections caused by the two types of movements will be mixed and integrated in the recording. "Integrated" recordings are acceptable if the researcher only wants to know if any eye movements at all have occurred during a recording session, irrespective of whether the eyes moved laterally or vertically. This is typically the situation when EEG and ERP recordings are made, because eye movements, of any kind, are a nuisance to be controlled for when the goal of the experiment is the recording of brain potentials.

Applications in Research

Although recordings of eye movements have a long history in psychophysiology (see Andreassi, 1989)—they have been used to link different kinds of eye movements to psychopathology, perception, learning, and problem solving—EOG recordings are today most often used as a control procedure in experiments designed for other kinds of recordings or stimulus presentations, like the experiments used in visual laterality research. One obvious exception to this is EOG applications in sleep research, where the recording of rapid eye movements (REMs) is a key measure in the identification of dream intervals.

Two other exceptions to this general picture are the studies by Pavlidis (e.g., 1981) on eye-movement disorders found in individuals with dyslexia and by Iacono and Lykken (1979) on saccadic and pursuit eye-movement patterns in twins reared apart. Pavlidis has argued that dyslexic children have faulty control over eye movements, that they cannot sustain fixation on the different words and letters for a long enough time. They also fixate at wrong positions when trying to look at words. The importance of eye-movement errors in dyslexia is, however, controversial, and others have argued that focusing on the eye movements of dyslexic children may be misleading.

Eye-tracking Dysfunction in Psychopathology

Holzman, Proctor, and Hughes (1973) found dysfunctions of eye movements in a majority of their schizophrenic patients and also in about 50 percent of the first-degree relatives of the patients. As argued by Holzman, the study of eye-movement dysfunctions in schizophrenia has both contributed to a neuropsychological understanding of

346 Collecting and Analyzing Data

schizophrenia and generated new hypotheses about the genetic transmission of schizophrenia. Typically, eye-movement dysfunctions occur in relation to smooth pursuit eye movements, the kind of eye movement needed to track a moving object. It should be noted, though, that abnormalities in pursuit movements may be caused by neurological disorders as well, and so it is difficult to make the specific claim that schizophrenia is primarily related to abnormal eye movements. It may be that these patients, in addition to being schizophrenic, have neurological or neuropsychological abnormalities that primarily relate to dysfunctional eye movements. In another study, Holzman, Proctor, Levy, et al. (1974) found abnormal eye movements in 55 percent of the parental pairs of schizophrenic patients, while only 17 percent of the parental pairs of manic-depressive patients showed a similar abnormality.

Thus, eye-movement dysfunction seems to be specific to schizophrenia among the major psychotic disorders. A study of the possibility that eye-movement function might be used as a marker of genetic transmission of schizophrenia was carried out by Holzman, Kringlen, Levy et al. (1978). They examined the sample of monozygotic and dizygotic twins studied by Kringlen in Norway for parent-sibling eye-movement dysfunction and found that the eye-tracking dysfunction was twice as concordant among the monozygotic twins as among the dizygotic twins. Thus, there seems to be some rather strong evidence for genetic transmission of schizophrenia, which can be indexed by eye-movement abnormality.

The Eyeblink Startle Reflex

The startle reflex is an involuntary response to unexpected stimuli that have strong intensity or a rapid onset. It is a multiresponse phenomenon characterized by gross body movements, changes in cardiovascular function, and desynchronization of the alpha wave in the EEG. A fast and reliable index of the startle reflex, though, is the closing of the eyelid in a blink response (Lang, Bradley, and Cuthbert, 1990). In general, the startle response is a compound of bodily responses that occur in rapid succession after the presentation of a stimulus in many species (see Davis, 1984, for an excellent review). In animals, like rats, the startle response can be measured via a stabilimeter as whole-body "jumps." In humans it can be measured via EMG recordings of eyelid closure or by recordings of the amplitude, and also latency, of responses in the obicularis oculi eye muscle elicited by the strong startle stimulus.

An important feature of the startle response is that it is easily measured yet provides valuable information about perceptual, cognitive, emotional, and sensorimotor processes. Recordings of changes in "startle amplitude" (the amplitude of EMG waves corresponding to the startle reflex) have also been used in various psychopathological studies. For example, it has been demonstrated that in schizophrenic patients the startle amplitude is not modified as a function of cognitive processing, indicating a deficit in attentional gating of a stimulus (Braff, Grillon, and Geyer, 1992; Dawson et al., 1993; see below for further explanation). Braff et al. (1992) suggested that the startle paradigm may yield different kinds of information regarding cognitive and sensorimotor status in various patient groups. First, one can assess *startle responsivity*, whether a patient responds at all to the startling stimulus. Second, if the patient responds, one can quantify the magnitude of the response to define a measure of *startle reactivity*. Third, one can examine the temporal characteristics of the response by assessing the *startle latency*, or the latency to the onset or the peak of the response. Fourth, the dynamics of startle allows investigators to assess sensorimotor gating, which is called *prepulse inhibition of startle*. Fifth, one can assess habituation (see Chapter 7), which is the decrement in startle response amplitudes over time after repeated stimulus presentations.

Graham (1975) has shown that the startle blink reflex may be facilitated or inhibited depending on whether the subject is actively attending to the startle stimulus or not. In these experiments, the subject focuses attention on a primary task in which he or she is engaged. Brief auditory startle stimuli are then presented during the attentional task at various intervals and the extent of the eyelid closure is measured with EMG techniques. A typical recording (see Figure 14.7) is from the orbicularis oculi, which is the muscle surrounding the eye and which contracts during an eyeblink.

When subjects are instructed to attend to the startle probe itself, the blink reflex is facilitated (Bohlin and Graham, 1977). On the other hand, when attention was directed to the primary task—for example, when the subject is waiting for the imperative stimulus to respond in a reaction-time task—the startle reflex is attenuated (Hackley and Graham, 1984). Thus, the startle blink may be modified by attention,

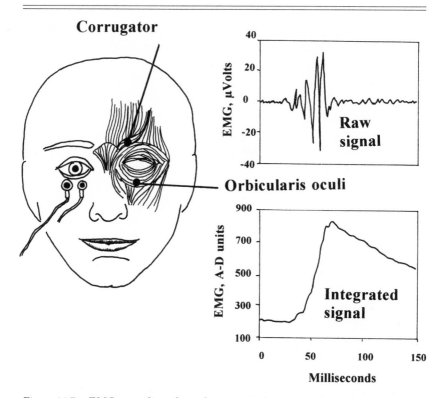

Figure 14.7. EMG recordings from the eye muscles (corrugator and orbicularis oculi) to startle stimuli. At top is the raw EMG signal with a typical "noise burst" and below it is the integrated EMG signal over time (150 msec). The integrated signal is expressed in an arbitrary unit (the *A-D unit*) that is used for converting the raw signal from analogue to digital values. (Adapted from Lang et al., 1990, with permission from the American Psychological Association and the authors.)

and this modification may be analyzed by comparing the amplitude of the blink reflex elicited in different attention-catching situations.

Graham (1975) observed that the blink amplitude is inhibited when the interval between the nonstartle and startle stimuli is between 60 and 240 msec and facilitated when the stimuli are presented at longer intervals, up to 1,000 msec (see also Anthony, 1985). Dawson (1990) suggested that the early inhibition process reflects protection of preattentive, automatic, *stimulus* processing, whereas the facilitation seen at longer intervals reflects sensory enhancement due to controlled, *cognitive* processing. The general explanation for these findings is that attentional resources are limited and may *a priori* be allocated away from the startle probe stimulus. Thus, when processing resources are allocated away from the modality in which the startle probe is presented, the blink reflex should be attenuated because there are less processing resources available to affect the reflex.

Using the prepulse inhibition paradigm—namely, presenting attended nonstartling stimuli before the startle stimulus—Dawson, Hazlett, Filion, et al. (1993) recently showed that the typical modulation of the blink reflex by prestartle attention was absent in a group of subjects with recent-onset schizophrenia. The expected modulation of the startle reflex to attended stimuli was present in a matched control group. Dawson et al. (1993) suggested that these findings showed traitlike attentional deficits in schizophrenia, and that the prepulse inhibition startle paradigm may be an important marker of vulnerability to schizophrenia. The prepulse inhibition paradigm typically involves a weak auditory prestimulus that is presented, for example, 100 msec prior to the strong startle-eliciting stimulus. The prestimulus reduces, or gates, the amplitude of the startle response elicited by the startle stimulus. The reduction of the amplitude of the startle response is termed *prepulse inhibition* or *reflex modification* (Flaten and Hugdahl, 1990).

Emotional Valence and Startle Eyeblinks

From the hypothesis that allocation of processing resources interacts with the amplitude of the startle blink reflex—that blink amplitudes are smaller when more processing resources are allocated to the primary task—it could be predicted also that the more interesting the primary task is, the smaller the blink amplitude.

The effects of emotional valence on startle modification has been extensively investigated by Peter Lang and his colleagues over the last couple of years (Lang et al., 1990; Bradley, Cuthbert, and Lang, 1991; Vrana, Spence, and Lang, 1988). The general experimental paradigm involves the presentation of series of slides with positive, neutral, and negative contents while brief auditory startle probes are presented during the "slide show." For this purpose, Lang, Öhman, and Vaitl (1988) have developed a test battery, the International Affective Picture System. Among the positive slides are pictures of a happy baby, an attractive nude, and a horse; among the neutral are pictures of a building, a neutral face, and a mushroom; and among the negative are pictures of a starving child, a snake, and violent death. Each slide is usually shown for 6 sec, with 16 to 24 sec between slides. The acoustic startle stimulus is presented for 50 msec as bursts of white noise with a very rapid rise time. The startle probes are presented several times, irregularly spaced across the 6 sec slide presentation.

In an early study (Vrana et al., 1988) it was found that the blink-reflex amplitude increased significantly from the pleasant to the neutral to the negative stimulus category. Thus, the hypothesis of resource allocation was empirically corroborated, as smaller blink amplitudes were recorded when there is an interesting, attention-getting stimulus foreground against which the startle probe is presented. The findings by Vrana et al. (1988) have been replicated several times (e.g., Bradley, Cuthbert, and Lang, 1988). Figure 14.8 includes results from these studies.

Laterality of Startle Modification

Of particular interest was the study by Bradley et al. (1988, 1991) which found that the amplitude of the blink reflex differed according to whether the startle probe was presented to the left or the right ear. The auditory system is lateralized in the brain, with more preponderant nerve fibers connecting one side of the brain with the contralateral ear. Thus, a stimulus in the right ear will have a greater effect on the left temporal cortex, and vice versa. The main finding was that only left-ear probes produced blink reflexes that varied significantly in amplitude according to the emotional valence of the stimulus foreground. This indicates that affective modulation of the startle blink reflex is mainly controlled from the right hemisphere of the brain.

A critique of this study is that the auditory system is not completely lateralized, which means that a monaural probe in the left or right ear will produce both ipsilateral and contralateral activation of the brain. This problem can easily be solved, however, by presenting dichotic stimuli, with the startle probe presented in one ear and another, non-startle stimulus simultaneously presented in the other ear. Such a procedure will preserve an initial unilateral activation of only the contralateral hemisphere in the brain.

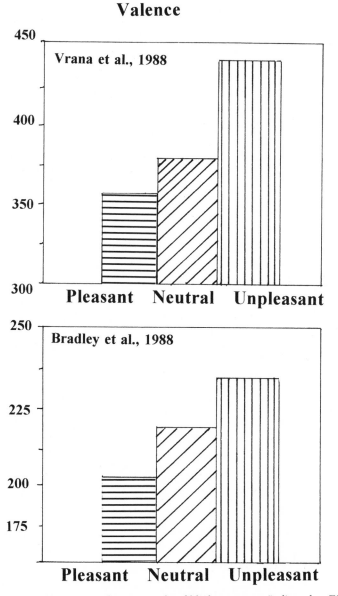

Figure 14.8. Differences in the magnitude of blink responses (indicated as EMG recordings in A-D units) to an auditory startle stimulus against a "foreground" of pleasant, neutral, and unpleasant emotional activation. (From Lang et al., 1990, with permission from American Psychological Association and the authors.)

Startle as a Cultural Phenomenon

The startle response to intense or rapid unexpected stimulation is observed in all species. It is also true that some individuals are more "readily" startled than others, although this is usually not seen as ay personality trait. Some individuals will react with a characteristic startle pattern when, for example, they realize that someone has entered a room without their noticing it. This may happen even if, for example, a wife knows her husband is home but is surprised to find him suddenly in the same room.

In some cultures, the startle phenomenon is viewed as the disposition of specific traits. Ronald Simons (1980) has revealed that in Malaysia, people who are known to startle readily and strongly are repetitively startled by others until they become extremely jumpy and flustered. A typical startle "trick" is to sneak up behind a person and poke him or her between the ribs. People who are easily startled may jump, drop objects they hold, and utter taboo words. In the Malaysian culture, they are also believed to obey the commands of others and to be, in general, inferior. The Malaysian word for this natural startle behavior is *latah*, and people who are easily startled are called "latahs." Simons (1980) reports that the condition of being a latah is a well-defined role in the Malaysian culture. Most latahs are women, and latahs are thought not to be responsible for their behavior when in the latah state. An interesting observation from neuroscience, which may explain this phenomenon, is that the startle response, for a fraction of a second, is a very profound trance state, during which the brain is inhibited for external input while the startle is executed. Although Simons (1988) has argued that the latah is a manifestation of a universal startle reflex, others have argued that it is a highly specific ethnographic behavior and has no universal meaning attached to it (Kenny, 1983).

Respiratory Psychophysiology

Respiratory psychophysiology may be the "most underrated variable in current psychophysiological research" (Hassett, 1978, p. 73). It has had relatively little impact on mainstream psychophysiology during the last decades.

Important exceptions are recent studies of panic attacks and anxiety and respiratory sinus arrhythmia (Porges, McCabe and Yonge, 1982) (see Chapter 9). Breathing problems experienced by individuals with anxiety disorders have gained renewed interest lately, especially since it was suggested that hyperventilation may elicit panic attacks in agoraphobic patients (Ley, 1985).

The Physiology of Breathing

For the purpose of psychophysiological studies, the respiratory system may be thought of as the mouth, the nose, the trachea, the bronchi (small passages) and the alveoli (small air sacs) in the lungs, and the passage of air and carbon dioxide to and from the lungs. The principal function of the respiratory system is to extract oxygen (O_2) from the air that enters the lungs, transport it to body tissues, and evacuate excess carbon dioxide (CO_2) and water. In anatomical terms, respiration involves the diaphragm, the intercostal muscles, and the abdominal muscles. All three structures are striated muscles basically under voluntary control, but respiration itself is both voluntary and involuntary, as the respiratory system is innervated also by the autonomic nervous system. We do not ordinarily think about normal breathing, although we can easily breathe faster or slower. Respiration is controlled from respiratory centers in the medulla, which also monitors the carbon dioxide content of the blood and activates respiratory reflex loops if the concentration exceeds normal limits.

Air is inhaled into the lungs and O_2 is extracted and supplied to the blood through gaseous exchange at the capillaries in the lungs. At the same time, CO_2 and other waste products are passed from the blood to the air in the lungs and removed through expiration. Oxygen is carried in the blood from the lungs to the heart and body tissues, where it supports metabolic processes necessary for the cells of the body to function. The rate of oxygen intake is directly related to the amount of muscular work done; it may normally vary between 0.2 liter per kilogram bodyweight per hour during rest to 4 l/kg/h during exercise.

Recording Techniques

Psychophysiological recordings of respiration may be obtained by attaching a strain gauge around the chest or abdomen, which records the expansion and reduction in circumference during inspiration and expiration as phasic changes on a polygraph chart. Another, less accurate method to measure patterns of inspiration and expiration is to attach a *thermistor* under the nose, which is sensitive to differences in temperature between inhaled and exhaled air. Since the exhaled air is warmer than the inhaled air (under normal circumstances), a display of the change in temperature will indicate the respiratory pattern. A third, more accurate, method is to use a *capnometer*, which analyzes the composition of gases in the exhaled air, particularly the concentration of CO_2.

Hyperventilation Syndrome and Anxiety

Capnometer recordings are frequently used in studies of *hyperventilation*, which is defined as breathing at a frequency higher than necessary to meet the metabolic demands of body tissue. Hyperventilation is characterized by lowered alveolar CO_2 pressure and blood alkalosis (pH higher than normal), because of the excessive loss of CO_2 due to overbreathing. The reduction in alveolar CO_2 pressure will reduce the diameter of the small pulmonary arteries and thus impede the flow of blood to body tissue. This may cause ischemic pain. The increase in blood pH reduces the amount of oxygen in the blood, and therefore reduces the amount of oxygen delivered to body cells. As a result, the heart must pump blood with greater force and frequency to compensate for the decrease in alveloar CO_2 pressure and the increase in pH. If hyperventilation continues long enough, symptoms of dyspnea, shortness of breath and breathing difficulty, will occur.

The hyperventilation syndrome is a collection of several symptoms affecting the cardiovascular, respiratory, musculoskeletal, endocrine, and gastrointestinal systems (see Fried and Grimaldi, 1993, for an updated discussion). From the perspective of psychophysiology, the symptom of interest is the elicitation of panic attacks in individuals with anxiety disorders, particularly agoraphobia (Ley, 1985; Fried and Grimaldi, 1993). Breathing is usually increased and intensified (deeper) in states of anxiety, as one might expect from the definition of anxiety as a state of tension signaling the potentiality of an impeding disaster and producing intense fear. The relationship between the hyperventilation syndrome and the panic attacks that occur in agoraphobic patients is described by Ley (1985, p. 79) as:

The panic attack consists of a synergistic interaction between hyperventilation and anxiety, the nature of which is a positively accelerated loop: with excessive expiration of CO_2, moderate overbreathing produces relatively mild symptoms (e.g. slight dizziness) which can be tolerated for prolonged periods. If, however, respiration rate increases somewhat, the symptoms of hyperventilatory hypocapnia increase in both number and intensity very rapidly to the point where tolerance gives way to alarm and fear. When fear is elicited, heightened sympathetic nervous system activity contributes to an increase in respiration rate and thereby increases the intensity of the hyperventilation syndrome, which in turn increases fear, which in turn increases respiration rate, and so on. The panic attack will in this way grow in intensity until the sufferer either falls into unconsciousness and thereby stops hyperventilating or engages in behavior which leads to a reduction in the amount of CO_2 dissipated.

As pointed out by Fried and Grimaldi (1993), there is still some controversy in the literature whether hyperventilation causes anxiety and panic attacks, or whether it is anxiety that causes the hyperventilation syndrome. It is beyond the scope of this book to dwell too much on this, but it seems clear that many patients suffering from anxiety with panic attacks will frequently hyperventilate, and hyperventilation should therefore be checked routinely in diagnosis and treatment of anxiety disorders. An interesting hypothesis is that hyperventilation may be a conditioned response in the Pavlovian sense. This was noted by Fried and Grimaldi (1993, p. 209): "chronic hyperventilators are a somato-autonomic type, in the Pavlovian sense. And both their reactions to the world, stress, and HV [hyperventilation] and their reaction to the effects of HV form a more or less closed feedback loop where components of the system become indistinguishable once the cycle is set into motion."

Summary

The present chapter has dealt with three measures of psychophysiological interactions that have been extensively used in psychosomatic medicine and in psychpathology. Disorders of muscle tension and of respiratory dysfunction is characteristic symptoms of stress and overactivation. Likewise, faulty eye movements have been suggested an important feature in psychotic behavior, indicating attentional deficits.

Eye movement recordings have also been extensively employed in research on reading and writing disorders, and in hyperactivity syndromes. Respiration patterns are also a characteristic feature of panic and anxiety disorders. It should finally be remembered that analysis of respiratory patterns may yield information about cardiovascular function (see Chapter 9), particularly in conjunction with recordings of heart rate variability, and sinus arrythmia.

The basic principles of psychophysiological recordings of muscle activity, EMG, were reviewed. Both basic muscle physiology and recording techniques are described, together with a brief, selective overview of some applications of the psychophysiology of the muscles, especially with regard to clinical and cognitive psychology. Psychophysiological studies of muscle activity have been focused on relaxation training in anxiety and emotional disorders, and the specific technique of biofeedback training. Biofeedback training with EMG has been applied to a variety of somatic disorders with a supposedly psychogenic origin, such as tension headache, migraine, and low back pain.

This overview of eye movements was concerned with different types of eye movements, how eye movements have been studied in the psychology of emotion, and studies of cognitive effects on eye-blink startle responses. The different eye-movements reviewed were saccades, smooth pursuit movements, nystagmus, and blinking. The major part of the chapter was concerned with reviewing recent research on startle reflexes by, in particular, Frances Graham and Peter Lang, showing how both affective and cognitive factors modify the amplitude of an eye-blink startle response. Peter Lang has shown that negative and positive affective valence, or mood, plays a critical role in startle amplitude. Also, Graham has shown how allocation of processing resources in the startle paradigm affects the eye-blink amplitude.

Epilogue

In this closing chapter I will provide a few summary statements about the use of psychophysiology in various disciplines involved in the study of brain-behavior relationships or stated, in a more generic way, disciplines that study the mind-body interface. Specifically, I will discuss how psychophysiology has been successfully applied in neuropsychology to investigate the physiological concomitants of brain damage and the cortical localization of function. Neuropsychology is today divided into at least two subdisciplines, one concerned with the localization of function (clinical neuropsychology), the other concerned solely with brain function (cognitive neuropsychology). I will also argue that psychophysiology shares with cognitive neuroscience both a broad scope and many points of interest, and that peripheral physiological processes are an integral part of the cognitive processes traditionally studied in cognitive neuroscience. Psychophysiology differs from cognitive neuroscience in that it has traditionally focused on emotions, stress, and other events that affect the peripheral physiology, whereas cognitive neuroscience has until now had little to say about the body half of the mind-body equation. Finally, I will provide some examples of how psychophysiology has been instrumental in specifying mediating mechanisms in major psychiatric disorders, like schizophrenia and depression.

The Psychophysiological Perspective on the Mind-Body Problem

The main focus in psychophysiology over the years has been the assessment and recording of physiological activity from the central, autonomic, and somatomotor nervous systems. Also of major concern in the field, however, has been the collection of subjective and behavioral data. Thus, psychophysiology has always maintained a strong interest in what may be called a "three-systems approach" (Chapter 1) to brain-behavioral relations. This approach promotes the integration of *physiological data* with *verbal reports* and *overt behavior*. Seen from a three-systems perspective, psychophysiology thus differs in scope and interest from both classic neurophysiology and physiological psychology). For neurophysiology and physiological psychology, the physiological domain is the primary area of interest, and behavior is studied only to evaluate relationships between physiological variables.

A similar view was stated by Öhman and Birbaumer (1993), who described the psychophysiologist's behavioral orientation to psychological phenomena and commitment to observe, measure, and influence rather than merely talk about behavior. The psychophysiologist also brings to psychological research a preference for grounding psychological research in natural science and biomedical research. Training in psychophysiology thus requires a broad knowledge not only of recording technology but also of general physiology.

The psychophysiology tradition has also emphasized measurement precision and advanced statistical analysis of recorded data. Perhaps the most important aspect of a psychophysiological approach to psychological phenomena, however, is the commitment to understand the physiological mechanisms mediating cognitive and emotional events. Thus, the psychophysiologist, the true proponent of the mind-body perspective, would argue against the disembodiment of thought and action. To the contrary, the psychophysiologist emphasizes the fact that the processing of information, or the function of the brain, is constrained by the location of the brain in the human body (cf. Jennings, 1992).

The Embodiment of Cognitions

The notion that the body may alter cognitive function has always been taken seriously in psychophysiological research. Lacey (e.g., 1967) put forward an elaborate theory on the relationship between cardiovascular events and information processing. In Lacey's view, the cardiovascular system modulates sensory input to the brain, either facilitating or inhibiting processing of new information depending on the quality of the stimulus (see also Chapter 10). One of the body's responses to novel, potentially interesting stimuli is a lowering of sensory thresholds that is accompanied by heart-rate deceleration. In situations of demanding cognitive activity, like mental arithmetic, however, there is a rejection of new sensory stimuli, accompanied by heart rate acceleration. Moreover, Lacey also speculated whether the change in heart rate, either deceleration or acceleration was directly linked to the increased intake or rejection of environmental stimuli through modulatory activity of the baroreceptors in the carotid artery in the neck. For Lacey (1967), an understanding of how the brain processes sensory information in situations of sensory intake or rejection was intimately linked to an understanding of not only how the brain works but also how the cardiovascular system works and how the two systems are related. In psychophysiology, there is a strong belief in the importance of physiological responses in both cognitive *and* emotional processes.

In his 1992 presidential address to the Society for Psychophysiological Research, Jennings (1992) argued that the interaction of autonomic and motor responses may reveal how information processing and physiological control are integrated. In his studies of the integration of behavior and physiological changes, Jennings has developed a simple experimental task: the subject is required to get ready to respond with a button press at the onset of a "ready signal" and to press the button quickly at the appearance of a "go signal" a few seconds later. This simple task involves several important features of the interaction of the brain and physiological activity. In the warning period there is an anticipation of the occurrence of the "go signal" along with the preparation for the motor response of pressing the button. Physiologically, a whole range of changes occurs in the anticipation period: heart-rate deceleration, respiration changes, muscle tonus quieting, skin-conductance response increases, and a slow negative wave in the brain EEG. What psychological processes may induce these physiological changes? As mentioned above, Lacey (1967) suggested that expectancy caused the heart to slow down, which in turn reduced input to the cardiovascular control centers in the brainstem. Lacey, moreover, believed that reduced afferent feedback to the brain from the cardiovascular system facilitated the integration of perceptual and motor activity, resulting in speeded responses to the "go signal." Obrist (1981), on the other hand, thought that the quieting of muscle activity in the foreperiod was a primary cause for heart-rate slowing. Thus, whereas Lacey thought anticipation and expectancy were directly linked to physiological changes, Obrist considered the changes in cardiovascular function a physiological consequence of the reaction in muscle tonus, which reduced the metabolic demands and, hence, caused the slowing of the heart.

The Emotions

The interaction between physiological responses and psychological phenomena has been most directly studied in the realm of emotions and emotional experiences. The well-known claim by James (1884) and Lange (1885) that emotions in fact *are* their accompanying bodily reactions implies not only that the physiological response is primary to the psychological experience in emotions, but also that there should be different physiological responses to different emotional experiences. In James's view, we feel sad because we cry, we feel afraid because the heart pounds. It may be of interest to note that James and Lange differed in their views on the physiological basis of emotions. James talked about bodily responses in a more general sense, and included motor activity as a significant response, whereas Lange restricted the physiological changes to the cardiovascular system, including changes in peripheral blood vessels. Cannon (1936) opposed both interpretations on the grounds that the autonomic nervous system was too slow to induce the kind of physiological changes that accompany emotions. Instead, Cannon suggested that the autonomic nervous system is engaged as part of an "emergency reaction" that supports a "fight" or "flight" reaction in situations that elicit anger or fear.

In more modern theories of emotion it is argued that physiological reactions are necessary inputs to a cognitive analysis of sensory events that result in an emotion (e.g., Mandler, 1975). As also mentioned in Chapter 1, psychophysiological recordings are frequently included in the definition of an emotional reaction, especially by those who work within the "three-systems" model of emotional behavior (e.g., Lang, 1968). The three-systems model of emotions holds that emotions are not unitary reactions and that they manifest themselves in at least three different response systems: verbal reports, overt behavior (often avoidance), and physiological responses. Different components may be of greater or lesser importance for different emotions. For example, whereas one phobic patient may experience extreme physiological reactivity in an anxiety-provoking situation, another patient may be more preoccupied with negative self-ruminations and thoughts about his or her ability to cope with the situation.

An Interdisciplinary and Interactionist Approach

As stated in the introductory chapters, psychophysiology is concerned with the study of physiological substrates of psychological processes. Although psychophysiology has traditionally focused on the study of the physiological basis of emotions, more modern approaches to psychophysiology also emphasize cognitive processes and the social context. Thus, psychophysiology covers a wide range of psychological processes and the bodily reactionsthat accompany them. A general view in psychophysiology is that activity in bodily response systems that participate in the execution and control of behavior may be detected by noninvasive recording devices. Psychophysiology furthermore seeks to understand both the physiological response systems themselves and the psychological context in which they occur. Thus, psychophysiology by necessity emphasizes the *interactions* between mind and body—it takes what may be called an "interactionist" perspective on the mind-body problem. In particular, it is important that the psychophysiologist understand both the physiological response system and the psychological context that generates physiological responses. In this sense, the psychophysiologist has to be both a physiologist and a psychologist.

In line with the view expressed by Coles, Donchin, and Porges (1986), the perspective taken in this book is that psychophysiological recordings are not only "surface" indexes of underlying physiological systems. The psychophysiologist should therefore have a thorough understanding of the underlying mechanisms, both from a physiological and a psychological point of view.

Physiological Psychology

The psychophysiologist attempts to monitor bodily events that result from manipulations of behavioral, cognitive, and emotional conditions. In this respect, psychophysiology is different from physiological psychology, which is mainly concerned with monitoring behavioral consequences after manipulations of physiological conditions. A typical experiment in physiological psychology might be to record behavioral dysfunction resulting from a lesion made to the brain or nervous system of an animal. The psychophysiologist, on the other hand, uses human subjects whose physiological responses are monitored noninvasively in an experimental setting in which perceptual, cognitive, or emotional stimuli are presented. Although psychophysiology traditionally has been defined as approaching the interface between the mind or brain and the body differently from the ways in which physiological psychology and neuropsychology do, a major theme in this book is that the time has now come for broader interaction among the various subdisciplines studying brain-behavior relationships.

Cognitive Neuroscience

The newly emerging discipline of cognitive neuroscience may be promising in this regard, since it has evolved out of a desire to understand the workings of the brain in complex cognitive tasks. It was pioneered by scientists from a variety of fields, including cognitive psychology, systems-level neuroscience, and artifical intelligence (see Kosslyn and Koening, 1992). Moreover, as stated by Gazzaniga (1989) in his editorial note in the first issue of the journal *Cognitive Neuroscience*, cognitive neuroscientists "believe that it is maximally fruitful to propose models of cognitive processes that can be assessed in neurobiologic terms. Likewise, it is no longer useful for neuroscientists to propose brain mechanisms underlying psychological processes without actually coming to grips with the complexity of psychological processes involved in any mental capacity examined" (p. 2). As should be clear by now, I have made the same argument in this book for the aim of psychophysiological investigations: we must understand the complex interaction of brain mechanisms, physiological responses, and mental activity if we are to understand the intricate nature of human behavior.

   An important research tool in cognitive neuroscience was the development of brain imaging techniques for the monitoring of regional blood flow in the brain during various psychological tasks (see Chapter 13). Through technologies like these, cognitive neuroscience is linked to psychophysiology both methodologically and conceptually. In the future, it should be as natural for the cognitive neuroscientist to use psychophysiological methods and techniques to monitor bodily events as it should be for the psychophysiologist to use brain imaging technology to monitor brain events. The use of event-related potentials (see Chapter 12) in psychophysiology to probe brain activity in response to cognitive challenges is another sign of the common interests and approaches in the two fields. By joining forces, psychophysiology and cognitive neuroscience should be able not only to develop new ways to ask questions about brain-behavior relationships but also to get better answers.

By recording, for example, ERPs from the brain simultaneously with or in close proximity to recordings of blood flow or glucose metabolism in the brain, we gain the advantage of high spatial resolution in the brain scans as well as the advantage of high temporal resolution of the electrophysiological responses. Similarly, by combining recordings of autonomic activity, like EDA or heart rate, with measures of brain function during cognitive and emotional tasks, we obtain access to a broader spectrum of activity in the same experimental context. These kinds of experiments may reveal how the brain regulates peripheral psychophysiological responses to mental challenges. It is my hope that such "joint" enterprises between cognitive neuroscience and psychophysiology will emerge in the future. For example, although human classical conditioning, the most elementary forms of learning, is perhaps is the most thoroughly studied phenomenon in the history of psychophysiology, we have very little knowledge about the brain areas involved in human conditioning. The new brain imaging techniques of PET and fMRI (see Chapter 13) would be well suited for a study of which brain areas are activated when a new association between two environmental events is learned. Similarly, although there is emerging evidence in cognitive neuroscience of which brain areas are involved in complex mental processes—from comparisons, for example, of the distribution of blood flow in the brain when the subject imagines seeing an object with blood-flow patterns when the subject really sees it (Kosslyn et al., 1993)—little is known about the peripheral consequences of these processes. Does the autonomic activity elicited by mental imagery resemble the activity elicited by perceiving the same emotional stimulus? To take another example: is it possible to inhibit, or even abolish, an orienting response or a startle response by hypnotizing the subject so that he or she cannot hear a tone stimulus? Answers to questions like these await closer collaborations among researchers working in the various subdisciplines.

Neuropsychology

In a similar way, it is time for psychophysiology to establish a closer relationship with neuropsychology and psychiatry. A study by Lehrer, Groveman, Randolph, et al. (1989) may serve as an example of how psychophysiology may enhance our understanding of cognitive and emotional dysfunction after brain injury. This study compared neuro-psychological and psychophysiological performance in a group of patients with closed head injuries with a normal control group. Among the neuropsychological tests were tests for short-term memory, finger-tapping speed, and arithmetic ability. Autonomic psychophysiological responses, including skin-conductance responses, heart rate, finger-pulse volume, muscle activity, and respiration, were recorded. By using psychophysiological recordings, the authors could evaluate two hypotheses regarding cognitive performance in patients with head injury. One hypothesis holds that the injured patients, as a consequence of brainstem compromise, would exhibit hypoarousal when exposed to cognitive challenges, which would explain their poor performance on the neuropsychological tests. The other hypothesis holds that patients with closed head injuries would exhibit increased arousal and activation while attempting cognitive tasks, because of the additional effort such tasks demand of injured patients. The patient group not only performed less well on the cognitive tasks but also had overall lower physiological activity. These results indicate that closed head injuries affect both cognitive function and the physiological modulation required for task performance. The attenuation of physiological modulation in the patient group may thus be primary to poor cognitive performance. The goals ofrehabilitation programs should therefore be not only to improve the skills required for cognitive tasks but also to maintain nonspecific arousal, which may be a prerequisite for improved cognitive function.

The Localization of Brain Function

As a discipline within the neuroscience family, neuropsychology is typically concerned with questions related to brain function—particularly to assessments of behavioral dysfunction after localized brain lesions, such as the loss of language skills after a stroke affecting the left side of the brain. An example of psychophysiology's more general interest in brain function is the question of the *localization* of brain function: What part or parts of the brain are involved in each of the myriad processes carried out in the "mind"? This question may be stated as, What are the interacting systems in the brain that organize the different parts of areas to promote behavior?

This is an old controversy in neuropsychology, and in neuroscience in general. According to one school of thought, perhaps best voiced through the work of Karl Lashley, the *entire* brain, not just a single part of it, participates in all different cognitive functions. This is reminiscent of Hughlings-Jackson's well-known argument that only lesions—not function—could be localized in the brain. Thus, removal of parts of the brain should produce a deficit in the performance of any given cognitive task that was proportional to the *amount* of tissue removed, not to the *location* of the removed tissue. This was called the *mass-action hypothesis*. According to another of Lashley's principles, the *equipotentiality hypothesis*, each area in the brain, and even each portion of an area, is able to produce the same behavior as any other portion of an area. The equipotentiality hypothesis cannot explain why other areas cannot take over a function that disappears after a localized lesion to a specific area in the brain. Interestingly, Lashley's work during the 1930s and 1940s (see Lashley, 1960) is still cited as showing the general principles of brain function, although modern brain imaging techniques and other research emphasizing functional systems has shown that he probably was wrong about localization of function in the brain.

I do not wish to imply that the concept of localization of function is without problems. There is ample evidence, accumulated by psychophysiologists as well as neurophysiologists and cognitive neuroscientists, of widespread activation in the brain during the performance of complex mental processes. The intricate involvement of thalamocortical projections and the amygdala in many different mental processes is a good example of the complexity of the functional organization of the brain. Furthermore, although recent blood-flow studies have demonstrated that regional increases in activity accompany specific types of cognitive activity, other studies have found a complex pattern of interaction among brain areas during mental processing (e.g., Lassen and Roland, 1983). Taken together, however, the evidence surely points to localization of primary sensory and motor functions, as well as specialization for vision and auditory function, although even these functions may best be described in a systems-related way.

Another area of research in localization is *hemispheric asymmetry* and the specialization of higher mental functions, like cognition, in the left and right cerebral hemispheres (see Hellige, 1993, for an update on asymmetry of cognitive function). Although research on hemispheric asymmetry has been a focus of neuropsychology for decades, much work still remains to be done on the exact nature of functional specialization in the brain. The specialization for language and visuospatial functions in the left and right hemispheres, respectively, may have an evolutionary basis in the need to communicate with members of the same species and to orient in the environment when hunting prey and avoiding predators. The evolutionary advantages of symbolic communication and orienting in three-dimensional space may have resulted in the development of specialized areas in the brain to deal with these particular functions. Moreover, because women had the greater responsibility for bringing up children and conveying the rules of social organization to them, they may have evolved a greater capacity for verbal skills than men have. In a similar way, the specialization for correct orientation in the environmentmay have resulted in men, the hunters in early human society, being more specialized, and lateralized, for visuospatial function than women are.

Psychophysiology is an important research and clinical tool for functional assessment, lesion diagnosis, and brain localization in neuropsychology. Assessment of motor disorders in neurodegenerative disorders like Parkinson's disease can be made with excellent precision if electromyographic (EMG) recordings are employed. Similarly, continuous recordings of eye-movement patterns with electrooculography (EOG) may help assess developmental disorders like dyslexia. Psychophysiological recordings of brain potentials (ERPs) have been of invaluable help in assessing neuropsychological disorders. Autonomic recordings, like electrodermal activity (EDA), have also been used in neuropsychological assessment. Kløve and Hole (1981) demonstrated that failure to show orienting reactions (ORs) to repeated presentations of a tone stimulus characterized hyperactive children; this observation is instrumental in theorizing that brainstem hypoactivity in these children may be compensated for by behavioral hyperactivity.

Psychophysiological parameters frequently reveal more subtle aspects of the intricate interplay between the left and right sides of the brain and the nervous system. The theoretical relevance of using, for example, electrodermal responding as a measure of hemispheric functioning might at first glance seem confusing. Why should a researcher interested in the specialized functioning of the hemispheres, which is a phenomenon of the central nervous system, look for differences in eccrine sweat-gland activity between the hands, which is a phenomenon of the autonomic nervous system? The answer is quite simple in the sense that lateralization in the brain is not strictly a cortical phenomenon. As discussed in previous chapters, most organs and structures in the brain and nervous system, with the exception of the pineal gland, have a left-right division. Thus, the issue of functional asymmetry should be as important to studies of subcortical structures as they are to studies of cortical structures. Crosson (1992) suggested that the dominant thalamus plays an important role in the gating, storage, and retrieval of verbal memory related to language function. Hugdahl, Wester, and Asbjørnsen (1990) found a reduction of the right-ear advantage in dichotic listening (indicative of left-hemisphere dysfunction) in Parkinson's patients who had surgery in the left thalamus compared with patients who had surgery in the right thalamus. Hugdahl et al. (1990) suggested that the left ventrolateral thalamus may act as an attention gate to facilitate or inhibit auditory signals from the contralateral ear. Thus, subcortical structures exhibit asymmetry of function in many respects similar to the asymmetries found at the cortical level.

It should therefore not come as a surprise that recordings of psychophysiological activity controlled from subcortical and peripheral structures could provide important information about functional specialization in the brain. In particular, when basic differences between the hemispheres are thought to reflect process variables, such as the task to be performed or the "cognitive strategy" used when the subject approaches a particular task, a psychophysiological approach to specialization in the brain may be valuable. When the basic nature of lateralization is conceptualized in terms of differences in processing strategy (e.g., Hellige, 1993), it is usually assumed that the asymmetry occurs at later, higher-order stages of information processing (e.g., Moscovitch, 1979). It then follows that attentional factors studied in psychophysiology, such as orienting and habituation, that involve higher-order processing of stimuli may be regarded as under asymmetrical cortical influences. In fact, Kinsbourne (e.g., 1973) has argued that observed asymmetries on the behavioral level merely reflect covert shifts of attention to the side of the more activated hemisphere for a particular task. This activity then "spills over" to motor centers that control activity on the contralateral side of the body. Since electrodermal activity is a sensitive indicator of attention and is frequently used in studies of orienting and habituation, it might be reasonable to relate EDA to hemispheric asymmetry.

This relationship could also be defended from a neuroanatomical and neurophysiological perspective. EDA is under the control of both excitatory and inhibitory centers located at the brainstem and at cortical levels (see Chapter 6). Wang (1964), for instance, found evidence of inhibitory effects on responses from the ventromedial reticular formation. Furthermore, Bloch and Bonvallet (1959) demonstrated an augmentation of responses when the mesencephalic reticular formation was stimulated, thus indicating a facilitory function. In addition, recent advances in psychophysiological research have revealed a number of important biological asymmetries related to immune function (Barneoud, Neveu, Vitiello, and Le Moal, 1987), neuroendocrine responses (Wittling and Pfluger, 1990), and autonomic function (e.g., Weisz, Szilagyi, Lang, and Adam, 1992). Wittling (1990) found that the cerebral hemispheres markedly differed in their ability to regulate blood pressure during emotionally laden situations. Both diastolic and systolic blood pressure was significantly increased during presentations to the right hemisphere of short film clips with emotional content. Similarly, Hugdahl, Wahlgren, and Wass (1982) reported that habituation of the electrodermal orienting response was delayed when visual stimuli were unilaterally presented to the right as compared to the left hemisphere.

It is therefore clear that hemispheric asymmetry affects more than just those higher mental functions residing in the cortex considered in the traditional view to be lateralized. It is also clear that vital physiological functions involving both endocrine and autonomic processes are influenced by functional asymmetry, although the exact nature of central regulation of, for example, autonomic function is still unclear (see Cechetto and Saper, 1990). We may therefore extend the familiar notion of cortical asymmetry to a broader concept of "neurobiological asymmetry," which may be thought of as operating through two different mechanisms: either the right and left cortical hemispheres differentially regulate outflow to the periphery, or peripheral mechanisms act asymmetrically by their own action. My view (see, e.g., Chapter 3) is that the sympathetic and parasympathetic branches of the autonomic nervous system are differently regulated from the right and left hemispheres of the brain. Predominant sympathetic activation is thought to be regulated from the right hemisphere, parasympathetic activation from the left hemisphere. For example, Heller, Lindsay, Metz, and Farnum (1990) showed that autonomic arousal was directly related to stimulation of the right hemisphere in a visual half-field paradigm. A similar finding (see Chapter 10) was reported by Hachinsky et al. (1992). In this study rats had either the left or right middle cerebral artery experimentally occluded, and heart rate, blood pressure, and plasma epinephrine and norepinephrine were monitored, among other variables. The experiment clearly showed greater sympathetic consequences after right-hemisphere lesions than after left-hemisphere lesions.

Studies of Brain Damage

Psychophysiology has also contributed to a deeper understanding of the neuropsychology of brain lesions. A now classic example is the study by Tranel and Damasio (1985) on patients who cannot recognize familiar faces, sometimes including their own. This phenomenon, called *prosopagnosia*, may occur after a stroke, although the exact nature of the condition is unknown, and patients may vary as to the localization and extent of the brain lesion. A typical feature of this syndrome is the inability to recognize someone by seeing his or her face, even if recognition by voice is possible, or the inability to distinguish a familiar from an unfamiliar face. Tranel and Damasio (1985) found that although patients with prosopagnosia could not verbally identify familiar faces when shown photographs of familiar and unfamiliar faces, they nevertheless showed larger electrodermal responses to the familiar faces. Thus, although explicit memory for recognition was impaired, a kind of implicit, unconscious memory was expressed in the autonomic nervous system, dissociated from consciousness.

A study related to the findings by Tranel and Damasio was the observation by Johnsen and Hugdahl (1993) that classical conditioning to facial expressions of happiness and anger was regulated from the right rather than the left hemisphere. Johnsen and Hugdahl (1993) had subjects look at pictures of happy and angry faces while presentation of one of the two faces was paired with a mildly aversive electric shock to the hand. After having established a conditioned electrodermal response to the shocked face, subjects were then exposed to the faces for just a few milliseconds, too brief a time to be able actually to see the faces. No shocks were presented during this phase of the experiment. On half of the trials, the faces were presented to the left visual field, with initial input only to the right hemisphere. On the other half of the trials the faces were presented in the right visual field, with initial input to the left hemisphere. Greater electrodermal responses were elicited by presentation of particularly angry faces that had previously been paired with an electric shock, especially when the stimulus was presented to the right hemisphere. Thus, although the subjects did not recognize the faces because they were presented for such a brief period of time, there was an implicit autonomic memory for the association of one of the faces with shock, and this memory was regulated from the right hemisphere of the brain. It is therefore evident that much information about brain-behavior relationships are dissociated from conscious experience and are therefore available only through recordings of psychophysiological parameters. This conclusion was also evident in a study by Kayser and Erdmann (1992), in which subjects looked at faces displaying some emotion presented in the left and right visual hemi-fields. Their findings also indicated that negative emotional arousal is modulated by right-hemisphere regulatory mechanisms. Of particular interest were the consistently larger electrodermal responses on the hand contralateral to the stimulated hemisphere.

Psychiatry and Clinical Psychology

Applications of psychophysiological techniques and methods to the diagnosis and treatment of psychiatric disorders and have been mentioned throughout this book (see, e.g., Chapters 7, 10, and 12). For example, as discussed at length in Chapter 7, the frequency of electrodermal responses to simple tone presentations has been used to identify a subgroup of schizophrenic "nonresponders" at greater risk for recurrent schizophrenic episodes and for chronic illness (Venables, 1984). A few other examples of the use of psychophysiology in psychiatric practice are provided here.

Recordings of event-related brain potentials (ERPs) following the presentation of auditory and visual stimuli have made it possible to investigate how the brain perceives and formulates cognitive decisions in psychiatric patients. Bruder and co-workers (e.g., Bruder, Towey, Stewart, et al., 1991) have shown that the latency of the P3 component of the ERP complex in a tone-discrimination task was significantly prolonged in patients with typical depressive disorders in comparison with normal controls. More important, the scalp distribution showed a characteristic asymmetrical pattern, implicating a specific right-hemisphere involvement in depressive disorders.

Using EMG recordings of eyeblink amplitudes, Dawson, Hazlett, Filion, et al. (1993) found that attentional modulation of the startle reflex is impaired in subjects with schizophrenia. The eyeblink startle reflex is elicited by stimuli with a rapid onset, like a sudden noise burst. This innate, reflexive response has been shown to be modified by attention to a nonstartling stimulus that shortly precedes the startle-eliciting stimulus, such as a tone that occurs shortly before the startling noise. The task of the subject is typically to pay close attention to some aspect of the nonstartling stimulus, for example, to count the number of tones. When the interval between the prepulse tone and the startle stimulus is short (in the range of 30 to 300 msec), the prepulse stimulus attenuates the amplitude of the startle reflex to the noise stimulus. This phenomenon is known as *prepulse inhibition* (Hoffman and Ison, 1980; see also Chapter 14). Prepulse inhibition is an unlearned, automatic gating that allows early information processing of the prepulse to proceed undisturbed by other stimulus events (Dawson et al., 1993; Graham, 1980). When the interval between the prepulse and startle stimuli are longer (more than 1,000 msec), however, the amplitude of the startle reflex is enhanced or facilitated, perhaps as a result of sensory enhancement associated with selective attention. Dawson et al. (1993) showed that attentional modulation of the startle reflex was clearly impaired in schizophrenic subjects: there was in these subjects no effect of the prepulse stimulus on the subsequent response to the startle stimulus. Because the subjects were relatively asymptomatic, Dawson et al. (1993) suggested that traitlike attentional deficits may be found in individuals with schizophrenia. The measurement of attentional modulation of the startle reflex may thus provide a nonverbal, reflexive, state-independent marker of vulnerability to schizophrenia. A marker of this kind—low-cost, noninvasive, and free of side effects—would be of great value in psychiatric practice and research.

Concluding Remarks

In closing, I want to stress the emerging consensus between psychophysiology and the other neurosciences—such as neuropsychology, physiological psychology, and cognitive psychology—on the relationship between mind and body, brain and behavior. In the past psychophysiology was seen as a discipline primarily concerned with recordings of bodily reactions to stress and emotional arousal, not with the functioning of the brain. It is my hope that this book will contribute to a broader definition of psychophysiology, one that puts emphasis not only on emotional processes but also on cognitive processes, like attention, language, and memory; we should recognize that these also have specific peripheral and central physiological consequences, such as phasic changes in heart rate, muscle tonus, electrodermal activity, and brain electrical activity. An understanding of how cognitive and emotional processes interact with physiological processes and with each other, and what specific processes modulate interactions between the brain and the periphery, is one of the great challenges facing researchers in biological psychology and the brain sciences. Modern recording techniques, from brain imaging to the analysis of apparently chaotic patterns of the heartbeat, have broken down the old barriers between the various biological subdisciplines interested in mind-body problems. The time has come for truly interdisciplinary collaboration among researchers in the brain and physiological sciences, for only by working together will we unravel the intricate mysteries of how the mind, brain, and body orchestrate our thoughts and feelings.

References

Author Index

General Index

References

Ader, R., and N. Cohen. 1985. CNS–immune system interactions: Conditioning phenomena. *Behavioral and Brain Sciences, 8,* 379–394.

———— 1993. Psychoneuroimmunology: Conditioning and stress. *Annual Review of Psychology, 44,* 53–85.

Ahonen, A., M. Hämäläinen, M. Kajola, J. Knuutila, P. Laine, O. V. Lounasmaa, J. Simola, C. Tesche, and V. A. Vilkman. 1992. 122-channel magnetometer covering the whole head. In *Proceedings of the Satellite Symposium on Neuroscience and Technology. Lyon, France: IEEE Engineering in Medicine and Biology Society,* pp. 16–20.

Ajilore, O., R. Stickgold, C. D. Rittenhouse, and J. A. Hobson. 1995. Nightcap: Laboratory and home-based evaluation of a portable sleep monitor. *Psychophysiology, 32,* 92–98.

Alexander, F. 1950. *Psychosomatic medicine.* New York: W. W. Norton.

Andreassi, J. L. 1989. *Psychophysiology: Human behavior and physiological response.* Hillsdale, NJ: Lawrence Erlbaum.

Andrykowski, M. A., and W. H. Redd. 1987. Longitudinal analysis of the development of anticipatory nausea. *Journal of Consulting and Clinical Psychology, 55,* 36–41.

Anthony, B. J. 1985. In the blink of an eye: Implications of reflex modification for information processing. In P. K. Ackles, J. R. Jennings, and M. G. H. Coles, eds., *Advances in psychophysiology,* vol. 1, pp. 167–218. Greenwich, CT: JAI Press.

Aserinsky, E., and N. Kleitman. 1953. Regularly occurring periods of eye motility and concurrent phenomena during sleep. *Science, 118,* 273–274.

Ax, A. 1953. The physiological differentiation between anger and fear in humans. *Psychosomatic Medicine, 15,* 433–442.

Baeyens, F., P. Eelen, G. Crombez, and O. Van den Bergh. 1992. Human evaluative conditioning: Acquisition trials, presentation schedule, evalua-

375

tive style and contingency awareness. *Behaviour Research and Therapy, 30,* 133–142.

Bagshaw, M. H., D. P. Kimble, and K. H. Pribram. 1965. The GSR of monkeys during orienting and habituation and after ablation of the amygdala, hippocampus and inferotemporal cortex. *Neuropsychologia, 3,* 111–119.

Bandettini, P. A., A. Jesmanovicz, E. C. Wong, and J. S. Hyde. 1993. Processing strategies for functional MRI of the human brain. *Magnetic Resonance in Medicine, 30,* 161–173.

Barneoud, P., P. J. Neveu, R. Vittal, and M. LeMoal. 1987. Functional heterogeneity of the right and left neocortex in modulation of the immune system. *Physiology and Behavior, 41,* 525–530.

Barry, R. J. 1982. Novelty and significance effects in the fractionation of phasic OR measures: A synthesis with traditional OR theory. *Psychophysiology, 19,* 28–35.

Barry, R. J., and E. N. Sokolov. 1993. Habituation of the phasic and tonic components of the orienting reflex. *International Journal of Psychophysiology, 15,* 39–42.

Basmajian, J. V. 1977. Motor learning and control: A working hypothesis. *Archives of Physical Medicine and Rehabilitation, 58,* 38–41.

Beck, E. C. 1963. The variability of potentials evoked by light in man: The effect of hypnotic suggestion. *Proceedings of the 3rd Annual Convention of the Utah Academy of Sciences, Arts, and Letters, 40,* 202–204.

Beck, A. T., and G. Emery. 1985. *Anxiety disorders and phobias: A cognitive perspective.* New York: Basic Books.

Becker, D. E., and D. Shapiro. 1981. Physiological responses to clicks during Zen, Yoga and TM meditation. *Psychophysiology, 18,* 694–699.

Begleiter, H., B. Porjesz, B. Bihari, and B. Kissin. 1984. Event-related potentials in boys at risk for alcoholism. *Science, 225,* 1493–1496.

Belliveau, J. W., D. N. Kennedy, R. C. McKinstry, B. R. Buchbinder, R. M. Weisskopf, S. M. Cohen, J. M. Vevea, T. J. Brady, and B. R. Rosen. 1991. Functional mapping of the human visual cortex by magnetic resonance imaging. *Science, 254,* 716–718.

Benson, H., J. F. Beary, and M. P. Carol. 1974. The relaxation response. *Psychiatry, 37,* 115–120.

Berger, H. 1929. Über das Elektroencephalogramm des Menschen. *Archiv für Psychiatrie und Nervenkrankheiten, 87,* 527–570.

Berlyne, D. E. 1958. The influence of complexity and novelty in visual figures on orienting responses. *Journal of Experimental Psychology, 55,* 289–296.

Bernstein, A. S. 1970. Phasic electrodermal orienting response in chronic schizophrenics II: Response to auditory signals of varying intensity. *Journal of Abnormal Psychology, 75,* 146–156.

Bernstein, A. S., K. W. Taylor, P. Starkey, S. Juni, J. Lubowski, and H. Paley.

1981. Bilateral skin conductance, finger pulse volume, and EEG orienting response to tones of differing intensities in chronic schizophrenics and controls. *Journal of Nervous and Mental Disease*, *169*, 513–528.

Bernstein, A. S., C. D. Frith, J. H. Gruzelier, T. Patterson, E. R. Straube, P. H. Venables, and T. P. Zahn. 1982. An analysis of skin conductance orienting responses in samples of British, American, and German schizophrenics. *Biological Psychology*, *14*, 155–211.

Berntson, G. G., S. T. Boysen, and J. T. Cacioppo. 1991. Cardiac orienting and defensive responses: Potential origin in autonomic space. In B. A. Campbell, ed., *Attention and information processing in infants and adults*, pp. 163–200. Hillsdale, NJ: Lawrence Erlbaum Publishers.

Berntson, G. G., J. T. Cacioppo, and K. S. Quigley. 1991. Autonomic determinism: The modes of autonomic control, the doctrine of autonomic space, and the laws of autonomic constraint. *Psychological Review*, *98*, 459–487.

Berntson, G. G., J. T. Cacioppo, K. S. Quigley, and V. J. Fabro. 1992. Autonomic space and cardiac chronotropy. Paper presented at the 32nd Annual Meeting of the Society for Psychological Research, San Diego, USA.

Berntson, G. G., J. T. Cacioppo, and K. S. Quigley. 1993. Respiratory sinus arrhythmia: Autonomic origins, physiological mechanisms, and psychophysiological implications. *Psychophysiology*, *30*, 183–196.

Birbaumer, N. 1977. Operant enhancement of EEG theta activity. In J. Beatty and H. Legewie, eds., *Biofeedback and behavior*, pp. 77–84. New York: Plenum Press.

Birk, L. 1973. *Biofeedback: Behavioral medicine*. New York: Grune and Stratton.

Bisiach, E., and G. Vallar. 1988. Hemineglect in humans. In F. Boller and J. Grafman, eds., *Handbook of neuropsychology*, vol. 1, pp. 195–222. New York: Elsevier Science Publishers.

Bjornæs, H., H. Smith-Meyer, H. Valen, K. Kristiansen, and H. Ursin. 1977. Plasticity and reactivity in unconscious patients. *Neuropsychologia*, *15*, 451–455.

Bloch, V., and M. Bonvallet. 1959. Controle cortico-reticulaire de l'activite electrodermale (response psychogalvanique). *Journal de Physiologie (Paris)*, *51*, 405–406.

Bogen, J. E. 1985. The callosal syndromes. In K. M. Heilman and E. Valenstein, eds., *Clinical neuropsychology*, pp. 295–338. New York: Oxford University Press.

Bohlin, G., and F. K. Graham. 1977. Cardiac deceleration and reflex blink facilitation. *Psychophysiology*, *14*, 423–430.

Bohlin, G., and A. Kjellberg. 1979. Orienting activity in two-stimulus paradigms as reflected in heart rate. In H. D. Kimmel, E. H. van Holst, and

J. F. Orlebeke, eds., *The orienting reflex in humans*, pp. 169–198. Hillsdale, NJ: Lawrence Erlbaum Publishers.

Booth-Kewley, S., and H. S. Friedman. 1987. Psychological predictors of heart disease: A quantitative review. *Psychological Bulletin, 101*, 343–362.

Boucsein, W. 1992. *Electrodermal activity.* New York: Plenum Press.

Boucsein, W., A. Valentin, and J. J. Furedy. 1993. Psychophysiological and behavioral differences as a function of age and Parkinson's disease. *Integrative Physiology and Behavioral Science, 28*, 213–225.

Bovbjerg, D. H., W. H. Redd, and L. A. Maier. 1990. Anticipatory immune suppression and nausea in women receiving cyclic chemotherapy for ovarian cancer. *Journal of Consulting and Clinical Psychology, 5*, 153–157.

Boyd, J. H., A. E. Pulver, and W. Stewart. 1986. Season of birth: Schizophrenia and bipolar disorder. *Schizophrenia Bulletin, 12*, 173–186.

Bradley, M. M., B. N. Cuthbert, and P. J. Lang. 1988. Lateral presentation of acoustic startle stimuli in a varying affective foreground. *Psychophysiology, 25*, 436 (Abstract).

———— 1991. Startle and emotion: Lateral acoustic probes and the bilateral blink. *Psychophysiology, 28*, 285–295.

Bradshaw, J. L., and N. C. Nettleton. 1981. The nature of hemispheric specialization in man. *Behavioral and Brain Sciences, 4*, 51–63.

Braff, D. L., C. Grillon, and M. A. Geyer. 1992. Gating and habituation of the startle reflex in schizophrenic patients. *Archives of General Psychiatry, 49*, 206–215.

Brener, J. 1974. A general model of voluntary control applied to phenomena of learned cardiovascular change. In P. A. Obrist, A. H. Black, J. Brener, and L. DiCara, eds., *Cardiovascular psychophysiology: Current issues in response mechanisms, biofeedback, and methodology*, pp. 365–391. Chicago: Aldine Press.

Broadbent, D. E. 1971. *Decision and stress.* London: Academic Press.

Brodal, A. 1981. *Neurological anatomy in relation to clinical medicine*, 3rd ed. New York: Oxford University Press.

Bruder, G. E., J. P. Towey, J. W. Stewart, D. Friedman, C. Tenke, and F. M. Quitkin. 1991. Event-related potentials in depression: Influence of task, stimulus hemifield and clinical features on P3 latency. *Biological Psychiatry, 28*, 92–98.

Brunia, C. H. 1993. Waiting in readiness: Gating in attention and motor preparation. *Psychophysiology, 30*, 327–339.

Brunia, C. H. M., and A. J. J. M. Vingerhouts. 1980. CNV and EMG preceding a plantar flexion of the foot. *Biological Psychology, 11*, 181–191.

Brunia, C. H. M., S. A. V. Haag, and J. G. M. Scheirs. 1985. Waiting to respond: Electrophysiological measurements in man during preparation for a voluntary movement. In H. Heuer, U. Kleinbeck, and K. H.

Schmidt, eds., *Motor behavior: Programming, control, and acquisition,* pp. 35–78. Berlin: Springer Verlag.

Brunia, C. H. M., J. Mocks, M. M. C. Berg-Lenssen, M. Coelho, M. G. H. Coles, T. Elbert, T. Gasserr, G. Gratton, E. C. Ifeachor, B. W. Jervis, W. Lutzenberger, L. Sroka, A. W. van Blokland- Vogelsang, G. van Driel, J. C. Woestenburg, P. Berg, W. C. McCallum, P. D. Tuan, P. V. Pocock, and W. T. Roth. 1989. Correction of ocular artifacts in the EEG: A comparison of several methods. *Journal of Psychophysiology, 3,* 1–50.

Buchsbaum, M. S., E. Hazlett, N. Sicotte, M. Stein, J. Wu, and M. Zetin. 1985. Topographic EEG changes with benzodiazepine administration in generalized anxiety disorder. *Biological Psychiatry, 20,* 832–842.

Byrne, E. A., and S. W. Porges. 1993. Beta-dependent filter characteristics of peak-valley respiratory sinus arrhythmia estimation: A cautionary note. *Psychopyhysiology, 30,* 397–404.

Cacioppo, J. T., and R. E. Petty. 1979. Lip and nonpreferred forearm EMG activity as a function of orienting task. *Biological Psychology, 9,* 103–113.

――― 1981. Electromyograms as measures of extent and affectivity of information processing. *American Psychologist, 36,* 441–456.

Cacioppo, J. T., G. G. Berntson, and B. L. Anderson. 1991. Psychophysiological approaches to the evaluation of psychotherapeutic process and outcome, 1991: Contribution from social psychophysiology. *Psychological Assessment, 3,* 321–336.

Cacioppo, J. T., D. J. Klein, G. G. Berntson, and E. Hatfield. 1993. The psychophysiology of emotion. In R. Lewis and J. M. Haviland, eds., *Handbook of emotions,* pp. 119–142. New York: Guilford Press.

Campbell, B. A., M. Kurtz, and R. Richardson. 1992. Paradoxical cardiac responses to intense auditory stimuli in the developing rat: Sympathetic and parasympathetic determinants. Paper presented at the 32nd Annual Meeting of the Society for Psychophysiological Research, San Diego.

Canavan, A. G. M. 1990. The contribution of psychophysiology to the understanding of Parkinson's disease. *Journal of Psychophysioogy, 4,* 85.

Cannon, W. B. 1936. *Bodily changes in pain, hunger, fear and rage.* New York: Appleton-Century-Crofts.

Carey, M. P., and T. G. Burish. 1988. Etiology and treatment of the psychological side effects associated with cancer chemotherapy: A critical review and discussion. *Psychological Bulletin, 104,* 307–325.

Cechetto, D. F., and C. B. Saper. 1990. Role of the cerebral cortex in autonomic functioning. In A. D. Loewy and K. M. Spyer, eds., *Central regulation of autonomic functioning,* pp. 208–223. New York: Oxford University Press.

Clinthorne, N. H., R. M. Leahy, T. H. Mareci, and W. W. Moses. 1992.

Fundamentals of medical imaging. Paper presented at the IEEE symposium on Fundamentals of Medical Imaging, Orlando, FL, October 1992.

Cohen, D. 1968. Magnetencephalography: Evidence of magnetic fields produced by alpha rhythm currents. *Science, 161,* 784–786.

Cohen, J. D., D. C. Noll, and W. Schneider. 1993. Functional magnetic resonance imaging: Overview and methods for psychological research. *Behavior Research Methods, Instruments and Computers, 25,* 101–113.

Cohn, R. 1948. The occipital alpha rhythm: A study of phase variations. *Journal of Neurophysiology, 11,* 31–37.

Coles, M. G. H. 1989. Modern mind-brain reading: Psychophysiology, physiology, and cognition. *Psychophysiology, 26,* 251–269.

Coles, M. G., and C. C. Duncan-Johnson. 1975. Cardiac activity and information processing: The effects of stimulus significance and detection and response requirements. *Journal of Experimental Psychology: Human Perception and Performance, 1,* 418–428.

Coles, M. G. H., and A. Gale. 1978. Psychophysiology. In B. M. Foss, ed., *Psychology Survey No. 1,* pp. 70–85. London: Allen and Unwin.

Coles, M. G. H., E, Donchin, and S. W. Porges. 1986. Preface. In Coles, M. G. H., E. Donchin, and S. W. Porges, eds., *Psychophysiology: Systems, processes, and applications,* pp. ix–x. Amsterdam: Elsevier.

Connelly, A., G. D. Jackson, S. J. Frackowiak, J. W. Belliveau, F. Vargha-Khadem, and D. G. Gadian. 1993. Functional mapping of activated human primary cortex with a clinical MR imaging system. *Radiology, 188,* 125–130.

Conway, J. 1984. Hemodynamic aspects of essential hypertension in humans. *Psychological Review, 64,* 617–660.

Cooper, R., J. W. Osselton, and J. C. Shaw. 1974. *EEG technology.* London: Butterworth.

Corteen, R. S., and B. Wood. 1972. Autonomic response to shock-associated words in an unattended channel. *Journal of Experimental Psychology, 94,* 308–313.

Craib, A., and M. M. Perry. 1975. *EEG handbook.* Schiller Park, IL: Beckman Instruments.

Crease, R. P. 1991. Images of conflict: MEG vs. EEG. *Science* (July), 374–375.

Crick, F., and G. Mitchison. 1983. The function of dream sleep. *Nature, 304,* 11–14.

Crider, A. 1993. Electrodermal response lability-stability: Individual difference correlates. In J. C. Roy, W. Boucsein, D. C. Fowles, and J. H. Gruzelier, eds., *Progress in electrodermal research,* pp. 173–186. New York: Plenum Press.

Crider, A., and R. Lunn. 1971. Electrodermal lability as a personality dimension. *Journal of Experimental Research in Personality, 5,* 145–150.

Crosson, B. 1992. *Subcortical functions in language and memory.* New York: The Guilford Press.

Crown, D. P., and D. Marlow. 1964. *The approval motive: Studies in evaluative dependence.* New York: Wiley and Sons.

Darrow, C. W. 1929. Differences in the physiological reactions to sensory and ideational stimuli. *Psychological Bulletin, 26,* 185–201.

——— 1937. Neural mechanisms controlling the palmar galvanic skin reflex and palmar sweating. *Archives of Neurology and Psychiatry, 37,* 641–663.

Daum, I., S. Channon, and A. Canavan. 1989. Classical conditioning in patients with severe memory problems. *Journal of Neurology, Neurosurgery, and Psychiatry, 52,* 47–51.

Daum, I., M. M. Schugens, H. Ackermann, W. Lutzenberger, J. Dichgans, and N. Birbaumer. 1993. Classical conditioning after cerebellar lesions in humans. *Behavioral Neuroscience, 107,* 1–9.

Davey, G. L. C., ed. 1987. *Cognitive processes and Pavlovian conditioning.* Chichester, UK: Wiley and Sons.

Davidson, R. J. 1984. Affect, cognition, and hemispheric specialization. In C. E. Izard, J. Kagan, and R. Zajonc, eds., *Emotion, cognition and behavior,* pp. 320–365. New York: Cambridge University Press.

——— 1992. Anterior cerebral asymmetry and the nature of emotion. *Brain and Cognition, 20,* 125–151.

——— 1993. The neuropsychology of emotion and affective style. In R. Lewis and J. M. Haviland, eds., *Handbook of emotions,* pp. 143–154. New York: Guilford Press.

Davidson, R. J., M. E. Horowitz, G. E. Schwartz, and D. M. Goodman. 1981. Lateral differences in the latency between finger tapping and the heart beat. *Psychophysiology, 18,* 36–41.

Davidson, R. J., and A. J. Tomarken. 1989. Laterality and emotion: An electrophysiological approach. In F. Boller and J. Grafman, eds., *Handbook of neuropsychology,* vol. 3, pp. 419–441. New York: Elsevier.

Davidson, R. J., J. P. Chapman, L. J. Chapman, and J. B. Henriques. 1990a. Asymmetrical brain electrical activity discriminates between psychometrically-matched verbal and spatial cognitive tasks. *Psychophysiology, 27,* 528–543.

Davidson, R. J., P. Ekman, C. D. Saron, J. A. Senulis, and W. V. Friesen. 1990b. Approach/withdrawal and cerebral asymmetry: Emotional expression and brain physiology I. *Journal of Personality and Social Psychology, 58,* 330–341.

Davidson, R. A., P. Fedio, B. D. Smith, E. Aureille, and A. Martin. 1992. Lateralized mediation of arousal and habituation: Differential bilateral electrodermal activity in unilateral temporal lobectomy patients. *Neuropsychologia, 30,* 1053–1063.

Davis, M. 1984. The mammalian startle response. In R. C. Eaton, ed., *Neural mechanisms of startle behavior*, pp. 287–342. New York: Plenum Press.

Davis, P. A. 1939. Effects of acoustic stimuli on the waking human brain. *Journal of Neurophysiology, 2,* 494–499.

Davis, R. C. 1939. Patterns of muscular activity during "mental work" and their constancy. *Journal of Experimental Psychology, 24,* 451–465.

——— 1940. *Set and muscular tension.* Indiana University Publications, Science Series, No. 10.

Dawson, G. D. 1954. A summation technique for the detection of of small evoked potentials. *Electroencephalography and Clinical Neurophysiology, 6,* 65–84.

Dawson, M. E. 1990. Psychophysiology at the interface of clinical science, cognitive science, and neuroscience. *Psychophysiology, 27,* 243–255.

Dawson, M. E., and P. Reardon. 1973. Construct validity of recall and recognition postconditioning measures of awareness. *Journal of Experimental Psychology, 98,* 308–315.

Dawson, M. E., and A. M. Schell. 1982. Electrodermal responses to attended and nonattended significant stimuli during dichotic listening. *Journal of Experimental Psychology: Human Perception and Performance, 8,* 82–86.

Dawson, M. E., A. M. Schell, J. R. Beers, and A. Kelly. 1982. Allocation of processing capacity during human autonomic classical conditioning. *Journal of Experimental Psychology: General, 111,* 273–295.

Dawson, M. E., and A. M. Schell. 1987. Human autonomic and skeletal classical conditioning: The role of conscious cognitive factors. In G. L. C. Davey, ed., *Cognitive processes and Pavlovian conditioning in humans*, pp. 27–55. Chichester, UK: Wiley.

Dawson, M. E., D. L. Filion, and A. M. Schell. 1989a. Is elicitation of the autonomic orienting response associated with allocation of processing resources? *Psychophysiology, 26,* 560–572.

Dawson, M. E., K. H. Neuchterlein, and R. M. Adams. 1989b. Schizophrenic disorders. In G. Turpin, ed., *Handbook of clinical psychophysiology*, pp. 393–418. Chichester, UK: Wiley.

Dawson, M. E., E. A. Hazlett, D. L. Filion, K. H. Neuchterlein, and A. M. Schell. 1993. Attention and schizophrenia: Impaired modulation of the startle reflex. *Journal of Abnormal Psychology, 102,* 633–641.

Dement, W., and N. Kleitman. 1957. The relationship of eye movements during sleep to dream activity: An objective method for the study of dreaming. *Journal of Experimental Psychology, 53,* 339–346.

Demonet, J. F., R. Wise, and R. S. J. Frackowiak. 1993. Language functions explored in normal subjects by positron emission tomography: A critical review. *Human Brain Mapping, 1,* 39–47.

DeYoe, E. A., P. Bandettini, J. Neitz, D. Miller, and P. Winans. 1994. Functional magnetic resonance imaging (fMRI) of the human brain. *Journal of Neuroscience Methods, 54,* 171–187.

Diehl, B. J. M., H. K. Meyer, P. Ulrich, and G. Meining. 1989. Mean hemispheric blood perfusion during autogenic training and hypnosis. *Psychiatry Research, 29,* 317–318.

Dimberg, U. 1982. Facial reactions to facial expressions. *Psychophysiology, 19,* 643–647.

———— 1990. Facial electromyography and emotional reactions. *Psychophysiology, 27,* 481–494.

Donchin, E., W. Ritter, and W. C. McCallum. 1978. Cognitive psychophysiology: The endogenous components of the ERP. In E. Callaway, P. Tueting, and S. H. Koslow, eds., *Event-related brain potentials in man,* pp. 1–79. New York: Academic Press.

Donchin, E., E. Heffley, S. A. Hillyard, N. Loveless, I. Maltzman, A. Öhman, F. Rösler, D. Ruchin, and D. Siddle. 1984. Cognition and event-related potentials II. The orienting reflex and P300. In R. Karrer, J. Cohen, and P. Tueting, eds., *Brain and information: Event-related potentials,* pp. 39–57. New York: New York Academy of Sciences.

Donchin, E., D. Karis, T. R. Bashore, M. G. H. Coles, and G. Gratton. 1986. Cognitive psychophysiology and human information processing. In M. G. H. Coles, E. Donchin, and S. W. Porges, eds., *Psychophysiology: Systems, processes and applications,* pp. 244–267. Amsterdam: Elsevier.

Donchin, E., and M. G. H. Coles. 1988. Is the P300 component a manifestation of context updating? *Behavioral and Brain Sciences, 11,* 355–372.

Dool, C. B., R. M. Stelmack, and B. P. Rourke. 1993. Event-related potentials in children with reading disabilities. *Journal of Clinical Child Psychology, 22,* 387–398.

Drevets, W. C., T. O. Videen, A. K. MacLeod, J. W. Haller, and M. E. Raichle. 1992. PET images of blood flow changes during anxiety: Correction. *Science, 256,* 1696.

Duffy, F. H., and G. B. McAnulty. 1985. Brain electrical activity mapping (BEAM): The search for a physiological signature of dyslexia. In F. H. Duffy and N. Geschwind, eds., *Dyslexia: A neuroscientific approach to clinical evaluation,* pp. 105–122. Boston: Little, Brown and Company.

Duncan-Johnson, C. C., and E. Donchin. 1977. On quantifying surprise: The variation of event-related potentials with subjective probability. *Psychophysiology, 14,* 456–467.

Dworkin, B. 1988. Hypertension as a learned response: The baroreceptor reinforcement hypothesis. In T. Elbert, W. Langosch, A. Steptoe, and D. Vaitl, eds., *Behavioral medicine in cardiovascular disorders,* pp. 17–47. Chichester, UK: Wiley and Sons.

Eckberg, D. L., Y. T. Kifle, and V. L. Roberts. 1980. Phase relationship between normal and human respiration and baroreceptor responsiveness. *Journal of Physiology, 304,* 489–502.

Edelberg, R. 1967. Electrical properties of the skin. In C. C. Brown, ed., *Methods in psychophysiology,* pp. 1–53. Baltimore: Williams and Williams.

—— 1968. Biopotentials from the skin surface: The hydration effect. In W. Fedor, ed., *Bioelectrodes. Annals of the New York Academy of Sciences, 148,* 252–262.

—— 1970. The information content of the recovery limb of the electrodermal response. *Psychophysiology, 6,* 527–539.

—— 1972. Electrical activity of the skin: Its measurement and uses in psychophysiology. In N. S. Greenfield and R. A. Sternbach, eds., *Handbook of psychophysiology,* pp. 367–418. New York: Holt, Rinehart, and Winston.

—— 1973. Mechanisms of electrodermal adaptations for locomotion, manipulation, or defense. In E. Stellar and J. M. Sprague, eds., *Progress in physiological psychology,* vol. 5, pp. 155–209. New York: Academic Press.

—— 1993. Electrodermal mechanisms: A critique of the two-effector hypothesis and a proposed replacement. In J. C. Roy, W. Boucsein, D. C. Fowles, and J. H. Gruzelier, eds., *Progress in electrodermal research,* pp. 7–30. New York: Plenum Press.

Ehrlichman, H., and A. Weinberger. 1978. Lateral eye movements and hemispheric asymmetry: A critical review. *Psychological Bulletin, 85,* 1080–1101.

Ehrlichman, H., and M. S. Wiener. 1979. Consistency of task-related EEG asymmetries. *Psychophysiology, 16,* 247–252.

Ehrlichman, H., J. S. Antrobus, and M. S. Wiener. 1985. EEG asymmetry and sleep during REM and NREM. *Brain and Cognition, 4,* 477–485.

Ekman, P. 1972. Universals and cultural differences in facial expressions of emotions. In J. K. Cole, ed., *Nebraska symposium on motivation,* vol. 19. Lincoln: University of Nebraska Press.

Ekman, P., and R. J. Davidson, eds. 1994. *The nature of emotion: Fundamental questions.* New York: Oxford University Press.

Ekman, P., and W. Friesen. 1976. *Pictures of facial affect.* Palo Alto, CA: Consulting Psychologists Press.

Ekman, P., and H. Oster. 1979. Facial expressions of emotion. *Annual Review of Psychology, 30,* 527–554.

Ekman, P., R. W. Levenson, and W. V. Friesen. 1983. Autonomic nervous system activity distinguishes among emotions. *Science, 221,* 1208–1210.

Elbert, T., N. Birbaumer, W. Lutzenberger, and B. Rockstroh. 1979. Biofeedback of slow cortical potentials: Self regulation of central autonomic patterns. In N. Birbaumer and H. D. Kimmel, eds., *Biofeedback and self-regulation,* pp. 321–342. Hillsdale, NJ: Lawrence Erlbaum Publishers.

Elbert, T., M. Tafil-Klawe, H. Rau, and W. Lutzenberger. 1991. Cerebral and cardiac responses to unilateral stimulation of carotid sinus baroreceptors. *Journal of Psychophysiology, 5,* 327–335.

Elias, M. F., M. A. Robbins, N. R. Schultz, and T. W. Pierce. 1990. Is blood pressure an important variable in research on aging and neuropsychological test performance? *Journal of Gerontology: Psychological Sciences, 45,* 128–135.

Ellsworth, P. 1994. William James and emotion: Is a century of fame worth a century of misunderstanding? *Psychological Review, 101,* 222–229.

Elmasian, R., H. Neville, D. Woods, M. Schuckit, and F. E. Bloom. 1982. Event-related brain potentials are different in individuals at high and low risk for developing alcoholism. *Proceedings of the National Academy of Sciences, 79,* 7900–7903.

Engel, B. T. 1960. Stimulus-response and individual-response specificity. *Archives of General Psychiatry, 2,* 305–313.

——— 1972. Response specificity. In N. S. Greenfield and R. A. Sternbach, eds., *Handbook of psychophysiolgy,* pp. 571–576. New York: Holt, Rinehart and Winston.

——— 1986. Psychosomatic medicine, behavioral medicine, just plain medicine. *Psychosomatic Medicine, 48,* 466–479.

Engel, B. T., and A. F. Bickford. 1961. Response specificity: Stimulus-response and individual-response specificity in essential hypertensives. *Archives of General Psychitary, 5,* 478–489.

Eppinger, H., and L. Hess. 1910. *Vagatonia.* New York: The Nervous and Mental Disease Publishing Company.

Eysenck, M. W., and M. T. Keane. 1990. *Cognitive psychology: A student's handbook.* Hillsdale, NJ: Erlbaum Associates.

Eriksen, L., and K. G. Götestam. 1984. Conditioned abstinence in alcoholics: A controlled experiment. *International Journal of the Addictions, 19,* 287–294.

Fahrenberg, J. 1986. Psychophysiological individuality: A pattern analytic approach to personality research and psychosomatic medicine. *Advances in Behaviour Research and Therapy, 8,* 43–100.

Farmer, M. E., S. J. Kittner, R. D. Abbott, M. M. Wolz, P. A. Wolf, and L. R. White. 1990. Longitudinally measured blood pressure, antihypertensive medication use, and cognitive performance: The Framingham study. *Journal of Clinical Epidemiology, 43,* 475–480.

Féré, C. 1888. Note sur les modifications de la résistance électrique sous l'influence des excitations sensorielles et des émotions. *Comptes Rendus des Séances de la Société de Biologie, 5,* 217–219.

Flaten, M. A., and K. Hugdahl. 1990. Reflex modification in the electrodermal system: Conceptual and methodological issues. *Biological Psychiatry, 30,* 3–12.

Flor-Henry, P. 1969. Psychosis and temporal lobe epilepsy: A controlled investigation. *Epilepsia, 10,* 363–395.

Folkow, B., G. Grimby, and O. Thulesius. 1958. Adaptive structural changes of the vascular walls in hypertension and their relation to the control of the peripheral resistance. *Acta Physiologica Scandinavica, 44*, 255–272.

Fowles, D. C. 1983. Motivational effects on heart rate and electrodermal activity: Implications for research on personality and psychopathology. *Journal of Research in Personality, 17*, 48–71.

———— 1988. Psychophysiology and psychopathology: A motivational approach. *Psychophysiology, 25*, 373–391.

———— 1993. Electrodermal activity and antisocial behavior: Empirical findings and theoretical issues. In J. C. Roy, W. Boucsein, D. C. Fowles, and J. H. Gruzelier, eds., *Progress in electrodermal research*, pp. 223–238. New York: Plenum Press.

Fowles, D. C., M. J. Christie, R. Edelberg, W. W. Grings, D. T. Lykken, and P. H. Venables. 1981. Publication recommendations for electrodermal measurements. *Psychophysiology, 18*, 232–239.

Frankenhaeuser, M. 1979. Psychoneuroendocrine approaches to the study of emotion as related to stress and coping. In H. E. Howe and R. A. Dienstbier, eds., *Nebraska symposium on motivation, 1978*, pp. 123–161. Lincoln: University of Nebraska Press.

———— 1983. The sympathetic-adrenal and pituitary-adrenal response to challenge: Comparison between sexes. In T. M. Dembroski, T. H. Schmidt, and G. H. Blumchen, eds., *Biobehavioral bases of coronary heart disease*, pp. 91–105. New York: Karger Press.

Frankenhaeuser, M., M. Rauste von Wright, A. Collins, J. von Wright, G. Sedvall, and C. G. Swahn. 1978. Sex differences in psychoneuroendocrine reactions to examination stress. *Psychosomatic Medicine, 40*, 334–343.

Frankenhaeuser, M., U. Lundberg, and L. Forsman. 1980. Dissociation between sympathetic-adrenal and pituitary-adrenal responses to an achievement situation characterized by high controllability: Comparison between Type A and Type B males and females. *Biological Psychology, 10*, 79–91.

Fredrikson, M. 1981. Orienting and defensive reactions to phobic and conditioned fear stimuli in phobics and normals. *Psychophysiology, 18*, 456–465.

Fredrikson, M., and K. A. Matthews. 1990. Cardiovascular responses to behavioral stress and hypertension: A meta-analytic review. *Annals of Behavioral Medicine, 12*, 30–39.

Fredrikson, M., G. Wik, T. Greitz, L. Eriksson, S. Stone-Elander, K. Ericson, and G. Sedvall, G. 1993a. Regional cerebral blood flow during experimental phobic fear. *Psychophysiology, 30*, 126–130.

Fredrikson, M., P. Annas, A. Georgiades, T. Hursti, and Z. Tersman. 1993b. Internal consistency and temporal stability of classically conditioned skin conductance responses. *Biological Psychology, 35*, 153–163.

Freixa-i-Baque, E., M. C. Catteau, Y. Miossec, and J. D. Roy. 1984. Asymmetry of electrodermal activity: A review. *Biological Psychology, 18,* 219–239.

Fridlund, A., and J. C. Caccioppo. 1986. Guidelines for human electromyographic research. *Psychophysiology, 23,* 567–589.

Fried, R., and J. Grimaldi. 1993. *The psychology and physiology of breathing.* New York: Plenum Press.

Friedman, B. H., J. F. Thayer, T. D. Borcovec, R. A. Tyrrell, B. H. Johnsen, and R. Columbo. 1993. Autonomic characteristics of nonclinical panic and blood phobia. *Biological Psychiatry, 34,* 298–310.

Friedman, D. 1990. ERPs during continous recognition memory for words. *Biological Psychology, 30,* 61–87.

Friedman, M., and R. H. Rosenman. 1959. Association of specific overt behavior pattern with blood and cardiovascular findings. *Journal of the American Medical Association, 169,* 1286–1296.

Friedman, M., C. E. Thoresen, J. J. Gill, L. H. Powell, D. Ulmer, L. Thompson, V. A. Price, D. D. Rabin, W. S. Breall, T. Dixon, R. Levy, and E. Bourg. 1984. Alteration of type A behavior and reduction in cardiac recurrences in postmyocardial infarction patients. *American Heart Journal, 108,* 237–248.

Friston, K. J. 1994. Statistical Parametric Mapping. In R. W. Thatcher, M. Hallett, T. Zetiro, E. R. John, and M. Huerta, eds., *Functional neuroimaging—Technical foundations,* pp. 79–93. San Diego: Academic Press.

Furedy, J. J. 1983. Operational, analogical, and genuine definition of psychophysiology. *International Journal of Psychophysiology, 1,* 13–19.

Furedy, J. J., and R. J. Heslegrave. 1983. A consideration of recent criticisms of the T-wave amplitude index of myocardial sympathetic activity. *Psychophysiology, 20,* 204–211.

Galambos, R., S. Makeig, and P. J. Talmachoff. 1991. A 40-Hz auditory potential recorded from the human scalp. *Procedings of the National Academy of Science, USA, 78,* 42–43.

Galin, D., and R. Ornstein. 1972. Lateral specialization of cognitive mode: An EEG study. *Psychophysiology, 8,* 412–418.

Gatchel, R. T., and K. P. Price, eds. 1979. *Clinical applications of biofeedback.* New York: Pergamon Press.

Gazzaniga, M. 1989. Editor's note. *Journal of Cognitive Neuroscience, 1,* 2.

Geenen, R., and F. J. R. Van De Vijver. 1993. A simple test of the law of initial values. *Psychophysiology, 30,* 525–530.

Gevins, A. S. 1987. Correlation analysis. In A. S. Gevins and A. Remond, eds., *Methods of analysis of brain electrical and magnetic signals. EEG handbook,* revised series, vol. 1, pp. 171–194. Amsterdam: Elsevier Publishers.

Gevins, A. S., G. M. Zeitlin, J. C. Doyle, C. D. Yingling, R. E. Schaffer, E.

Callaway, and C. L. Yeager. 1979. Electroencephalogram correlates of higher cortical functions. *Science, 203,* 665–668.

Gevins, A. S., R. E. Schaffer, J. C. Doyle, B. A. Cutillo, R. S. Tannenhill, and S. L. Bressler. 1983. Shadows of thought: Shifting lateralization of human brain electrical patterns during brief visuomotor tasks. *Science, 220,* 97–99.

Gevins, A. S., and S. L. Bressler. 1988. Functional topography of the human brain. In G. Pfurtscheller and F. H. Lopes da Silva, eds., *Functional brain imaging,* pp. 99–116. Toronto: Hans Huber Publishers.

Gold, P. W., F. K. Goodwin, and G. P. Chrousos. 1988. Clinical and bio-chemical manifestations to depression: Relation to the neurobiology of stress. *New England Journal of Medicine, 319,* 413–420.

Goldberger, A. 1991. Is the normal heartbeat chaotic or homeostatic? *NIPS, 6,* 87–91.

Goldman-Rakic, P. S. 1987. Circuitry of primate prefrontal cortex and regula-tion of behavior by representational knowledge. In F. Plum and V. B. Mountcastle, eds., *Handbook of physiology,* section 1: *The nervous system,* volume 5: *Higher functions of the brain.* Bethesda, MD: American Physio-logical Society.

——— 1988. Topography of cognition: Parallel distributed networks in pri-mate association cortex. *Annual Review of Neuroscience, 11,* 137–156.

Goldstein, D. S. 1983. Plasma catecholamines and essential hypertension: An analytical review. *Hypertension, 3,* 551–556.

Grace, W. J., and D. T. Graham. 1952. Relationships of specific attitudes and emotions to certain bodily diseases. *Psychosomatic Medicine, 14,* 243–251.

Graham, D. T. 1972. Psychosomatic medicine. In N. S. Greenfield and R. A. Sternbach, eds., *Handbook of psychophysiology,* pp. 839–924. New York: Holt, Rinehart and Winston.

Graham, D. T., and S. Wolf. 1950. Pathogenesis of urticaria: Experimental study of life situations, emotions, and cutaneous vascular reactions. *Jour-nal of the American Medical Association, 143,* 1396–1402.

Graham, D. T., J. D. Kabler, and L. Lundsford. 1961. Vasovagal fainting: A diphasic response. *Psychosomatic Medicine, 23,* 319–326.

Graham, F. K. 1973. Habituation and dishabituation of responses innervated by the autonomic nervous system. In H. S. Peeke and M. J. Hertz, eds., *Habituation,* vol. 1, pp. 163–218. New York: Academic Press.

——— 1975. The more or less startling effects of weak prestimulation. *Psycho-physiology, 12,* 238–248.

——— 1980. Control of reflex blink excitability. In R. F. Thompson, L. H. Hicks, and V. B. Shryrkov, eds., *Neural mechanisms of goal directed behavior and learning,* pp. 511–519. San Diego: Academic Press.

Graham, F. K., and R. K. Clifton. 1966. Heart-rate change as a component of the orienting response. *Psychological Bulletin, 65,* 305–320.

Greenfield, N. S., and R. A. Sternbach, eds. 1972. *Handbook of psychophysiology.* New York: Holt, Rinehart and Winston.

Grings, W. W., and M. E. Dawson. 1973. Complex variables in conditioning. In W. F. Prokasy and D. C. Raskin, eds., *Electrodermal activity in psychological research,* pp. 204–245. New York: Academic Press.

Gross, C. G., and M. Mishkin. 1977. The neural basis of stimulus equivalence across retinal translation. In S. Harnad, R. Doty, J. Jaynes, L. Goldstein, and G. Krauthamer, eds., *Lateralization in the nervous system,* pp. 109–122. New York: Academic Press.

Grossman, P. 1992. Respiratory and cardiac rhythms as windows to central and autonomic biobehavioral regulation: Selection of window frames, keeping the panes clean and viewing the neural topography. *Biological Psychology, 34,* 131–161.

Grossman, P., and S. Svebak. 1987. Respiratory sinus arrhythmia as an index of parasympathetic cardiac control during active coping. *Psychophysiology, 24,* 228–235.

Groves, P. M., and R. F. Thompson. 1970. Habituation: A dual process theory. *Psychological Review, 77,* 419–450.

Grueninger, W. E., D. P. Kimble, J. Grueninger, and S. Levine. 1965. GSR and corticosteroid response in monkeys with frontal ablations. *Neuropsychologia, 3,* 205–216.

Gruzelier, J. H. 1973. Bilateral asymmetry of skin conductance orienting activity and levels in schizophrenics. *Biological Psychology, 1,* 21–41.

——— 1983. Disparate syndromes in psychosis delineated by direction of electrodermal response lateral asymmetry. In P. Flor-Henry and J. Gruzelier, eds., *Laterality and psychopathology,* pp. 525–538. Amsterdam: Elsevier.

Gruzelier, J. H., and P. H. Venables. 1973. Skin conductance responses to tones with and without attentional significance in schizophrenic and nonschizophrenic psychiatric patients. *Neuropsychologia, 11,* 221–230.

——— 1974. Bimodality and lateral asymmetry of skin conductance orienting activity in schizophrenics: Replication and evidence of lateral asymmetry in patients with depression and disorders of personality. *Biological Psychiatry, 8,* 55–73.

Gruzelier, J. H., T. Brow, A. Perry, J. Rhonder, and M. Thomas. 1984. Hypnotic susceptibility: A lateral predisposition and altered cerebral asymmetry under hypnosis. *International Journal of Hypnosis, 2,* 131–139.

Gruzelier, J. H., and T. D. Brow. 1985. Psychophysiological evidence for a state theory of hypnosis and hypnotic susceptibility. *Journal of Psychosomatic Research, 29,* 287–302.

Gur, R. E., and G. D. Pearlson. 1993. Neuroimaging in schizophrenia. *Schizophrenia Bulletin, 19,* 337–353.

Guyton, A. C. 1992. *Textbook of medical physiology.* Philadelphia: W. B. Saunders and Co.

Hachinsky, V. C., S. M. Oppenheimer, J. X. Wilson, C. Guiraudon, and D. F. Cechetto. 1992. Asymmetry of sympathetic consequences of experimental stroke. *Archives of Neurology, 49,* 697–702.

Hackley, S. A., and F. K. Graham. 1984. Early selective attention effects on cutaneous and acoustic blink reflexes. *Physiological Psychology, 11,* 235–242.

Halgren, E., N. K. Squires, C. L. Wilson, J. W. Rohrbaugh, T. L. Babb, and P. H. Crandall. 1980. Endogenous potentials generated in the human hippocampal formation and amygdala by infrequent events. *Science, 210,* 803–805.

Halliday, A. M., W. I. McDonald, and J. Mushin. 1973. Visual evoked response in the diagnosis of multiple sclerosis. *British Medical Journal, 4,* 661–664.

Hallman, G. L., L. L. Leatherman, R. D. Leachman, D. G. Rochelle, D. L. Bricker, R. D. Bloodwell, and D. Cooley. 1969. Function of the transplanted human heart. *Journal of Thoracic and Cardiovascular Surgery, 58,* 319–325.

Hämäläinen, M., R. Hari, R. Ilmoniemi, J. Knuutila, and O. V. Lounasmaa. 1993. Magnetoencephalography: Theory, instrumentation, and applications to noninvasive studies of the working human brain. *Reviews of Modern Physics, 65,* 413–498.

Hamilton, V., and D. M. Warburton, eds. 1979. *Human stress and cognition: An information processing perspective.* Chichester, U.K.: Wiley and Sons.

Hansen, J. C., and S. A. Hillyard. 1980. Endogenous brain potentials associated with selective auditory attention. *Electroencephalography and Clinical Neurophysiology, 49,* 277–290.

Hantas, M. N., E. S. Katkin, and S. D. Reed. 1984. Cerebral lateralization and heart beat discrimination. *Psychophysiology, 21,* 274–278.

Hare, R. D. 1978. Psychopathy and electrodermal responses to nonsignal stimulation. *Biological Psychology, 6,* 237–246.

Hare, R. D., and G. Blevings. 1975. Conditioned orienting and defensive responses. *Psychophysiology, 12,* 89–97.

Hari, R. 1990. The neuromagnetic method in the study of the human auditory cortex. In F. Grandori, M. Hoke, and G. L. Romani, eds., *Auditory evoked magnetic fields and electric potentials,* vol. 6, *Advances in audiology,* pp. 222–282. Basel: Karger.

Hari, R., and R. Ilmoniemi. 1986. Cerebral magnetic fields. *CRC Critical Reviews in Biomedical Engineering, 14,* 93–126.

Hart, J. D. 1974. Physiological responses of anxious and normal subjects to simple signal and non-signal auditory stimuli. *Psychophysiology, 11,* 443–451.

Hartshorne, M. F. 1995. Positron emission tomography. In W. W. Orrison, Jr., J. D. Lewine, J. A. Sanders, and M. F. Hartshorne, eds., *Functional brain imaging.* St. Louis: Mosby Publishers.

Hassett, J. 1978. *A primer of psychophysiology.* San Francisco: Freeman Press.

Hastrup, J. L. 1979. Effects of electrodermal lability and introversion on vigilance decrement. *Psychophysiology, 16,* 302–310.

Hausken, T., S. Svebak, I. Wilhelmsen, T. T. Haug, K. Olafsen, E. Pettersson, K. Hveem, and A. Berstad. 1993. Low vagal tone and antral dysmotility in patients with functional dyspepsia. *Psychosomatic Medicine, 55,* 12–22.

Haynes, S. N. 1991. Clinical applications of psychophysiological assessment: An introduction and overview. *Psychological Assessment, 3,* 307–308.

Heilman, K. M., and R. T. Watson. 1977. Mechanisms underlying the unilateral neglect syndrome. In E. A. Weinstein and R. F. Friedland, eds., *Advances in neurology,* vol. 18, pp. 93–105. New York: Raven Press.

Heilman, K. M., H. D. Schwartz, and R. T. Watson. 1978. Hypoarousal in patients with the neglect syndrome and emotional indifference. *Neurology, 28,* 229–232.

Heller, W., D. L. Lindsey, J. Metz, and D. M. Farnum. 1990. Individual differences in right-hemisphere activation are associated with arousal and autonomic response to lateralized stimuli. *Journal of Clinical and Experimental Neuropsychology, 13,* 95.

Hellige, J. B. 1993. *Hemispheric asymmetry: What's right and what's left.* Cambridge, MA: Harvard University Press.

Henriques, J. B., and R. J. Davidson. 1990. Regional brain electric asymmetries discriminate between previously depressed and healthy control subjects. *Journal of Abnormal Psychology, 99,* 22–31.

Henry, C. E. 1965. Electroencephalographic correlates with personality. In W. P. Wilson, ed., *Application of electroencephalography in psychiatry,* pp. 3–18. Durham, NC: Duke University Press.

Henry, J. P., and P. M. Stephens. 1977. *Stress, health, and the social environment.* New York: Springer.

Heslegrave, R. J., and J. J. Furedy. 1980. Carotid dP/dt as a psychophysiological index of sympathetic myocardial effects: Some considerations. *Psychophysiology, 17,* 482–494.

Hess, E. H. 1965. Attitude and pupil size. *Scientific American, 212,* 46–54.

Hillyard, S. A. 1993. Electrical and magnetic brain recordings: Contributions to cognitive neuroscience. *Current Opinion in Neurobiology, 3,* 217–224.

Hillyard, S. A., R. F. Hink, V. L. Schwent, and T. W. Picton. 1973. Electrical signs of selective attention in the human brain. *Science, 182,* 177–180.

Hillyard, S. A., and M. Kutas. 1983. Electrophysiology of cognitive processing. *Annual Review of Psychology, 34,* 33–61.

Hillyard, S. A., and J. C. Hansen. 1986. Attention: Electrophysiological approaches. In M. G. H. Coles, E. Donchin, and S. W. Porges, eds., *Psychophysiology: Systems, processes and applications,* pp. 227–243. Amsterdam: Elsevier.

Hobson, J. A. 1990. Sleep and dreaming. *Journal of Neuroscience, 10,* 371–382.

Hobson, J. A., and R. W. McCarley. 1977. The brain as a dream state generator: An activation-synthesis hypothesis of the dream process. *American Journal of Psychiatry, 134,* 1335–1348.

Hoffman, H. S., and J. R. Ison. 1980. Reflex modification in the domain of startle: 1.: Some empirical findings and their implications for how the nervous system processes sensory input. *Psychological Review, 87,* 175–189.

Holmes, D. S. 1984. Meditation and somatic arousal reduction. *American Psychologist, 39,* 1–10.

Holzman, P. S., L. R. Proctor, and D. W. Hughes. 1973. Eye-tracking patterns in schizophrenia. *Science, 181,* 179.

Holzman, P. S., L. R. Proctor, D. L. Levy, N. J. Yasillo, H. Y. Meltzer, and S. W. Hurt. 1974. Eye-tracking dysfunctions in schizophrenic patients and their relatives. *Archives of General Psychiatry, 31,* 143.

Holzman, P. S., E. Kringlen, D. L. Levy, L. R. Proctor, and S. Haberman. 1978. Smooth pursuit eye movements in schizophrenia: Evidence for a genetic marker. *Archives of General Psychiatry, 34,* 802–.

Hugdahl, K. 1981. The three-systems model of fear and emotion: A critical examination. *Behaviour Research and Therapy, 19,* 75–85.

——— 1984. Hemispheric asymmetry and bilateral electrodermal recordings: A review of the evidence. *Psychophysiology, 24,* 371–394.

——— 1987. Pavlovian conditioning and hemispheric asymmetry: A perspective. In G. L. C. Davey, ed., *Cognitive processes and Pavlovian conditioning in humans,* pp. 147–182. Chichester, UK: Wiley.

——— 1988. Electrodermal asymmetries: Past hopes and future prospects. *International Journal of Psychophysiology, 39,* 33–44.

——— 1992. Dichotic listening in brain lateralization studies. *Neuroscience Year: Supplement to the Encyclopedia of Neuroscience,* pp. 23–26. Boston: Birkhauser Inc.

——— 1995. Classical conditioning and implicit learning: The right hemisphere hypothesis. In R. J. Davidson and K. Hugdahl, eds., *Brain asymmetry,* pp. 235–268. Cambridge, MA: MIT Press.

Hugdahl, K., and A. Öhman. 1977. Effects of instruction on acquisition and extinction of electrodermal responses to potentially phobic stimuli. *Journal of Experimental Psychology: Human Learning and Memory, 3,* 608–618.

Hugdahl, K., M. Fredrikson, and A. Öhman. 1977. "Preparedness" and "arousability" as determinants of electrodermal responses to potentially phobic stimuli. *Behaviour Research and Therapy, 15,* 345–353.

Hugdahl, K., and J. Ternes. 1981. An electrodermal measure of arousal in opiate addicts to drug-related stimuli. *Biological Psychology, 12,* 291–298.

Hugdahl, K., C. Wahlgren, and T. Wass. 1982. Habituation of the electrodermal orienting reaction is dependent on the cerebral hemisphere initially stimulated. *Biological Psychology, 15,* 49–62.

Hugdahl, K., M. Franzon, B. Andersson, G. Walldebo. 1983. Heart rate responses (HRR) to lateralized visual stimuli. *Pavlovian Journal of Biological Science, 18,* 186–198.

Hugdahl, K., K. O. Fagerström, and C. G. Brobeck. 1984. Effects of cold and mental stress on finger temperature in vasospastics and normal subjects. *Behaviour Research and Therapy, 22,* 471–476.

Hugdahl, K., and C. G. Brobeck. 1986. Hemispheric asymmetry and human electrodermal conditioning: The dichotic extinction paradigm. *Psychophysiology, 23,* 491–499.

Hugdahl, K., G. Kvale, H. Nordby, and J. B. Overmier. 1987. Hemispheric asymmetry and human classical conditioning to verbal and non-verbal visual CSs. *Psychophysiology, 24,* 557–565.

Hugdahl, K., K. Wester, and A. Asbjørnsen. 1990. The role of the left and right thalamus in language asymmetry: Dichotic listening in Parkinson-patients undergoing stereotactic thalamotomy. *Brain and Language, 39,* 1–13.

Hugdahl, K., and B. H. Johnsen. 1993. Brain asymmetry and autonomic conditioning: Skin conductance responses. In J. C. Roy, W. Boucsein, D. C. Fowles, and J. H. Gruzelier, eds., *Progress in electrodermal research,* pp. 271–288. New York: Plenum Press.

Hugdahl, K., and H. Nordby. 1994. Electrophysiological correlates to cued attentional shifts in the visual and auditory modalities. *Behavioral and Neural Biology, 62,* 21–32.

Hugdahl, K., A. Berardi, W. L. Thompson, S. M. Kosslyn, R. Macy, D. P. Baker, N. M. Alpert, and J. E. LeDoux. 1995. Brain mechanisms in human classical conditioning: A PET blood flow study. *NeuroReport, 6,* 1723–1728.

Hurwitz, B. E. 1993. Issues in methodology and application if impedance cardiography: An introduction. *Biological Psychology, 36,* 1–2.

Hygge, S., and K. Hugdahl. 1985. Skin conductance recordings and the NaCl concentration of the electrolyte. *Psychophysiology, 22,* 365–367.

Iacono, W. G. 1982. Bilateral electrodermal habituation-dishabituation and resting EEG in remitted schizophrenics. *Journal of Nervous and Mental Disease, 170*, 91–101.

——— 1985. Psychophysiologic markers of psychopathology: A review. *Canadian Psychology, 26*, 96–112.

Iacono, W. G., and D. T. Lykken. 1979. Electro-oculographic recording and scoring of smoth pursuit and saccadic eye tracking: A parametric study using monozygotic twins. *Psychophysiology, 16*, 94–107.

Iacono, W. G., D. T. Lykken, L. J. Peloquin, A. E. Lumry, R. H. Valentine, and V. B. Tuason. 1983. Electrodermal activity in euthymic unipolar and bipolar affective disorders. *Archives of General Psychiatry, 40*, 557–565.

Iacono, W. G., and J. W. Ficken. 1989. Research strategies employing psychophysiological measures: Identifying using psychophysiological markers. In G. Turpin, ed., *Handbook of Clinical Psychophysiology*, pp. 45–70. Chichester, UK: Wiley and Sons.

Ingvar, D. H., and J. Risberg. 1965. Influence of mental activity upon regional cerebral blood flow in man. *Acta Neurologica Scandinavica, 41* (Supplementum 14), 93–96.

Itil, T. M., A. Mucci, and E. Eralp. 1991. Dynamic brain mapping methodology and application. *International Journal of Psychophysiology, 10*, 281–291.

Ivancevich, J. M., and M. T. Matteson. 1988. Type A behaviour and the healthy individual. *British Journal of Medical Psychology, 61*, 37–56.

James, W. 1884; 1969. What is an emotion? In *Collected essays and reviews*. New York: Russell and Russell.

——— 1890. *The principles of psychology*. New York: Holt, Rinehart and Winston.

Jasper, H. H. 1958. The Ten-Twenty Electrode System of the International Federation. *Electroencephalography and Clinical Neurophysiology, 10*, 371–375.

Jasper, H. H., and C. Shagass. 1941. Conditioning of the occipital alpha rhythm in man. *Journal of Experimental Psychology, 28*, 373–388.

Jenkins, C. D. 1971. Psychologic and social precursors of coronary disease. *New England Journal of Medicine, 284*, 244–255, 307–317.

Jennings, J. R. 1986. Bodily changes during attention. In M. G. H. Coles, E. Donchin, and S. W. Porges, eds., *Psychophysiology: Systems, processes, and applications*, pp. 268–289. Amsterdam: Elsevier.

——— 1992. Is it important that the mind is in a body? Inhibition and the heart. *Psychophysiology, 29*, 369–383.

Jennings, J. R., J. R. Averill, E. M. Opton, and R. S. Lazarus. 1970. Some parameters of heart rate change: Perceptual versus motor task requirements, noxiousness, and uncertainity. *Psychophysiology, 7*, 194–212.

Jennings, J. R., A. J. Tahmoush, and D. P. Redmond. 1980. Non-invasive measurement of peripheral vascular activity. In I. Martin and P. H. Venables, eds., *Techniques in psychophysiology*, pp. 70–131. Chichester, UK: Wiley and Sons.

Jennings, J. R., W. K. Berg, J. S. Hutcheson, P. Obrist, S. Porges, and G. Turpin. 1981. Publication guidelines for heart rate studies in man. *Psychophysiology, 18*, 226–231.

Jennings, J. R., and S. Choi. 1983. An arterial to peripheral pulse wave velocity measure. *Psychophysiology, 20*, 410–418.

Jennings, J. R., and K. A. Matthews. 1984. The impatience of youth: Phasic cardiovascular response in Type A and Type B elementary school-aged boys. *Psychosomatic Medicine, 46*, 498–511.

Jennings, J. R., and M. G. H. Coles, eds. 1991. *Handbook of cognitive psychophysiolgy*. Chichester, UK: Wiley and Sons.

Johanson, A. M., J. Risberg, P. Silfverskiöld, and G. Smith. 1986. Regional changes in cerebral blood flow during increased anxiety in patients with anxiety disorders. In U. Hentschel, G. Smith, and J. G. Draguns, eds., *The roots of perception*, pp. 353–366. Amsterdam: Elsevier North Holland.

John, E. R., L. S. Prichep, J. Fridman, and P. Easton. 1988. Neurometrics: Computer-assisted differential diagnosis of brain dysfunctions. *Science, 239*, 162–169.

Johnsen, B. H., and K. Hugdahl. 1991. Hemispheric asymmetry in conditioning to facial emotional expressions. *Psychophysiology, 28*, 154–162.

——— 1993. Right hemisphere representation of autonomic conditioning to facial emotional expressions. *Psychophysiology, 30*, 274–278.

Jones, G. E. 1994. Perception of visceral sensations: A review of recent findings, methodologies, and future directions. *Advances in Psychophysiology, 5*, 55–192.

Jones, G. E., and J. G. Hollandsworth. 1981. Heart rate discrimination before and after exercise-induced augmented cardiac activity. *Psychophysiology, 18*, 252–257.

Jutai, J. W. 1984. Cerebral asymmetry and the psychophysiology of attention. *International Journal of Psychophysiology, 1*, 219–25.

Kahneman, D. 1973. *Attention and effort*. Englewood Cliffs, NJ: Prentice-Hall.

Kamyia, J. 1969. Operant control of the EEG alpha rhythm and some of its reported effects on consciousness. In C. Tart, ed., *Altered states of consciousness*. New York: Wiley and Sons.

Katkin, E. S. 1985. Blood, sweat, and tears: Individual differences in autonomic self-perception. *Psychophysiology, 22*, 125–137.

Katkin, E. S., and E. N. Murray. 1968. Instrumental conditioning of autonomically mediated behavior: Theoretical and methodological issues. *Psychological Bulletin, 70*, 52–68.

Katkin, E. S., and R. J. McCubbin. 1969. Habituation of the orienting response as a function of individual differences in anxiety and autonomic lability. *Journal of Abnormal Psychology, 74,* 54–60.

Katkin, E. S., J. Blascovich, and S. Goldband. 1981. Empirical assessment of visceral self-perception: Individual and sex differences in the acquisition of heartbeat discrimination. *Journal of Personality and Social Psychology, 40,* 1095–1101.

Katkin, E. S., M. A. Morell, S. Goldband, G. L. Bernstein, and J. A. Wise. 1982. Individual differences in heartbeat discrimination. *Psychophysiology, 19,* 160–166.

Kaufman, L., and S. J. Williamson. 1986. The neuromagnetic field. In R. Q. Cracco and I. Bodis-Wollner, eds., *Frontiers of clinical neuroscience: Evoked potentials,* vol. 3, pp. 85–98). New York: Alan R. Liss.

Kayser, J., and G. Erdmann. 1992. Lateralization and autonomic reactivity with emotional stimulation. Research Report of The Institute of Psychology, Technical University of Berlin, Germany, No. 92/10.

Kenny, M. G. 1983. Paradox lost—The Latah problem revisited. *Journal of Nervous and Mental Disease, 171,* 159–167.

Keys, A. 1966. The individual risk of coronary heart disease. *Annals of the New York Academy of Science, 134,* 1046–1063.

Kilpatrick, D. G. 1972. Differential responsiveness of two electrodermal indices to psychological stress performance and performance of a complex cognitive task. *Psychophysiology, 9,* 218–226.

Kimble, G. A. 1961. *Hilgard and Marquis' conditioning and learning.* New York: Appleton Century Croft.

Kimmel, H. D. 1966. Inhibition of the unconditioned response in classical conditioning. *Psychological Review, 73,* 232–240.

——— 1967. Instrumental conditioning of autonomically mediated behavior. *Psychological Bulletin, 67,* 337–345.

Kinsbourne, M. 1973. The control of attention by interaction between the cerebral hemispheres. In S. Kornblum, ed., *Attention and performance, IV.* New York: Academic Press.

Kløve, H., and K. Hole. 1981. The hyperkinetic syndrome: Criteria for diagnosis. Unpublished manuscript, University of Bergen, Norway.

Köhler, T., J. Dunker, and O. Zander. 1992. The number of active palmar sweat glands (palmar sweat index, PSI) as an activation measure in field studies. *Behavior Research Methods, Instruments, and Computers, 24,* 519–522.

Kopp, M. S. 1984. Electrodermal characteristics in psychosomatic patients groups. *International Journal of Psychophysiology, 2,* 73–85.

Koriath, J. J., and E. Lindholm. 1986. Cardiac-related cortical inhibition during a fixed free period reaction time task. *International Journal of Psychophysiology, 4,* 183–195.

Kornhuber, H. H., and L. Deecke. 1965. Hirnpotentialanderungen bei Will-

kurberwegungen und passiven Berwegungen des Menschen: Bereit-
schaftspotential und reafferente Potentiale. *Pflugers Archives Gesamte
Physiologie, 284,* 1–17.

Kosslyn, S. M., and O. Koening. 1992. *Wet mind: The new cognitive neuroscience.* New York: Free Press.

Kosslyn, S. M., N. M. Alpert, W. L. Thompson, V. Maljokovic, S. B. Weise,
C. F. Chabris, S. E. Hamilton, S. L. Rauch, and F. S. Buonanno. 1993.
Visual mental imagery activates topographically organized visual cortex:
PET investigations. *Journal of Cognitive Neuroscience, 5,* 263–287.

Kosslyn, S. M., K. Hugdahl, R. J. Davidson, D. Spiegel, J. A. Hobson, R.
Rose, and M. J. Horowitz. 1995. Information processing by the brain:
A cognitive neuroscience model. Submitted.

Krantz, D. S., J. M. Arabian, J. E. Davia, and J. S. Parker. 1982. Type A
behavior and coronary artery bypass surgery: Intraoperative blood pressure and perioperative complications. *Psychosomatic Medicine, 44,* 273–
284.

Krantz, D. S., and S. B. Manuck. 1984. Acute psychophysiologic reactivity
and risk of cardiovascular disease: A review and methodologic critique.
Psychological Bulletin, 96, 435–464.

Kreezer, G. 1940. The relation of intelligence level and the electroencephalogram. *National Society for the Study of Education, Yearbook 39,* 130–133.

Kreuger, J. M., J. Walter, C. A. Dinarello, and L. Chedid. 1985. Induction
of slow-wave sleep by Interleukin-1. In *The Physiologic, Metabolic, and Im-
munologic Actions of Interleukin-1,* pp. 161–170. New York: Liss.

Kubicek, W. G., R. P. Patterson, D. A. Witsoe, and R. H. Mattson. 1966.
Development and evaluation of an electric impedance cardiac output system. *Aerospace Medicine, 37,* 1208–1212.

Kuhn, W. F., M. H. Davis, and S. B. Lippman. 1988. Emotional adjustment
to cardiac transplantation. *General Hospital Psychiatry, 10,* 108–113.

Kulli, J., and C. Koch. 1991. Does anesthesia cause loss of consciousness.
Trends in Neurosciences, 14, 6–10.

Kutas, M., and S. A. Hillyard. 1980. Reading senseless sentences: Brain potentials reflect semantic incongruity. *Science, 207,* 203–205.

Kvale, G., K. Hugdahl, A. Asbjørnsen, B. Rosengren, and K. Lothe. 1991.
Anticipatory nausea and vomiting in cancer-patients undergoing chemotherapy. *Journal of Consulting and Clinical Psychology, 59,* 894–898.

Kwong, K. K., J. W. Belliveau, D. A. Chesler, I. E. Goldberg, R. M.
Weisskopf, B. P. Poncelet, D. N. Kennedy, B. E. Hoppel, M. S.
Cohen, R. Turner, H. M. Cheng, T. Brady, and B. R. Rosen. 1992. Dynamic magnetic resonance imaging of human brain activity during primary sensory stimulation. *Proceedings of the National Academy of Sciences,
89,* 5675–5679.

Laberg, J. C. 1990. What is presented, and what is prevented in cue exposure and response prevention with alcohol dependent subjects? *Addictive Behaviors, 15*, 367–386.

Laberg, J. C., K. Hugdahl, K. M. Stormark, H. Nordby, and H. Aas. 1992. Effects of visual alcohol cues on alcoholic's autonomic arousal. *Psychology of Addictive Behaviors, 6*, 181–187.

Lacey, J. I. 1958. Psychophysiological approaches to the evaluation of psychotherapeutic process and outcome. In E. A. Rubinstein and M. B. Parloff, eds., *Research in psychotherapy*, pp. 160–208. Washinton, D.C.: APA Press.

────── 1967. Somatic response patterning and stress: Some revisions of activation theory. In M. H. Appley and R. Trumbull, eds., *Psychological stress: Issues in research*, pp. 14–42. New York: Appleton-Century-Crofts.

Lacey, J. I., J. Kagan, B. C. Lacey, and H. A. Moss. 1963. The visceral level: Situational determinants and behavioral correlates of autonomic response patterns. In P. H. Knapp, ed., *Expression of emotion in man*, pp. 161–196. New York: International University Press.

Lacey, J., and B. Lacey. 1970. Some autonomic-central nervous system interrelationships. In P. H. Black, ed., *Physiological correlates of emotion*, pp. 205–227. New York: Academic Press.

Lacey, B. C., and J. I. Lacey. 1974. Studies of heart rate and other bodily processes in sensorimotor behavior. In P. A. Obrist, A. H. Black, J. Brener, and L. V. DiCara, eds., *Cardiovascular psychophysiology*, pp. 538–564. Chicago: Aldine Press.

Lacroix, J. M., and P. Comper. 1979. Lateralization in the electrodermal system as a function of cognitive/hemispheric manipulation. *Psychophysiology, 16*, 116–129.

Lader, M. H. 1967. Palmar skin conductance measures in anxiety and phobic states. *Journal of Psychosomatic Research, 11*, 271–281.

Lader, M. H., and J. D. Montagu. 1962. The psycho-galvanic reflex: A pharmacological study of the peripheral mechanism. *Journal of Neurological and Neurosurgical Psychiatry, 25*, 126–133.

Lader, M. H., and L. Wing. 1964. Habituation of the psycho-galvanic reflex in patients with anxiety states and in normal subjects. *Journal of Neurology, Neurosurgery, and Psychiatry, 27*, 210–218.

Lane, R. D., and G. Schwartz. 1987. Induction of lateralized sympathetic input to the heart by CNS during emotional arousal: A possible neurophysiologic trigger of sudden cardiac death. *Psychosomatic Medicine, 49*, 274–284.

Lane, R. D., and J. R. Jennings. 1995. Hemispheric asymmetry, autonomic asymmetry and the problem of sudden cardiac death. In R. J. Davidson and K. Hugdahl, eds., *Brain asymmetry*, pp. 271–304. Cambridge, MA: MIT Press.

Lang, P. J. 1968. Fear reduction and fear behavior: Problems in treating a construct. In J. M. Schlien, ed., *Research in psychotherapy*, vol. 3, pp. 90–102. Washington, DC: American Psychological Association.

——— 1979. Emotional imagery and visceral control. In R. J. Gatchel and K. P. Price, eds., *Clinical applications of biofeedback: Appraisal and status*, pp. 12–27. New York: Pergamon Press.

Lang, P. J., L. A. Sroufe, and J. E. Hastings. 1967. Effects of feedback and instructional set on the control of cardiac rate variability. *Journal of Experimental Psychology*, 75, 425–431.

Lang, P. J., M. J. Kozak, G. A. Miller, D. N. Levin, A. McLean, Jr. 1980. Emotional imagery: Conceptual structure and pattern of somatovisceral response. *Psychophysiology*, 17, 179–192.

Lang, P. J., A. Öhman, and D. Vaitl. 1988. *The International Affective Picture System* (photographic slides). Gainesville, FL: University of Florida, Center for Research in Psychophysiology.

Lang, P. J., M. M. Bradley, and B. N. Cuthbert. 1990. Emotion, attention, and the startle reflex. *Psychological Review*, 97, 377–395.

Lange, C. G. 1885. *Om sindsbevegelser: Et psykofysiologisk studium*. København.

Lashley, K. 1960. Functional determinants of cerebral localization. In F. A. Beach, D. O. Hebb, C. T. Morgan, and H. W. Nissen, eds., *The neuropsychology of Lashley*, pp. 328–344. New York: McGraw-Hill.

Lassen, N. A., and D. H. Ingvar. 1961. The blood flow of the cerebral cortex determined by radioactive Krypton-85. *Experentia*, 17, 42–50.

Lassen, N. A., and P. E. Roland. 1983. Localization of cognitive function with cerebral blood flow. In A. Kertez, ed., *Localization in neuropsychology*, pp. 41–152. New York: Academic Press.

Lawler, K. A., and Schmied, L. A. 1992. A prospective study of women's health: The effects of stress, hardiness, locus of control, Type A behavior, and physiological reactivity. *Women Health*, 19, 27–41.

Lawler, K. A., T. C. Harraldson, C. A. Armstead, and L. A. Schmied. 1993. Gender and cardiovascular responses: What is the role of hostility? *Journal of Psychosomatic Disease*, 37, 603–613.

Lazarus, R. S., and R. McCleary. 1951. Autonomic discrimination without awareness: A study of subception. *Psychological Review*, 58, 113–122.

LeDoux, J. E., J. Iwata, P. Cicchetti, and D. Reis. 1988. Different projections of the central amygdaloid nucleus mediate autonomic and behavioral correlates of conditioned fear. *Journal of Neuroscience*, 8, 2517–2529.

Lehrer, P. M., A. Groveman, C. Randolph, M. H. Miller, and I. Pollack. 1989. Physiological response patterns to cognitive testing in adults with closed head injuries. *Psychophysiology*, 26, 668–675.

Levenson, R. W., P. Ekman, and W. V. Friesen. 1990. Voluntary facial action generates emotion-specific autonomic nervous system activity. *Psychophysiology*, 27, 363–384.

Levine, M. J., and M. Gueramy. 1991. Application of psychophysiology in clinical neuropsychology. *Annals of the New York Academy of Sciences, 620,* 208–216.

Ley, R. 1985. Agoraphobia, the panic attack, and the hyperventilation syndrome. *Behaviour Therapy and Research, 23,* 79–81.

Lindsley, D. B. 1944. Electroencephalography. In J. McV. Hunt, ed., *Personality and the behavior disorders,* pp. 1033–1106. New York: Ronald Press.

——— 1960. Attention, consciousness, sleep, and wakefulness. In J. Field, H. W. Magoun, and V. E. Hall, eds., *Handbook of physiology,* vol. 3, pp. 1553–1593. Washington, DC: American Physiology Society.

Lippold, O. C. J. 1967. Electromyography. In P. H. Venables and I. Martin, eds., *A manual of psychophysiological methods,* pp. 245–298. Amsterdam: North-Holland Publishing Company.

Lockhart, R. A. 1966. Comments regarding multiple response phenomena in long interstimulus interval conditioning. *Psychophysiology, 3,* 108–114.

Loewy, A. D. 1990. Anatomy of the autonomic nervous system: An overview. In A. D. Loewy and K. M. Spyer, eds., *Central regulation of autonomic functions,* pp. 3–16. New York: Oxford University Press.

Lovallo, W. R., and M. F. Wilson. 1992. The role of cardiovascular reactivity in hypertension risk. In J. R. Turner, A. Sherwood, and K. C. Light, eds., *Individual differences in cardiovascular response to stress,* pp. 165–186. New York: Plenum Press.

Loveless, N. E. 1983. Event-related brain potentials and human performance. In A. Gale, ed., *Physiological correlates of human behavior,* pp. 80–97. London: Academic Press.

Lu, S. T., M. Hämäläinen, R. Hari, R. J. Ilmoniemi, O. V. Lounasmaa, M. Sams, and V. Vilkman. 1991. Seeing faces activates three separate areas outside the occipital visual cortex in man. *Neuroscience, 43,* 287–290.

Lundberg, U. 1983. Note on type A behavior and cardiovascular response to challenge in 3- to 6-year-old children. *Journal of Psychosomatic Research, 27,* 39–42.

Lundervold, A., L. Ersland, K. I. Gjesdal, A. I. Smievoll, T. Tillung, H. Sundberg, and K. Hugdahl. 1995. Functional magnetic resonance imaging of primary visual processing using a 1.0 Tesla scanner. *International Journal of Neuroscience, 81,* 151–168.

Luria, A. R., and E. D. Homskaya. 1970. Frontal lobes and the regulation of arousal processes. In D. I. Mostofsky, ed., *Attention: Contemporary theory and analysis,* pp. 303–330. New York: Appleton-Century-Crofts.

Lykken, D. T. 1957. A study of anxiety in the sociopathic personality. *Journal of Abnormal Psychology, 55,* 6–10.

——— 1968. Neuropsychology and psychophysiology in personality research. In E. F. Borgatta and W. W. Lambert, eds., *Handbook of personality theory and research*, part 2, pp. 413–509. Chicago: Rand McNally.

Lynn, R. 1966. *Attention, arousal, and the orientation reaction.* Oxford: Pergamon Press.

MacLeod-Morgan, C., and L. Lack. 1982. Hemispheric specificity: A physiological concomitant of hypnotizability. *Psychophysiology, 23*, 71–75.

Mäkelä, J. P., A. Ahonen, M. Hämäläinen, R. Hari, R. Ilmoniemei, M. Kajola, J. Knuutila, O. V. Lounasmaa, L. McEvoy, R. Salmelin, O. Salonen, M. Sams, J. Simola, C. Tesche, and J. P. Vasama. 1993. Functional differences between auditory cortices of the two hemispheres revealed by whole-head neuromagnetic recordings. *Human Brain Mapping, 1*, 48–56.

Malmo, R. B., and C. Shagass. 1949. Physiologic study of symptom mechanisms in psychiatric patients under stress. *Psychosomatic Medicine, 11*, 25–29.

Malmo, R. B. 1975. *On emotions, needs and our archaic brain.* New York: Holt, Rinehart and Winston.

Maltzman, I., J. Gould, O. J. Barnett, D. C. Raskin, and C. Wolff. 1979. Habituation of the GSR and digital vasomotor components of the orienting reflex as a consequence of task instructions and sex differences. *Physiological Psychology, 7*, 213–220.

Mamelak, A., and J. A. Hobson. 1989. Nightcap: A home-based sleep monitoring system. *Sleep, 12*, 157–166.

Mandler, G. 1975. *Mind and emotion.* New York: Wiley.

Mandler, G., J. M. Mandler, and E. T. Uviller. 1958. Autonomic feedback: The perception of autonomic activity. *Journal of Abnormal and Social Psychology, 37*, 367–373.

Mangun, G. R., J. C. Hansen, and S. A. Hillyard. 1987. The spatial orientation of attention: Sensory facilitation or response bias? In R. Johnson, Jr., J. W. Rorbaugh, and R. Parasuraman, eds., *Current trends in event-related potential rersearch*, pp. 118–124. Amsterdam: Elsevier Publishers.

Mangun, G. R., S. A. Hillyard, and S. J. Luck. 1993. Physiological bases of visual selective attention. In D. E. Meyer and S. Kornblum, eds., *Attention and performance, XIV: Synergies in experimental psychology, artificial intelligence, and cognitive neuroscience*, pp. 219–243. Cambridge, MA: MIT Press.

Manuck, S. B., and D. S. Krantz. 1986. Psychophysiologic reactivity in coronary heart disease and essential hypertension. In K. A. Matthews, S. M. Weiss, T. Detre, T. M. Dembroski, B. Falkner, S. B. Manuck, and R. B. Williams, eds., *Handbook of stress, reactivity and cardiovascular disease*, pp. 11–34. New York: Wiley and Sons.

Manuck, S. B., A. L. Kasprowicz, and M. F. Muldoon. 1990. Behaviorally evoked cardiovascular reactivity and hypertension: Conceptual issues and potential associations. *Annals of Behavioral Medicine, 12,* 17–29.

Margraf, J., C. B. Taylor, A. Ehlers, W. T. Roth, and W. S. Agras. 1987. Panic attacks in the natural environment. *Journal of Nervous and Mental Disease, 175,* 558–565.

Marinkovich, K., A. M. Schell, and M. E. Dawson. 1989. Awareness of the CS-UCS contingency and classical conditioning of skin conductance responses with olfactory CSs. *Biological Psychology, 29,* 39–60.

Marks, I. 1969. *Fears and phobias.* London: Heineman Medical Books.

—— 1981. *Cure and care of neuroses.* New York: Wiley and Sons.

Martin, I., and A. B. Levey. 1987. Learning what will happen next: Conditioning, evaluation, and cognitive processes. In G. C. L. Davey, ed., *Cognitive processes and Pavlovian conditioning in humans,* pp. 57–82. New York: Wiley and Sons.

Martin, D. G., M. Stambrook, D. J. Tataryn, and H. Biehl. 1984. Conditioning in the unattended left ear. *International Journal of Neuroscience, 23,* 95–102.

Mathews, A., and C. MacLeod. 1985. Selective processing of threat cues in anxiety states. *Behaviour Research and Therapy, 23,* 563–569.

Matthews, K. A. 1982. Psychological perspectives on the Type A behavior pattern. *Psychological Bulletin, 91,* 293–323.

—— 1986. Summary, conclusions, and implications. In K. A. Matthews, S. M. Weiss, T. Detre, T. M. Dembroski, B. Falkner, S. B. Manuck, and R. B. Williams, eds., *Handbook of stress, reactivity and cardiovascular disease,* pp. 461–473. New York: Wiley and Sons.

—— 1988. Coronary heart disease and Type A behaviors: Update on and alternative to the Booth-Kewley and Friedman (1987) quantitative review. *Psychological Bulletin, 104,* 373–380.

Matthews, K. A., and J. R. Jennings. 1984. Cardiovascular responses of boys exhibiting the Type A behavior pattern. *Psychosomatic Medicine, 46,* 484–497.

Matthews, K. A., S. B. Manuck, and, P. G. Saab. 1986. Cardiovascular responses of adolescents during a naturally occurring stressor and their behavioral and psychophysiological predictors. *Psychophysiology, 23,* 198–209.

McCann, B. S., R. C. Veith, R. S. Schwartz, N. Lewis, J. J. Albers, G. R. Warnick, and R. H. Knopp. 1988. Cardiovascular, neuroendocrine, and lipoprotein changes during stress in hyperlipidemic and normolipidemic men. *Psychophysiology, 25,* 421.

McCarthy, G., A. M. Blamire, G. Bloch, D. L. Rothman, and R. G. Shulman. 1993. Echo planar MRI studies of frontal cortex during word generation. *Proceedings of the Society of Magnetic Resonance in Medicine,* vol. 3, 1412.

McGuigan, F. J. 1978. *Cognitive psychophysiology: Principles of covert behavior.* Englewood Cliffs, NJ: Prentice-Hall.

McGuigan, F. J., B. Keller, and E. Stanton. 1964. Covert language responses during silent reading. *Journal of Educational Psychology, 55,* 339–343.

McGurk, H., and J. MacDonald. 1976. "Hearing lips and seeing voices." *Science, 264,* 746–748.

McKeever, W. F. 1986. Tachistoscopic methods in neuropsychology. In J. F. Hannay, ed., *Experimental techniques in human neuropsychology,* pp. 167–211. New York: Oxford University Press.

Mednick, S. A., and F. Schulsinger. 1974. Studies of children at high risk for schizophrenia. In S. A. Mednick, F. Schulsinger, J. Higgins, and B. Bell, eds., *Genetics, environment, and psychopathology,* pp. 109–116. Amsterdam: Elsevier.

Melzack, R., and P. D. Wall. 1965. Pain mechanisms: A new theory. *Science, 150,* 971–979.

Merrin, E. L., G. Fein, T. C. Floyd, and C. D. Yingling. 1986. EEG asymmetry in schizophrenic patients before and during neuroleptic treatment. *Biological Psychiatry, 21,* 455–464.

Mikulincer, M. H., H. Babkoff, T. Caspy, and H. Sing. 1989. The effects of 72 hours of sleep loss on psychological variables. *British Journal of Psychological, 80,* 145–162.

Miller, N. E. 1964. Learning of visceral and glandular responses. *Science, 163,* 434–445.

Miller, T. Q., C. W. Turner, R. S. Tindale, E. J. Posavac, and B. L. Dugoni. 1991. Reasons for the trend toward null findings in research on Type A behavior. *Psychological Bulletin, 110,* 469–485.

Milner, B. 1964. Some effects of frontal lobectomy in man. In J. M. Warren and K. Ackert, eds., *The frontal granular cortex and behavior,* pp. 313–334. New York: McGraw-Hill.

Milner, P. M. 1970. *Physiological psychology.* New York: Holt, Rinehart, and Winston.

Montagu, J. D., and E. M. Coles. 1966. Mechanism and measurement of the galvanic skin response. *Psychological Bulletin, 65,* 261–279.

Morgan, A. H., H. MacDonald, and E. Hilgard. 1974. EEG alpha: Lateral asymmetry related to task, and hypnotizability. *Psychophysiology, 11,* 275–282.

Moscovitch, M. 1979. Information processing in the cerebral hemispheres. In M. S. Gazzaniga, ed., *Handbook of human neurobiology,* vol. 2, pp. 379–446. New York: Plenum Press.

Näätänen, R. 1967. Selective attention and evoked potentials. *Annals of the Academy Scientarium Fennicae, 151,* 1–266.

—— 1990. The role of attention in auditory information processing as revealed by event-related potentials and other measures of cognitive function. *Behavioral and Brain Sciences, 13,* 201–288.

———— 1992. *Attention and brain function.* Hillsdale, NJ: Lawrence Erlbaum.

Näätänen, R., A. W. K. Gaillard, and S. Mäntysalo. 1978. Early selective attention effect on evoked potential reinterpreted. *Acta Psychologica, 42,* 313–329.

Näätänen, R., K. Ahlo, and M. Sams. 1985. Selective information processing and event-related brain potentials. In F. Klix, R. Näätänen, and K. Zimmer, eds., *Psychophysiological approaches to human information processing,* pp. 73–92. Amsterdam: Elsevier Science Publishers.

Näätänen, R., and T. W. Picton. 1987. The N1 wave of the human electric and magnetic response to sound: A review and an analysis of the component structure. *Psychophysiology, 24,* 375–425.

Näätänen, R., P. Paavalainen, and K. Reinikainen. 1989. Do event-related potentials to infrequent decrements in duration of auditory stimuli demonstrate a memory trace in man? *Neuroscience Letters, 107,* 347–352.

Naveteur, J., and H. Sequiera-Martinho. 1990. Reliability of bilateral differences in electrodermal activity. *Biological Psychology, 31,* 47–56.

Neuchterlein, K. H., and M. E. Dawson. 1984. Information processing and attentional functioning in the developmental course of schizophrenic disorders. *Schizophrenia Bulletin, 10,* 160–203.

Neville, H. J., M. Kutas, and A. Schmidt. 1982. Event-related potential studies of cerebral specialization during reading II. Studies of congenitally deaf adults. *Brain and Language, 16,* 316–337.

Nordby, H., W. T. Roth, and A. Pfefferbaum. 1988. Event-related potentials to time-deviant and pitch-deviant tones. *Psychophysiology, 25,* 249–261.

Nordby, H., K. Hugdahl, R. Stickgold, K. Bronnick, and J. A. Hobson. Event-related potential (ERP) recordings to auditory stimuli during wake and different stages of sleep. Unpublished manuscript.

Nunez, P. L. 1981. *Electrical fields of the brain.* New York: Oxford University Press.

Nussbaum, P. D., and G. Goldstein. 1992. Neuropsychological sequelae of heart transplantation: A preliminary review. *Clinical Psychology Review, 12,* 475–483.

O'Gorman, J. G. 1983. Individual differences in the orienting response. In D. Siddle, ed., *Orienting and habituation: Perspectives in human research,* pp. 431–448. Chichester, UK: Wiley and Sons.

O'Keefe, J., and L. Nadel. 1978. *The hippocampus as a cognitive map.* Oxford: Oxford University Press.

O'Leary, A. 1990. Stress, emotion, and human immune function. *Psychological Bulletin, 108,* 363–382.

Obrist, P. A. 1963. Skin resistance levels and galvanic skin response: Unilateral differences. *Science, 139*, 227–228.

———— 1976. The cardiovascular-behavioral interaction as it appears today. *Psychophysiology, 13*, 95–107.

———— 1981. *Cardiovascular psychophysiology: A perspective.* New York: Plenum.

Obrist, P. A., R. A. Webb, and J. R. Sutterer. 1969. Heart rate and somatic changes during aversive conditioning and a simple reaction time task. *Psychophysiology, 8*, 696–703.

Obrist, P. A., K. C. Light, J. A. McCubbin, J. S. Hutcheson, and J. L. Hoffer. 1979. Pulse transit time: Relationship to blood pressure and myocardial performance. *Psychophysiology, 16*, 292–301.

Öhlund, L. S., A. Öhman, T. Alm, L. G. Öst, and L. H. Lindström. 1990. Season of birth and electrodermal unresponsiveness in male schizophrenics. *Biological Psychiatry, 27*, 328–340.

Öhman, A. 1971. Differentiation of conditioned and orienting response components in electrodermal conditioning. *Psychophysiology, 8*, 7–22.

———— 1979a. The orienting response, attention and learning: An information-processing perspective. In H. D. Kimmel, E. H. van Olst, and J. F. Orlebeke, eds., *The orienting reflex in humans*, pp. 443–471. Hillsdale, NJ: Erlbaum.

———— 1979b. Fear-relevance, autonomic conditioning and phobias: A laboratory model. In P. O. Sjödén, S. Bates, and W. Dockens III, eds., *Trends in behavior therapy*, pp. 107–133. New York: Academic Press.

———— 1981. Electrodermal activity and vulnerability to schizophrenia: A review. *Biological Psychology, 12*, 87–145.

———— 1983. The orienting response during Pavlovian conditioning. In D. Siddle, ed., *Orienting and habituation: Perspectives in human research*, pp. 315–370. Chichester, UK: Wiley and Sons.

———— 1986. Face the beast and fear the face: Animal and social fears as prototypes for evolutionary analyses of emotion. *Psychophysiology, 23*, 123–146.

———— 1992. Orienting and attention: Preferred preattentive processing of potentially phobic stimuli. In B. A. Campbell, H. Hayne, and R. Richardson, eds., *Attention and information processing in infants and adults*, pp. 263–295. Hillsdale, NJ: Lawrence Erlbaum.

Öhman, A., M. Fredrikson, K. Hugdahl, and P. A. Rimmö. 1976. The premise of equipotentiality in human classical conditioning: Conditioned electrodermal responses to potentially phobic stimuli. *Journal of Experimental Psychology: General, 103*, 313–337.

Öhman, A., M. Fredrikson, and K. Hugdahl. 1978. Towards an experimental model for simple phobic reactions. *Behaviour Analysis and Modification, 2*, 234–239.

Öhman, A., L. S. Öhlund, T. Alm, J. M. Wieselgren, L. G. Öst, and L. H. Lindström. 1989. Electrodermal nonresponding, premorbid adjustment, and symptomatology as predictors of long-term social functioning in schizophrenics. *Journal of Abnormal Psychology, 98,* 426–435.

Öhman, A., and N. Birbaumer. 1993. Psychophysiological and cognitive-clinical perspectives on emotion: Introduction and overview. In A. Öhman and N. Birbaumer, eds., *The structure of emotion: Psychophysiological, cognitive and clinical aspects,* pp. 3–17. Seattle: Hogrefe and Huber Publishers.

Oscar-Berman, M., and A. Gade. 1979. Electrodermal measures of arousal in humans with cortical or subcortical brain damage. In H. D. Kimmel, E. H. van Olst, and J. F. Orlebeke, eds., *The orienting reflex in humans,* pp. 665–676. Hillsdale, NJ: Erlbaum.

Öst, L. G. 1989. Panic disorder, agoraphobia, and social phobia. In G. Turpin, ed., *Handbook of clinical psychophysiology,* pp. 309–328. Chichester, UK: Wiley and Sons.

Öst, L. G., and K. Hugdahl. 1981. Acquisition of phobias and anxiety response patterns in clinical patients. *Behaviour Research and Therapy, 19,* 439–447.

Öst, L. G., V. Sterner, and I. L. Lindahl. 1984. Physiological responses in blood phobics. *Behaviour Research and Therapy, 22,* 445–460.

Öst, L. G., and L. Jansson. 1986. Methodological issues in cognitive-behavioral treatments of anxiety disorders. In L. Michelson and M. Ascher, eds., *Cognitive-behavioral assessment and treatment of anxiety disorders,* pp. 105–145. New York: Guilford.

Pagani, M., F. Lombardi, S. Guzzetti, O. Rimoldi, R. Furlan, P. Pizzinelli, G. Sandrone, G. Malfatto, S. Dell'Orto, E. Piccaluga, et al. 1986. Power spectral analysis of heart rate and arterial pressure variabilities as a marker of sympathovagal interaction in man and conscious dog. *Circulation Research, 59,* 178–193.

Papanicolou, A. C., D. W. Loring, G. Deutsch, and H. M. Eisenberg. 1986. Task-related EEG asymmetries: A comparison of alpha blocking and beta enhancement. *International Journal of Neuroscience, 30,* 81–85.

Pardo, J. V., P. T. Fox, and M. E. Raichle. 1991. Localization of a human system for sustained attention by positron emission tomography. *Nature, 349,* 61–64.

Pavlidis, G. T. 1981. Sequencing, eye movements and the early objective diagnosis of dyslexia. In G. T. Pavlidis and T. R. Miles, eds., *Dyslexia: Research and its applications to education,* pp. 99–164. Chichester, UK.: Wiley and Sons.

Pavlov, I. P. 1927. *Conditioned reflexes.* Trans. G. V. Anrep. New York: Dover Publications.

Petersen, S. E., P. T. Fox, M. I. Posner, M. A. Mintun, and M. E. Raichle. 1988. Positron emission tomographic studies of the cortical anatomy of single word processing. *Nature, 331,* 585–589.

Picton, T. W. 1980. The use of human event-related potentials in psychology. In I. Martin and P. H. Venables, eds., *Techniques in psychophysiology*, pp. 357–395. Chichester, UK: Wiley and Sons.

Picton, T. W., D. R. Stapells, and K. B. Campbell. 1981. Auditory evoked potentials from the human cochlea and brainstem. *Journal of Otolaryngology, 10*, 1–41.

Pivik, R. T., R. J. Broughton, R. Coppola, R. J. Davidson, N. Fox, and M. R. Nuwer. 1993. Guidelines for the recording and quantitative analysis of electroencephalographic activity in research contexts. *Psychophysiology, 30*, 547–558.

Polich, J. 1989. Habituation of P300 from auditory stimuli. *Psychobiology, 17*, 19–28.

———— 1990. P300, probability, and interstimulus interval. *Psychophysiology, 27*, 396–402.

Polich J., and F. E. Bloom. 1988. Event-related brain potentials in individuals high and low at risk for developing alcoholism: Failure to replicate. *Alcoholism: Clinical and Experimental Research, 12*, 368–272.

Polich, J., V. E. Pollock, and F. E. Bloom. 1994. Meta-analysis of P300 amplitude from males at risk for alcoholism. *Psychological Bulletin, 115*, 55–73.

Porges, S. W. 1986. Respiratory sinus arrhythmia: Physiological basis, quantitative methods, and clinical implications. In P. Grossman, K. Janssen, and D. Vaitl, eds., *Cardiorespiratory and cardiosomatic psychophysiology*, pp. 101–115. New York: Plenum Press.

———— 1988. Neonate vagal tone: Diagnostic and prognostic implications. In P. N. Vietze and H. G. Vaughn, eds., *Early identification of infants with developmental disabilities*, pp. 147–159. Philadelphia: Grune and Stratton.

Porges, S. W., P. M. McCabe, and B. G. Yonge. 1982. Respiratory-heart rate interactions: Psychophysiology—Implications for pathophysiology and behavior. In J. T. Cacioppo and R. E. Petty, eds., *Perspectives in cardiovascular psychophysiology*. New York: Guilford Press.

Porges, S. W., and A. A. Byrne. 1992. Research methods for measurement of heart rate and respiration. *Biological Psychology, 34*, 93–130.

Porges, S. W., and A. K. Maiti. 1992. The smart and vegetative vagi: Implications for specialization and laterality of function. Paper presented at the 32nd Annual Meeting of the Society for Psychophysiological Research, San Diego, CA.

Posner, M. I. 1986. A framework for relating cognitive to neural systems. In W. C. McCallum, R. Zappolli, and F. Denoth, eds., *Cerebral Psychophysiology: Studies in Event-Related Potentials*, EEG Suppl. 38, pp. 155–166. Amsterdam: Elsevier.

———— 1988. Structures and functions of selective attention. In T. Boll and D. K. Bryant, eds., *Clinical neuropsychology and brain function: Research assessment and practice*, pp. 173–202. Washington, DC: APA.

———— 1992. Attention as a cognitive and neural system. *Current Directions in Psychological Science, 1,* 11–14.

———— 1993. Seeing the mind. *Science, 262,* 673–674.

Posner, M. I., and C. R. Snyder. 1975. Facilitation and inhibition in the processing of signals. In P. M. Rabbit, ed., *Attention and Performance V.* New York: Academic Press

Posner, M. I., J. A. Walker, F. A. Friedrich, and R. D. Rafal. 1987. How do the parietal lobes direct covert attention? *Neuropsychologia, 25,* 135–147.

Posner, M. I., T. S. Early, E. Reiman, P. J. Pardo, and M. Dhawan. 1988. Asymmetries in hemispheric control of attention in schizophrenia. *Archives of General Psychiatry, 45,* 814–821.

Posner, M.I., and S. E. Petersen. 1990. The attention system of the human brain. *Annual Review of Neuroscience, 13,* 25–42.

Posner, M. I., and J. Driver. 1992. The neurobiology of selective attention. *Current Biology, 2,* 165–169.

Posner, M. I. and M. E. Raichle. 1994. *Images of mind.* New York: Scientific American Library.

Powers, W. J., and M. E. Raichle. 1985. Positron emission tomography and its application to the study of cerebrovascular disease in man. *Stroke, 16,* 361–375.

Pribram, K., and D. McGuinness. 1975. Arousal, activation, and affect in the control attention. *Psychological Review, 82,* 116–149.

Prokasy, W. F., and K. L. Kumpfer. 1973. Classical conditioning. In W. F. Prokasy and D. C. Raskin, eds., *Electrodermal activity in psychological research,* pp. 157–196. New York: Academic Press.

Putnam, F. W., T. P. Zahn, and R. M. Post. 1990. Differential autonomic nervous system activity in multiple personality disorder. *Psychiatry Research, 31,* 251–260.

Rachman, S., and R. I. Hodgson. 1974. Synchrony and desynchrony in fear and avoidance. *Behaviour Research and Therapy, 12,* 311–318.

Raichle, M. E. 1986. Neuroimaging. *Trends in Neurosciences,* October, 525–529.

Raine, A., and P. H. Venables. 1984. Electrodermal nonresponding, antisocial behavior, and schizoid tendencies in adolescents. *Psychophysiology, 21,* 424–433.

Raine, A., G. P. Reynolds, and C. Sheard. 1991. Neuroanatomical correlates of skin conductance orienting in normal humans: A magnetic resonance imaging study. *Psychophysiology, 28,* 548–558.

Randall, W. C., J. A. Armour, W. P. Geis, and D. B. Lippincott. 1972. Regional cardiac distribution of the sympathetic nerves. *Federation Proceedings: Federation of American Societies for Experimental Biology, 32,* 1119–1208.

Raskin, D. C., H. Kotses, and J. Bever. 1969. Autonomic indicators of orienting and defensive reflexes. *Journal of Experimental Psychology, 80,* 423–433.

Rau, H., T. Elbert, B. Geiger, and W. Lutzenberger. 1992. PRES: The controlled noninvasive stimulation of the carotid baroreceptors in humans. *Psychophysiology, 29,* 165–172.

Rau, H., P. Pauli, S. Brody, T. Elbert, and N. Birbaumer. 1993. Baroreceptor stimulation alters cortical activity. *Psychophysiology, 30,* 322–325.

Ray, J. J. 1991. If "A–B" does not predict heart disease, why bother with it? A comment on Ivancevich and Matteson. *British Journal of Medical Psychology, 64,* 85–90.

Razran, G. 1961. The observable unconscious and the inferable conscious in current Soviet psychophysiology. *Psychological Review, 68,* 81–147.

Rechtschaffen, A., B. M. Bergmann, C. A. Everson, C. A. Kushida, and M. A. Gilliland. 1989. Sleep deprivation in the rat: X. Integration and discussion of the findings. *Sleep, 12,* 68–87.

Reiman, E. M., M. E. Raichle, F. K. Butler, P. Herscovitch, and E. Robins. 1984. A focal brain abnormality in panic disorder, a severe form of anxiety. *Nature, 310,* 683–685.

Rescorla, R. A. 1980. *Pavlovian second-order conditioning.* New York: Academic Press.

Rescorla, R. A., and A. R. Wagner. 1972. A theory of Pavlovian conditioning: Variations in the effectiveness of reinforcement and nonreinforcement. In A. Black and W. F. Prokasy, eds., *Classical conditioning II: Current theory and research,* pp. 64–99. New York: Appleton-Century-Crofts.

Richards, J. E. 1988. Heart rate offset responses to visual stimuli in infants from 14 to 26 weeks of age. *Psychophysiology, 25,* 278–291.

Rippon, G. 1985. Bilateral electrodermal activity: Effects of differential hemisphere activation. Paper presented at the 25th Annual Meeting of the Society for Psychophysiological Research, Houston, Texas, October.

——— 1990. Individual differences in electrodermal and electroencephalographic asymmetries. *International Journal of Psychophysiology, 8,* 309–320.

——— 1993. Hemispheric differences and electrodermal asymmetry: Task and subject effects. In J. C. Roy, W. Boucsein, D. C. Fowles, and J. H. Gruzelier, eds., *Progress in electrodermal research,* pp. 297–310. New York: Plenum Press.

Risberg, J. 1986. Regional cerebral blood flow. In J. H. Hannay, ed., *Experimental techniques in human neuropsychology,* pp. 514–544. New York: Oxford University Press.

Risberg, J., J. H. Halsey, E. L. Wills, and E. M. Wilson. 1975. Hemispheric specialization in normal man studied by bilateral measurements of the regional cerebral blood flow. *Brain, 98,* 511–524.

Risberg, J., and L. Gustafson. 1983. 133Xe cerebral blood flow in dementia and in neuropsychiatry research. In P. Magistretti, ed., *Functional radionuclide imaging of the brain*, pp. 151–160. New York: Raven Press.

Rockstroh, B., T. Elbert, N. Birbaumer, and W. Lutzenberger. 1982. *Slow brain potentials and behavior*. Baltimore and Munich: Urban and Schwarzenberg.

Rockstroh, B., T. Elbert, W. Lutzenberger, N. Birbaumer, and L. Roberts. 1988. Bilateral electrodermal and electrocortical activity in anticipation of sensorimotor tasks. *Psychophysiology, 25*, 185–192.

Rogers, M. C., G. Battit, B. McPeek, and D. Todd. 1978. Lateralization of sympathetic control of the human sinus node. *Anesthesiology, 48*, 139–141.

Rogers, W. A. 1993. Age-related differences in learning. Paper presented at the APA Third Annual Scientific Psychology Forum, Washington, D.C., March, 1993.

Rogozea, R., and V. Florea-Ciocoui. 1982. Habituation of the orienting reaction in patients with post-meningioencephalitic epilepsy. *Electroencephalography and Clinical Neurophysiology, 53*, 115–118.

Rohrbaugh, J. W., K. Syndulko, and D. B. Lindsbley. 1976. Brain wave components of the contingent negative variation in humans. *Science, 191*, 1055–1057.

Roman, F., F. A. Garcia-Sanchez, J. M. Martinez-Selva, J. Gomez-Amor, and E. Carrillo. 1989. Sex differences and bilateral electrodermal activity: A replication. *Pavlovian Journal of Biological Science, 24*, 150–155.

Roman, F., E. Carrillo, and F. A. Garcia-Sanchez. 1992. Responsiveness patterns and handedness differences in bilateral electrodermal asymmetry. *International Journal of Psychophysiology, 12*, 71–79.

Roth, W. T., and E. H. Cannon. 1972. Some features of the auditory evoked response in schizophrenics. *Archives of General Psychiatry, 27*, 466–471.

Rugg, M. 1985. The effects of semantic priming and word repetition on event-related potentials. *Psychophysiology, 22*, 642–647.

Rugg, M., and M. E. Nagy. 1987. Lexical contribution to non-word repetition effects: Evidence from event-related potentials. *Memory and Cognition, 15*, 473–481.

Sams, M., P. Paavalainen, K. Alho, and R. Näätänen. 1985. Auditory frequency discrimination and event-related potentials. *Electroencephalography and Clinical Neuropsychology, 62*, 437–448.

Sams, M., M. Aulanko, R. Hämäläinen, R. Hari, O. V. Lounasmaa, S. T. Lu, and J. Simola. 1991. Seeing speech: Visual information from lip movements modifies activity in the human auditory cortex. *Neuroscience Letters, 127*, 141–145.

Sato, K. 1977. The physiology, pharmacology, and biochemistry of the eccrine sweat gland. *Reviews of Physiology, Biochemistry, and Pharmacology*, *79*, 51–131.

Schachter, S., and J. Singer. 1962. Cognitive, social and physiological determinants of emotional state. *Psychological Review*, *69*, 379–399.

Schackel, B. 1967. Eye-movement recording by electro-oculography. In P. H. Venables and I. Martin, eds., *A manual of psychophysiological methods*, pp. 299–334. Amsterdam: North-Holland Publishing Company.

Schalling, D. 1978. Psychopathy-related personality variables and the psychophysiology of socialization. In R. D. Hare and D. Schalling, eds., *Psychopathic behavior: Approaches to research*, pp. 85–106. New York: Wiley and Sons.

Schandry, R. 1981. Heart beat perception and emotional experience. *Psychophysiology*, *18*, 483–488.

Scherg, M. 1989. Fundamentals of dipole source potential analysis. In F. Grandori and F. Romani, eds., *Auditory evoked electric and magnetic field: Topographic mapping and functional localization*, pp. 40–69. Basel: Karger.

Schliack, H., and R. Schiffter. 1979. Neurophysiologie und Pathophysiologie der Schweißsekretion. In E. Schwarz, H. W. Spier, and G. Stüttgen, eds., *Handbuch der Haut- und Geschlechtskrankheiten*, vol. 1/4A, pp. 483–486. Berlin: Springer Verlag.

Schmidt, R. F., and G. Thews. 1980. *Physiologie des Menschen*. Berlin: Springer Verlag.

Schwartz, G. E., and S. M. Weiss. 1978. Yale conference on behavioral medicine: A proposed definition and statement of goals. *Journal of Behavioral Medicine*, *1*, 3–12.

Schwartz, G. E., L. Ahern, and S. L. Brown. 1979. Lateralized facial muscle response to positive and negative emotional stimuli. *Psychophysiology*, *16*, 561–571.

Schwartz, P. J., and T. Weiss. 1983. T-wave amplitude as an index of cardiac sympathetic activity: A misleading concept. *Psychophysiology*, *20*, 696–701.

Seer, P. 1979. Psychological control of essential hypertension: Review of the literature and methodological critique. *Psychological Bulletin*, *86*, 1015–1044.

Seligman, M. E. P. 1971. Phobias and preparedness. *Behavior Therapy*, *2*, 307–321.

——— 1975. *Helplessness: On depression, development and death*. San Francisco: Freeman.

Sequiera-Martinho, H., J. D. Roy, and S. Ba-M'Hamed. 1986. Cortical and pyramidal stimulation elicit nonlateralized skin potential responses in the cat. *Biological Psychology*, *23*, 85–86.

Shagass, C. 1972. Electrical activity of the brain. In N. S. Greenfield and R. A. Sternbach, eds., *Handbook of psychophysiology*, pp. 263–328. New York: Holt, Rinehart and Winston.

Shagass, C., and M. Schwartz. 1964. Recovery-functions of somato-sensory peripheral nerve and cerebral evoked responses in man. *Electroencephalography and Clinical Neurophysiology*, 17, 126–135.

Shannahoff-Khalsa, D. 1991. Lateralized rhythms of the central and autonomic nervous systems. *International Journal of Psychophysiology*, 11, 225–251.

Sherwood, A., M. T. Allen, and J. Fahrenberg, R. M. Kelsey, W. R. Lovallo, and L. J. P. van Doornen. 1990. Methodological guidelines for impedance cardiography. *Psychophysiology*, 27, 1–23.

Sherwood, A., and J. R. Turner. 1992. A conceptual and methodological overview of cardiovascular reactivity research. In J. R. Turner, A. Sherwood, and K. C. Light, eds., *Individual differences in cardiovascular response to stress*, pp. 3–32. New York: Plenum Press.

Siddle, D. A. T. 1991. Orienting, habituation, and resource allocation: An associative analysis. *Psychophysiology*, 28, 245–259.

Siddle, D. A. T., and P. A. Heron. 1976. Reliability of electrodermal habituation measures under two conditions of stimulus intensity. *Journal of Research in Personality*, 10, 195–200.

Sideroff, S. I., and M. E. Jarvik. 1980. Conditioned responses to a videotape showing heroin-related stimuli. *International Journal of the Addictions*, 15, 529–536.

Siegel, S. 1979. The role of conditioning in drug tolerance and addiction. In J. D. Keehn, ed., *Psychopathology in animals: Research and clinical implications*, pp. 143–168. San Diego, CA: Academic Press.

Skolnick, B. E., N. Sussman, and R. Gur. 1986. Selective hemispheric barbituration and electrodermal asymmetry. *Psychophsyiology*, 23, 463 (Abstract).

Silberman, E. K., and H. Weingartner. 1986. Hemispheric lateralization of functions related to emotion. *Brain and Cognition*, 5, 322–353.

Simons, R. A. 1980. The resolution of the LATAH paradox. *Journal of Nervous and Mental Disease*, 168, 195–206.

Skinner, B. F. 1953. *Science and human behavior*. New York: Macmillan Press.

Sobotta, J., and H. Becher. 1990. In H. Ferner and J. Straubesand, eds., *Atlas of human anatomy*, vol. 3. Munich and Berlin: Urban and Schwarzenberg.

Sokolov, E. N. 1960. Neuronal models and the orienting reflex. In M. A. Brazier, ed., *The central nervous system and behavior*, pp. 187–276. New York: J. Macey.

——— 1963. *Perception and the conditioned reflex*. London: Pergamon Press.

Spence, K. W. 1960. *Behavior theory and conditioning.* New Haven, CN: Prentice-Hall.

Sperry, R. W. 1974. Lateral specialization in the surgically separated hemisphere. In F. O. Schmitt and F. G. Worden, eds., *The neurosciences: Third study program*, pp. 5–19. Cambridge, MA: MIT Press.

Spiegel, D. 1991. Neurophysiological correlates of hypnosis and dissociation. *Neuropsychiatric Practice and Opinion, 3,* 440–445.

Spiegel, D., S. Cutcomb, C. Ren, and K. Pribram. 1985. Hypnotic hallucination alters evoked potentials. *Journal of Abnormal Psychology, 94,* 249–255.

Spinks, J. A., and D. A. T. Siddle. 1983. The functional significance of the orienting response. In D. A. T. Siddle, ed., *Orienting and habituation: Perspectives in human research*, pp. 237–314. Chichester, UK: Wiley.

Squire, L. R., and P. C. Slater. 1978. Anterograde and retrograde memory impairment in chronic amnesia. *Neuropsychologia, 16,* 313–322.

Squires, N. K., and C. Ollo. 1986. Human evoked potential techniques: Possible applications to neuropsychology. In J. H. Hannay, ed., *Experimental techniques in human neuropsychology*, pp. 386–418. New York: Oxford University Press.

Squires, K. C., N. K. Squires, and S. A. Hillyard. 1975. Decision-related cortical potentials during an auditory signal detection task with cued observation intervals. *Journal of Experimental Psychology: Human Perception and Perfromance, 1,* 268–279.

Steinhauer, S. R., J. R. Jennings, D. P. Van P., and J. Zubin. 1992. Beat-by-beat cardiac responses in normals and schizophrenics to events varying in conditional probability. *Psychophysiology, 29,* 223–231.

Stemmler, G., and J. Fahrenberg. 1989. Psychophysiological assessment: Conceptual, psychometric, and statistical issues. In G. Turpin, ed., *Handbook of Clinical Psychophysiology*, pp. 71–104. Chichester, UK: Wiley and Sons.

Steptoe, A., H. Smulyan, and B. Gribbin. 1976. Pulse wave velocity and blood pressure change: Calibration and applications. *Psychophysiology, 13,* 488–493.

Stern, J. A. 1964. Toward a definition of psychophysiology. *Psychophysiology, 1,* 90–91.

Sternbach, R. 1966. *Principles of psychophysiology.* New York: Academic Press.

Stewart, J., H. de Wit, and R. Eikelboom. 1984. The role of unconditioned and conditioned drug effects in the self-administration of opiates and stimulants. *Psychological Review, 91,* 251–268.

Stoney, C. M., and K. Matthews. 1988. Characteristics associated with lipid and lipoprotein responses to acute behavioral stress. *Psychophysiology, 25,* 420–421.

Stormark, K. M., K. Hugdahl, and M. I. Posner. 1994. Emotional modulation of covert spatial attention. Submitted for publication.

Stormark, K. M., J. C. Laberg, T. Bjerland, H. Nordby, and K. Hugdahl. 1995. Attentional processes and autonomic function in alcoholics: The effect of olfactory stimuli. *Psychology of Addictive Behaviors, 7,*

Stroop, J. R. 1935. Studies of interference in serial verbal reactions. *Journal of Experimental Psychology, 18,* 643–662.

Sudhir, K., G. L. Jennings, and M. D. Esler, et al. 1989. Hydrocortisone-induced hypertension in humans: Pressor responsiveness and sympathetic function. *Hypertension, 13,* 416–421.

Sutarman, X., and M. L. Thomson. 1952. A new technique for enumerating active sweat glands in man. *Journal of Physiology* (London), *117,* 51–52.

Sutton, S. 1979. P300—Thirteen years later. In H. Begleiter, ed., *Evoked brain potentials and behavior,* pp. 107–126. New York: Plenum Press.

Sutton, S., M. Braren, J. Zubin, and E. R. John. 1965. Evoked potential correlates of stimulus uncertainty. *Science, 150,* 1187–1188.

Svebak, S. 1986. Patterns of cardiovascular-somatic-respiratory interactions in the continuous perceptual-motor task paradigm. In P. Grossman and K. H. Janssen, eds., *Cardiorespiratory and cardiosomatic psychophysiology,* pp. 219–230. New York: Plenum.

Svebak, S., K. Dalen, and O. Storfjell. 1981. The psychological significance of task-induced tonic changes in somatic and autonomic activity. *Psychophysiology, 18,* 403–409.

Svebak, S., S. Knardahl, H. Nordby, and A. Aakvaag. 1992. Components of Type A behavior pattern as predictors of neuroendocrine and cardiovascular reactivity in challenging tasks. *Personality and Individual Differences, 13,* 733–744.

Svensson, T. H. 1987. Peripheral, autonomic regulation of locus coeruleus noradrenergic neurons in brain: Putative implications for psychiatry and psychopharmacology. *Psychopharmacology, 92,* 1–7.

Talairach, J., and P. Tournoux. 1988. *Co-planar stereotaxic atlas of the human brain.* New York: Thieme Medical Publishers Inc.

Tarchanoff, J. 1890. Über die galvanischen Erscheinungen an der Haut des Menschen dei Reizung der Sinnesorgane und bei verschiedenen Formen der psychischen Tätigkeit. *Plügers Archiv für die gesamte Physiologie des Menschen und der Tiere, 46,* 46–55.

Tassinary, L. G., J. T. Cacioppo, and T. R. Geen. 1989. A psychometric study of surface electrode placements for facial electromyographic recording: I. The brow and cheek muscle regions. *Psychophysiology, 26,* 1–16.

Telles, S., and T. Desiraju. 1993. Autonomic changes in Brahmakumaris Raja youga meditation. *International Journal of Psychophysiology, 15,* 147–152.

Thompson, R. F. 1988. The neural basis of associative learning of discrete behavioral responses. *Trends in Neurosciences, 11*, 142–155.

Thompson, R. F., and W. A. Spencer. 1966. Habituation: A model phenomenon for the study of neuronal substratrates of behavior. *Psychological Review, 73*, 16–43.

Tranel, D., and A. R. Damasio. 1985. Knowledge without awareness: An autonomic index of facial recognition by prosopagnosics. *Science, 228*, 1453–1454.

Tranel, D., and H. Damasio. 1989. Intact electrodermal skin conductance responses after bilateral amygdala damage. *Neuropsychologia, 27*, 381–390.

——— 1994. Neuroanatomical correlates of electrodermal skin conductance responses. *Psychophysiology, 31*, 427–438.

Turkkan, J. S. 1989. Classical conditioning: The new hegemony. *Behavioral and Brain Sciences, 12*, 121–179.

Turkkan, J. S., and J. Brady. 1985. Meditational theory of the placebo effect: Discussion. In L. White, B. Tursky, and G. E. Schwartz, eds., *Placebo: Theory, research and mechanisms.* New York: Guilford Press.

Turpin, G. 1985. Ambulatory psychophysiological monitoring: Techniques and applications. In D. Papakospoulos, S. Butler, and I. Martin, eds., *Clinical and experimental neuropsychophysiology,* pp. 695–728. London: Croom Helm.

——— ed. 1989. *Handbook of clinical psychophysiology.* Chichester, UK: Wiley and Sons.

——— 1991. The psychophysiological assessment of anxiety disorders: Three-systems measurement and beyond. *Psychological Assessment, 3*, 366–375.

Turpin, G., and K. Clements. 1993. Electrodermal activity and psychopathology: The development of the palmar sweat index (PSI) as an applied measure for use in clinical settings. In J. C. Roy, W. Boucsein, D. C. Fowles, and J. H. Gruzelier, eds., *Progress in electrodermal research,* pp. 49–60. New York: Plenum Press.

Tursky, B., and L. D. Jamner. 1982. Measurement of cardiovascular functioning. In J. T. Cacioppo and R. E. Petty, eds., *Perspectives in cardiovascular psychophysiology,* pp. 19–92. New York: Guilford Press.

Ursin, H., E. Baade, and S. Levine. 1978. *Psychobiology of stress: A study of coping men.* New York: Academic Press.

Vaughn, H. G., and W. Ritter. 1970. The sources of auditory evoked responses recorded from the human scalp. *Electroencephalography and Clinical Neurophysiology, 28*, 360–367.

Vaughn, H. G., and J. C. Arezzo. 1988. The neural basis of event-related potentials. In T. W. Picton, ed., Human event-related potentials, *Handbook of electroencephalography and clinical neurophysiology*, rev. ser., vol. 3, pp. 45–96. Amsterdam: Elsevier Science Publishers.

Vaughan, K. B., and J. T. Lanzetta. 1980. Vicarious instigation and conditioning of facial expressive and autonomic responses to model's expressive display of pain. *Journal of Personality and Social Psychology, 38*, 909–923.

van Doornen, L. J. P., H. Snieder, E. C. J. de Geus, and D. I. Boomsma. 1993. Cardiovascular reactivity and lipid levels. Paper presented at the 33rd Annual Meeting of the Society for Psychophysiological Research, Rotach-Egern, Germany, October.

Venables, P. H. 1983. Some problems and controversies in the psychophysiological investigation of schizophrenia. In A. Gale and J. A. Edwards, eds., *Physiological correlates of human behaviour*, vol. 3, pp. 207–232. London: Academic Press.

——— 1984. Cerebral mechanisms, autonomic responsiveness, and attention in schizophrenia. In W. D. Spaulding and J. K. Cole, eds., *Theories of schizophrenia and psychosis: Nebraska Symposium on Motivation 1983*, pp. 47–91. Lincoln: University of Nebraska Press.

——— 1991. Autonomic activity. *Annals of the New York Academy of Sciences, 620*, 191–207.

——— 1993. Electrodermal markers as markers for the development of schizophrenia. In J. C. Roy, W. Boucsein, D. C. Fowles, and J. H. Gruzelier, eds., *Progress in electrodermal research*, pp. 187–206. New York: Plenum Press.

Venables, P. H., and M. J. Christie. 1973. Mechanisms, instrumentation, recording techniques and quantification of responses. In W. F. Prokasy and D. C. Raskin, eds., *Electrodermal activity in psychological research*, pp. 2–125. New York: Academic Press.

——— 1980. Electrodermal activity. In I. Martin and P. H. Venables, eds., *Techniques in electrodermal research*, pp. 3–67. Chichester, UK: Wiley and Sons.

Verrier, R., and B. D. Nearing. 1994. Electrophysiologic basis for T wave alternans as an index of vulnerability to ventricular fibrillation. *Journal of Cardiovascular Electrophysiology, 5*, 445–461.

Vrana, S. R., E. L. Spence, and P. J. Lang. 1988. The startle probe response: A new measure of emotion. *Journal of Abnormal Psychology, 97*, 487–491.

Waldstein, S. R., S. B. Manuck, C. M. Ryan, and M. F. Muldoon. 1991. Neuropsychological correlates of hypertension: Review and methodologic considerations. *Psychological Bulletin, 110*, 451–468.

Walker, B. B., and Sandman, C. A. 1979. Human visual evoked responses are related to heart rate. *Journal of Comparative and Physiological Psychology, 93*, 717–729.

Walker, B. B., and C. A. Sandman. 1982. Visual evoked potentials change as heart rate and carotid pressure change. *Psychophysiology, 19*, 520–7.

Wallace, R. K. 1970. Physiological effects of transcendental meditation. *Science, 167*, 1751–1754.

Wallin, B. G. 1981. Sympathetic nerve activity underlying electrodermal and cardiovascular reactions in man. *Psychophysiology, 18*, 470–476.

Wallin, B. G., and J. Fagius. 1986. The sympathetic nervous system in man: Aspects derived from microelectrode recordings. *Trends in Neurosciences*, February, 63–66.

Walter, W. G., R. Cooper, V. J. Aldridge, W. C. McCallum, and A. L. Winter. 1964. Contingent negative variation. *Nature, 203*, 380–384.

Wang, G. H. 1964. *The neural control of sweating*. Madison: University of Wisconsin Press.

Wardlaw, K. A., and N. E. Kroll. 1976. Autonomic responses to shock-associated words in nonattended message: A failure to replicate. *Journal of Experimental Psychology: Human Perception and Performance, 2*, 357–360.

Wardle, J., and M. Jarvis. 1981. The paradoxical fear response to blood, injury and illness—a treatment report. *Behavioral Psychotherapy, 9*, 13–24.

Weise, F., F. Heydenreich, and U. Runge. 1987. Contributions of sympathetic and vagal mechanisms to the genesis of heart rate fluctuations during orthostatic load: A spectral analysis. *Journal of Autonomic Nervous System, 21*, 127–134.

Weiskrantz, L. 1986. *Blindsight: A case study and its implications*. New York: Oxford University Press.

Weisz, J., N. Szilagyi, E. Lang, and G. Adam. 1992. The influence of monocular viewing on heart period variability, *International Journal of Psychophysiology, 12*, 11–18.

Weitkunat, R., and R. Schandry. 1990. Motivation and heartbeat evoked potentials. *Journal of Psychophysiology, 4*, 33–40.

Wenger, M. A. 1941. The measurement of individual differences in autonomic balance. *Psychosomatic Medicine, 3*, 427–434.

Wenger, M. A., B. T. Engel, and T. L. Clemens. 1957. Studies of autonomic response patterns: Rationale and methods. *Behavioral Science, 2*, 216–221.

Werntz, D. A., R. G. Bickford, and D. Shannahoff-Khalsa. 1987. Selective hemispheric stimulation by unilateral forced nostril breathing. *Human Neurobiology, 6*, 165–171.

Whitehead, W. E., V. M. Drescher, P. Heiman, and B. Blackwell. 1977. Relation of heart rate control to heartbeat perception. *Biofeedback and Self Regulation, 2*, 371–392.

Wilcott, R. C., and H. H. Bradley. 1970. Low-frequency electrical stimulation of the cat's anterior cortex and inhibition of skin potential changes. *Journal of Comparative and Physiological Psychology, 72*, 351–355.

Wilder, J. 1967. *Stimulus and response: The law of initial value.* Bristol, UK: Wright.

Windholz, G. 1992. Pavlov's conceptualization of learning. *American Journal of Psychology, 105,* 459–469.

Wittling, W. 1990. Psychophysiological correlates of human brain asymmetry: Blood pressure changes during lateralized presentation of an emotionally laden film. *Neuropsychologia, 28,* 457–470.

Wittling, W., and M. Pfluger. 1990. Neuroendocrine hemisphere asymmetries: Salivary cortisol secretion during lateralized viewing of emotion-related and neutral films. *Brain and Cognition, 14,* 243–265.

Woldorff, M. G., C. C. Gallen, S. A. Hampson, S. A. Hillyard, C. Pantev, D. Sobel, and F. E. Bloom. 1993. Modulation of early sensory processing in human auditory cortex during auditory selective attention. *Proceedings of the National Academy of Sciences, 90,* 8722–8726.

Wolpe, J. 1982. *The practice of behavior therapy.* New York: Pergamon Press.

Wood, C. C., G. McCarthy, N. K. Squires, H. G. Vaughn, D. L. Woods, and W. C. McCallum. 1984. Anatomical and physiological substrates of event-related potentials: Two case studies. *Annals of the New York Academy of Sciences, 425,* 681–721.

Wright, J. M. von, K. Andersson, and U. Stenman. 1975. Generalization of conditioned GSRs in dichotic listening. In P. M. Rabbit and S. Dornic, eds., *Attention and performance,* vol. 5, pp. 194–204. London: Academic Press.

Yokoyama, K., R. Jennings, P. Ackles, P. Hood, and F. Boller. 1987. Lack of heart rate changes during an attention-demanding task after right hemisphere lesions. *Neurology, 36,* 624–630.

Zahn, T. P. 1986. Psychophysiological approaches to psychopathology. In M. G. H. Coles, E. Donchin, and S. W. Porges, eds., *Psychophysiology: Systems, processes, applications,* pp. 508–610. Amsterdam: Elsevier.

Zahn, T. P., J. I. Nurnberger, and W. H. Berretini. 1989. Electrodermal activity in young adults at genetic risk for affective disorder. *Archives of General Psychiatry, 46,* 1120–1124.

Zeki, S. M. 1978. Functional specialization in the visual cortex of the rhesus monkey. *Nature, 274,* 423–428.

Zoccolotti, P., D. Scabini, and C. Violani. 1982. Electrodermal responses in patients with unilateral brain damage. *Journal of Clinical Neuropsychology, 4,* 143–150.

Zoccolotti, P., C. Caltagirone, A. Peccinenda, and E. Troisi. 1993. Electrodermal activity in patients with unilateral brain damage. In J. C. Roy, W. Boucsein, D. C. Fowles, and J. H. Gruzelier, eds., *Progress in electrodermal research,* pp. 311–326. New York: Plenum Press.

Author Index

419

General Index

Acetylcholine (ACh), 55, 88
ACTH, 78
Action potential, 53
Activation, activation theory, 44, 254
Adrenal gland, 78
Afferent, 84
Aggressivity, 214
Agoraphobia, 352
Alcohol dependence, 162–3
Alcoholism, 302
Alpha rhythm (wave), 242–244
Altered states. *See* Consciousness
Ambulatory recordings. *See* Recordings
Amino acids, 326
Angina pectoris, 206
ANS. *See* Autonomic nervous system
Anxiety, 159, 187
Anxiety disorders 4, 6; panic attacks, 352
Aorta, 168–170
Approach-avoidance, 259
Arousal, 10, 44, 140
Arrythmia, respiratory sinus, 183
Arteries: brain, 76; pulmonary, 168
Aspartate, 325
Asymmetry. *See* Laterality
Atherosclerosis, 206
Atrioventricular (AV) node, 170
Attention, 226, 311, 315; shift, 5; visual cuing, 289, 291; facilitation, 292; inhibition, 292
Auditory system, 60-62
Automatic processing. *See* Information processing
Autonomic balance, 41

Autonomic space, 93–95
Autonomic nervous system (ANS), 84, 85, 95, 219, 308
Autonomic Perception Questionnaire (APQ), 215
AV node. *See* Atrioventricular node

Baroreceptors, 194, 196
Basal ganglia, 58, 73–74
BEAM. *See* Topographical mapping
Behavioral medicine, 4, 22
Behaviorism, 143
BESA, 271
Beta-blockers, 172
Beta rhythm (wave), 243, 244
Bicuspid valve, 169
Biofeedback, 39–41
Blood flow, 188–189, 310, 312, 317
Blood oxygenation, 323
Blood pressure, 188–189, 193, 194; diastolic, 172, 189, 203; systolic, 172, 189, 203; mean arterial, 188
BOLD, 323
Brain, 63–83; potentials, 234–237; mapping, 250, 251; imaging, 309; function, 323; localization of function, 364; damage, 369
Brain electrical activity mapping (BEAM). *See* Topographical mapping
Brain electric source analysis (BESA), 271
Brainstem potentials, auditory (ABR), 280
Bundle of His, 170–171

425